R. Gupta's®

National Testing Agency (NTA)

UGC-NET

Junior Research Fellowship & Assistant Professor Eligibility Exam

PAPER-I

Previous Years' Papers

Solved

by

RPH Editorial Board

2021
EDITION

RAMESH PUBLISHING HOUSE, New Delhi

Published by
O.P. Gupta *for* Ramesh Publishing House

Admin. Office
12-H, New Daryaganj Road, Opp. Officers' Mess,
New Delhi-110002 ✆ 23261567, 23275224, 23275124

E-mail: info@rameshpublishinghouse.com
Website: www.rameshpublishinghouse.com

Showroom
- Balaji Market, Nai Sarak, Delhi-6 ✆ 23253720, 23282525
- 4457, Nai Sarak, Delhi-6, ✆ 23918938

Book Code: R-1960

ISBN: 978-93-87604-64-3

HSN Code: 49011010

REVISED SCHEME

As per the revised Scheme, the test will consist of two papers as below:

Paper	Marks	Number of Question
I	100	50 questions. All are compulsory
II	200	100 questions. All are compulsory

- **Paper-I** shall consist of 50 objective type compulsory questions each carrying 2 marks. The questions which will be of general nature, intended to assess the teaching/research aptitude of the candidate. It will primarily be designed to test reasoning ability, comprehension, divergent thinking and general awareness of the candidate.
- **Paper-II** shall consist of 100 objective type compulsory questions each carrying 2 marks which will be based on the **subject selected by the candidate.**

CONTENTS

PREVIOUS PAPERS (SOLVED)

Previous Years' Paper (Solved)

National Testing Agency (NTA)

UGC-NET (JRF) Online Exam, December-2019*

PAPER–I

1. Successful educational communication is dependent upon the skills of

(*a*) Understanding the negative characteristics of the audience

(*b*) Verbal communication and body language

(*c*) Estimating time for audience impact

(*d*) Analyzing the audience needs

Choose the correct answer from the options given below:

A. (*a*) and (*b*) only B. (*b*) and (*c*) only
C. (*c*) and (*d*) only D. (*b*) and (*d*) only

2. Consider the following with reference to the Indian School of Logic.

(*a*) It is related to form of the argument only.

(*b*) It is related to the content of the argument only.

(*c*) It is related to perceptual knowledge alone.

(*d*) It is related to presenting analogies alone.

Choose the correct answer from the options given below:

A. (*a*) only B. (*b*) only
C. Both (*a*) and (*b*) D. Both (*c*) and (*d*)

3. In an intervention based action research process, which of the following is the usually recommended sequence?

A. Plan, Act, Observe and Reflect
B. Observe, Plan, Act and Reflect
C. Reflect, Plan, Act and Plan
D. Observe, Act, Reflect and Plan

4. Determing the term 'X' in the following series

2, 9, 20, 35, 54, 77, 'X'

A. 104 B. 102
C. 89 D. 110

5. Effective educational communication is:

A. Non-reciprocal
B. Repetitive
C. Continuous
D. Coercive

6. Which of the following will be considered key teaching behaviour belonging to the category of effectiveness?

(*a*) Making ideas clear to learners who may be at different level of understanding.

(*b*) Showing enthusiasm and animation through variation in eye contact, voice and gestures.

(*c*) Using student ideas by acknowledging and summarizing.

(*d*) Probing through general questions and shifting a discussion to some higher thought level.

(*e*) Using meaningful verbal praise to get and keep students actively participating in the learning process.

Choose the correct answer from the options given below:

A. (*a*), (*b*) and (*c*) only
B. (*a*), (*b*) and (*e*)
C. (*b*), (*c*) and (*d*) only
D. (*c*), (*d*) and (*e*) only

7. The main purpose of using ICT for classroom teaching is to

A. Making the classroom instructions interesting
B. Divert students' attention in the class
C. Keep students engaged in the class
D. Optimize learning outcomes of teaching

* *Online Exam held on 06 December, 2019.*

8. In the Statement "No dogs are reptiles", which term are distributed?

A. Only subject term
B. Only predicate term
C. Both subject and predicate terms
D. Neither subject nor predicate term

9. "Mr. X lives in slum and is unemployed. Therefore, Mr. X deserves to be a minister."

Which kind of fallacy is committed in this argument?

A. Fallacy of Composition
B. Ad misericordium
C. Fallacy of Division
D. Fallacy of Accident

10. The two cities P and Q are 360 km apart from each other. A car goes from P to Q with a speed of 40 km/hr and returns to P with a speed of 60 km/hr. What is the average speed of the car?

A. 45 km/hr B. 48 km/hr
C. 50 km/hr D. 55 km/hr

11. The compositional skills and creativity in presentation of students can be most effectively evaluated by which of the following tests?

A. Objective type tests
B. Essay type tests
C. Short answer tests
D. Projective type tests

12. At the stage of data analysis, in which quantitative techniques have been used by a researcher, the evidence warrants the rejection of Null Hypothesis (H_0). Which of the following decisions of the researcher will be deemed appropriate?

A. Rejecting the (H_0) and also the substantive research hypothesis
B. Rejecting the (H_0) and accepting the substantive research hypothesis
C. Rejecting the (H_0) without taking any decision on the substantive research hypothesis
D. Accepting the (H_0) and rejecting the substantive research hypothesis

13. A student obtains overall 78% marks in his examination consisting of Physics, Chemistry, Mathematics, Computer Science and General English. Marks obtained in each subject and the maximum marks are indicated in the following table.

Subject	**Physics (200 max marks)**	**Chemistry (100 max marks)**	**Mathematics (200 max marks)**	**Computer Science (200 max marks)**	**General English (100 max marks)**
Marks Obtained	155	80	165	140	X

The marks (X) obtained by the student in General English would be:

A. 68
B. 74
C. 84
D. 90

14. A circle has the same area as that of a square of diagonal of length 11.0 cm. What is the diameter of the circle?

A. ~ 8.7 cm
B. ~ 17.4 cm
C. ~ 7.8 cm
D. ~ 15.6 cm

15. Assertion (A): Pedagogy and social interaction are two major result-oriented activities of a teacher.

Reason (R) : Communication has a limited role in both these activites.

Choose the correct answer from the options given below:

A. Both (A) and (R) are true and (R) is the correct explanation of (A)
B. Both (A) and (R) are true but, (R) is NOT the correct explanation of (A)
C. (A) is true but, (R) is false
D. (A) is false but, (R) is true

16. Which of the following is not necessary step when you present an argument based on inference before the others according to the Classical Indian School of Logic?

A. Nigamana B. Upamana
C. Upanaya D. Udaharana

17. A college teacher presents a research paper in a seminar. The research paper cites references which are pretty old. This situation will be described as the case of:

A. Technical lapse
B. Ethical lapse
C. Academic ignorance
D. Inability of updating research source

18. The converse of "All cats are mammals" is

A. Some mammals are not cats
B. No mammals are cats
C. Some mammals are cats
D. All mammals are cats

19. Which of the following theories can be applied to classroom communication?

A. Theory of Social Constructivism
B. Audience Marginalization Theory
C. Ritualistic Theory
D. Theory of Hegemony

20. Identify the sequence which correctly indicates the order for ensuring teaching-learning activities in a constructivist approach

A. Explore, Explain, Engage, Extend and Evaluate
B. Evaluate, Extend, Engage, Explain and Explore
C. Explain, Engage, Explore, Evaluate and Extend
D. Engage, Explore, Explain, Evaluate and Extend

21. Match Set I with Set II:

Set-I (Research Tools)	**Set-II (Measurement Scale)**
(*a*) Questionnaire and Interview	(*i*) Ratio scale of measurement
(*b*) Intelligence and Aptitude Tests	(*ii*) Ordinal Scale of measurement
(*c*) Attitude and Value Tests	(*iii*) Interval Scale of measurement
(*d*) Speed and Frequency Tests	(*iv*) Nominal Scale of measurement

Code:

	(*a*)	(*b*)	(*c*)	(*d*)
A.	(*i*)	(*ii*)	(*iii*)	(*iv*)
B.	(*iii*)	(*i*)	(*iv*)	(*ii*)
C.	(*iv*)	(*iii*)	(*ii*)	(*i*)
D.	(*ii*)	(*iii*)	(*i*)	(*iv*)

22. A shopkeeper sells a refrigerators for ₹ 22,000.00 and makes a profit of 10%. If he desires to make a profit of 18%, what should be his selling price?

A. ₹ 23,600 B. ₹ 39,600
C. ₹ 36,000 D. ₹ 24,600

23. Which of the following factors have been labelled as 'social competence' in influencing learning?

(*a*) Socio-economic status
(*b*) Motivation
(*c*) Intelligence - general and specific
(*d*) Emotional well-being
(*e*) Inability to translate thoughts into action

Choose the correct answer from the options given below:

A. (*a*), (*b*) and (*c*) only
B. (*b*), (*c*) and (*d*) only
C. (*a*), (*b*) and (*d*) only
D. (*c*), (*d*) and (*e*) only

24. Which of the following will help overcome communication barriers?

A. Focused listening
B. Neglecting semantic noise
C. Top-down command structure
D. Use of cliched idioms

25. If data has been recorded using technical media, which among the following is a necessary step on the way to its interpretation?

A. Transcription
B. Structural Equation Modelling
C. Sequential Analysis
D. Sampling

Directions (Qs. No. 26 to 30): *Read the information carefully and answer the questions.*

The table shows the percentage (%) profit earned by the Company A, income of Company B and expenditure of Company B during the years, 2013-18 as well as formula to compute percentage (%) profit.

Years wise financial details (in ₹ Lakhs)

Year	% Profit of A	Income of B (in ₹ lakhs)	Expenditure of B (in ₹ lakhs)
2013	40%	48.6	36
2014	25%	35	25
2015	60%	62.4	48
2016	40%	77	44
2017	10%	80	50
2018	20%	72	45

where $\text{Profit (\%)} = \dfrac{(\text{Income} - \text{Expenditure})}{(\text{Expenditure})} \times 100$

26. If the income of the Company A in the year 2014 happened to be ₹ 32.5 lakhs, then what was the sum of the net profit (in ₹ lakhs) of Company A and Company B in 2014?
A. ₹ 12.8 lakhs B. ₹ 13.2 lakhs
C. ₹ 15 lakhs D. ₹ 16.5 lakhs

27. The percent profit of Company B was maximum in the year?
A. 2014 B. 2015
C. 2016 D. 2017

28. What is the difference between percent (%) profit of Company A and Company B in the year 2013?
A. 5% B. 7%
C. 12% D. 15%

29. If the income of Company A in the year 2018 was ₹ 90 lakhs, then the net profit (in ₹ lakhs) of Company B in 2018 is what percent more than the net profit (in ₹ lakhs) of Company A?
A. 30% B. 60%
C. 75% D. 80%

30. If the expenditure of Company A in year 2017 was ₹ 45 lakhs, then the net profit (in ₹ lakhs) of Company A is what percent of net profit (in ₹ lakhs) of Company B in the same year?
A. 15% B. 25%
C. 40% D. 75%

31. Which of the following sequences of disposal options for low hazardous solid waste from industrial and urban sources is in order of increasing desirability?
A. Indiscriminate dumping < Landfill < Incineration < Reuse
B. Composting < Landfill < Reuse < Incineration
C. Landfill < Composting < Reuse < Incineration
D. Incineration < Composting < Reuse < Landfill

32. Which among the following recommended the establishment of State Council for Higher Education in each state?
A. Report of the Estimates Committee (1965 - 66)
B. Review Committee on UGC (1977), Ministry of Education
C. National Policy on Education (1986)
D. Report of the UGC Committee (1990)

33. As per provisions of Paris Agreement, the Intended Nationally Determined Contributions (INDCs) are to be reviewed every
A. 15 years B. 10 years
C. 5 years D. 3 years

34. Suppose the concentration of Carbondioxide, a greenhouse gas responsible for climate change, is 400 ppm. What is its concentration in air in percentage terms?
A. 0.04% B. 0.4%
C. 0.004% D. 4.0%

35. Identify the correct group of diseases caused by polluted water.
A. Cholera, Acute Diarrhoea, Typhoid and Polio
B. Cholera, Typhoid, Enteritis and Tuberculosis

C. Typhoid, Enteritis and Tuberculosis
D. Cholera, Acute Diarrhoea, Typhoid and Tuberculosis

36. The National Skills Qualifications Framework is based on which of the following?
A. Competency
B. Technology
C. Economic development
D. Evaluation

37. Which among the following is a Massive Open Online Course platform created by the Ministry of Human Resource Development, Government of India?
A. PRATHAM
B. SWAYAM
C. FUTURELEARN
D. OPEN LEARN

38. Which among the following is the statutory function of the UGC?
A. To appoint teaching faculty in universities
B. To control the conduct of examination in universities
C. To determine and maintain the standards of teaching and research in universities
D. To develop curriculum for university courses

39. Select the option that contains exclusively the text file formats.
A. JPEG, MP3, RTF
B. CSV, RTF, TXT
C. GIF, JPEG, MP3
D. CSV, MP3, PDF

40. Which of the following statements is/are correct?
(a) A Local Area Network (LAN) is usually located on one brand of computer
(b) The acronym 'ISP' stands for Internet Standard Provider

Choose the correct answer from the options given below:
A. (*a*) only
B. (*b*) only
C. Both (*a*) and (*b*)
D. Neither (*a*) nor (*b*)

41. Assertion (A) : The clock speed of CPUs has not increased significantly in recent years.
Reason (R) : Software now being used is faster and therefore processors do not have to be faster.

Choose the correct answer from the options given below:
A. Both (A) and (R) are true and (R) is the correct explanation of (A)
B. Both (A) and (R) are true but, (R) is NOT the correct explanation of (A)
C. (A) is true, but (R) is false
D. (A) is false, but (R) is true

42. Identify the correct sequence of biomass fuels in terms of their energy content per unit mass:
A. Dung (dry) > Coconut Shells > Unsorted domestic refuse
B. Unsorted domestic refuse > Coconut Shells > Dung (dry)
C. Wood (dry) > Coconut Shells > Unsorted domestic refuse
D. Coconut Shells > Dung (dry) > Unsorted domestic refuse

43. Who among the following scholars carried back scriptures from Nalandas University and wrote about architecture and learning of this university?
A. Kim Huang (Korea)
B. Jin Tan Yang (Korea)
C. Xuan Zang (China)
D. Junha Meng (China)

44. Match List I with List II.

List I (Software)	**List II (Description)**
(*a*) Web browser	(*i*) Prepare written documents
(*b*) Word processor	(*ii*) Create and edit web pages
(*c*) Spreadsheet	(*iii*) Connect to websites and display web pages
(d) Web authoring	(*iv*) Analyze and summarize numerical data

Code:

	(*a*)	(*b*)	(*c*)	(*d*)
A.	(*ii*)	(*iv*)	(*i*)	(*iii*)
B.	(*iii*)	(*i*)	(*iv*)	(*ii*)
C.	(*iii*)	(*i*)	(*ii*)	(*iv*)
D.	(*ii*)	(*i*)	(*iv*)	(*iii*)

45. Which of the following statements is/are correct?

(*a*) The clock speed of CPU is measured in hertz (Hz).

(*b*) Bluetooth technology consumes more power than Wi-Fi technology.

Choose the correct answer from the options given below:

A. (*a*) only B. (*b*) only

C. Both (*a*) and (*b*) D. Neither (*a*) nor (*b*)

Directions (Qs. No. 46 to 50): *Read the passage carefully and answer the questions.*

The motives for direct investments abroad are generally the same as earning higher returns, possibly resulting from higher growth rates abroad, more favorable tax treatment or greater availability of infrastructure and diversifying risks. Indeed, it has been found that firms with a strong international orientation, either through exports of through foreign production and/or sales facilities, are more profitable, and have a much smaller variability in profits than purely domestic firms. Although these reasons are sufficient to explain international investments they leave one basic question unanswered with regard to direct foreign investments. That is, they cannot explain why the residents of a nation do not borrow from other nations and themselves make real investments in their own nation rather than accept direct investment from abroad. After all, the residents of a nation can be expected to be more familiar with local conditions, and thus to be at a competitive advantage with respect to foreign investors. There are several explanations for this. The most important is that many large corporations, usually in monopolistic and oligopolistic markets, often have some unique production knowledge or managerial skill that could easily and profitably be utilized abroad and over which the corporation wants to retain direct control. In such a situation, the firm will make direct investments abroad. This involves horizontal integration or the production abroad of a differentiated product that is also produced at home. This helps serve the foreign market better by adapting to local conditions than through exports.

46. What advantage do large corporations have in oligopolistic markets?

A. Direct control over profitability

B. Large production of undifferentiated products

C. Localization of managerial skills

D. Eliminating barriers to higher profits

47. In the case of direct foreign investmens, what factor remains unaddressed?

A. Acceptance of foreign investment

B. Non-acceptance of foreign investment

C. Absence of competitive edge

D. Role of monopolistic corporations

48. The possible reasons for direct foreign investment can be:

(*a*) Higher returns

(*b*) Better tax regimes

(*c*) Availability of infrastructure

(*d*) Risk mitigation

(*e*) Financial support from local investors

Choose the correct answer from the options given below:

A. (*a*), (*d*) and (*e*) only

B. (*b*), (*c*) and (*d*) only

C. (*a*), (*b*) and (*c*) only

D. (*d*), (*e*) and (*f*) only

49. The passage focuses on the aspects mainly related to:

A. Indirect control over investments

B. International orientation of investment

C. Sales facilities

D. Risks involved in integration of production

50. Purely domestic firms are affected by:

A. Low interest rates

B. Small variability of profits

C. Large variability of profits

D. Export controls

ANSWERS

1	2	3	4	5	6	7	8	9	10
D	C	A	A	C	B	D	C	B	B
11	**12**	**13**	**14**	**15**	**16**	**17**	**18**	**19**	**20**
B	B	C	A	C	B	D	C	A	D
21	**22**	**23**	**24**	**25**	**26**	**27**	**28**	**29**	**30**
C	A	C	A	A	D	C	A	D	A
31	**32**	**33**	**34**	**35**	**36**	**37**	**38**	**39**	**40**
A	C	C	A	A	A	B	C	B	D
41	**42**	**43**	**44**	**45**	**46**	**47**	**48**	**49**	**50**
C	D	C	B	A	A	B	B, C	B	C

Explanatory Answers

1. Successful educational communication is dependent upon the skills of

(*a*) Listening

(*b*) Verbal Communication

(*c*) Nonverbal Communication

(*d*) Emotional Awareness

(*e*) Written Communication

(*f*) Communicating in Difficult Situations

2. Indian school of logic is related to form of the argument and content of the argument.

Logic has always intrigued mankind for its sheer scope of immense arguments and discussions. It is the scientific study of 'reasoning'. Scientific here, does not mean anything related to the basic sciences. The usage is primarily more as an adjective meant to qualify the manner in which the study is undertaken. Indian logic, for that matter, has been differently viewed in different ages. Academicians have discussed Indian Logic as a system by compartmentalizing 'Buddhist logic' from it. It not only diminishes the scope of the study but it also narrows the relevance of Indian Logic. It must be studied as the form of correct arguments and inference patterns, developed in India from the methodology of philosophical debate. Therefore, it is generally accepted as a valid knowledge established either by means of perception (using the six senses) or inference.

4. 2 $\xrightarrow{+7}$ 9 $\xrightarrow{+11}$ 20 $\xrightarrow{+15}$ 35 $\xrightarrow{+19}$ 54 $\xrightarrow{+23}$ 77 $\xrightarrow{+27}$ X

Therefore, X = 77 + 27 = 104

5. Effective educational communication is continuous. Communication has great value for humans. People with good communication skills are able to convey their thoughts, knowledge, ideas, etc., effectively to other people. As in all dimensions of social life, in educational organizations, good communication is crucial. For an active, qualified, and productive education, effective communication skills are needed among school managers and teachers, both in the school environment and outside of it. Communication in educational administration includes manager-employee, student-employee, teacher-teacher, and teacher-student relationships. Effective communication in a school setting influences the motivations and satisfaction of managers, teachers, and students. Managers with effective communi-cation skills make it easier for the organization to reach targets.

Effective communication between teachers can be even more fruitful. Employees, managers, and teachers in schools should analyse the communication process, and use it effectively in educational activities. This case will not only help the school achieve its objectives, but also play an important role in socializing students.

6. Effective teaching behaviour/skills includes:

- making oneself clear to all learners regardless of their individual differences.
- using effective non-verbal communication such as enthusiasm and animation through variation in eye contact, voice and gestures to keep students engaged/ involved in the learning process.
- using meaningful verbal phrase to maintain active participation of students.

On the other hand,

- acknowledging and summarising students' ideas is not effective in learning; using those to connect/build further ideas is.
- probing general questions or shifting a discussion to higher thought level defeats the planned learning objectives; teaching must be appropriate for the specific topic as well as the specific class level.

7. Information and Communication Technology (ICT) in education is the mode of education that use information and communications technology to support, enhance, and optimize the delivery of information.

Worldwide research has shown that ICT can lead to an improved student learning and better teaching methods. A report made by the National Institute of Multimedia Education in Japan, proved that an increase in the use of ICT in education with integrating technology to the curriculum has a significant and positive impact on students' achievements. The results specifically showed that the students who are continuously exposed to technology through education has better 'knowledge', presentation skills, innovative capabilities, and are ready to take more efforts into learning as compared to their counterparts.

8. Distribution is the status of a term in regard to extension. The subject-term is distributed in statements whose quantity is universal and undistributed in statements whose quantity is particular. The given statement is universal as it includes 'No' with the subject 'Dog'; so, the subject is distributed.

In affirmative propositions the predicate-term is always taken particularly (and therefore undistributed) and in negative propositions the predicate is always taken universally (and therefore distributed). The given statement is a negative proposition so, the predicate 'are reptiles' is universal and distributed.

10. The distance between two cities P and Q are 360 km

P •———360 km———• Q

Time taken by a car during travelling from P to Q

$$t_1 = \frac{S}{V_1} = \frac{360}{40} = 9 \text{ hr}$$

Time taken by a car during travelling from Q to P

$$t_2 = \frac{S}{V_2} = \frac{360}{60} = 6 \text{ hr}$$

Therefore, average speed of the car

$$\overline{V} = \frac{2S}{t_1 + t_2} = \frac{2 \times 360}{9+6} = \frac{720}{15}$$

$$= 48 \text{ km/hr}$$

11. The compositional skills and creativity in presentation of students can be most effectively evaluated by Essay type tests. Essay questions provide a complex prompt that requires written responses, which can vary in length from a couple of paragraphs to many pages. Like short answer questions, they provide students with an opportunity to explain their understanding and demonstrate creativity, but make it hard for students to arrive at an acceptable answer by bluffing. They can be constructed reasonably, quickly and easily but marking these questions can be time-consuming and grader agreement can be difficult.

Essay questions differ from short answer questions in that the essay questions are less structured. This openness allows students to demonstrate that they can integrate the course material in creative ways. As a result, essays are a favoured approach to test higher levels of cognition including analysis, synthesis and evaluati-on. However, the requirement that the students provide most of the structure increases the amount of work required to respond effectively. Students often take longer to compose a five paragraph essay than they would take to compose five one paragraph answers to short answer questions. This increased workload limits the number of essay questions that can be posed on a single exam and thus can restrict the overall scope of an exam to a few topics or areas. To ensure that this doesn't cause students to panic or blank out, consider giving the option of answering one of two or more questions.

12. At the stage of data analysis, in which quantitative techniques have been used by a researcher, the evidence warrants the rejection of Null Hypothesis (H_0). Rejecting the (H_0) and accepting the substantive research hypothesis will be deemed appropriate. Null hypothesis testing is a formal approach to deciding between two interpretations of a statistical relationship in a sample. One interpretation is called the null hypothesis (often symbolized H_0 and read as "H-naught"). This is the idea that there is no relationship in the population and that the relationship in the sample reflects only sampling error. Informally, the null hypothesis is that the sample relationship "occurred by chance." The other interpretation is called the alternative hypothesis (often symbolized as H_1). This is the idea that there is a relationship in the population and that the relationship in the sample reflects this relationship in the population.

Again, every statistical relationship in a sample can be interpreted in either of these two ways: It might have occurred by chance, or it might reflect a relationship in the population. So researchers need a way to decide between them. Although there are many specific null hypothesis testing techniques, they are all based on the same general logic. The steps are as follows:

- Assume for the moment that the null hypothesis is true. There is no relationship between the variables in the population.
- Determine how likely the sample relationship would be if the null hypothesis were true.
- If the sample relationship would be extremely unlikely, then reject the null hypothesis in favour of the alternative hypothesis. If it would not be extremely unlikely, then retain the null hypothesis.

13. Total maximum marks

$$= 200 + 100 + 200 + 200 + 100$$
$$= 800$$

Total marks obtained

$$= 155 + 80 + 165 + 140 + X$$
$$= 540 + X$$

According to question,

$$800 \times \frac{78}{100} = 540 + X$$

$$\Rightarrow \quad 624 = 540 + X$$
$$\Rightarrow \quad X = 624 - 540$$
$$\Rightarrow \quad X = 84$$

Therefore, the marks obtained by the student in General English would be 84.

14. Length of the diagonal of a square = 11 cm

As a formula, diagonal = $\sqrt{S^2 + S^2}$

[where S is side]

$$\Rightarrow \quad 11 = \sqrt{2S^2}$$

Squaring both sides we get,

$$\Rightarrow \quad 121 = 2S^2$$

$$\Rightarrow \quad \frac{121}{2} = S^2$$

$$\therefore \quad S = \frac{11}{\sqrt{2}}$$

$\therefore$ Area of square = $S^2 = \frac{121}{2}$

According to question, $\pi R^2 = S^2$

$$\Rightarrow \quad \pi R^2 = \frac{121}{2}$$

$$\Rightarrow \quad R^2 = \frac{121}{2\pi} = \frac{121 \times 7}{2 \times 22}$$

$$\therefore \quad R^2 = \frac{77}{4}$$

$$\therefore \quad R = \sqrt{\frac{77}{4}} = \frac{8.77}{2} = 4.39$$

$\therefore$ Diameter of the circle = 2R = 8.7 cm

15. Pedagogy and social interaction are two major result-oriented activities of a teacher is true but communication has a limited role in both these activities is false. There are several factors that contribute to the explanation of the learning outcomes, among them, pedagogical interaction such as teacher competencies or student-student interaction. These factors are considered fundamental for creating effective learning environments, likely to improve the learning outcomes of students.

Pedagogical interaction has been proposed as one of the key parts of any learning experience. Despite the interpersonal relationship in classroom, empathy between students and teachers with students is one of the most relevant factors to establish an efficient interactional environment, promoting the development of meaningful learning and allowing the emergence of attitudes of trust, security and openness.

16. The methodology of inference involves a combination of induction and deduction by moving from particular to particular via generality. It has five steps, as in the example shown:

- There is fire on the hill (called Pratijna, required to be proved)
- Because there is smoke there (called *Hetu,* reason)
- Wherever there is smoke, there is fire, e.g. in a kitchen (called Udaharana, example of vyapti)
- The hill has smoke that is pervaded by fire (called *Upanaya,* reaffirmation or application)
- Therefore, there is fire on the hill (called *Nigamana,* conclusion)

17. Research studies are meant not only to answer research questions but also stand as reference/ guidance for further research in the same or related area(s). A researcher must be able to produce results which are contemporary and relevant. For this, it is imperative to use updated data and resources. By citing old references, the academic/scholar/researcher shows that they have not cared to update the materials/resources used for their research study and thereby, has committed the serious lapse of carelessness which will undermine the relevance of the study.

Technical lapse refers to the lapse relates particular subject, art, or craft, or its techniques.

Ethical lapse relates to compromise with the moral aspects involved.

Academic ignorance means lack of knowledge about education and/or scholarship.

19. Theory of social constructivism can be applied to classroom communication. Social constructivism is a variety of cognitive constructivism that emphasizes the collaborative nature of much learning. Social constructivism was developed by post-revolutionary Soviet psychologist Lev Vygotsky. Vygotsky was a cognitivist, but rejected the assumption made by cognitivists such as Piaget and Perry that it was possible to separate learning from its social context. He argued that all cognitive functions originate in (and must therefore be explained as products of) social interactions and that learning did not simply comprise the assimilation and accommodation of new knowledge by learners; it was the process by which learners were integrated into a knowledge community. According to Vygotsky (1978),

Every function in the child's cultural development appears twice: first, on the social level and, later on, on the individual level; first, between people (interpsychological) and then inside the child (intrapsychological). This applies equally to voluntary attention, to logical memory, and to the formation of concepts. All the higher functions originate as actual relationships between individuals.

Vygotsky's theory of social learning has been expanded upon by numerous later theorists and researchers.

20. Engage, Explore, Explain, Evaluate and Extend correctly indicates the order for ensuring teaching-learning activities in a constructivist approach. Constructivism is an epistemology, or a theory, used to explain how people know what they know. The basic idea is that problem solving is at the heart of learning, thinking, and development. As people solve problems and discover the consequences of their actions—through reflecting on past and immediate experiences–they construct their own understanding. Learning is thus an active process that requires a change in the learner. This is achieved through the activities the learner engages in, including the consequences of those activities, and through reflection. People only deeply understand what they have constructed.

22. Let C.P. = 100

Profit = 10%

Then, S.P. = 100 + 10 = 110

Applying unitary method

If S.P. is 110, then C.P. is 100

If S.P. is 1, then C.P. is = $\frac{100}{110}$

If S.P. is 22000, then C.P. is

$$= \frac{100}{110} \times 22000$$

$$= 20000$$

Now shopkeeper wants profit of 18% on 20000

$$\therefore\ 18\% \text{ of } 20000 = \frac{18}{100} \times 20000$$

$$= 3600$$

∴ We must sell the refrigerator at

$$= 20000 + 3600 = ₹\ 23600$$

23. Social competence refers to the social, emotional, and cognitive skills and behaviuors that children need for successful social adaptation. Despite this simple definition, social competence is an elusive concept, because the skills and behaviuors required for healthy social development vary with the age of the child and with the demands of particular situations. A socially competent preschool child behaves in a much different manner than a socially competent adolescent; conversely, the same behaviours (e.g., aggression, shyness) have different implications for social adaptation depending upon the age of the child and the particulars of the social context.

A child's social competence depends upon a number of factors including the child's social skills, social awareness, and self-confidence. Social skills is a term used to describe the child's knowledge of, and ability to use, a variety of social behaviours that are appropriate to a given interpersonal situation and that are pleasing to others in each situation. The capacity to inhibit egocentric, impulsive, or negative social behaviour is also a reflection of a child's social skills. The term emotional intelligence refers to the child's ability to understand others' emotions, perceive subtle social cues, "read" complex social situations, and demonstrate insight about others' motivations and goals. Children who have a wide repertoire of social skills and who are socially aware and perceptive are likely to be socially competent. Social competence is the broader term used to describe a child's social effectiveness—a child's ability to establish and maintain high quality and mutually satisfying relationships and to avoid negative treatment or victimization from others. In addition to social skills and emotional intelligence, factors such as the child's self-confidence or social anxiety can affect his/her social competence. Social competence can also be affected by the social context and the extent to which there is a good match between the child's skills, interests, and abilities and those of the other children in his/her environment. For example, a quiet and studious boy may appear socially incompetent in a peer group full of raucous athletes, but may do fine socially if a better peer group "niche" can be found for him, such as a group of peers who share his interests in quiet games or computers.

24. Measures to overcome the barriers to effective communication are:

1. Clarify the Ideas before Communication,
2. Communicate According to the Need of Receiver,
3. Consult others before Communicating,
4. Be aware of Language, Tone and Content of Message,
5. Convey Things of Help and Value to Listeners,
6. Ensure Proper Feedback,
7. Communicate for Present as well as Future,
8. Follow up Communications,
9. Be a Good Listener!

25. Qualitative research in primary care deepens understanding of phenomena such as health, illness and health care encounters. Many qualitative studies collect audio or video data (e.g. recordings of interviews, focus groups or talk in consultation), and these are usually transcribed into written form for closer study. Transcribing appears to be a straightforward technical task, but in fact involves judgements about what level of detail to choose (e.g. omitting non-verbal dimensions of interaction), data interpretation (e.g. distinguishing 'I don't, no' from 'I don't know') and data representation (e.g. representing the verbalization 'hwarryuhh' as 'How are you?').

Representation of audible and visual data into written form is an interpretive process which is therefore the first step in analysing data. Different levels of detail and different representations of data will be required for projects with differing aims and methodological approaches.

32. The National Policy on Education (NPE) was adopted by Parliament in May, 1986. A committee was set up under the chairmanship of Acharya Ramamurti in May, 1990 to review NPE and to make recommendations for its modifications. That Committee submitted its report in December, 1990. At the request of the Central Advisory Board of Education (CABE) a committee was set up in July, 1991 under the chairmanship of

Shri N. Janardhana Reddy, Chief Minister of Andhra Pradesh, to consider modifications in NPE taking into consideration the report of the Ramamurti Committee and other relevant developments having a bearing on the Policy, and to make recommendations regarding modifications to be made in the NPE. This Committee submitted its report in January, 1992. The report of the Committee was considered by the CABE in its meeting held on 5-6 May, 1992. While broadly endorsing the NPE, CABE has recommended a few changes in the Policy.

The policy spells out the following:

(*a*) Autonomous colleges will be developed in large numbers. The creation of autonomous departments within universities on a selective basis will be given a fillip.

(*b*) The courses and programmes of college education will be redesigned to meet the demands of specialization better. There would be given emphasis on linguistic competence and course combination.

(*c*) State level planning and co-ordination will be done through Councils of Higher Education. The UGC and these Councils will develop method jointly to keep a watch on standards.

(*d*) Admission will be regulated according to capacity.

(*e*) Methods of teaching will be supplemented by audio-visual aids and electronic gadgets. Development of latest curricula and material, research and teacher orientation will receive close attention.

33. As per provisions of Paris Agreement, the Intended Nationally Determined Contributions (INDCs) are to be reviewed every 5 years. Countries across the globe adopted an historic international climate agreement at the U.N. Framework Convention on Climate Change (UNFCCC) Conference of the Parties (COP21) in Paris in December 2015. In anticipation of this moment, countries publicly outlined what post-2020 climate actions they intended to take under the new international agreement, known as their Intended Nationally Determined Contributions (INDCs). The climate actions communicated in these INDCs largely determine whether the world achieves the long-term goals of the Paris Agreement: to hold the increase in global average temperature to well below 2°C, to pursue efforts to limit the increase to 1.5°C, and to achieve net zero emissions in the second half of this century.

34. Suppose the concentration of Carbondioxide, a greenhouse gas responsible for climate change, is 400 ppm. The concentration of Carbondioxide in air in percentage terms is 0.04%. Concentrations of CO_2 in the atmosphere were as high as 4,000 parts per million (ppm, on a molar basis) during the Cambrian period about 500 million years ago to as low as 180 ppm during the Quaternary glaciation of the last two million years. Reconstructed temperature records for the last 420 million years indicate that atmospheric CO_2 concentrations peaked at ~2000 ppm during the Devonian period, and again in the Triassic period. Global annual mean CO_2 concentration has increased by more than 45% since the start of the Industrial Revolution, from 280 ppm during the 10,000 years up to the mid-18th century to 415 ppm as of May, 2019.

35. Waterborne diseases are caused by drinking contaminated or dirty water. Contaminated water can cause many types of diarrheal diseases, including Cholera, and other serious illnesses such as Guinea worm disease, Typhoid, Dysentery, Polio, Arsenicosis, Trachoma, etc.

36. The National Skills Qualifications Framework (NSQF) is a competency-based framework that organizes all qualifications according to a series of levels of knowledge, skills and aptitude. These levels, graded from one to ten, are defined in terms of learning outcomes which the learner must possess regardless of whether they are obtained through formal, non-formal or informal learning. NSQF in India was notified on 27th December, 2013. All otherframeworks, including the NVEQF (National Vocational Educational Qualification Framework) released by the Ministry of HRD, stand superceded by the NSQF.

Under NSQF, the learner can acquire the certification for competency needed at any level through formal, non-formal or informal learning. In that sense, the NSQF is a quality assurance framework. Presently, more than 100 countries have, or are in the process of developing national qualification frameworks.

The NSQF is anchored at the National Skill Development Agency (NSDA) and is being implemented through the National Skills Qualifications Committee (NSQC) which comprises of all key stakeholders. The NSQC's functions amongst others include approving NOSs/QPs, approving accreditation norms, prescribing guidelines to address the needs of disadvantages sections, reviewing inter-agency disputes and alignment of NSQF with international qualification frameworks.

37. SWAYAM is a Massive Open Online Course platform created by the Ministry of Human Resource Development, Government of India. SWAYAM (Study Webs of Active–Learning for Young Aspiring Minds) is a programme initiated by Government of India and designed to achieve the three cardinal principles of Education Policy viz., access, equity and quality. The objective of this effort is to take the best teaching learning resources to all, including the most disadvantaged. SWAYAM seeks to bridge the digital divide for students who have hitherto remained untouched by the digital revolution and have not been able to join the mainstream of the knowledge economy. This is done through an indigenous developed IT platform that facilitates hosting of all the courses taught in classrooms to be accessed by anyone, anywhere at any time. All the courses are interactive, prepared by the best teachers in the country and are available, free of cost to the residents in India.

SWAYAM platform is developed by Ministry of Human Resource Development (MHRD) and NPTEL, IIT Madras with the help of Google Inc. and Persistent Systems Ltd. It would be ultimately capable of hosting 2000 courses and 80000 hours of learning: covering school, under-graduate, post-graduate, engineering, law and other professional courses.

38. UGC Role and Functions: The prime functions of the University Grants Commission are as follows:

- It provides funds to the various higher educational institutes.
- It carries out the function of coordination, determination and maintenance of standards in institutions of higher education.

In addition to these the University Grants Commission also performs the following functions as well:

- Promoting and coordinating university education.
- Determining and maintaining standards of teaching, examination and research in universities.
- Framing regulations on minimum standards of education.
- Monitoring developments in the field of collegiate and university education; disbursing grants to the universities and colleges.
- Serving as a vital link between the Union and state governments and institutions of higher learning.

- Advising the Central and State governments on the measures necessary for improvement of university education.
  Finally it can be concluded saying that the UGC looks after the proper development and fostering of higher education in the country.

39. Text files contain textual data and may be saved in plain text or rich text formats. While most text files are documents created and saved by users, they can also be used by software developers to store program data. Examples of text files include word processing documents, log files, and saved email messages.

Common text file extensions include .TXT, .RTF, .LOG, and .DOCX.

40. A local-area network (LAN) is a computer network that spans a relatively small area. Most often, a LAN is confined to a single room, building or group of buildings, however, one LAN can be connected to other LANs over any distance via telephone lines and radio waves.

Most LANs connect workstations and personal computers. Each node (individual computer) in a LAN has its own CPU with which it executes programs, but it also is able to access data and devices anywhere on the LAN. This means that many users can share expensive devices, such as laser printers, as well as data. Users can also use the LAN to communicate with each other, by sending email or engaging in chat sessions.

LANs are capable of transmitting data at very fast rates, much faster than data can be transmitted over a telephone line; but the distances are limited and there is also a limit on the number of computers that can be attached to a single LAN.

An ISP stands for Internet Service Provider and IP address means Internet Protocol Address.

41. There was once a time when CPU clock speed increased dramatically from year to year. In the 90s and early 2000s processors increased at incredible speeds, shooting from 60 MHz Pentium chips to gigahertz-level processors within a decade. But around 2005, the top CPU clock speed of the high-end processors settled around 4 GHz and hasn't increased much since then. Now greater improvements in power come from multi-core processor designs. As a result, we see chips like AMD's recent offerings, with a dramatically increased number of cores. These modern transistors and Chips have increased the power of processors. Thus CPU clock speed need not to increase.

42. Biomass fuels generate energy from things that once lived such as wood products, dried vegetation, crop residues, aquatic plants, and even garbage. When plants lived, they used a lot of the sun's energy to make their own food (photosynthesis). They stored the foods in the plants in a form of chemical energy. As the plants died, the energy became entrapped in the remains. This trapped energy is usually released by burning and can be converted into biomass energy. Wood remains the largest biomass energy source to date. Industrial biomass can be grown from numerous types of plants, including miscanthus, switchgrass, hemp, corn, poplar, willow, sorghum, sugarcane, bamboo, and a variety of tree species, ranging from eucalyptus to oil palm. Burning materials like wood, waste, and other plant matters releases stored chemical energy in the form of heat, which can be used to turn shaft to produce electricity.

43. Xuanzang carried back scriptures from Nalanda University and wrote about architecture and learning of this university. Xuanzang (c. 602 – 664) was a Chinese Buddhist monk, scholar, traveller, and translator who travelled to India in the seventh century and described the interaction between Chinese Buddhism and Indian Buddhism during the early Tang dynasty.

During the journey he visited many sacred Buddhist sites in what are now Pakistan, India, Nepal, and Bangladesh. He was born in what is now Henan province around 602, from boyhood he took to reading religious books, including the Chinese classics and the writings of ancient sages.

He became famous for his seventeen-year overland journey to India (including Nalanda), which is recorded in detail in the classic Chinese text *Great Tang Records on the Western Regions*, which in turn provided the inspiration for the novel *Journey to the West* written by Wu Cheng'en during the Ming dynasty, around nine centuries after Xuanzang's death.

44. A web browser is a software application for accessing information on the World Wide Web. A word processor is a device or computer program that provides for input, editing, formating and output of text, often with some additional features. A spreadsheet is a computer application for organization, analysis and storage of data in tabular form. Web authoring software is a type of desktop publishing tool that allows users to navigate the tricky environment of HTML and web coding by offering a different kind of graphical user interface.

45. CPU clock speed, or clock rate, is measured in Hertz-generally in gigahert z(GHz). A CPU's clock speed rate is a measure of how many clock cycles a CPU can perform per second. For example, a CPU with a clock rate of 1.8 GHz can perform 1,800,000 clock cycles per second. This seems simple on its face. The more clock cycles a CPU can perform, the more things it can get done.

Modern CPUs also aren't fixed at a single speed, particularly laptop, smartphone, tablet and other mobile CPUs where power efficiency and heat production are major concerns. Instead, the CPU runs at a slower speed when idle (or when you]re not doing too much) and a faster speed under load. The CPU dynamically increases and decreases its speed when needed. When doing something demanding, the CPU will increase its clock rate, get the work donw as quickly as possible, and get back to the slower clock rate that allows it to save more power.

Previous Years' Paper (Solved)

National Testing Agency (NTA)

UGC-NET (JRF) Online Exam, June-2019*

PAPER–I

1. Which among the following best describes the Emotional Intelligence of learners?

(*a*) Understand the emotion of other people and your own

(*b*) Express oneself very strongly

(*c*) Being rational in thinking

(*d*) Adjusting one's emotion as per situation

(*e*) Being creative and open to criticism

(*f*) Accepting other people as they are

Choose your answer from the options given below:

A. (*a*), (*d*) and (*f*) B. (*d*), (*e*) and (*f*)

C. (*a*), (*b*) and (*c*) D. (*b*), (*c*) and (*d*)

2. Which of the following statements explains the concepts of inclusive teaching?

A. Teacher facilitates the learning of the gifted students

B. Teacher facilitates the learning of the weak students

C. Teacher takes support of parents of the students to make them learn

D. Teacher makes the students of different backgrounds to learn together in the same

3. Who developed the theory of 'Multiple Intelligence'?

A. Alfred Binet B. L. Thurstone

C. Charles Spearman D. Howard Gardner

4. Bibliography given in a research report

A. Helps those interested in further research

B. Shows the vast knowledge of the researcher

C. Makes the report authentic

D. Is an optional part of the report

5. From the list of the effective teaching behaviours, identify those which are called key behaviours.

(*i*) Direct, audible and oral delivery to all students

(*ii*) Encouraging students to elaborate on an answer

(*iii*) Warm and nurturing relationships with learners

(*iv*) Varying modes of presentation

(*v*) Preventing misbehaviour with a minimum of class disruption

(*vi*) Organising what is to come and summarising what has gone before.

Select your answer from the options given below:

A. (*i*), (*iv*) and (*v*)

B. (*i*), (*ii*) and (*iii*)

C. (*ii*), (*iii*) and (*iv*)

D. (*iv*), (*v*) and (*vi*)

6. Through which research method, the manipulation of an independent variable and its effect on dependent variable is examined with reference to a hypothesis under controlled conditions?

A. Ex-post facto research

B. Descriptive research

C. Case study research

D. Experimental research

7. Which of the following is a plagiarism checking website?

A. http://go.turnitin.com

B. http://www.researchgate.com

C. http://www.editorial.elsevier.com

D. http://www.grammarly.com

* *Online Exam held on 24 June, 2019.*

8. The research design is specifically related to which of the following features in research?

(*i*) Sample selection

(*ii*) Formulation of a plan

(*iii*) Deciding about the tool for data collection

(*iv*) Hypothesis making

(*v*) Choice of a field of inquiry

Select your answer from the options given below:

A. (*ii*), (*iii*) and (*iv*) B. (*i*), (*ii*) and (*iii*)

C. (*ii*), (*iv*) and (*v*) D. (*iii*), (*iv*) and (*v*)

9. To organize discussion method in teaching effectively, which of the following conditions should be met?

(*a*) Topic be easy

(*b*) Topic be declared in advance

(*c*) Topic of common interest

(*d*) Availability of more than one teacher

(*e*) Language facility of participants

Select appropriate answer from the options given below:

A. (*b*), (*c*) and (*e*) B. (*a*), (*b*) and (*c*)

C. (*a*), (*b*) and (*e*) D. (*c*), (*d*) and (*e*)

10. In which of the following research studies interpretation and meaning get more attention than formulation of generalisations?

(*i*) Historical studies

(*ii*) Survey studies

(*iii*) Philosophical studies

(*iv*) Ethnographic studies

(*v*) Hypothetico — deductive studies

(*vi*) Ex-post facto studies

Choose your answer from the options given below:

A. (*i*), (*ii*) and (*iii*) B. (*iv*), (*v*) and (*vi*)

C. (*ii*), (*iv*) and (*v*) D. (*i*), (*iii*) and (*iv*)

Directions (Qs. No. 11 to 15): *Read the comprehension carefully and answer these question.*

COMPREHENSION

Michaelangelo is famous for having successfully interpreted the human body. His great achievement is that of the painting of David whose hands reach out as a sign of human capability and potential. It is assumed that the time he lived was ripe for exchange of knowledge, development in science and matured enough to advance the horizon of investigation in all fields. Renaissance humanism stressed on a serious rethink on the nature of art that focussed on accurate details. In painting and sculpture, artists focussed on not so casual but verifiable and minute details. Michaelangelo's paintings are no exception to it. In a study published in the journal of the royal Society of medicine, a group of surgeons are of the opinion that the great master was "afflicted by an illness involving his joints". They have used his portraits as evidence to argue their view. During his life, he complained of what he felt to be 'gout'. Later he complained of his sore and stiff hands which the doctors would find to be natural for someone who was engaged in handmade art. The doctors found corroboration of those claims in portraits of the artist that show a hanging left hand with both degenerative and non-degenerative changes. They attribute the pain not just to arthritis, but to the stress of hammering and chiseling and note that though the master was seen hammering days before his death at an old age, he did not write or sign his own letters before his death. In recent times there have been attempts to diagnose famous artists with diseases that were not known during their time. This practice has raised many questions, especially on the issue of ethics in research. It is also inferred from authentic analysis that Michaelangelo persisted in his work until his last days. This theory would emphasize that his artistic subject defied his physical infirmities.

11. Renaissance painting in Europe was sceptical of

A. The obsessive medieval method of accuracy

B. The classical simplicity and lack of control

C. The case and decorative excess of earlier art

D. Expressionist technique

12. What actually may be concluded from the above passage?

A. Physical infirmities do dissuade people with capabilities from excelling
B. Excellence in any form triumphs over extraneous factors including physical ailments
C. Michaelangelo's gout and other ailments lessened his efficiency
D. The diseases Michaelangelo faced were due to constant hammering

13. Michaelangelo lived during a time that lets us know that
A. Human aspirations are limitless and open to new vistas of knowledge
B. Cross cultural exchange in ideas is the only way for human progress
C. It is progress of science and anatomy that contributes to civilizations exclusively
D. Human beings possess language which is the only key to knowledge

14. What generalisations do people subscribe to?
A. Establishing facts by DNA tests
B. Inferring the essence of character from famous people's handwriting
C. Carbon dating of the hair of celebrities to draw conclusion on their physical structure
D. To retroactively diagnose famous artists and public figures of conditions that were not prevalent during their time

15. The controversy that the passage above refers to is whether
A. Michaelangelo worked under duress
B. Michaelangelo could contain his physical infirmity by artistic excellence
C. Michaelangelo submitted to disease
D. Michaelangelo survived different diseases before pursuing art

16. In a classroom situation, a teacher organises group discussion to help arrive at a solution of a problem. In terms of a model of communication used, it will be called
A. A transactional model
B. An interaction model
C. A horizontal model
D. A linear model

17. In a new budget, the price of petrol rose by 25%. By how much per cent must a person reduce his consumption so that his expenditure on it dows not increase?
A. 10% B. 15%
C. 20% D. 25%

18. Today's media-society equation is largely
A. Mystical
B. Morally bound
C. Consumer conscious
D. Tradition centric

19. The dance of the honeybee conveying to other bees where nector will be found is an example of
A. Mass communication
B. Group communication
C. Interpersonal communication
D. Intrapersonal communication

20. Which of the following is a function of mass media?
A. To transmit culture
B. To formulate national policies
C. To help the judiciary take its decisions
D. To stabilise the share market

21. Choose the correct sequence of communication from the options given below:
A. Information – exposure – persuasion – behavioural change
B. Persuasion – information – behavioural change – exposure
C. Exposure — information – persuasion – behavioural change
D. Behavioural change – information – persuasion – exposure

22. Given below are two premises with four conclusions drawn from them. Which of the following conclusions could be validly drawn from the premises?

Premises :
(*i*) No paper is pen.
(*ii*) Some paper are handmade.

Conclusions :

1. All paper are handmade
2. Some handmade are pen
3. Some handmade are not pen
4. All handmade are paper

A. 1 B. 2
C. 3 D. 4

23. For all integers $y > 1, \langle y \rangle = 2y + (2y-1) + (2y-2) + ... + 1$. What is the value of $\langle 3 \rangle \times \langle 2 \rangle$? Where × is a multiplication operator?

A. 116 B. 210
C. 263 D. 478

24. The proposition 'No historians are non-mathematician' is equivalent to which of the following proposition?

A. All historians are mathematicians
B. No historians are mathematicians
C. Some historians are mathematicians
D. Some historians are not mathematicians

25. A sum of money doubles at compound interest in 6 years. In how many years will it become 16 times?

A. 16 years B. 24 years
C. 48 years D. 96 years

26. If the proposition 'Houses are not bricks' is taken to be False then which of the following propositions can be True?

(*a*) All houses are bricks
(*b*) No house is brick
(*c*) Some houses are bricks
(*d*) Some houses are not bricks

Select the correct answer from the options given below:

A. (*b*) and (*c*) B. (*a*) and (*d*)
C. (*b*) only D. (*c*) only

27. 'All republics are grateful' and 'Some republics are not grateful' cannot both be true, and they can not both be false. This is called as

A. contraries B. contradictories
C. subaltern D. super altern

28. Identify the reasoning in the following argument: 'Use of teaching aids in the classroom to enhance learning is important in a similar way as that of the use of ICT for production of knowledge'.

A. Hypothetical B. Analogical
C. Inductive D. Deductive

29. Oar is to rowboat as foot is to

A. running B. sneaker
C. skateboard D. jumping

30. If 152 is divided into four parts proportional to 3, 4, 5 and 7, then the smallest part is

A. 29 B. 26
C. 25 D. 24

Directions (Qs. No. 31 to 35): *Consider the following table that shows the number (in lakhs) of different sizes of LED television sets sold by a company over the last seven years from 2012 to 2018. Answer the questions based on the data contained in the table.*

Sale of LED Television sets (in lakhs) of different sizes (in inches)

Year	**Size of LED Television sets (in inches)**				
	22"	**24"**	**32"**	**40"**	**49"**
2012	85	154	124	112	118
2013	100	136	112	94	136
2014	106	124	85	115	145
2015	115	100	160	100	85
2016	100	85	145	85	100
2017	115	70	175	55	130
2018	125	95	170	110	155

31. What is the difference in the number of 40-inch Television sets sold in 2013 and 2018?

A. 1,600,000 B. 1,500,000

C. 15,000,000 D. 16,000,000

32. What was the approximate percentage increase/decrease in the sales of 32-inch LED Television sets in 2017 compared to that in 2013?

A. 36% B. 56%

C. 57% D. 64%

33. What is the total sale of Television sets of size 49-inches (in lakhs) over all the seven years?

A. 912 B. 896

C. 879 D. 869

34. For which LED Television set is the total sales of all the seven years the minimum?

A. 22-inch Television

B. 24-inch Television

C. 49-inch Television

D. 40-inch Television

35. For which size LED Television sets is the total sales of all the seven years the maximum?

A. 22-inch Television

B. 24-inch Television

C. 32-inch Television

D. 49-inch Television

36. Algal blooms in oligotrophic lakes are

A. very frequent B. frequent

C. very rare D. widespread

37. The Education Commission of India that first took serious note of the problem of Brain Drain was

A. The Education Commission of India

B. The University Education Commission

C. The Calcutta University Commission

D. The Sargeant Commission

38. In the last few years, India has been affected by which of the following tropical cyclones?

A. Gaja, Hudhud, Bhima

B. Hudhud, Bhima, Ockhi

C. Gaja, Hudhud, Ockhi

D. Gaja, Bhima, Ockhi

39. Which one of the following pairs LEAST matches in respect of computers?

A. 1 Giga Byte : (1024) × (1024) × (1024) × 8 bits

B. CRT : Cathode Ray Tube

C. ROM : Rapid Online Memory

D. CPU : Central Processing Unit

40. Which one of the followig instructional designs is not a part of SWAYAM launched by Government of India?

A. E-tutorial

B. E-Content

C. Physical interaction

D. Discussion Forum

41. **Assertion (A):** Methemoglobinemia is a condition in which blood is not able to carry and deliver enough oxygen to the body.

Reason (R): Consuming drinking water with high nitrate levels may cause methemoglobinemia.

Choose the correct answer from the options given below:

A. Both (A) and (R) are true and (R) is the correct explanation of (A).

B. Both (A) and (R) are true but (R) is not the correct explanation of (A).

C. (A) is true and (R) is false.

D. (A) is false but (R) is true.

42. The present form of Inter University Board that was previously established for promoting cooperation and coordination among Universities is

A. UGC B. AIU

C. NUEPA D. ICSSR

43. Select the true statement about an Operating System (OS)?

A. An OS controls peripherals, allocates memory and organises data into fields and records

B. An OS provides protection against viruses and controls peripherals

C. An OS controls peripheral, and allocates memory and processor time

D. An OS controls the processor and peripherals and allows the user to connect to the Internet

44. **Assertion (A):** High concentration of ozone in the lower troposphere is desirable.
Reason (R): Ozone present in the atmosphere protects the living organisms on the surface of earth from the harmful ultra-violet radiation of the sun.
Choose the correct answer from the options given below:
A. Both (A) and (R) are true and (R) is the correct explanation of (A).
B. Both (A) and (R) are true but (R) is not the correct explanation of (A).
C. (A) is true and (R) is false.
D. (A) is false but (R) is true.

45. Which of the following NOT correctly matched?
(*i*) Gyan darshan — Satellite based educational TV Channel
(*ii*) Gyan vani — Educational FM Radio network
(*iii*) MOOCs — Massive Open Online Credits
Choose the correct answer from the options given below:
A. Only (*i*) and (*ii*)
B. Only (*ii*) and (*iii*)
C. Only (*iii*)
D. Only (*i*) and (*iii*)

46. In post independence India, which one of the following Committee/Commission's report deals with all levels of education in India?
A. Sargeant Commission
B. Hartog Committee
C. Kothari Commission
D. Radhakrishnan Commission

47. Which of the following statement(s) is/are True in respect of Wireless Technology?
P : Bluetooth is a wireless technology which can be used to connect a headset to a mobile phone.
Q : Bluetooth is a long range wireless technology and is a low cost means of data transfer.
A. P only B. Q only
C. Both P and Q D. Neither P nor Q

48. Which of the following is a type of malware intentionally inserted into a software system that will setoff a malicious function when specified conditions are met?
A. Worm B. Trojan
C. Spyware D. Logic bomb

49. Select the option that shows the storage devices in order of capacity from lowest to highest
A. CD-ROM, DVD-ROM, Blu-ray
B. Blu-ray, CD-ROM, DVD-ROM
C. DVD-ROM, Blu-ray, CD-ROM
D. DVD-ROM, CD-ROM, Blu-ray

50. Which of the following are priority areas in relation to the Sustainable Development Goals?
(*a*) No poverty
(*b*) Zero hunger
(*c*) Reducing urbanization
(*d*) Peace, justice and strong institutions
Choose the correct answer from the options given below:
A. (*a*), (*b*), (*c*) B. (*a*), (*c*), (*d*)
C. (*b*), (*c*), (*d*) D. (*a*), (*b*), (*d*)

ANSWERS

1	**2**	**3**	**4**	**5**	**6**	**7**	**8**	**9**	**10**
A	D	D	A	A	D	D	B	A	D
11	**12**	**13**	**14**	**15**	**16**	**17**	**18**	**19**	**20**
C	B	A	D	B	A	C	C	B	A
21	**22**	**23**	**24**	**25**	**26**	**27**	**28**	**29**	**30**
C	C	B	A	B	D	B	B	C	D

31	32	33	34	35	36	37	38	39	40
A	B	D	D	C	C	A	C	C	C
41	**42**	**43**	**44**	**45**	**46**	**47**	**48**	**49**	**50**
A	B	C	D	C	C	A	D	A	D

Explanatory Answers

1. Emotional intelligence is different from general or common intelligence. It's the ability of an individual to monitor their own emotions, to monitor the emotions of others, to understand the differences between them, and to use all of this information in order to guide their actions. This is about accurately understanding the emotions of oneself and others, as well as expressing emotions in a way that's accessible.

A high level of emotional intelligence is an essential aspect of learning. The ability to develop the skill of emotional understanding is a driver not only in the realm of relationships but also in the realm of education. The following four dimensions of emotional intelligence can help teachers and administrators to better understand and support student learning.

- Understanding
- Management
- Relationships
- Empathy

2. Inclusive teaching posits cultural diversity, or differences related to identity and experience, as crucial to learning. The practice of inclusive teaching involves consciously working to foster learning across differences, for example by acknowledging and challenging biases and stereotypes that can impede understanding and undermine a student's sense of belonging to the discipline or institution. The practice of inclusive teaching also involves keeping accessibility and transparency in mind when designing courses and assignments, as well as being aware of power differences within the classroom and of psycho-social factors that can affect learning.

3. The theory of multiple intelligences was developed in 1983 by Dr. Howard Gardner, professor of education at Harvard University. It suggests that the traditional notion of intelligence, based on I.Q. testing, is far too limited. Instead, Dr. Gardner proposes eight different intelligences to account for a broader range of human potential in children and adults. These intelligences are:

- Linguistic intelligence ("word smart")
- Logical-mathematical intelligence ("number/reasoning smart")
- Spatial intelligence ("picture smart")
- Bodily-Kinesthetic intelligence ("body smart")
- Musical intelligence ("music smart")
- Interpersonal intelligence ("people smart")
- Intrapersonal intelligence ("self smart")
- Naturalist intelligence ("nature smart").

4. Bibliography given in a research report helps those interested in further research and studying the problem from another angle.

6. Experimental research is any research conducted with a scientific approach, where a set of variables are kept constant while the other set of variables are being measured as the subject of experiment. Experimental research is one of the founding quantitative research methods.

The simplest example of an experimental research is conducting a laboratory test. As long as research is being conducted under scientifically acceptable conditions – it qualifies as an experimental research. A true experimental research is considered to be successful only when the researcher confirms that a change in the dependent variable is solely due to the manipulation of the independent variable.

7. Plagiarism is the representation of another person's work as one's own. It can be intentional, which normally happens when students and inexperienced writers copy other people's content in an effort to save themselves the time spent in conducting real research. Plagiarism can also be unintentional. Just about everything we do has been influenced by someone along the way. A writer can, therefore, have a style that has been influenced by an author they admire. That could result in unintentional plagiarism through similarity of style.

List of best plagiarism Checker Tool

- Scribbr (Uses Turnitin plagiarism detection technology)
- Plagiarism Checker (Grammarly Writing Assistant and Plagiarism checker; Used in universities)
- PWA (Safe plagiarism checker with Grammar assistant; Supports Mac)
- Turnitin (Used by universities and Colleges)
- Prowritingaid (Grammar and Plagiarism checking tool)
- Plagiarisma (Plagiarism checker tool)
- Plagiarismcheckerx (Safe Desktop Plagiarism Checking tool for students and professors)
- Bibme (Web based Plagiarism Checking tool)
- Copyscape (Plagiarism checker tool)
- MOSS (Measure of Software Similarity).

8. Research design is a general plan about what you will do to answer the research question. Important elements of research design include research strategies and methods related to data collection and analysis.

Research design can be divided into two groups: exploratory and conclusive. Exploratory research, according to its name merely aims to explore specific aspects of the research area. Exploratory research does not aim to provide final and conclusive answers to research questions. The researcher may even change the direction of the study to a certain extent, however not funda-mentally, according to new evidences gained during the research process.

Conclusive research can be divided into two categories: descriptive and causal. Descriptive research design, as the name suggests, describes specific elements, causes, or phenomena in the research area. Causal research design, on the other hand, is conducted to study cause-and-effect relationships.

16. Models of communication have evolved significantly since Shannon and Weaver first proposed their well- known conceptual model over sixty years ago. One of the most useful models for understanding public speaking is Barnlund's transactional model of communication. In the transactional model, communication is seen as an ongoing, circular process. We are constantly affecting and are affected by those we communicate with. The transactional model has a number of interdependent processes and components, including the encoding and decoding processes, the communicator, the message, the channel and noise. Although not directly addressed in Barnlund's (2008) original transactional model, participants' worldviews and the context also play an important role in the communication process.

17. If the price of petrol increases by R%, then the reduction in consumption so as not to increase the expenditure is $\left[\frac{R}{100+R}\times 100\right]\%$

Here, R = 25

Hence, % decrease in the consumption of petrol

$$= \left[\frac{25}{100+25}\times 100\right]\%$$

$$= 20\%$$

18. Today's media-society equation is largely consumer conscious. Society is influenced by media in so many ways. It is the media for the masses that helps them to get information about a lot of things and also form opinions and make a judgement regarding various issues. It is the media, which keep people updated and informed about what is happening around them and the world that everyone draws something from it.

19. The dance of the honeybee, conveying to other bees where nector will be found is an example of group communication. Group communication as the word says is communicating in groups. There are different type of groups, family, friends, relatives, acquaintances, co-workers, etc. Any kind of communication among the group is said to be group communication.

20. Almost everyone gets his or her information about world, national, and local affairs from the mass media. This fact gives both print and broadcast journalism important functions that include influencing public opinion, determining the political agenda, providing a link between the government and the people, acting as a government watchdog, and affecting socialization.

The mass media, most significantly through its news, reporting, and analysis, affects what and how we learn about politics and our own political views. Along with family, schools, and religious organizations, television also becomes part of the process by which people learn society's values and come to understand what society expects from them. In this regard, the impact comes primarily from entertainment programming.

25. As we know that for time t_1 money becomes n_1 and in time t_2 it becomes n_2.

So, relation between them is,

$$n_2 = (n_1)^{\frac{t_2}{t_1}}$$

$$\Rightarrow 16 = (2)^{\frac{t_2}{6}}$$

$$\Rightarrow (2)^4 = (2)^{\frac{t_2}{6}}$$

$$\Rightarrow 4 = \frac{t_2}{6}$$

$$\Rightarrow t_2 = 24 \text{ years}$$

30. According to the question, there must be some small factor x which, when multiplied by the 4 numbers and summed, adds upto 152.

So, $3x + 4x + 5x + 7x = 152$

$\Rightarrow 19x = 152$

$\therefore x = \frac{152}{19} = 8$

So, the smallest part $3x = 3 \times 8 = 24$

36. An oligotrophic lake is a lake with low primary productivity, as a result of low nutrient content. These lakes have low algal production, and consequently, often have very clear waters, with high drinking-water quality. The bottom waters of such lakes typically have ample oxygen; thus, such lakes often support many fish species such as lake trout, which require cold, well-oxygenated waters. The oxygen content is likely to be higher in deep lakes, owing to their larger hypolimnetic volume.

Ecologists use the term oligotrophic to distinguish unproductive lakes, characterised by nutrient deficiency, from productive, eutrophic lakes, with an ample or excessive nutrient supply. Oligotrophic lakes are most common in cold regions underlain by resistant igneous rocks.

39. Read-only memory (ROM) is a type of storage medium that permanently stores data on personal computers (PCs) and other electronic devices. It contains the programming needed to start a PC, which is essential for boot-up; it performs major input/output tasks and holds programs or software instructions.

Because ROM is read-only, it cannot be changed; it is permanent and non-volatile, meaning it also holds its memory even when power is removed. By contrast, random access memory (RAM) is volatile; it is lost when power is removed.

There are numerous ROM chips located on the motherboard and a few on expansion boards. The chips are essential for the basic input/output system (BIOS), boot up, reading and writing to peripheral devices, basic data management and the software for basic processes for certain utilities.

40. SWAYAM (Study Webs of Active–Learning for Young Aspiring Minds) is a programme initiated by Government of India and designed to achieve the three cardinal principles of Education Policy viz., access, equity and quality. The objective of this effort is to take the best teaching learning resources to all, including the most disadvantaged. SWAYAM seeks to bridge the digital divide for students who have hitherto remained untouched by the digital revolution and have not been able to join the mainstream of the knowledge economy. This is done through an indigenous developed IT platform that facilitates hosting of all the courses taught in classrooms to be accessed by anyone, anywhere at any time. All the courses are interactive, prepared by the best teachers in the country and are available, free of cost to the residents in India.

SWAYAM platform is developed by Ministry of Human Resource Development (MHRD) and NPTEL, IIT Madras with the help of Google Inc. and Persistent Systems Ltd. It would be ultimately capable of hosting 2000 courses and 80000 hours of learning: covering school, under-graduate, post-graduate, engineering, law and other professional courses.

The courses hosted on SWAYAM is in 4 quadrants

- video lecture
- specially prepared reading material that can be downloaded/printed
- self-assessment tests through tests and quizzes and
- an online discussion forum for clearing the doubts.

41. Methemoglobinemia is a blood disorder that occurs when too little oxygen is delivered to the cells of the body. There are two kinds of methemoglobinemia — congenital and acquired.

Babies can inherit it from their parents; this is called congenital MetHb. Sometimes it is called blue baby syndrome, as one of the symptoms can be a blue tinge to the skin.

People can develop acquired MetHb after exposure to certain drugs or chemicals. Acquired MetHb is also rare, but it is usually mild and resolves after the person has identified and removed the cause. Acquired MetHb is more common than the inherited forms. It occurs in some people after they are exposed to certain chemicals and medicines, including:

- Anesthetics such as benzocaine
- Nitrobenzene
- Certain antibiotics (including dapsone and chloroquine)
- Nitrites (used as additives to prevent meat from spoiling).

42. The Association of Indian Universities (AIU) acts as a centre for Indian Universities. It was originated in our country according to the recommendations of Saddler Commission-1917. The Commission had recommended for establishing an inter-university board in the country for maintaining proper liaison and coordination between the universities. So, the board took final shape in a conference of the vice-chancellors of Universities convened by the then viceroy of India at Shimla in 1924.

The Inter-University Board (IUB) of India subsequently formed on March 23, 1925, to promote university activities, by sharing information and co-operation in the field of education, culture, sports and allied areas. The Board acquired a legal status with its registration in 1967 as a society under the Societies Registration Act, 1860. In 1973, it assumed it present name "The Association of Indian University (AIU)''.

43. An operating system (OS) is system software that manages computer hardware and software resources and provides common services for computer programs.

Time-sharing operating systems schedule tasks for efficient use of the system and may also include accounting software for cost allocation of processor time, mass storage, printing, and other resources.

For hardware functions such as input and output and memory allocation, the operating system acts as an intermediary between programs and the computer hardware, although the application code is usually executed directly by the hardware and frequently makes system calls to an OS function or is interrupted by it. Operating systems are found on many devices that contain a computer –from cellular phones and video game consoles to web servers and supercomputers.

44. Ozone or trioxygen, is an inorganic molecule with the chemical formula O_3. It is a pale blue gas with a distinctively pungent smell. It is an allotrope of oxygen that is much less stable than the diatomic allotrope O_2, breaking down in the lower atmosphere to O_2 (dioxygen). Ozone is formed from dioxygen by the action of ultraviolet light (UV) and electrical discharges within the Earth's atmosphere. It is present in very low concentrations throughout the latter, with its highest concentration high in the ozone layer of the stratosphere, which absorbs most of the Sun's ultraviolet (UV) radiation. Ozone present in the atmosphere protects the living organisms on the surface of earth from the harmful ultraviolet radiation of the sun.

45. A massive open online course (MOOC) is an online course aimed at unlimited participation and open access via the web. In addition to traditional course materials, such as filmed lectures, readings, and problem sets, many MOOCs provide interactive courses with user forums to support community interactions among students, professors, and teaching assistants (TAs), as well as immediate feedback to quick quizzes and assignments. MOOCs are a recent and widely researched development in distance education, first introduced in 2006 and emerged as a popular mode of learning in 2012.

Early MOOCs often emphasized open-access features, such as open licensing of content, structure and learning goals, to promote the reuse and remixing of resources. Some later MOOCs use closed licenses for their course materials while maintaining free access for students.

46. In post independence India, Kothari Commission's report deals with all levels of education in India. 'Indian Education Commisison (1964-66)' popularly known as Kothari Commission, was an adhoc Commisison setup by the Government of India to examine all aspects of the educational sector in India, to evolve a general pattern of education and to advise guideline and policies for the development of education in India. It was formed on 14 July, 1964 under the chairmanship of Daulat Singh Kothari, then chairman of the UGC.

It consisted of 16 members, 11 being Indians and 5 foreign experts. The terms of reference of the Commission was to formulate the general priciples and guidelines for the development of education from primary level to the highest and advise the government on a standardized national pattern of education in India. However, the medical and legal studies were excluded from the purview of the Commission. The tenancy of the Commission was from 1964 to 1966 and the report was submitted by the Commission on 29 June, 1966.

47. Bluetooth is a wireless technology standard for exchanging data between fixed and mobile devices over short distances using short-wavelength UHF radio waves in the industrial, scientific and medical radio bands, from 2.400 to 2.485 GHz, and building personal area networks (PANs). It was originally conceived as a wireless alternative to RS-232 data cables.

48. A logic bomb is a piece of code intentionally inserted into a software system that will set off a malicious function when specified conditions are met. For example, a programmer may hide a piece of code that starts deleting files (such as a salary database trigger), should they ever be terminated from the company.

Software that is inherently malicious, such as viruses and worms, often contain logic bombs that execute a certain payload at a pre-defined time or when some other condition is met. This technique can be used by a virus or worm to gain momentum and spread before being noticed. Some viruses attack their host systems on specific dates, such as Friday the 13th or April Fools' Day. Trojans and other computer viruses that activate on certain dates are often called "time bombs".

To be considered a logic bomb, the payload should be unwanted and unknown to the user of the software. As an example, trial programs with code that disables certain functionality after a set time are not normally regarded as logic bombs.

50. The Sustainable Development Goals (SDGs), otherwise known as the Global Goals, are a universal call to action to end poverty, protect the planet and ensure that all people enjoy peace and prosperity.

These 17 Goals build on the successes of the Millennium Development Goals, while including new areas such as climate change, economic inequality, innovation, sustainable consumption, peace and justice, among other priorities. The goals are interconnected – often the key to success on one will involve tackling issues more commonly associated with another.

The SDGs came into effect in January 2016, and they will continue to guide UNDP policy and funding until 2030. As the lead UN development agency, UNDP is uniquely placed to help implement the Goals through our work in some 170 countries and territories.

Our strategic plan focuses on key areas including poverty alleviation, democratic governance and peacebuilding, climate change and disaster risk, and economic inequality. UNDP provides support to governments to integrate the SDGs into their national development plans and policies. This work is already underway, as we support many countries in accelerating progress already achieved under the Millennium Development Goals.

Our track record working across multiple goals provides us with a valuable experience and proven policy expertise to ensure we all reach the targets set out in the SDGs by 2030. But we cannot do this alone.

Achieving the SDGs requires the partnership of governments, private sector, civil society and citizens alike to make sure we leave a better planet for future generations.

Previous Years' Paper (Solved)

National Testing Agency (NTA)

UGC-NET (JRF) Online Exam, December-2018*

PAPER–I

1. Which of the following is an indicator of key behaviour in effective teaching as evident from researches?

A. teacher affect in developing teacher-learner relationship
B. engagement in learning by students
C. using students ideas and contributions
D. use of process and content questions during teaching

2. In the following statements identify those which relate to 'Norm-Referenced Testing' (NRT). Select from the code to give your answer.

(*a*) Covering a large domain of learning tasks with just a few items measuring specific tasks.
(*b*) Emphasizing discrimination among individuals in terms of relative level of learning.
(*c*) Focusing on a specified domain of learning tasks with a large number of items measuring specific tasks.
(*d*) Interpretation requires a clearly defined group.
(*e*) Interpretation requires a clearly defined achievement domain.
(*f*) Emphasizing description of learning tasks which individuals can and cannot perform.

Code:

A. (*a*), (*b*) and (*d*) B. (*b*), (*c*) and (*f*)
C. (*a*), (*b*) and (*c*) D. (*d*), (*e*) and (*f*)

3. In the two sets given below, Set-I provides the different levels of teaching and learning while Set-II gives their examplars and concerns. Match the two sets and select from the code to indicate your answer.

Set-I (Levels of teaching and learning)	**Set-II (Examplars and concerns)**
(*a*) Memory level	(*i*) Encourages critical thinking based cognitive interchange.
(*b*) Understanding level	(*ii*) Protects personal interest and attitudinal concerns
(*c*) Reflective level	(*iii*) Facilitates recalling and recognizing of facts
	(*iv*) Enhances scope for seeing of relationships and meanings

Code:

	(*a*)	(*b*)	(*c*)
A.	(*i*)	(*ii*)	(*iii*)
B.	(*iii*)	(*ii*)	(*iv*)
C.	(*iii*)	(*iv*)	(*i*)
D.	(*iv*)	(*iii*)	(*ii*)

4. From the following list, identify the indicators of commitment areas of teachers and learners. Select from the code to give your answer.

(*a*) 'Do it well' approach
(*b*) Developing contact with community
(*c*) Enhancing performance in classroom including teaching-learning processes
(*d*) Concern for the allround development and readiness to help
(*e*) Acquiring curricular and content competency
(*f*) Respecting impartiality, objectivity and intellectual honesty.

Code:

A. (*a*), (*b*) and (*c*) B. (*b*), (*c*) and (*d*)
C. (*a*), (*d*) and (*f*) D. (*d*), (*e*) and (*f*)

* *Online Exam held on 19 December, 2018.*

5. In which of the following methods of research the independent variable has to be selected rather than manipulated?

A. Descriptive survey method
B. Experimental method
C. Ex post facto method
D. Exegetic research

6. In the list of statements given below which of them offer a suitable definition of research? Give your answer by selecting from the code:

(*a*) Research means a repeated search.
(*b*) Research is basically an answer to a question.
(*c*) Research provides an authentic solution to a problem.
(*d*) Research is an endeavour to prove one's hypothesis.
(*e*) Research is a meaning–giving process.
(*f*) Research means drawing a sample from a defined population.

Code:

A. (*a*), (*b*) and (*c*) B. (*b*), (*c*) and (*f*)
C. (*a*), (*d*) and (*f*) D. (*b*), (*c*) and (*e*)

7. Ability to see and size up the situation creatively is most relevant at which stage of research?

A. At the stage of identifying and defining a research problem.
B. In determining the research design and its execution.
C. In formulating research hypotheses and procedures for testing them.
D. In deciding and identifying the sampling procedures to ensure their representative character.

8. 'Research ethics' is of critical importance in which of the following areas? Select your answer from the code given below:

(*a*) Data collecting
(*b*) Preparing a seminar paper
(*c*) Data analysis
(*d*) Participation in a conference
(*e*) Writing a thesis/dissertation
(*f*) Selecting a research problem

A. (*a*), (*b*) and (*c*) B. (*a*), (*c*) and (*e*)
C. (*d*), (*e*) and (*f*) D. (*a*), (*b*) and (*f*)

9. While presenting the research outcomes and sharing the same with others, in which of the following research type, the style has to be impersonal?

A. Ethnographic studies
B. Action research based studies
C. Causal comparative based Ex post facto studies
D. Narrative studies

10. Which of the following methods of teaching will encourage indirect learning?

A. Lecturing with examples
B. Team teaching
C. Demonstration on a subject
D. Collaborative projects

Directions (Qs. No. 11 to 15): *Read the passage carefully and answer these question.*

In noting the nature of human lives, we have reason to be interested not only in the various things we succeed in doing, but also in the freedoms that we actually have to choose between different kinds of lives. The freedom to choose our lives can make a significant contribution to our well-being, but going beyond the perspective of well-being, the freedom itself may be seen as important. Being able to reason and choose is a significant aspect of human life. In fact, we are under no obligation to seek only our own well-being. It is for us to decide what we have good reason to pursue. We need not have to be a great leader to recognise that we can have aims or priorities that differ from the single-minded pursuit of our own well-being only. The freedoms and capabilities we enjoy can also be valuable to us. It is ultimately for us to decide how to use the freedom we have. It is important to emphasise that if social realisations are assessed in terms of capabilities that people actually have, rather than in terms of their utilities or happiness. First, human lives are then seen inclusively, taking note of the substantive freedoms that people enjoy, rather than ignoring everything other than pleasures or utilities they end up having. There is also a second significant aspect of freedom: it makes us accountable for what we do. Freedom to choose gives us the opportunity to decide what we should do, but with that opportunity comes the responsibility for what we do—to the extent that they are chosen actions. Since a capability is the power to do something, the accountability that emanates from that ability—that power—is a part of the capability perspective, and this can make room for demands of duty—what can be broadly called deontological demands. There is an overlap here between agency-centred concerns and the implications of a capability based approach. The perspective of social realisations will take us to further issues central to the analysis of justice in the world.

11. Why freedom is seen as important?
   A. To succeed in doing things.
   B. To have different life styles.
   C. To understand the perspective of one's well-being.
   D. To go beyond the perspective of one's own well-being.

12. Why should we go beyond considerations of our own well-being?
   A. To follow in the footsteps of great leaders.
   B. To think of freedoms of others.
   C. To appreciate that our aims can differ from self-interest.
   D. To be able to enjoy our freedoms.

13. What is of no value for assessing social realisations?
   A. Capabilities of people
   B. Utilities
   C. Inability to use the freedom given
   D. Ignoring the values of freedom

14. What is the inherent aspect of freedom?
   A. Pleasures of freedom
   B. Absence of actions
   C. Accountability
   D. Well-being of the self

15. The central idea of the passage is:
   A. Emphasis on variety of personal issues
   B. Use of power for freedom
   C. Responsibility for individual happiness
   D. Need for securing justice to all

16. When students place themselves close to certain communication sources, it will lead to:
   A. Source domination
   B. Selective exposure
   C. Negative choices
   D. Impersonal behaviour

17. **Assertion (A):** Classroom communication involves the clear decoding of messages by the students.
   Reason (R) : By increasing redundancy, we can improve the fidelity of communication.
   A. Both (A) and (R) are true.
   B. Both (A) and (R) are true, but (R) is not the correct explanation of (A).
   C. (A) is true, but (R) is false.
   D. (A) is false, but (R) is true.

18. Fleeting changes that occur in facial expressions of teachers in a classroom are described as:
   A. Significant – momentary movements
   B. Informational – momentary movements
   C. Macro – momentary movements
   D. Micro – momentary movements

19. Identify the correct sequence of decoding process of communication in the classroom.
   A. Evaluation, Interpretation, Sensory involvement, Feedback
   B. Feedback, Sensory involvement, Interpretation, Evaluation
   C. Sensory involvement, Interpretation, Evaluation, Feedback
   D. Interpretation, Evaluation, Feedback, Sensory involvement

20. Match the following:
Given below are two sets. Set-I embodies the types of communication while set-II provides their exemplification. Select your answer from the code given:

Set-I (Types of Communication)	**Set-II (Exemplification)**
(*a*) Linear communication	(*i*) Members are given themes on which they are required to hold discussion.
(*b*) Interactive communication	(*ii*) A teacher in the classroom presents a structured content

(*c*) Transactional communication — (*iii*) The principal of a college holds the staff meeting for understanding their problems.

(*iv*) The teacher and students in a college go on rampage.

Code:

	(*a*)	(*b*)	(*c*)
A.	(*iii*)	(*i*)	(*ii*)
B.	(*iv*)	(*ii*)	(*iii*)
C.	(*ii*)	(*iii*)	(*i*)
D.	(*i*)	(*iv*)	(*iii*)

21. In the sequence of numbers 5, 19, 49, 101, 181, 295, *x*, ..., the term *x* is:

A. 401 B. 351
C. 449 D. 501

22. If NTA14 and NTA15 one 5-digit numbers such that their sum is 157229, then N + T + A would be:

A. 15 B. 21
C. 25 D. 72

23. A's mother is sister of B and daughter of C. D is daughter of B and sister of E. How is C related to E?

A. Sister-in-law B. Aunt
C. Grandmother D. Mother

24. You have recently joined a new office. Walking at 5 km/hour, you reach the office from your house 15 minutes early and walking at 3 km/hour, you are late by 9 minutes. The distance between your house and office is:

A. 5 km B. 8 km
C. 3 km D. 2 km

25. Choose the correct alternative to replace the question mark (?).

42 → 26 71 → 78
33 → 16 62 → ?

A. 68 B. 54
C. 38 D. 39

26. A cluster of propositions with a structure that exhibits some inference is called:

A. An implication B. An argument
C. An explanation D. A description

27. Given below are two premises. Four conclusions are drawn from them (taking singly or together). Select the code that states the validly drawn conclusions.

Premises : (*i*) Some flowers are red.
(*ii*) All roses are flowers.

Conclusions: (*a*) Some roses are red.
(*b*) Some red things are flowers.
(*c*) Some flowers are roses.
(*d*) All roses are red.

Code:

A. (*a*), (*b*) and (*c*) only
B. (*a*) and (*b*) only
C. (*b*) and (*c*) only
D. (*c*) and (*d*) only

28. Consider the statements (*a*), (*b*), (*c*) and (*d*) given below. Which one of the codes contains the correct statements only?

(*a*) Venn diagram is a clear method of notation.
(*b*) To diagram a standard form of a categorical proposition, three overlapping circles are drawn.
(*c*) To test a categorical syllogism, two overlapping circles are drawn.
(*d*) Venn diagram is a method of testing the validity of categorical syllogisms.

Code:

A. (*a*) and (*b*) only
B. (*a*), (*b*) and (*c*) only
C. (*a*), (*b*), (*c*) and (*d*)
D. (*a*) and (*d*) only

29. If the proposition 'No dog is quadruped' is false which one among the following propositions can be claimed certainly to be true?

A. All dogs are quadruped.
B. Some dogs are quadruped.
C. Some dogs are not quadruped.
D. All dogs are biped.

30. A deductive argument is invalid if:

A. Its premises and conclusions are all true.
B. Its premises and conclusions are all false.
C. Its premises are all true but its conclusion is false.
D. Its premises are all false but its conclusion is true.

Directions (Qs. No. 31 to 35): *The following table shows the percentage of marks (%) obtained by five students A–E in six subjects S1-S6. Maximum marks in all the six subjects S1-S6 are 80, 75, 100, 120, 125 and 150 respectively. In accordance with the table given below, answer the questions that follow.*

Percentage of marks (%) obtained by five students in six subjects

Subject → / Students ↓	S1 (Out of 80 marks)	S2 (Out of 75 marks)	S3 (Out of 100 marks)	S4 (Out of 120 marks)	S5 (Out of 125 marks)	S6 (Out of 150 marks)
A	80	72	76	80	50	65
B	60	70	88	90	65	72
C	45	65	44	72	72	82
D	50	75	72	84	64	70
E	65	45	68	60	80	66

31. The approximate average percentage of marks obtained by student A comes out to be:
A. 65% B. 74%
C. 75% D. 70%

32. The difference in the total marks obtained by student A in the subjects S3 and S4 taken together and student E in the subjects S3 and S4 taken together, is:
A. 30 B. 36
C. 28 D. 32

33. The average percentage of marks obtained by all the five students together in subject S6, is:
A. 71% B. 69%
C. 64% D. 75%

34. The average of marks obtained by all the five students together in subject S1, is:
A. 48 B. 50
C. 49 D. 51

35. The difference in the marks obtained by all the five students together in the subjects S3 and S1, is:
A. 48 B. 98
C. 108 D. 110

36. Which one of the following pairs least matches in respect of Computers?
A. 1 Gigabyte : (1024) × (1024) × (1024) Bytes
B. LCD : Light Crystal Display
C. USB : Universal Serial Bus
D. GUI : Graphical User Interface

37. Amit has decided to use either a DVD-RW or DVD-R. Select statements that are TRUE for these storage devices.
P : Both DVD-R and DVD-RW are read only.
Q : DVD-R can be written to only once.
R : DVD-RW can be written to many times.
S : Both DVD-R and DVD-RW can be written to only once.
A. P only B. S only
C. P and R only D. Q and R only

38. The following list indicates different types of computer networks. Arrange them in an ascending order on the basis of geographical space implied.
A. LAN, WAN, MAN
B. WAN, LAN, MAN
C. MAN, LAN, WAN
D. LAN, MAN, WAN

39. Computer peripherals are external devices connected to a computer. Which list contains input peripheral devices only?
A. Speakers, Scanners, Mouse, Modem
B. Keyboard, Projector, Mouse, Flash drive
C. Microphones, Track-ball mouse, Scanner, Touch screen
D. Laser printer, Graphic tablet, Barcode reader, Hard disk

40. Read the following spreadsheet (MS-EXCEL)

EXCEL Spreadsheet

	A	B	C
1	10	16	
2	20		
3	8		
4	12		
5	0		

The equation in cell B2 is = A2 + B1. This equation is then copied and pasted to cells B3, B4 and B5. What should be the value in B5?

A. 36 B. 24
C. 44 D. 56

41. The tsunami that occurred in south and south-east Asia in December, 2004 was caused due to:

A. An earthquake B. A volcanic eruption
C. A hurricane D. A tropical cyclone

42. Which of the following gases initiates a chain reaction that breaks-down ozone in the upper atmosphere?

A. Nitrogen dioxide B. Carbon dioxide
C. Hydrogen sulphide D. Chlorine

43. High level lead (Pb) exposures in humans through inhalations or food consumption may cause:

(*a*) Mental retardation
(*b*) High blood pressure
(*c*) Disorder of central nervous system

Select the correct answer from the code given below:

A. (*a*) and (*b*) only B. (*b*) and (*c*) only
C. (*c*) and (*a*) only D. (*a*), (*b*) and (*c*)

44. In a human population, which is undergoing the demographic transition, which of the following generally decreases first?

A. Life expectancy B. Level of education
C. Death rate D. Birth rate

45. **Assertion (A):** The ecosystem surrounding a river gets damaged due to construction of a dam.

Reason (R): The area gets inundated with large volume of water.

Choose the correct code:

A. Both (A) and (R) are correct and (R) is the correct explanation of (A).
B. Both (A) and (R) are correct and (R) is not the correct explanation of (A).
C. (A) is true and (R) is false.
D. (A) is false and (R) is true.

46. Which one of the following has larger scope for the possibility of hands on experience?

A. Seminar B. Conference
C. Workshop D. Symposium

47. Which one of the following is less oriented towards knowledge dissemination?

A. Seminar B. Classroom
C. Field work D. Journal

48. Which of the following body is empowered with the role of appointment and approval of teachers in a University System in India?

A. Board of Management/Executive Council/ Syndicate
B. Academic Council
C. Board of Studies
D. University Court/Senate

49. Which of the following is entrusted with the responsibility for coordination and quality of higher education in India?

A. Bar Council of India
B. Association of Indian Universities
C. University Grants Commission
D. NITI Ayog

50. Who is the administrative and academic head of Indian University System?

A. Chancellor of a University
B. Vice-chancellor of a University
C. Registrar of a University
D. Dean of studies in a University

ANSWERS

1	2	3	4	5	6	7	8	9	10
B	A	C	C	C	D	C	B	C	D
11	**12**	**13**	**14**	**15**	**16**	**17**	**18**	**19**	**20**
D	C	B	C	D	B	A	D	C	C

21	22	23	24	25	26	27	28	29	30
C	B	C	C	C	B	C	D	B	C
31	**32**	**33**	**34**	**35**	**36**	**37**	**38**	**39**	**40**
D	D	A	A	C	B	D	D	C	D
41	**42**	**43**	**44**	**45**	**46**	**47**	**48**	**49**	**50**
A	D	D	C	B	C	C	A	C	B

Explanatory Answers

2. A **Norm-Referenced Test** (**NRT**) is a type of test, assessment, or evaluation which yields an estimate of the position of the tested individual in a predefined population, with respect to the trait being measured. The estimate is derived from the analysis of test scores and possibly other relevant data from a sample drawn from the population. That is, this type of test identifies whether the test taker performed better or worse than other test takers, not whether the test taker knows either more or less material than is necessary for a given purpose.

Norm-referenced refers to **standardized tests** that are designed to compare and rank test takers in relation to one another. Norm-referenced tests report whether test takers performed better or worse than a hypothetical average student, which is determined by comparing scores against the performance results of a statistically selected group of test takers, typically of the same age or grade level, who have already taken the exam.

5. The ex-post facto research is a kind of research in which the researcher predicts the possible causes behind an effect that has already occurred. For example, if a child is delinquent (that is, one who indulges in criminal activities), then in order to find the basic reason behind such delinquency, the researcher would try to find out the various events that have occurred and the many possibilities that could have contributed to the concerned delinquent behaviour. The expected possibilities may be lack of discipline at school/family history/peer effect/ neighbourhood or socialisation.

Thus, an ex-post facto research can be defined as an empirically based investigation which does not involve the researchers' direct control over the independent variables because they have already led to effects which can no Ex-Post Facto Research more be manipulated. The conclusions regarding the relationship between the variables are inferred without intervening or varying the independent or dependent variable.

6. Research is a systematic problem analysis, model building and fact finding for the purpose of important decision-making and control for the process of study undertaken. It is a well-planned, systematic process which implies that it needs planning at all the stages. It uses scientific methods. It is an objective process as it attempts to provide accurate authentic information. It is sometimes defined as the application of scientific methods in the solution of problems.

Another definition of research is given by Creswell, who states that, "Research is a process of steps used to collect and analyze information to increase our understanding of a topic or issue". It consists of three steps: (*i*) Pose a question, (*ii*) Collect data to answer the question, and (*iii*) Present an answer to the question.

7. A **research design** is the set of methods and procedures used in collecting and analyzing measures of the variables specified in the research problem research. The design of a study defines the study type (descriptive, correlation, semi-experimental, experimental, review, meta-analytic) and sub-type (*e.g.*, descriptive-longitudinal case study), research problem, hypotheses, independent and dependent variables, experimental design, and, if applicable, data collection methods and a statistical analysis plan. A research design is a framework that has been created to find answers to research questions.

Hypothesizing is done only after survey of relevant literature and learning the present status of the field of research. It can be formulated based on previous research and observation. To formulate a hypothesis the researcher should acquire enough knowledge in the topic of research and a reasonably deep insight about the problem. In formulating a hypothesis construct operational definitions of variables in the research problem. Hypothesis is due to an intelligent guess or for inspiration which is to be tested in the research work rigorously through appropriate methodology. Testing of hypothesis leads to explanation of the associated phenomenon or event.

9. A causal-comparative design is a research design that seeks to find relationships between independent and dependent variables after an action or event has already occurred. The researcher's goal is to determine whether the independent variable affected the outcome, or dependent variable, by comparing two or more groups of individuals. There are similarities and differences between causal-comparative research, also referred to as *ex post facto research*, and both correlational and experimental research.

Causal research uses different terms: *ex post facto* studies gather data retrospectively (*e.g.* given the obvious effects of smoking, the researcher will look in the past to find the potential cause), causal comparison where data are gathered from pre-formed groups and the independent variable is not manipulated in the experiment.

10. Collaborative projects method of teaching will encourage indirect learning.

Collaborative learning strategy to develop teamwork among the students. In this method, they can work in partnerships to solve a problem or a puzzle related to a subject. This allows them to think individually as well as to share ideas to come up with a solution. They can discuss the ideas with their allotted partner before sharing it with a larger group.

Collaboration allows student to actively participate in the learning process by talking with each other and listening to others opinions. Collaboration establishes a personal connection between students and the topic of study and it helps students think in a less personally biased way. Group projects and discussions are examples of this teaching method. Teachers may employ collaboration to assess student's abilities to work as a team, leadership skills, or presentation abilities.

16. **Selective exposure** is a theory within the practice of psychology, often used in media and communication research, that historically refers to individuals' tendency to favour information which reinforces their pre-existing views while avoiding contradictory information. Selective exposure has also been known and defined as "congeniality bias" or "confirmation bias" in various texts throughout the years.

Selective exposure relies on the assumption that one will continue to seek out information on an issue even after an individual has taken a stance on it. The position that a person has taken will be coloured by various factors of that issue that are reinforced during the decision-making process. When student themselves close to certain communication sources, it will lead to selective exposure.

19. Human Communication involves encoding and decoding. The process of encoding consists of two essential parts: Formulation of a message and adaptation of the message to the characteristics of the intended receiver(s). Once the message has been transmitted, the receiver must attend to the message and engage in the process of decoding. The latter involves four phases: Sensory involvement, interpretation, evaluation and feedback.

A theory of communication which may deal with the classroom situation may consist of five elements: Source (teachers and students); message; channel; receiver (teacher and students); and feedback.

The source of communication may be either a teacher or student(s) the textbooks, films, records or tapes. The message in the classroom communication consists of what the teacher says and what the students say and the way they say something.

20. **Linear communication:** There's a bit of a debate about the Linear Communication model and how it recognizes (or doesn't recognize) the concept of feedback. The linear model's behaviour is belied by its name, where a sender encodes a message via a channel and the message is decoded by the receiver. It is straight-line communication found typically in mass communication; think television, radio, newspapers, etc. According to this model, there is no means for immediate feedback. In linear communication a teacher in the classroom presents a structured content.

Interactive Communication Model: Simply put, the Interactive Model takes the Linear Model and multiplies it times two with a quick flip of the return message. It now allows for a feedback element because after a message is encoded and sent to the decoding receiver, the roles then reverse and the receiver encodes and sends a response to the original sender who has now turned receiver. In Interactive communication the principle of a collage holds the staff meeting for understanding their problems.

Transactional Communication Model: The Transactional Model becomes more sophisticated yet. This model depicts face-to-face interaction, or "trans-action" as a dynamic and changeable process that is not limited to simple definition. In the Transactional Model, receiver and sender can play the same roles simultaneously, as sometimes happens, as messages can be sent back and forth simultaneously. In Transactional communication members are given themes on which they are required to hold discussion.

21. 5 19 49 101 181 295 [449]

+14 +30 +52 +80 +114 +154

+16 +22 +28 +34 +40

+6 +6 +6 +6

22.

$$\begin{array}{r} N\ T\ A\ 1\ 4 \\ +\ N\ T\ A\ 1\ 5 \\ \hline 1\ 5\ 7\ 2\ 2\ 9 \\ \hline \end{array}$$

Taking A = 6, A + A = 12 ← carry

Taking T = 8, T + T = 8 + 8 = 16 + 1

= 17 ← carry

Taking N = 7, N + N = 7 + 7 = 14 + 1 = 15

∴ A = 6, T = 8 and N = 7

N + T + A = 7 + 8 + 6 = 21.

23.

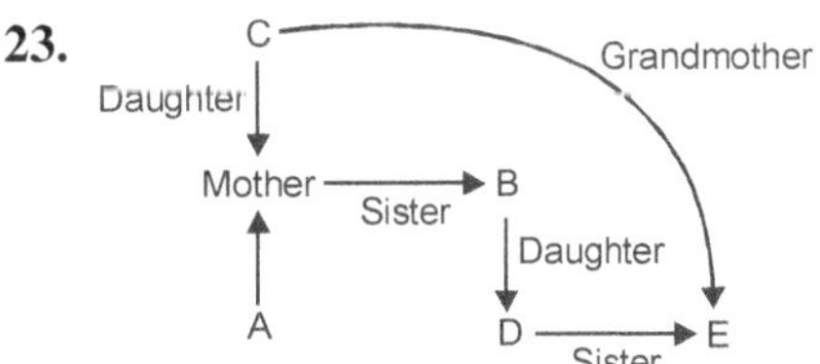

24. Required distance

$$= \frac{S_1 \times S_2}{S_1 - S_2}(T_1 \sim T_2)$$

$$= \frac{5 \times 3}{5-3}\left(\frac{24}{60}\right) = \frac{15}{2} \times \frac{24}{60} = 3 \text{ km.}$$

25. As

42 → (4 ÷ 2) . (4 + 2) = 26

71 → (7 ÷ 1) . (7 + 1) = 78

33 → (3 ÷ 3) . (3 + 3) = 16

Similarly,

62 → (6 ÷ 2) . (6 + 2) = 38.

26. With propositions as building blocks, we construct arguments. In any argument we affirm one proposition on the basis of some other propositions. In doing this, an inference is drawn. Inference is a process that may tie together a cluster of propositions. Some inferences are warranted (or correct); others are not. The logician analyzes these clusters, examining the propositions with which the process begins and with which it ends, as well as the relations among these propositions. Such a cluster of propositions constitutes an argument. Arguments are the chief concern of logic.

Argument is a technical term in logic. It need not involve disagreement, or controversy. In logic, argument refers strictly to any group of propositions of which one is claimed to follow from the others, which are regarded as providing support for the truth of that one. For every possible inference there is a corresponding argument.

27. 

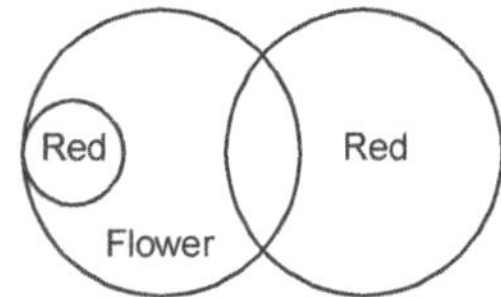

(*b*) Some red things are flowers.

(*c*) Some flowers are roses.

28. A Venn diagram uses overlapping circles or other shapes to illustrate the logical relationships between two or more sets of items. Often, they serve to graphically organize things, highlighting how the items are similar and different.

In order to use a Venn diagram to test a syllogism, the diagram must be filled in to reflect the contents of the premises. Remember, shading an area means that area is empty, the term represented has no extension in that area. What one is looking for in a Venn diagram test for validity is an accurate diagram of the **conclusion** of the argument that **logically follows** from a diagram of the premises. Since each of the premises of a categorical syllogism is a categorical proposition, diagram the premise sentences independently and then see whether the conclusion has already been diagramed. If so, the argument is valid. If not, then it is not. Venn diagram is a method of testing the validity of categorical syllogism.

31. Marks obtained by student A

In Subject S_1, $80 \times 80\% = 64$

In Subject S_2, $75 \times 72\% = 54$

In Subject S_3, $100 \times 76\% = 76$

In Subject S_4, $120 \times 80\% = 96$

In Subject S_5, $125 \times 50\% = 62.5$

In Subject S_6, $150 \times 65\% = 97.5$

Total percentage

$$= \frac{64+54+76+96+62.5+97.5}{80+75+100+120+125+150} \times 100$$

$$= \frac{450}{650} \times 100 = 69.23\% \sim 70\%.$$

32. By Student A,

Total marks obtained in Subject S_3 and S_4

$= 100 \times 76\% + 120 \times 80\%$

$= 76 + 96 = 172$

By student E,

Total marks obtained in subject S_3 and S_4

$= 100 \times 68\% + 120 \times 60\%$

$= 68 + 72 = 140$

$\therefore$ Required difference $= 172 - 140 = 32$.

33. Required Average marks in subject S_6 of all students

$$= \frac{65+72+82+70+66}{5} = \frac{355}{5} = 71\%.$$

34. In Subject S_1, Marks obtained by A

$= 80 \times 80\% = 64$

In Subject S_1, Marks obtained by B

$= 80 \times 60\% = 48$

In Subject S_1, Marks obtained by C

$= 80 \times 45\% = 36$

In Subject S_1, Marks obtained by D

$= 80 \times 50\% = 40$

In Subject S_1, Marks obtained by E

$= 80 \times 65\% = 52$

Required Average

$$= \frac{64+48+36+40+52}{5} = \frac{240}{5} = 48.$$

35. In subject S_3, the sum of marks obtained by all five students

$= 100 \times 76\% + 100 \times 88\% + 100 \times 44\% + 100 \times 72\% + 100 \times 68\%$

$= 76 + 88 + 44 + 72 + 68 = 348$

In Subject S_1, the Sum of marks obtained by all five students

$= 80 \times 80\% + 80 \times 60\% + 80 \times 45\% + 80 \times 50\% + 80 \times 65\%$

$= 64 + 48 + 36 + 40 + 52 = 240$

Required difference = 348 – 240 = 108.

36. A **liquid-crystal display (LCD)** is a flat-panel display or other electronically modulated optical device that uses the light-modulating properties of liquid crystals. Liquid crystals do not emit light directly, instead using a backlight or reflector to produce images in colour or monochrome.

38. There are several different types of computer networks. Computer networks can be characterized by their size as well as their purpose.

The size of a network can be expressed by the geographic area they occupy and the number of computers that are part of the network. Networks can cover anything from a handful of devices within a single room to millions of devices spread across the entire globe.

Some of the different networks based on size are:

- Personal area network, or PAN
- Local area network, or LAN
- Metropolitan area network, or MAN
- Wide area network, or WAN

39. A **computer peripheral** is a device that is connected to a computer but is not part of the core computer architecture. The core elements of a computer are the central processing unit, power supply, motherboard and the computer case that contains those three components. Technically speaking, everything else is considered a peripheral device. However, this is a somewhat narrow view, since various other elements are required for a computer to actually function, such as a hard drive and random-access memory (or RAM).

Three categories of peripheral devices exist based on their relationship with the computer:

1. an *input device* sends data or instructions to the computer, such as a mouse, keyboard, graphics tablet, image scanner, barcode reader, game controller, light pen, light gun, microphone, digital camera, webcam, dance pad, touch screen and read-only memory);
2. an *output device* provides output from the computer, such as a computer monitor, projector, printer, headphones, and computer speaker); and
3. an *input/output device* performs both input and output functions, such as a computer data storage device (including a disk drive, USB flash drive, memory card, and tape drive).

42. **Chlorine**, which is released by CFC's and catalyzes a **chain reaction that breaks down ozone in the upper atmosphere**. The major biological source of dissolved oxygen in the ocean comes from: Photosynthesis by phytoplankton, which converts CO_2 into organic compounds using the energy from sunlight.

The chlorine radicals are continuously regenerated and cause the breakdown of ozone. Thus, CFCs are transporting agents for continuously generating chlorine radicals into the stratosphere and damaging the ozone layer.

43. Although children are primarily at risk, lead poisoning is also dangerous for adults. Signs and symptoms in adults might include:

- High blood pressure
- Joint and muscle pain
- Difficulties with memory or concentration
- Headache
- Abdominal pain
- Mood disorders
- Reduced sperm count and abnormal sperm
- Miscarriage, stillbirth or premature birth in pregnant women

45. The environmental consequences of large dams are numerous and varied, and includes direct impacts to the biological, chemical and physical properties of rivers and riparian (or "stream-side") environments.

The flooding of surrounding habitat around dams kills trees and other plant life that then decomposes and releases large amounts of carbon into the atmosphere. Because the river is no longer flowing freely, the water becomes stagnant and the bottom of the reservoir becomes depleted of oxygen.

This lack of oxygen creates a situation where methane (a very potent greenhouse gas) is produced from the decomposition of the plant materials at the bottom of the reservoir that eventually gets released into the atmosphere, contributing to global climate change.

Dammed rivers create a reservoir upstream from the dam, which spills out into the surrounding environments and floods ecosystems and habitats that once existed there. Such flooding can kill or displace many different organisms, including plants, wildlife, and humans.

46. **A Seminar** is a form of academic instruction, either at a university or offered by a commercial or professional organization. It has the function of bringing together small groups for recurring meetings, focusing each time on some particular subject, in which everyone present is requested to actively participate.

A Conference refers to a formal meeting where participants exchange their views on various topics. Conference can take place in different fields, and it need not be academic in nature all the time. Thus, we have parent teacher conferences, sport conferences, a trade conference, a conference of journalists, conference of doctors, a conference of research scholars, and so on. A conference is a meeting that has been prearranged and involves consultation and discussion on a number of topics by the delegates.

A Workshop includes all the elements of the Seminar, but with the largest portion being emphasized on "hand-on-practice" or laboratory work. The Lab work is designed to reinforce, imprint and bring forward an immediate functioning dimension to the participant's eye and hands by implementing and practicing the actual concept or technique that was taught through the lecture and demonstration process.

A Symposium is a formal gathering in an academic setting where participants are experts in their fields. These experts present or deliver their opinions or viewpoints on a chosen topic of discussion. It would be correct to label a symposium as a small scale conference as the number of delegates is smaller.

47. Knowledge management has been described as 'getting the right knowledge to the right people in the right place at the right time'. Knowledge dissemination is a crucial part of knowledge management because it ensures knowledge is available to those who need it.

49. India's higher education system is the third largest in the world, next to the United States and China. The main governing body at the tertiary level is the University Grants Commission, which enforces its standards, advises the government, and helps coordinate between the centre and the state. The UGC is entrusted with the responsibility of taking on novel initiatives to enhance the overall quality of education.

50. A **chancellor** is a leader of a college or university, usually either the executive or ceremonial head of the university or of a university campus within a university system.

In most Commonwealth and former Commonwealth nations, the chancellor is usually a ceremonial non-resident head of the university. In such institutions, the chief executive of a university is the **vice-chancellor**, who may carry an additional title, such as "president & vice-chancellor". The chancellor may serve as chairman of the governing body; if not, this duty is often held by a chairman who may be known as a pro-chancellor.

Previous Years' Paper (Solved)

UGC-NET (JRF) Exam July, 2018*

PAPER–I

Note : • This paper consists of **Fifty (50)** objective type questions of **Two (2)** marks each. **All** questions are **compulsory**. ***(50 × 2 = 100 marks.)***

1. Which of the following set of statements best describes the nature and objectives of teaching?

Indicate your answer by selecting from the code.

(*a*) Teaching and learning are integrally related.

(*b*) There is no difference between teaching and training.

(*c*) Concern of all teaching is to ensure some kind of transformation in students.

(*d*) All good teaching is formal in nature.

(*e*) A teacher is a senior person.

(*f*) Teaching is a social act whereas learning is a personal act.

Code :

A. (*a*), (*b*) and (*d*) B. (*b*), (*c*) and (*e*)
C. (*a*), (*c*) and (*f*) D. (*d*), (*e*) and (*f*)

2. Which of the following learner characteristics is highly related to effectiveness of teaching?

A. Prior experience of the learner
B. Educational status of the parents of the learner
C. Peer groups of the learner
D. Family size from which the learner comes

3. In the two sets given below Set-I indicates methods of teaching while Set-II provides the basic requirements for success/effectiveness. Match the two sets and indicate your answer by choosing from the code:

Set-I *(Method of teaching)*	**Set-II** *(Basic requirements for success/effectiveness)*
(*a*) Lecturing	(*i*) Small step presentation with feedback provided
(*b*) Discussion in groups	(*ii*) Production of large number of ideas
(*c*) Brainstorming	(*iii*) Content delivery in a lucid language
(*d*) Programmed Instructional procedure	(*iv*) Use of teaching-aids
	(*v*) Theme based interaction among participants

Code:

	(*a*)	(*b*)	(*c*)	(*d*)
A.	(*i*)	(*ii*)	(*iii*)	(*iv*)
B.	(*ii*)	(*iii*)	(*iv*)	(*v*)
C.	(*iii*)	(*v*)	(*ii*)	(*i*)
D.	(*iv*)	(*ii*)	(*i*)	(*iii*)

4. From the list of evaluation procedures given below identify those which will be called 'formative evaluation'. Indicate your answer by choosing from the code:

(*a*) A teacher awards grades to students after having transacted the course work.

(*b*) During interaction with students in the classroom, the teacher provides corrective feedback.

* Exam held on 08/07/2018.

(*c*) The teacher gives marks to students on a unit test.

(*d*) The teacher clarifies the doubts of students in the class itself.

(*e*) The overall performance of a students is reported to parents at every three months interval.

(*f*) The learner's motivation is raised by the teacher through a question-answer session.

Code:

A. (*a*), (*b*) and (*c*) B. (*b*), (*c*) and (*d*)

C. (*a*), (*c*) and (*e*) D. (*b*), (*d*) and (*f*)

5. Assertion (*a*): All teaching should aim at ensuring learning.

Reason (R): All learning results from teaching.

Choose the correct answer from the following code:

A. Both (A) and (R) are true, and (R) is the correct explanation of (A).

B. Both (A) and (R) are true, but (R) is not the correct explanation of (A).

C. (A) is true, but (R) is false.

D. (A) is false, but (R) is true.

6. There are two sets given below. Set-I specifies the types of research, while Set-II indicates their characteristics. Match the two and give your answer by selecting the appropriate code.

Set-I ***(Research types)***	**Set-II** ***(Characteristics)***
(*a*) Fundamental research	(*i*) Finding out the extent of perceived impact of an intervention
(*b*) Applied research	(*ii*) Developing an effective explanation through theory building
(*c*) Action research	(*iii*) Improving an existing situation through use of interventions
(*d*) Evaluative research	(*iv*) Exploring the possibility of a theory for use in various situations
	(*v*) Enriching technological resources

Code:

	(*a*)	(*b*)	(*c*)	(*d*)
A.	(*ii*)	(*iv*)	(*iii*)	(*i*)
B.	(*v*)	(*iv*)	(*iii*)	(*ii*)
C.	(*i*)	(*ii*)	(*iii*)	(*iv*)
D.	(*ii*)	(*iii*)	(*iv*)	(*v*)

7. Which of the sets of activities best indicate the cyclic nature of action research strategy ?

A. Reflect, Observe, Plan, Act

B. Observe, Act, Reflect, Plan

C. Act, Plan, Observe, Reflect

D. Plan, Act, Observe, Reflect

8. Which of the following sequences of research steps is nearer to scientific method ?

A. Suggested solution of the problem, Deducing the consequences of the solution, Perceiving the problem situation, Location of the difficulty and Testing the solutions.

B. Perceiving the problem situation, Locating the actual problem and its definition, Hypothesizing, Deducing the consequences of the suggested solution and Testing the hypothesis in action.

C. Defining a problem, Identifying the causes of the problem, Defining a population, Drawing a sample, Collecting data and Analysing results.

D. Identifying the causal factors, Defining the problem, Developing a hypothesis, Selecting a sample, Collecting data and arriving at generalizations and Conclusions.

9. The problem of 'research ethics' is concerned with which aspect of research activities?

A. Following the prescribed format of a thesis

B. Data analysis through qualitative or quantitative techniques

C. Defining the population of research

D. Evidence based research reporting

10. In which of the following activities, potential for nurturing creative and critical thinking is relatively greater?

A. Preparing research summary

B. Presenting a seminar paper

C. Participation in research conference

D. Participation in a workshop

Directions (Qs. 11 to 15): *Read the following passage carefully and answer questions.*

If India has to develop her internal strengths, the nation has to focus on the technological imperatives, keeping in mind three dynamic dimensions : the people, the overall economy and the strategic interests. These technological imperatives also take into account a 'fourth' dimension, time, an offshoot of modern day dynamism in business, trade, and technology that leads to continually shifting targets. We believe that technological strengths are especially crucial in dealing with this fourth dimension underlying continuous change in the aspirations of the people, the economy in the global context, and the strategic interests. The progress of technology lies at the heart of human history. Technological strengths are the key to creating more productive employment in an increasingly competitive market place and to continually upgrade human skills. Without a pervasive use of technologies, we cannot achieve overall development of our people in the years to come. The direct linkages of technology to the nation's strategic strengths are becoming more and more clear, especially since 1990s. India's own strength in a number of core areas still puts it in a position of reasonable strength in geo-political context. Any nation aspiring to become a developed one needs to have strengths in various strategic technologies and also the ability to continually upgrade them through its own creative strengths. For people-oriented actions as well, whether for the creation of large scale productive employment or for ensuring nutritional and health security for people, or for better living conditions, technology is the only vital input. The absence of greater technological impetus could lead to lower productivity and wastage of precious natural resources. Activities with low productivity or low value addition, in the final analysis hurt the poorest most. The technological imperatives to lift our people to a new life, and to a life they are entitled to is important. India, aspiring to become a major economic power in terms of trade and increase in GDP, cannot succeed on the strength of turnkey projects designed and built abroad or only through large-scale imports of plant machinery, equipment and know how. Even while being alive to the short-term realities, medium and long-term strategies to develop core technological strengths within our industry are vital for envisioning a developed India.

11. According to the above passage, which of the following are indicative of the fourth dimension?

(*a*) Aspirations of people
(*b*) Modern day dynamism
(*c*) Economy in the global context
(*d*) Strategic interests

Code:

A. (*a*), (*b*) and (*c*) only
B. (*b*), (*c*) and (*d*) only
C. (*a*), (*c*) and (*d*) only
D. (*a*), (*b*) and (*d*) only

12. More productive employment demands:

A. Pervasive use of technology
B. Limiting competitive market place
C. Geo-political considerations
D. Large industries

13. Absence of technology would lead to:

(*a*) Less pollution
(*b*) Wastage of precious natural resources
(*c*) Low value addition
(*d*) Hurting the poorest most

Code:

A. (*a*), (*b*) and (*c*) only
B. (*b*), (*c*) and (*d*) only
C. (*a*), (*b*) and (*d*) only
D. (*a*), (*c*) and (*d*) only

14. The advantage of technological inputs would result in:

A. Unbridled technological growth
B. Importing plant machinery
C. Sidelining environmental issues
D. Lifting our people to a life of dignity

15. Envisioning a developed India requires :

A. Aspiration to become a major economic player
B. Dependence upon projects designed abroad
C. Focus on short-term projects
D. Development of core technological strengths

16. Differentiation between acceptance and non-acceptance of certain stimuli in classroom communication is the basis of:

A. selective expectation of performance
B. selective affiliation to peer groups
C. selective attention
D. selective morality

17. **Assertion (A):** The initial messages to students in the classroom by a teacher need not be critical to establish interactions later.

Reason (R): More control over the communication process means more control over what the students are learning.

Code:

A. Both (A) and (R) are true, and (R) is the correct explanation of (A).
B. Both (A) and (R) are true, but (R) is not the correct explanation of (A).
C. (A) is true, but (R) is false.
D. (A) is false, but (R) is true.

18. **Assertion (A):** To communicate well in the classroom is a natural ability.

Reason (R): Effective teaching in the classroom demands knowledge of the communication process.

Code:

A. Both (A) and (R) are true, and (R) is the correct explanation of (A).
B. Both (A) and (R) are true, but (R) is not the correct explanation of (A).
C. (A) is true, but (R) is false.
D. (A) is false, but (R) is true.

19. **Assertion (A):** Classroom communication is a transactional process.

Reason (R): A teacher does not operate under the assumption that students' responses are purposive.

Select the correct code for your answer :

A. Both (A) and (R) are true, and (R) is the correct explanation of (A).
B. Both (A) and (R) are true, but (R) is not the correct explanation of (A).
C. (A) is true, but (R) is false.
D. (A) is false, but (R) is true.

20. Which of the following set of statements is correct for describing the human communication process?

(*a*) Non-verbal communication can stimulate ideas.
(*b*) Communication is a learnt ability.
(*c*) Communication is not a universal panacea.
(*d*) Communication cannot break-down.
(*e*) More communication means more effective learning by students.
(*f*) Value of what is learnt through classroom communication is not an issue for students.

Code:

A. (*a*), (*c*), (*e*) and (*f*)
B. (*b*), (*d*), (*e*) and (*f*)
C. (*a*), (*b*), (*c*) and (*d*)
D. (*a*), (*d*), (*e*) and (*f*)

21. The next term in the series
–1, 5, 15, 29, __?__, ...
is:

A. 36 B. 47
C. 59 D. 63

22. The next term in the series

ABD, DGK, HMS, MTB, SBL, __?__, ...
is :

A. ZKU B. ZCA
C. ZKW D. KZU

23. If VARANASI is coded as WCUESGZQ, then the code of KOLKATA will be:

A. LOQOZEH B. HLZEOOQ
C. ZELHOQO D. LQOOFZH

24. Introducing Rakesh to her husband a women said, "His brother's father is the only son of my grandfather". The woman is related to Rakesh as:

A. Aunt B. Mother
C. Sister D. Daughter

25. Two numbers are in the ratio 2 : 5. If 16 is added to both the numbers, their ratio becomes 1 : 2. The numbers are:

A. 16, 40 B. 20, 50
C. 28, 70 D. 32, 80

26. Superiority of intellect depends upon its power of concentration on one theme in the same way as a concave mirror collects all the rays that strike upon it into one point.

What type of reasoning is entailed in the above statement?

A. Mathematical B. Psychological
C. Analogical D. Deductive

27. Given below are two premises (A and B). Four conclusions are drawn from them. Select the code that states validly drawn conclusion(s) (taking the premises individually or jointly).

Premises:

(*a*) Most of the dancers are physically fit.
(*b*) Most of the singers are dancers.

Conclusions:

(*a*) Most of the singers are physically fit.
(*b*) Most of the dancers are singers.
(*c*) Most of the physically fit persons are dancers.
(*d*) Most of the physically fit persons are singers.

Code:

A. (*a*) and (*b*) B. (*b*) and (*c*)
C. (*c*) and (*d*) D. (*d*) and (*a*)

28. Which one among the following is a presupposition in inductive reasoning?

A. Law of identity
B. Unchangeability in nature
C. Harmony in nature
D. Uniformity of nature

29. If the proposition 'domestic animals are hardly ferocious' is taken to be false, which of the following proposition/propositions can be claimed to be certainly true ? Select the correct code:

Propositions:

(*a*) All domestic animals are ferocious.
(*b*) Most of the domestic animals are ferocious.
(*c*) No domestic animal is ferocious.
(*d*) Some domestic animals are non-ferocious.

Code:

A. (*a*) and (*b*) B. (*a*) only
C. (*c*) and (*d*) D. (*b*) only

30. Which one of the following statements is not correct in the context of Venn diagram method?

A. It is a method of testing the validity of arguments.
B. It represents both the premises of a syllogism in one diagram.
C. It requires two overlapping circles for the two premises of a standard-form categorical syllogism.
D. It can be used to represent classes as well as propositions.

Directions (Qs. 31-35): *The table below embodies data on the production, exports and per capita consumption of rice in country P for the five years from 2012 to 2016. Answer questions based on the data contained in the table.*

Year-wise Production, Exports and Per Capita Consumption of Rice

Year	Production (in million kg)	Exports (in million kg)	Per Capita Consumption (in kg)
2012	186.5	114	36.25
2013	202	114	35.2
2014	238	130	38.7
2015	221	116	40.5
2016	215	88	42

Where, Per Capita Consumption = (Consumption in million kg) ÷ (Population in million) and consumption (in million kg) = Production–Exports.

31. The percentage increase in the consumption of rice over the previous year was the highest in which year?

A. 2013 B. 2014
C. 2015 D. 2016

32. What is the population of the country in the year 2014 (in million)?

A. 2.64 B. 2.72
C. 2.79 D. 2.85

33. The ratio of exports to consumption in the given period was the highest in the year:

A. 2012 B. 2013
C. 2014 D. 2015

34. In which year, the population of country was the highest ?

A. 2013 B. 2014
C. 2015 D. 2016

35. What is the average consumption of rice (in million kg) over the years 2012-2016?

A. 104 B. 102.1
C. 108 D. 100.1

36. Which of the following statements, regarding the term ICT is/are TRUE?

P : ICT is an acronym that stands for Indian Classical Technology.

Q : Converging technologies that exemplify ICT include the merging of audio-visual, telephone and computer networks through a common cabling system.

A. P only B. Q only
C. P and Q D. Neither P nor Q

37. A new Laptop has been produced that weighs less, is smaller and uses less power than previous Laptop models.

Which of the following technologies has been used to accomplish this?

A. Universal Serial Bus Mouse
B. Faster Random Access Memory
C. Blu Ray Drive
D. Solid State Hard Drive

38. Given the following email fields, which of the email addresses will 'swami' be able to see when he receives the message?

To...	ram@test.com
Cc...	raj@test.com; ravi@test.com
Bcc...	swami@test.com; rama@test.com

A. ram@test.com
B. ram@test.com; raj@test.com; ravi@test.com
C. ram@test.com; rama@test.com
D. ram@test.com; rama@test.com; raj@test.com; ravi@test.com

39. Put the following units of storage into the correct order, starting with the smallest unit first and going down to the largest unit:

(*a*) Kilobyte (*b*) Byte
(*c*) Megabyte (*d*) Terabyte
(*e*) Gigabyte (*f*) Bit

Give your answer from the following code:

A. (*f*), (*b*), (*a*), (*c*), (*d*), (*e*)
B. (*f*), (*b*), (*a*), (*d*), (*e*), (*c*)
C. (*f*), (*b*), (*a*), (*c*), (*e*), (*d*)
D. (*f*), (*b*), (*a*), (*d*), (*c*), (*e*)

40. With regard to computer memory, which of the following statement(s) is/are TRUE?

P : Read Only Memory (ROM) is 'volatile' memory.

Q : Random Access Memory (RAM) is 'volatile' memory.

R : Secondary Memory is 'volatile' memory.

A. P only B. Q only
C. P and Q only D. P and R only

41. 'Fly ash' produced in thermal power plants is an ecofriendly resource for use in :

(*a*) agriculture as micro-nutrient
(*b*) wasteland development
(*c*) dam and water holding structures
(*d*) brick industry

Choose the **correct** answer from the code given below:

A. (*a*), (*b*) and (*d*) only
B. (*b*), (*c*) and (*d*) only
C. (*a*), (*c*) and (*d*) only
D. (*a*), (*b*), (*c*) and (*d*)

42. Which of the following types of natural disasters has no definite beginning and end?

A. Earthquakes B. Landslides
C. Hurricanes D. Droughts

43. **Assertion (A):** Indoor air pollution is a serious health hazard.

Reason (R): The dispersal of air pollutants is rather limited in indoor environment.

Choose the **correct** answer from the code given below:

A. Both (A) and (R) are true and (R) is the correct explanation of (A).
B. Both (A) and (R) are true but (R) is not the correct explanation of (A).
C. (A) is true and (R) is false.
D. Both (A) and (R) are false.

44. In terms of their contribution to the total power generation in India, identify the correct sequence of energy sources - Thermal Power Plants (TPP), Large Hydropower Projects (LHP), Nuclear Energy (NE) and Renewable Energy (RE) which includes solar energy, wind energy, biomass and small hydropower projects.

A. TPP > RE > LHP > NE
B. TPP > LHP > RE > NE
C. LHP > TPP > RE > NE
D. LHP > TPP > NE > RE

45. Which of the following is considered as major source of pollution in rivers of India?

A. Unregulated small scale industry
B. Untreated sewage
C. Agricultural run-off
D. Thermal power plants

46. India has the largest Higher Education System in the World after :

(*a*) The United States of America
(*b*) Australia
(*c*) China
(*d*) United Kingdom (U.K.)

Select the **correct** answer from the code given below:

A. (*a*), (*b*), (*c*) and (*d*) B. (*a*), (*b*) and (*c*) only
C. (*a*), (*c*) and (*d*) only D. (*a*) and (*c*) only

47. Prime Minister Research Fellowship is for students pursuing Ph.D programme in:

A. State and Central Universities
B. Central Universities, IISc, IITs, NITs, IISERs and IIITs
C. IISc, IITs, NITs, IISERs, IIITs, State and Central Universities
D. IITs and IISc

48. Leader of the Opposition is a member of committees which select:

(*a*) the Central Information Commissioner
(*b*) the Central Vigilance Commissioner
(*c*) the Chairperson of National Human Rights Commission
(*d*) the Chairperson of National Commission for Women

Select the **correct** answer from the code given below:

A. (*a*), (*b*), (*c*) and (*d*) B. (*a*), (*b*) and (*c*) only
C. (*a*), (*c*) and (*d*) only D. (*a*), (*b*) and (*d*) only

49. Which of the following statements are **correct** about gender budgeting?

(*a*) It is a separate budget addressing the specific needs of women.
(*b*) It assesses the impact of government budget on women.
(*c*) It is an accounting exercise.
(*d*) It is another budgeting innovation.

Select the **correct** answer from the code given below:

A. (*b*) and (*d*) only B. (*a*) and (*d*) only
C. (*a*), (*c*) and (*d*) only D. (*b*), (*c*) and (*d*) only

50. Which of the following are the barriers to citizen-centric administration in India?

(*a*) Wooden and inflexible attitude of the civil servants
(*b*) Ineffective implementation of laws and rules
(*c*) Awareness of rights and duties of citizens
(*d*) Lack of job opportunities for the youth

Select the **correct** answer from the code given below:

A. (*a*), (*b*), (*c*) and (*d*)
B. (*a*), (*b*) and (*c*) only
C. (*a*), (*b*) and (*d*) only
D. (*a*) and (*b*) only

ANSWERS

1	2	3	4	5	6	7	8	9	10
C	A	C	D	C	A	D	B	D	C
11	**12**	**13**	**14**	**15**	**16**	**17**	**18**	**19**	**20**
C	A	B	D	D	C	D	D	C	C
21	**22**	**23**	**24**	**25**	**26**	**27**	**28**	**29**	**30**
B	C	D	C	D	C	B	D	A	C
31	**32**	**33**	**34**	**35**	**36**	**37**	**38**	**39**	**40**
B	C	A	D	D	B	D	B	C	B
41	**42**	**43**	**44**	**45**	**46**	**47**	**48**	**49**	**50**
D	D	A	A	B	D	D	B	A	D

EXPLANATORY ANSWERS

1. Teaching is the process of attending to people's needs, experience and feelings, and making specific interventions to help them particular things.

Nature of Teaching: In its broadest sense, teaching is a process that facilitates learning. Teaching is the specialized application of knowledge, skills and attributes designed to provide unique service to meet the educational needs of the individual and of society. The choice of learning activities whereby the goals of education are realized in the school is the responsibility of the teaching profession.

Objectives of Teaching: Teacher education has to become more sensitive to the emerging demands from the school system. For this, it has to prepare teachers for a dual role of;

Encouraging, supportive and humane facilitator in teaching learning situations who enables learners (students) to discover their talents, to realize their physical and intellectual potentialities to the fullest, to develop character and desirable social and human values to function as responsible citizens; and,

An active member of the group of persons who make conscious effort to contribute towards the process of renewal of school curriculum to maintain its relevance to the changing societal needs and personal needs of learners, keeping in view the experiences gained in the past and the concerns and imperatives that have emerged in the light of changing national development goals and educational priorities.

2. Prior experience of the learner characteristics is highly related to effectiveness of teaching.

The adult's experience is a key resource in any learning effort. Adults have a greater reservoir of life experiences simply because they have lived longer and seen and done more. This is a critical distinction between adults and traditional learners. Consciously or unconsciously, adults tend to link any new learning to their prior learning, a body of knowledge that is rooted in their life experiences.

3. A **teaching method** comprises the principles and methods used by teachers to enable student learning. These strategies are determined partly on subject matter to be taught and partly by the nature of the learner.

The lecture method is just one of several teaching methods, though in schools it's usually considered the primary one. The lecture method is convenient for the institution and cost-efficient, especially with larger classroom sizes.

Discussion methods are a variety of forums for open-ended, collaborative exchange of ideas among a **teacher** and students or among students for the purpose of furthering students thinking, learning, problem solving, understanding, or literary appreciation.

Brainstorming is a large or small group activity that encourages students to focus on a topic and contribute to the free flow of ideas.

1. The **teacher** may begin a **brainstorming** session by posing a question or a problem, or by introducing a topic.
2. Students then express possible answers, relevant words and ideas.

Programmed instruction is a **method** of presenting new subject matters to students in a graded sequence of controlled steps. Students work through the **programmed** material by themselves at their own speed and after each step test their comprehension by answering an examination question or filling in a diagram.

4. Formative Evaluations are evaluations for learning. They are often ungraded and informal. Their aim is to provide both the students and instructor with a gauge of where their level of understanding is at the current moment, and enable the instructor to adjust accordingly to meet the emerging needs of the class.

Formative evaluations are particularly important because they allow you to make changes that affect the current students, while the end of term forms only affect future classes. In addition, formative evaluations signal your class that you are indeed interested in what and how they're learning, and in their responses to your teaching.

Formative evaluation includes any form of classroom interaction that generates information on student learning, which is then used by faculty and students to fine-tune their teaching and learning strategies, respectively, during the teaching-learning process.

6. Educational research refers to the systematic collection and analysis of data related to the field of education. Research may involve a variety of methods. Research may involve various aspects of education including student learning, teaching methods, teacher training, and classroom dynamics.

Fundamental research, also known as **basic research** or **pure research** does not usually generate findings that have immediate applications in a practical level. Fundamental research is driven by curiosity and the desire to expand knowledge in specific research area. This type of research makes a specific contribution to the academic body of knowledge in the research area.

Applied research is a methodology used to solve a specific, practical problem of an individual or group. The study and **research** is used in business, medicine and education in order to find solutions that may cure diseases, solve scientific problems or develop technology.

Action research is either research initiated to solve an immediate problem or a reflective process of progressive problem solving led by individuals working with others in teams or as part of a "community of practice" to improve the way they address issues and solve problems.

Evaluation research can be defined as a type of **study** that uses standard social **research** methods for **evaluative** purposes, as a specific **research** methodology, and as an assessment process that employs special techniques unique to the **evaluation** of social programs.

10. In participation in research conference activities, potential for nurturing creative and critical thinking is relatively greater.

The main reasons for researchers to participate in scientific conferences are the following:

- to get informed about the state-of-the-art
- to present their own research, and get reactions from peers

- to have their paper published in the conference proceedings
- to meet others working in the same domain

16. Differentiation between acceptance and non-acceptance of certain stimuli in classroom communication is the basis of selective attention.

Selective attention is the process of focusing on a particular object in the environment for a certain period of time. Attention is a limited resource, so selective attention allows us to tune out unimportant details and focus on what really matters.

19. The transaction model of communication describes communication as a process in which communicators generate social realities within social, relational, and cultural contexts. This model includes participants who are simultaneously senders and receivers and accounts for how communication constructs our realities, relationships, and communities.

Classroom communication is a transactional communication.

A transactional model is perhaps the most simple and applicable forms of communication, and it can be used to describe communication at many levels including human verbal, human nonverbal, electronic communications, and even communication in the animal kingdom. In the transactional model, a sender represents the individual who has important information that needs to reach someone else.

Teachers are more inclined to regard students as active participants in the process of acquiring knowledge than to see the teacher's main role as the transmission of information and demonstration of "correct solutions". A teacher does operate under the assumption that students' responses are purposive.

21. –1 5 15 29 [47]

+ 6 + 10 + 14 + 18

+ 4 + 4 + 4

Therefore '47' will be the next term in the series.

22. 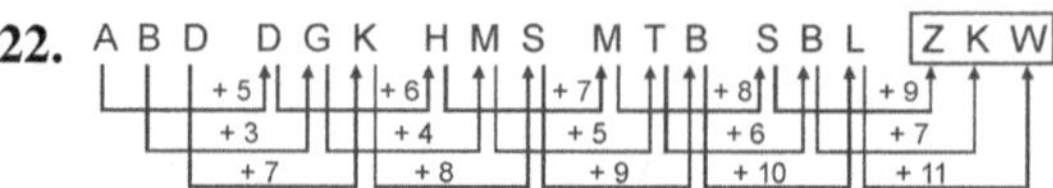

Therefore, 'ZKW' will be the next term in the series.

23. As,

V A R A N A S I

+1 +2 +3 +4 +5 +6 +7 +8

W C U E S G Z Q

Similarly,

K O L K A T A

+1 +2 +3 +4 +5 +6 +7

L Q O O F Z H

Therefore, KOLKATA is coded as LQOOFZH.

24. 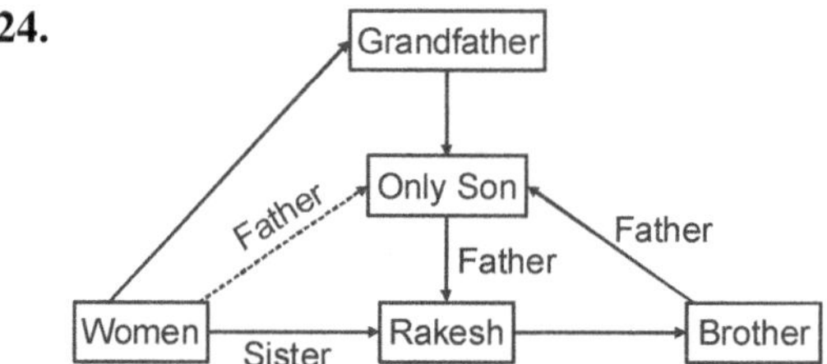

Clearly from the above diagram, women is the sister of Rakesh.

25. Let the Numbers are $2x$ and $5x$

According to question,

$$\frac{2x+16}{5x+16} = \frac{1}{2}$$

$$4x + 32 = 5x + 16$$

$$5x - 4x = 32 - 16$$

$$x = 16$$

Therefore, Numbers are, 32 and 80.

31. $\because$ Consumption (in million kg)
= Production – Export

Consumption in 2012 = 186.5 – 114
= 72.5 million kg

Consumption in 2013 = 202 – 114
= 88 million kg

Consumption in 2014 = 238 – 130
= 108 million kg

Consumption in 2015 = 221 – 116
= 105 million kg

Consumption in 2016 = 215 – 88
= 127 million kg

Percentage increase in consumption in 2013

$$= \frac{88-72.5}{72.5}\times 100 = 21.38\%$$

Similarly,

In 2014 = $\frac{108-88}{88}\times 100 = 22.73\%$

In 2015 = $\frac{105-108}{108}\times 100 = -2.78\%$

In 2016 = $\frac{127-105}{105}\times 100 = 20.95\%$.

32. Let the population in 2014 be x million

Then, Consumption = Production – Export

= 238 – 130

= 108 million kg

Per capita consumption

$$= \frac{\text{Consumption (in million kg)}}{\text{Population (in million)}}$$

$$38.7 = \frac{108}{x}$$

$$\therefore \quad x = \frac{108}{38.7} = 2.79 \text{ million}$$

33. In 2012, Required Ratio = $\frac{114}{72.5} = \frac{228}{145} = 1.57$

In 2013, Required Ratio = $\frac{114}{88} = \frac{57}{44} = 1.29$

In 2014, Required Radio = $\frac{130}{108} = \frac{65}{54} = 1.2$

In 2015, Required Ratio = $\frac{116}{105} = 1.10$

Therefore, Highest Ratio was in 2012.

34. $\because$ Per capita consumption = $\frac{\text{Consumption}}{\text{Population}}$

$\therefore$ Population = $\frac{\text{Consumption}}{\text{Per capita consumption}}$

In 2012, population = $\frac{72.5}{36.25}$ = 2 million

In 2013, population = $\frac{88}{35.2}$ = 2.5 million

In 2014, population = $\frac{108}{38.7}$ = 2.79 million

In 2015, population = $\frac{105}{40.5}$ = 2.59 million

In 2016, population = $\frac{127}{42}$ = 3.02 million

Therefore highest population was in 2016.

35. Required average consumption of rice (in million kg) over the years 2012-2016

$$= \frac{72.5+88+108+105+127}{5}$$

$$= \frac{500.5}{5} = 100.1 \text{ million kg.}$$

36. **Information and communication technology (ICT)** is another/extensional term for information technology (IT) that stresses the role of unified communications and the integration of telecommunications, computers as well as necessary enterprise software, middleware, storage, and audio-visual systems, which enable users to access, store, transmit, and manipulate information.

Converging technologies that exemplify ICT include the merging of audio-visual, telephone and computer networks through a common cabling system.

39.

Unit	Abbreviation	Storage
Bit	B	Binary Digit, Single 1 or 0
Nibble	–	4 bits
Byte/Octet	B	8 bits
Kilobyte	KB	1024 bytes
Megabyte	MB	1024 KB
Gigabyte	GB	1024 MB
Terabyte	TB	1024 GB
Petabyte	PB	1024 TB
Exabyte	EB	1024 PB
Zettabyte	ZB	1024 EB
Yottabyte	YB	1024 ZB

40. Volatile memory is computer storage that only maintains its data while the device is powered.

Most RAM (random access memory) used for primary storage in personal computers is volatile memory. RAM is much faster to read from and write to than the other kinds of storage in a computer, such as the hard disk or removable media.

Read-only memory (**ROM**) is a type of non-volatile memory used in computers and other electronic devices. Data stored in ROM can only be modified slowly, with difficulty, or not at all, so it is mainly used to store firmware or application software in plug-in cartridges.

Secondary memory is computer memory that is non-volatile and persistent in nature and is not directly accessed by a computer/processor. It allows a user to store data that may be instantly and easily retrieved, transported and used by applications and services.

41. **Fly ash**, is a coal combustion product that is composed of the particulates (fine particles of burned fuel) that are driven out of coal-fired boilers together with the flue gases. Ash that falls to the bottom of the boiler is called bottom ash.

Fly ash technology is providing relief to the overstressed resource base of soils being mined for the production of fired-bricks. Fly ash has proved to be an economical substitute for expensive adsorbents as well as a suitable raw material for brick manufacturing, zeolite synthesis, etc. Fly ash is a reservoir of essential minerals but is deficient in nitrogen and phosphorus.

42. Drought is the unusual dryness of soil caused by levels of rainfall significantly below average over a prolonged period. Hot dry winds, shortage of water, high temperatures and consequent evaporation of moisture from the ground can also contribute to conditions of drought. Droughts result in crop failure and shortages of water.

The beginning of a drought is difficult to determine. Several weeks, months, or even years might pass before people know that a drought is occurring. The end of a drought can occur as gradually as it began.

Drought is a complex phenomenon which is difficult to monitor and define. Hurricanes, for example, have a definite beginning and end and can easily be seen as they develop and move. Drought, on the other hand, is the *absence* of water. It is a creeping phenomenon that slowly sneaks up and impacts many sectors of the economy, and operates on many different time scales.

43. Indoor air pollution is a concern in the developed countries, where energy efficiency improvements sometimes make houses relatively airtight, reducing ventilation and raising pollutant levels. Indoor air problems can be subtle and do not always produce easily recognized impacts on health. Indoor air pollution is a serious health hazards.

Pollutants are any harmful contaminants in the air; therefore, **indoor air pollution** is when pollutants from things such as gases and particles contaminate the air indoors.

Indoor air pollution is a very real and dangerous thing because indoor air is far more concentrated with pollutants than outdoor air.

The dispersal of air pollutants is rather limited in Indoor environment.

44. **Sources of energy in India-**
Thermal power plant—59%
Large hydropower project—17%
Renewable Energy—12%
Natural gas—9%
Nuclear Energy—2%

45. Water pollution is a major environmental issue in India. The largest source of **water pollution in India** is untreated sewage. Other sources of pollution include agricultural runoff and unregulated small scale industry. Most rivers, lakes and surface water in India are polluted.

Eighty per cent of sewage in India is untreated and flows directly into the nation's rivers, polluting the main sources of drinking water, a study by an environment watchdog .

"The untreated waste dumped into rivers seeps into groundwater, thereby creating a ticking health bomb in India," concludes the report.

46. India's higher education system is the third largest in the world, next to the United States and China. The main governing body at the tertiary level is the University Grants Commission, which enforces its standards, advises the government, and helps coordinate between the centre and the state.

Previous Years' Paper (Solved)

UGC-NET (JRF) Exam November, 2017*

PAPER–I

Note : • This paper consists of **Fifty (50)** objective type questions of **two (2)** marks each. All questions are compulsory. ***(50 × 2 = 100 marks.)***

1. Which of the following set of statements best represents the nature and objective of teaching and learning?

(*a*) Teaching is like selling and learning is like buying.

(*b*) Teaching is a social act while learning is a personal act.

(*c*) Teaching implies learning whereas learning does not imply teaching.

(*d*) Teaching is a kind of delivery of knowledge while learning is like receiving it.

(*e*) Teaching is an interaction and is triadic in nature whereas learning is an active engagement in a subject domain.

Code:

A. (*a*), (*d*) and (*e*)

B. (*b*), (*c*) and (*e*)

C. (*a*), (*b*) and (*c*)

D. (*a*), (*b*) and (*d*)

2. From the list given below identify the learner characteristics which would facilitate teaching learning system to become effective. Choose the correct code to indicate your answer.

(*a*) Prior experience of learner

(*b*) Learner's family lineage

(*c*) Aptitude of the learner

(*d*) Learner's stage of development

(*e*) Learner's food habits and hobbies

(*f*) Learner's religious affiliation

Code:

A. (*a*), (*c*) and (*d*)

B. (*d*), (*e*) and (*f*)

C. (*a*), (*d*) and (*e*)

D. (*b*), (*c*) and (*f*)

3. **Assertion (A):** All teaching implies learning.
Reason (R) : Learning to be useful must be derived from teaching.

Choose the correct answer from the following:

A. Both (A) and (R) are true and (R) is the correct explanation of (A).

B. Both (A) and (R) are true, but (R) is not the correct explanation of (A).

C. (A) is true, but (R) is false.

D. (A) is false, but (R) is true.

4. On the basis of summative tests, a teacher is interpreting his/her students, performance in terms of their wellness life style evident in behaviour. This will be called:

A. Formative testing

B. Continuous and comprehensive evaluation

C. Norm-referenced testing

D. Criterion-referenced testing

5. Which one of the following is a key behaviour in effective teaching?

A. Using student ideas and contribution

B. Structuring

C. Instructional variety

D. Questioning

* Held on 5 November, 2017.

6. Which of the following research types focuses on ameliorating the prevailing situations?
A. Fundamental Research
B. Applied Research
C. Action Research
D. Experimental Research

7. A researcher attempts to evaluate the effect of method of feeding on anxiety - proneness of children. Which method of research would be appropriate for this?
A. Case study method
B. Experimental method
C. Ex-post-facto method
D. Survey method

8. In which of the following arrangements a wider spectrum of ideas and issues may be made possible?
A. Research Article
B. Workshop mode
C. Conference
D. Symposium

9. In finalizing a thesis writing format which of the following would form part of supplementary pages?
A. List of tables and figures
B. Table of contents
C. Conclusions of the study
D. Bibliography and Appendices

10. Which of the following is susceptible to the issue of research ethics?
A. Inaccurate application of statistical techniques
B. Faulty research design
C. Choice of sampling techniques
D. Reporting of research findings

Directions (Qs. No. 11-15): *Read the passage carefully and answer the questions.*

Climate change is considered to be one of the most serious threats to sustainable development, with adverse impacts on the environment, human health, food security, economic activity, natural resources and physical infrastructure. Global climate varies naturally.

According to the Intergovernmental Panel on Climate Change (IPCC), the effects of climate change have already been observed, and scientific findings indicate that precautionary and prompt action is necessary. Vulnerability to climate change is not just a function of geography or dependence on natural resources; it also has social, economic and political dimensions which influence how climate change affects different groups.

Poor people rarely have insurance to cover loss of property due to natural calamities *i.e.,* drought, floods, super cyclones etc. The poor communities are already struggling to cope with the existing challenges of poverty and climate variability and climate change could push many beyond their ability to cope or even survive. It is vital that these communities are helped to adapt to the changing dynamics of nature. Adaptation is a process through which societies make themselves better able to cope with an uncertain future.

Adapting to climate change entails taking the right measures to reduce the negative effects of climate change (or exploit the positive ones) by making the appropriate adjustments and changes. These range from technological options such as increased sea defences or flood - proof houses on stilts to behavioural change at the individual level, such as reducing water use in times of drought. Other strategies include early warning systems for extreme events, better water management, improved risk management, various insurance options and biodiversity conservation. Because of the speed at which climate change is happening due to global temperature rise, it is urgent that the vulnerability of developing countries to climate change is reduced and their capacity to adapt is increased and national adaptation plans are implemented. Adapting to climate change will entail adjustments and changes at every level from community to national and international.

Communities must build their resilience, including adopting appropriate technologies while making the most of traditional knowledge, and diversifying their livelihoods to cope with current and future climate stress. Local coping strategies and knowledge need to be used in synergy with government and local interventions. The need of adaptation interventions depends on national circumstances. There is a large body of knowledge and experience within local communities on coping with climatic variability and extreme weather events. Local communities have always aimed to adapt to variations in their climate. To do so, they have made preparations based on their resources and their knowledge accumulated through experience of past weather patterns.

This includes times when they have also been forced to react to and recover from extreme events, such as floods, drought and hurricanes. Local coping strategies are an important element of planning for adaptation. Climate change is leading communities to experience climatic extremes more frequently, as well as new climate conditions and extremes. Traditional knowledge can help to provide efficient, appropriate and time-tested ways of advising and enabling adaptation to climate change in communities who are feeling the effects of climate changes due to global warming.

11. Given below are the factors of vulnerability of poor people to climate change. Select the code that contains the correct answer.

(*a*) Their dependence on natural resources
(*b*) Geographical attributes
(*c*) Lack of financial resources
(*d*) Lack of traditional knowledge

Code:

A. (*a*), (*b*) and (*c*) B. (*b*), (*c*) and (*d*)
C. (*a*), (*b*), (*c*) and (*d*) D. (*c*) only

12. Adaptation as a process enables societies to cope with:

(*a*) An uncertain future
(*b*) Adjustments and changes
(*c*) Negative impact of climate change
(*d*) Positive impact of climate change

Select the most appropriate answer from the following code:

A. (*a*), (*b*), (*c*) and (*d*) B. (*a*) and (*c*)
C. (*b*), (*c*) and (*d*) D. (*c*) only

13. To address the challenge of climate change, developing countries urgently require:

A. Imposition of climate change tax
B. Implementation of national adaptation policy at their level
C. Adoption of short-term plans
D. Adoption of technological solutions

14. The traditional knowledge should be used through:

A. Its dissemination
B. Improvement in national circumstances
C. Synergy between government and local interventions
D. Modern technology

15. The main focus of the passage is on:

A. Combining traditional knowledge with appropriate technology
B. Co-ordination between regional and national efforts
C. Adaptation to climate change
D. Social dimensions of climate change

16. The interaction between a teacher and students creates a zone of proximal:

A. Difference B. Confusion
C. Development D. Distortion

17. The spatial audio reproduction in a classroom can reduce the students:

A. Cognitive load in understanding
B. Respect for the teacher
C. Motivation for excellence
D. Interest in technology-orientation

18. The classroom communication should essentially be:

A. Contrived
B. Empathetic
C. Abstract
D. Non-descriptive

19. A good communicator begins his/her presentation with a:

A. Complex question
B. Non-sequitur
C. Repetitive phrase
D. Ice-breaker

20. In a classroom, the probability of message reception can be enhanced by:
A. Establishing a viewpoint
B. Exposing the ignorance of students
C. Increasing the information load
D. Using high decibel audio tools

21. In the series 1, 6, 15, 28, 45, ... the next term will be:
A. 66 B. 76
C. 56 D. 84

22. The next term in the series ABD, DGK, HMS, MTB, ... is:
A. NSA B. SBL
C. PSK D. RUH

23. In certain code, "COVALENT" is coded as BWPDUOFM. The code of "ELEPHANT" will be:
A. MFUIQRTW B. QMUBIADH
C. QFMFUOBI D. EPHNTEAS

24. Ajay is a friend of Rakesh. Pointing to an old man Ajay asked Rakesh who is he? Rakesh said "His son is my son's uncle". The old man is related to Rakesh as:
A. Grandfather
B. Father-in-law
C. Father
D. Uncle

25. A postman walked 20 m straight from his office, turned right and walked 10 m. After turning left he walked 10 m and after turning right walked 20 m. He again turned right and walked 70 m. How far he is from his office?
A. 50 m B. 40 m
C. 60 m D. 20 m

26. It is Truism to say that no one was there when life first appeared on earth. Any assertion about life's origin, thus, should be treated as a theory. The above two statements constitute:
A. A historical explanation
B. A narrative
C. An argument
D. A conjecture

27. Given below are four statements. Among them two are related in such a way that they can both be true but they cannot both be false. Select the code that indicates those two statements:
Statements:
(*a*) Honest people never suffer.
(*b*) Almost all honest people do suffer.
(*c*) Honest people hardly suffer.
(*d*) Each and every honest person suffers.
Code:
A. (*a*) and (*b*) B. (*a*) and (*c*)
C. (*a*) and (*d*) D. (*b*) and (*c*)

28. A deductive argument is invalid if:
A. Its premises and conclusion are all true.
B. Its premises and conclusion are all false.
C. Its premises are all false but its conclusion is true.
D. Its premises are all true but its conclusion is false.

29. Given below are two premises (*a* and *b*). From those two premises four conclusions (*i*), (*ii*), (*iii*) and (*iv*) are drawn. Select the code that states the conclusion/conclusions drawn validly (taking the premises singularly or jointly).
Premises : (*a*) All bats are mammals.
(*b*) No birds are bats.
Conclusions: (*i*) No birds are mammals.
(*ii*) Some birds are not mammals.
(*iii*) No bats are birds.
(*iv*) All mammals are bats.
Code:
A. (*i*) only B. (*i*) and (*ii*) only
C. (*iii*) only D. (*iii*) and (*iv*) only

30. Just as melting ice-cubes do not cause a glass of water to overflow, melting sea-ice does not increase oceanic volume.
What type of argument is it?
A. Analogical
B. Hypothetical
C. Psychological
D. Statistical

Directions (Qs. No. 31-35): *Answer the questions based on the data given in the table below.*

Table: Number of registered vehicles in India and India's population.

Year	*Total vehicles (Lakhs)*	*Two wheelers (Lakhs)*	*Cars, Jeeps, Taxis (Lakhs)*	*Buses (Lakhs)*	*Goods vehicles (Lakhs)*	*Others (Lakhs)*	*Population (India) (Millions)*
1961	6.65	0.88	3.1	0.57	1.68	0.42	439.23
1971	18.65	5.76	6.82	0.94	3.43	1.70	548.15
1981	53.91	26.18	11.60	1.62	5.54	8.97	683.32
1991	213.74	142.00	29.54	3.31	13.56	25.33	846.42
2001	549.91	385.56	70.58	6.34	29.48	57.95	1028.73
2011	1417.58	1018.65	191.23	16.04	70.64	121.02	1210.19

31. The maximum decadal growth in population of India is registered in the period:
A. 1961 - 1971
B. 1991 - 2001
C. 2001 - 2011
D. 1981 - 1991

32. In which year the decadal growth (%) in number of cars surpassed that of the two wheelers?
A. 1991 B. 2001
C. 1981 D. 2011

33. What was the average decadal growth in the number of cars during 1961 - 2011?
A. ~ 131% B. ~ 68%
C. ~ 217% D. ~ 157%

34. In the year 2001, out of total number of vehicles, the number of passenger vehicles (4 wheelers) accounted for:
A. ~ 14% B. ~ 24%
C. ~ 31% D. ~ 43%

35. What was the per capita ownership of two wheelers in India in the year 2011?
A. ~ 0.084% B. ~ 0.0084%
C. ~ 0.84% D. ~ 0.068%

36. What is the name for a webpage address?
A. Domain B. Directory
C. Protocol D. URL

37. The data storage hierarchy consists of:
A. Bytes, bits, fields, records, files and databases
B. Bits, bytes, fields, records, files and databases
C. Bits, bytes, records, fields, files and databases
D. Bits, bytes, fields, files, records and databases

38. Which of the following domains is used for - profit businesses?
A. .org B. .net
C. .edu D. .com

39. What is the full form of USB as used in computer related activities?
A. Ultra Security Block
B. Universal Security Block
C. Universal Serial Bus
D. United Serial Bus

40. Which of the following represents billion characters?
A. Terabytes B. Megabytes
C. Kilobytes D. Gigabytes

41. Which of the following pollutants is the major cause of respiratory diseases?
A. Suspended fine particles
B. Nitrogen oxides
C. Carbon monoxide
D. Volatile organic compounds

42. **Assertion (A):** In urban areas, smog episodes occur frequently in winters.

Reason (R) : In winters, a lot of biomass is burnt by people for heating purposes or to keep themselves warm.

Choose the correct answer from the code given below:

A. Both (A) and (R) are true and (R) is the correct explanation of (A)
B. Both (A) and (R) are true, but (R) is not the correct explanation of (A)
C. (A) is true and (R) is false
D. Both (A) and (R) are false

43. Occurrence of natural hazards is affected by:

(*a*) Land use changes
(*b*) Drainage and construction
(*c*) Ozone depletion
(*d*) Climate change

Choose the correct answer from the code given below:

A. (*a*), (*c*) and (*d*)
B. (*a*), (*b*) and (*c*)
C. (*a*), (*b*) and (*d*)
D. (*b*), (*c*) and (*d*)

44. Which of the following pollutant gases is **not** produced both naturally and as a result of industrial activity?

A. Chlorofluoro carbon
B. Nitrous oxide
C. Methane
D. Carbon dioxide

45. Among the following fuels of energy, which is the most environment friendly?

A. Ethanol
B. Biogas
C. CNG
D. Hydrogen

46. Which of the following are the goals of higher education in India?

(*a*) Access
(*b*) Equity
(*c*) Quality and Excellence
(*d*) Relevance
(*e*) Value based education
(*f*) Compulsory and free education

Select the correct answer from the code given below:

A. (*a*), (*b*) and (*e*) only
B. (*a*), (*b*), (*e*) and (*f*)
C. (*a*), (*b*), (*c*), (*d*) and (*e*)
D. (*a*), (*b*), (*c*), (*d*), (*e*) and (*f*)

47. Which of the following has been ranked the best college in the country (2017) as per the National Institutional Ranking Framework (NIRF)?

A. Miranda House, Delhi
B. St. Stephen's College, Delhi
C. Fergusson College, Pune
D. Maharaja's College, Mysore

48. Which of the following universities has received the Visitor's Award for the best Central University in India in Feb. 2017?

A. Jawaharlal Nehru University
B. Banaras Hindu University
C. Tezpur University
D. University of Hyderabad

49. Who among the following can be removed by the President without Parliament's resolution?

A. Judge of a High Court
B. Governor of a State
C. Chief Election Commissioner
D. Comptroller and Auditor-General

50. Which of the following come(s) within the ambit of the term 'corruption'?

(*a*) Misuse of official position
(*b*) Deviation from rules, laws and norms
(*c*) Non-action when action is required
(*d*) Harm to public good

Select the correct answer from the code given below:

A. (*a*) only
B. (*a*) and (*b*) only
C. (*a*), (*b*) and (*d*)
D. (*a*), (*b*), (*c*) and (*d*)

ANSWERS

1	2	3	4	5	6	7	8	9	10
B	A	C	D	C	C	C	C	D	D
11	**12**	**13**	**14**	**15**	**16**	**17**	**18**	**19**	**20**
A	A	B	C	C	C	A	B	D	A
21	**22**	**23**	**24**	**25**	**26**	**27**	**28**	**29**	**30**
A	B	C	C	A	C	D	D	C	A
31	**32**	**33**	**34**	**35**	**36**	**37**	**38**	**39**	**40**
A	D	A	A	*	D	B	D	C	D
41	**42**	**43**	**44**	**45**	**46**	**47**	**48**	**49**	**50**
A	B	C	A	D	C	A	A	B	D

* *Error in Questions*

EXPLANATORY ANSWERS

4. A **criterion-referenced test** is a style of test which uses test scores to generate a statement about the behaviour that can be expected of a person with that score.

Most tests and quizzes that are written by school teachers can be considered criterion-referenced tests.

Criterion-referenced tests (or CRTs) differ in that each examinee's performance is compared to a pre-defined set of criteria or a standard. The goal with these tests is to determine whether or not the candidate has the demonstrated mastery of a certain skill or set of skills.

5. Key behaviours for effective teaching and some indicators pertaining to them are the following:

- **Lesson clarity:** Logical, step-by-step order; clear and audible delivery free of distracting mannerisms.
- **Instructional variety:** Variability in instructional materials, questioning, types of feedback, and teaching strategies.
- **Task orientation:** Achievement (content) orientation as opposed to process orientation, maximum content coverage, and time devoted to instruction.
- **Student engagement:** Limiting opportunities for distraction and getting students to work on, think through, and inquire about the content.
- **Success rate:** 60% to 70% of time spent on tasks that afford moderate-to-high levels of success, especially during expository or didactic instruction.

Instructional variety is a description of the flexibility of an instructor when presenting a lesson.

For a teacher, this means being able to shift from one form of instruction to another in order to maintain the focus of students. This is not easy and is considered a valuable skill in education. If a teacher teaches the same way regardless of what the lesson demands or the students need, this indicates a lack of a variety. This inability to provide instruction in a variety of ways suggest that there may be a lower level of teacher effectiveness.

6. **Action research** is either research initiated to solve an immediate problem or a reflective process of progressive problem solving led by individuals working with others in teams or as part of a "community of practice" to improve the way they address issues and solve problems.

Action research helps educators be more effective at what they care most about—their teaching and the development of their students. Seeing students grow is probably the greatest joy educators can experience.

When teachers have convincing evidence that their work has made a real difference in their students' lives, the countless hours and endless efforts of teaching seem worthwhile.

The Action Research Process

Educational action research can be engaged in by a single teacher, by a group of colleagues who share an interest in a common problem, or by the entire faculty of a school. Whatever the scenario, action research always involves the same seven-step process.

These seven steps, which become an endless cycle for the inquiring teacher, are the following:

1. Selecting a focus
2. Clarifying theories
3. Identifying research questions
4. Collecting data
5. Analyzing data
6. Reporting results
7. Taking informed action

7. Researcher attempts to evaluate the effect of method of feeding on anxiety-proneness of children. Ex-post-facto method of research would be appropriate for this.

An ex-post-facto research design is a method in which groups with qualities that already exist are compared on some dependent variable.

Also known as "after the fact" research, an ex-post-facto design is considered quasi-experimental because the subjects are not randomly assigned - they are grouped based on a particular characteristic or trait.

Although differing groups are analyzed and compared in regards to independent and dependent variables it is not a true experiment because it lacks random assignment. The assignment of subjects to different groups is based on whichever variable is of interest to the researchers.

8. **A conference** is a gathering of people with a common interest or background, with the purposes of allowing them to meet one another and to learn about and discuss issues, ideas and work that focus on a topic of mutual concern.

The Latin roots of the word "conference" mean, literally, "Bring together." A conference brings together people and ideas.

In the cases of health and community work, conferences often have the goal of generating or working toward solutions to problems or broader social change.

Conferences may be held in places other than the workplaces and neighbourhoods of their participants, so that the people attending can focus on the topic at hand without distractions. Some conferences are even held in another area of the country or the world.

9. A thesis (or dissertation) may be arranged as a thesis by publication or a monograph, with or without appended papers, respectively, though many graduate programs allow candidates to submit a curated collection of published papers.

An ordinary monograph has a title page, an abstract, a table of contents, comprising the various chapters (*e.g.,* introduction, literature review, methodology, results, discussion), and a bibliography or (more usually) a references section.

They differ in their structure in accordance with the many different areas of study (arts, humanities, social sciences, technology, sciences, etc.) and the differences between them. In a thesis by publication, the chapters constitute an introductory and comprehensive review of the appended published and unpublished article documents.

10. **Research** that involves human subjects or participants raises unique and complex ethical, legal, social and political issues.

Research ethics is specifically interested in the analysis of **ethical** issues that are raised when people are involved as participants in research. There are three objectives in research ethics.

16. The **zone of proximal development** is the difference between what a learner can do without help and what he or she cannot do.

The zone of proximal development (ZPD) of a child is not a naturally existing phenomenon that arises by itself every time an adult helps a child achieve greater independence. It is a special form of interaction in which the action of the adult is aimed at generating and supporting the child's initiative.

18. Empathy—the power to understand perspectives other than your own—is an essential skill for all children to master, and it's one of an important set of **teaching strategies** teachers should focus on.

Empathy is foundational for building bridges between individuals, understanding each others' complex emotions, gaining a diverse perspective, and leveraging relationships for collaboration and progress.

19. An ice-breaker is an activity, game, or event that is used to welcome and warm up the conversation among participants in a meeting, training class, team building session, or another event.

Any event that requires people to comfortably interact with each other and a facilitator is an opportunity to use an ice-breaker.

21. 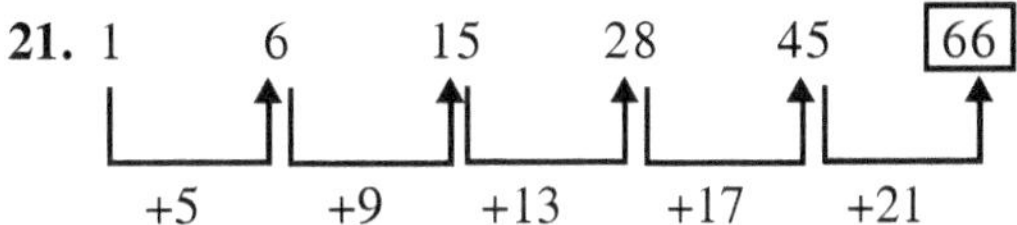

Hence, the next term will be 66.

22. ABD, DGK, HMS, MTB ......

Hence, next term in the series is SBL.

23. C O V A L E N T is coded as

↓ ↓ ↓ ↓ ↓ ↓ ↓ ↓

B W P D U O F M

Similarly,

E L E P H A N T is coded as

↓ ↓ ↓ ↓ ↓ ↓ ↓ ↓

Q F M F U O B I

24. The oldman is related to Rakesh as Father.

25. 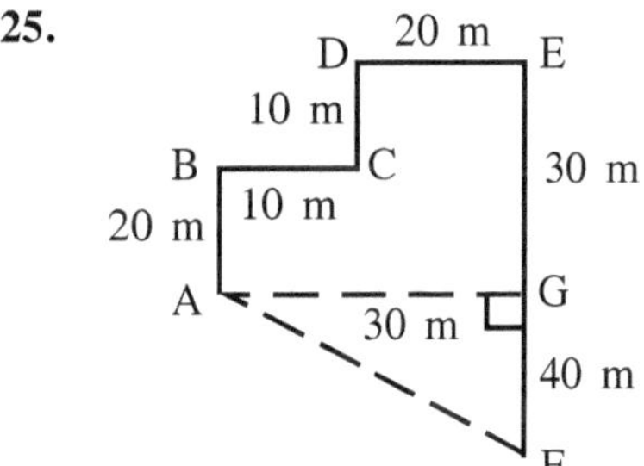

In right Δ AGF,

$$AF^2 = (40)^2 + (30)^2$$

$$= 1600 + 900$$

$$\Rightarrow \quad AF^2 = 2500$$

$$\Rightarrow \quad AF = 50 \text{ m}$$

Hence, Postman is 50 m away from his office.

28. **A deductive argument** is said to be valid if and only if it takes a form that makes it impossible for the premises to be true and the conclusion nevertheless to be false. Otherwise, **a deductive argument** is said to be **invalid**.

A deductive argument is *sound* if and only if it is both valid, and all of its premises are *actually true*. Otherwise, a deductive argument is *unsound*.

37. Data is organized in a **data storage hierarchy** of increasingly complex levels: bits, bytes (characters), fields, records, files, and databases. A **character** is a letter, number, or special character. A **field** consists of one or more characters (bytes). A **record** is a collection of related fields.

A **file** is a collection of related records. A database is, as mentioned, an organized collection of integrated files. Important to data organization is the key field, a field used to uniquely identify a record so that it can be easily retrieved and processed.

38. .com be used primarily for commercial businesses, .net for network related organizations and .org for nonprofit groups. This quickly became unworkable and consequently, in the case of.com, .net and .org, a decision was made to rely on registrants to choose the TLD *(Top Level Domain)* they wish. In fact, many registrants *(domain owners)* order their domain name as .com, .net and .org.

39. USB, short for Universal Serial Bus, is an industry standard that defines cables, connectors and communications protocols for connection, communication, and power supply between computers and devices.

USB was designed to standardize the connection of computer peripherals (including keyboards, pointing devices, digital cameras, printers, portable media players, disk drives and network adapters) to personal computers, both to communicate and to supply electric power.

It has largely replaced a variety of earlier interfaces, such as serial ports and parallel ports, as well as separate power chargers for portable devices—and has become commonplace on a wide range of devices.

Created in the mid-1990s, it is currently developed by the USB Implementers Forum (USB IF).

40. A gigabyte (GB) is a measure of computer data storage capacity that is roughly equivalent to 1 billion bytes. A gigabyte is two to the 30th power or 1,073,741,824 in decimal notation.

41. There is clear evidence that atmospheric pollution is associated with troublesome respiratory symptoms in children but what is less clear is whether specific pollutants have a causal role in the pathogenesis of respiratory diseases.

The principal pollutants of the external (outdoor) environment include nitrogen oxides (NO, NO_2), ozone, sulphur dioxide (SO_2) and particulates.

Respirable suspended particulates or PM10, can get deep into the lungs and cause a broad range of health effects, in particular, respiratory and cardiovascular illnesses, including –

- Increasing respiratory symptoms, such as irritation of the air-ways, coughing, or difficulty in breathing;
- Decreasing lung function;
- Aggravation of asthma;
- Development of chronic bronchitis;
- Adverse effects on the cardiovascular system;
- Premature death in people with heart or lung disease.

People with heart or lung disease, children and the elderly are most likely to be affected by particulate pollution.

43. Natural hazards are naturally occurring phenomena that have disastrous impact on humanity.

These phenomena had been in existence even before the advent of humanity. The hazardous dimension of these natural phenomena are in the context of the impact that such a phenomenon would have on human population in the area affected by that phenomenon.

Geophysical hazards encompass geological and meteorological phenomena such as earthquakes, volcanic eruptions, wildfires, cyclonic storms, floods, droughts, and landslides.

44. Chlorofluoro carbon (CFC) is an organic compound that contains carbon, chlorine, and fluorine, produced as a volatile derivative of methane, ethane and propane.

The properties of CFCs make them useful for a variety of commercial and industrial purposes: as a propellant in aerosol sprays (now banned in the US and Europe), in refrigeration and air conditioning systems, in foams, in cleaning solvents and in electrical components.

Most CFCs have been released to the atmosphere through the use of aerosols containing them and as leakages from refrigeration equipment. Other releases may occur from industry producing and using them and other products containing them. There are not thought to be any natural sources of CFCs to the environment.

45. An Eco-Friendly Fuel is an ecologically friendly fuel. Its production and use has a minimum impact on the environment.

Hydrogen fuel is a zero-emission fuel when burned with oxygen, if one considers water not to be an emission. Hydrogen has been touted as an environmentally friendly wonder fuel that can be used in vehicles and burns to produce only water as a by product. The problem with hydrogen is that producing it is far from environmentally friendly and storing it in a fuel tank is extremely hazardous.

46. India's higher education system is the third largest in the world. The main governing body at the tertiary level is the University Grants Commission, which enforces its standards, advises the government, and helps coordinate between the centre and the state.

The objectives of higher education are:

- **Wisdom and knowledge:** Since education is both a training of minds and training of souls, it should give both knowledge and wisdom. No amount of factual information would take ordinarily into educated men unless something is awakened in them.
- **Aims of the social order:** Our education system must find its guiding principle in the aims of the social order for which it prepares. Unless we preserve the value of democracy, justice, liberty, equality and fraternity, we cannot preserves our freedom.
- **Love for higher values of life:** The greatness of a country does not depend on the extent of its territory, the length of its communication or the amount of its wealth, but on the love for higher values of life. We must develop thought for the poor and sufferings, regards and respect for women, faith in brotherhood regardless of race, colour, religion etc.
- **Training for leadership:** One of the important aims of higher education is the training for leadership in the profession and public life. It is the function of universities to train men and women for wise leadership.

47. The Ministry of Human Resource Development released the NIRF rankings, 2017 as per which the Indian Institute of Science at Bengaluru in Karnataka is No. 1 higher educational institute while the Indian Institute of Management at Ahmedabad in Gujarat is the top management institute.

The Indian Institute of Technology (IIT) Madras has been ranked as the best engineering college in India. Deemed university Jamia Hamdard in Delhi is numero uno in pharmacy category, while Miranda House in the national capital has been ranked the best college in the country.

Bengaluru's IISc has also been ranked as the top university in India, as per the second edition of India Rankings under the National Institutional Ranking Framework (NIRF) released by Union Human Resource Development Minister Prakash Javadekar. The Jawaharlal Nehru University (JNU) secured second spot in the top university rankings in India.

In the list of best colleges in India, Miranda House in Delhi was followed by Loyola college in Chennai. This is the first time general colleges have been ranked in the NIRF.

49. The **governors and lieutenant-governors** of the states and union territories of India have similar powers and functions at the state level as that of the President of India at Union level. Governors exist in the states while lieutenant-governors exist in union territories and in the National Capital Territory of Delhi.

The governors and **lieutenant-governors** are appointed by the **President** for a term of **five years**.

The term of governor's office is normally 5 years but it can be terminated earlier by:

- Dismissal by the president (usually on the advice of the prime minister of the country) at whose pleasure the governor holds office. Dismissal of Governors without valid reason is not permitted. However, it is the duty of the President to dismiss a Governor whose acts are upheld by courts as unconstitutional and in bad faith.
- Resignation by the governor: There is no provision for impeachment, as it happens for the president.

50. Corruption is the misuse of *public* power (by elected politician or appointed civil servant) for private gain.

Corruption is a deviation from normal human behaviour in a geopolitical setting whereby causing the derailment of individual and institutional accountability, transparency and natural justice.

Corruption is a barometer of a nations' development and decline which determines its stanching stature and estimation among the country of nation-states. But of late, corruption has become a way of national life and has already been institutionalized beyond the comprehension of ordinary human imagination.

Previous Years' Paper (Solved)

UGC-NET (JRF) EXAM JANUARY, 2017*

PAPER–I

Note :
- This paper contains **Sixty (60)** multiple choice questions, each question carrying **two (2)** marks.
- Candidate is expected to answer any **Fifty (50)** questions.
- In case more than **Fifty (50)** questions are attempted, only the first **Fifty (50)** questions will be evaluated.

1. The principal of a school conducts an interview session of teachers and students with a view to explore the possibility of their enhanced participation in school programmes. This endeavour may be related to which type of research?

A. Evaluation Research
B. Fundamental Research
C. Action Research
D. Applied Research

2. In doing action research what is the usual sequence of steps?

A. Reflect, observe, plan, act
B. Plan, act, observe, reflect
C. Plan, reflect, observe, act
D. Act, observe, plan, reflect

3. Which sequence of research steps is logical in the list given below?

A. Problem formulation, Analysis, Development of Research design, Hypothesis making, Collection of data, Arriving at generalizations and conclusions.
B. Development of Research design, Hypothesis making, Problem formulation, Data analysis, Arriving at conclusions and data collection.
C. Problem formulation, Hypothesis making, Development of a Research design, Collection of data, Data analysis and formulation of generalizations and conclusions.
D. Problem formulation, Deciding about the sample and data collection tools, Formulation of hypothesis, Collection and interpretation of research evidence.

4. Below are given two sets – research methods (Set-I) and data collection tools (Set-II). Match the two sets and indicate your answer by selecting the correct code :

Set-I (Research Methods)	**Set-II (Data Collection Tools)**
(*a*) Experimental method	(*i*) Using primary and secondary sources
(*b*) Ex post-facto method	(*ii*) Questionnaire
(*c*) Descriptive survey method	(*iii*) Standardized tests
(*d*) Historical method	(*iv*) Typical characteristic tests

Codes:

	(*a*)	(*b*)	(*c*)	(*d*)
A.	(*ii*)	(*i*)	(*iii*)	(*iv*)
B.	(*iii*)	(*iv*)	(*ii*)	(*i*)
C.	(*ii*)	(*iii*)	(*i*)	(*iv*)
D.	(*ii*)	(*iv*)	(*iii*)	(*i*)

* *Exam held on 22 January, 2017.*

5. The issue of 'research ethics' may be considered pertinent at which stage of research?

A. At the stage of problem formulation and its definition

B. At the stage of defining the population of research

C. At the stage of data collection and interpretation

D. At the stage of reporting the findings.

6. In which of the following, reporting format is formally prescribed?

A. Doctoral level thesis

B. Conference of researchers

C. Workshops and seminars

D. Symposia

Read the following passage carefully and answer questions from 7 to 12:

The last great war, which nearly shook the foundations of the modern world, had little impact on Indian literature beyond aggravating the popular revulsion against violence and adding to the growing disillusionment with the 'humane pretensions' of the Western World. This was eloquently voiced in Tagore's later poems and his last testament, Crisis in Civilisation. The Indian intelligentsia was in a state of moral dilemma. On the one hand, it could not help sympathising with England's dogged courage in the hour of peril, with the Russians fighting with their backs to the wall against the ruthless Nazi hordes, and with China groaning under the heel of Japanese militarism; on the other hand, their own country was practically under military occupation of their own soil, and an Indian army under Subhas Bose was trying from the opposite camp to liberate their country. No creative impulse could issue from such confusion of loyalties. One would imagine that the achievement of Indian Independence in 1947, which came in the wake of the Allies' victory and was followed by the collapse of colonialism in the neighbouring countries of South-East Asia, would have released an upsurge of creative energy. No doubt it did, but unfortunately it was soon submerged in the great agony of partition, with its inhuman slaughter of the innocents and the uprooting of millions of people from their homeland, followed by the martyrdom of Mahatma Gandhi. These tragedies, along with Pakistan's invasion of Kashmir and its later atrocities in Bangladesh, did indeed provoke a poignant writing, particularly in the languages of the regions most affected, Bengali, Hindi, Kashmiri, Punjabi, Sindhi and Urdu. But poignant or passionate writing does not by itself make great literature. What reserves of enthusiasm and confidence survived these disasters have been mainly absorbed in the task of national reconstruction and economic development. Great literature has always emerged out of chains of convulsions. Indian literature is richer today in volume, range and variety than it ever was in the past.

Based on the passage answer the following questions from 7 to 12:

7. What was the impact of the last great war on Indian literature?

A. It had no impact.

B. It aggravated popular revulsion against violence.

C. It shook the foundations of literature.

D. It offered eloquent support to the Western World.

8. What did Tagore articulate in his last testament?

A. Offered support to Subhas Bose.

B. Exposed the humane pretensions of the Western World.

C. Expressed loyalty to England.

D. Encouraged the liberation of countries.

9. What was the stance of Indian intelligentsia during the period of great war?

A. Indifference to Russia's plight.

B. They favoured Japanese militarism.

C. They prompted creativity out of confused loyalties.

D. They expressed sympathy for England's dogged courage.

10. Identify the factor responsible for the submergence of creative energy in Indian literature.

A. Military occupation of one's own soil.
B. Resistance to colonial occupation.
C. Great agony of partition.
D. Victory of Allies.

11. What was the aftermath that survived tragedies in Kashmir and Bangladesh?
A. Suspicion of other countries
B. Continuance of rivalry
C. Menace of war
D. National reconstruction

12. The passage has the message that
A. Disasters are inevitable.
B. Great literature emerges out of chains of convulsions.
C. Indian literature does not have a marked landscape.
D. Literature has no relation with war and independence.

13. Effective communication pre-supposes
A. Non-alignment B. Domination
C. Passivity D. Understanding

14. When verbal and non-verbal messages are contradictory, it is said that most people believe in
A. indeterminate messages
B. verbal messages
C. non-verbal messages
D. aggressive messages

15. The typical feature of an information-rich classroom lecture is in the nature of being
A. Sedentary B. Staggered
C. Factual D. Sectoral

16. Expressive communication is driven by
A. Passive aggression
B. Encoder's personality characteristics
C. External clues
D. Encoder-decoder contract

17. Positive classroom communication leads to
A. Coercion B. Submission
C. Confrontation D. Persuasion

18. Classroom communication is the basis of
A. Social identity
B. External inanities
C. Biased passivity
D. Group aggression

19. The missing term in the series 1, 4, 27, 16, ?, 36, 343, ... is
A. 30 B. 49
C. 125 D. 81

20. The next term in the following series
YEB, WFD, UHG, SKI, _?_ will be
A. TLO B. QOL
C. QLO D. GQP

21. If A is coded as C, M as I, N as P, S as O, I as A, P as N, E as M, O as E and C as S, then the code of COMPANIES will be
A. SPEINMOAC B. NCPSEIOMA
C. SMOPIEACN D. SEINCPAMO

22. Among the following, identify the continuous type of data:
A. Number of languages a person speaks
B. Number of children in a household
C. Population of cities
D. Weight of students in a class

23. Ali buys a glass, a pencil box and a cup and pays ₹ 21 to the shopkeeper. Rakesh buys a cup, two pencil boxes and a glass and pays ₹ 28 to the shopkeeper. Preeti buys two glasses, a cup and two pencil boxes and pays ₹ 35 to the shopkeeper. The cost of 10 cups will be
A. ₹ 40 B. ₹ 60
C. ₹ 80 D. ₹ 70

24. Out of four cities given below three are alike in some manner while the fourth one is different. Identify the odd one
A. Lucknow B. Rishikesh
C. Allahabad D. Patna

25. Given below are some characteristics of reasoning. Select the code that states a characteristic which is not of deductive reasoning:
A. The conclusion must be based on observation and experiment.
B. The conclusion should be supported by the premise/premises.
C. The conclusion must follow from the premise/premises necessarily.
D. The argument may be valid or invalid.

26. If two standard form categorical propositions with the same subject and predicate are related in such a manner that if one is undetermined the other must be undetermined, what is their relation?

A. Contrary B. Subcontrary
C. Contradictory D. Sub-altern

27. Men and woman may have different reproductive strategies but neither can be considered inferior or superior to the other, any more than a bird's wings can be considered superior or inferior to a fish's fins. What type of argument it is?

A. Biological B. Physiological
C. Analogical D. Hypothetical

28. Among the following propositions two are related in such a way that they cannot both be true but can both be false. Select the code that states those two propositions.

Propositions:

(*a*) Every student is attentive.
(*b*) Some students are attentive.
(*c*) Students are never attentive.
(*d*) Some students are not attentive.

Codes:

A. (*a*) and (*b*) B. (*a*) and (*c*)
C. (*b*) and (*c*) D. (*c*) and (*d*)

29. Given below are two premises (*a*) and (*b*). From those two premises four conclusions (*i*), (*ii*), (*iii*) & (*iv*) are drawn. Select the code that states the conclusions validly drawn from the premises (taking singly or jointly).

Premises: (*a*) Untouchability is a curse.
(*b*) All hot pans are untouchable.

Conclusions:

(*i*) All hot pans are curse.
(*ii*) Some untouchable things are hot pans.
(*iii*) All curses are untouchability.
(*iv*) Some curses are untouchability.

Codes:

A. (*i*) and (*ii*) B. (*ii*) and (*iii*)
C. (*iii*) and (*iv*) D. (*ii*) and (*iv*)

30. If the statement 'None but the brave wins the race' is false which of the following statements can be claimed to be true?

Select the correct code:

A. All brave persons win the race.
B. Some persons who win the race are not brave.
C. Some persons who win the race are brave.
D. No person who wins the race is brave.

The table below embodies data on the sales revenue (₹ in lakh) generated by a publishing house during the years 2012-15 while selling books, magazines and journals as three categories of items. Answer questions 31 – 33 based on the data contained in the table.

	Sales Revenue (₹ in lakh)			
Year→ / Items ↓	**2012**	**2013**	**2014**	**2015**
Journals	46	47	45	44
Magazines	31	39	46	51
Books	73	77	78	78
Total				

31. In 2015, approximately what percent of total revenue came from books?

A. 45% B. 55%
C. 35% D. 25%

32. The number of years in which there was an increase in revenue from at least two categories of items, is

A. 0 B. 1
C. 2 D. 3

33. If the year 2016 were to show the same growth in terms of total sales revenue as the year 2015 over the year 2014, then the revenue in the year 2016 must be approximately:

A. ₹ 194 lakh B. ₹ 187 lakh
C. ₹ 172 lakh D. ₹ 177 lakh

A University professor maintains data on MCA students tabulated by performance and gender of the students. The data is kept on a computer hard disk, but accidently some of it is lost because of a computer virus. Only the following could be recovered:

Performance → / Gender ↓	Number of MCA Students			
	Average	Good	Excellent	Total
Male			10	
Female				32
Total		30		

Panic buttons were pressed but to no avail. An expert committee was formed, which decided that the following facts were self evident:

(*a*) Half the students were either excellent or good.

(*b*) 40% of the students were females.

(*c*) One-third of the male students were average.

*Answer questions **34 – 36** based on the data given above:*

34. How many female students are excellent?

A. 0 B. 8
C. 16 D. 32

35. What proportion of female students are good?

A. 0 B. 0.25
C. 0.50 D. 0.75

36. Approximately, what proportion of good students are male?

A. 0 B. 0.73
C. 0.43 D. 0.27

37. Which of the following statement(s) is/are TRUE?

S1: The decimal number 11 is larger than the hexadecimal number 11.

S2: In the binary number 1110.101, the fractional part has the decimal value as 0.625.

A. S1 only B. S2 only
C. Both S1 and S2 D. Neither S1 nor S2

38. Read the following two statements:

I: Information and Communication Technology (ICT) is considered a subset of Information Technology (IT).

II: The 'right to use' a piece of software is termed as copyright.

Which of the above statement(s) is/are CORRECT?

A. Both I and II B. Neither I nor II
C. II only D. I only

39. Which of the following correctly lists computer memory types from highest to lowest speed?

A. Secondary Storage; Main Memory (RAM); Cache Memory; CPU Registers
B. CPU Registers; Cache Memory; Secondary Storage; Main Memory (RAM)
C. CPU Registers; Cache Memory; Main Memory (RAM); Secondary Storage
D. Cache Memory; CPU Registers; Main Memory (RAM); Secondary Storage

40. Which of the following is a characteristic of Web2.0 applications?

A. Multiple users schedule their time to use Web2.0 applications one by one.
B. Web2.0 applications are focused on the ability for people to collaborate and share information online.
C. Web2.0 applications provide users with content rather than facilitating users to create it.
D. Web2.0 applications use only static pages.

41. With regard to a word processing software, the process of combining static information in a publication together with variable information in a data source to create one merged publication is called

A. Electronic mail B. Data sourcing
C. Mail merge D. Spam mail

42. DVD technology uses an optical media to store the digital data. DVD is an acronym for

A. Digital Vector Disc
B. Digital Volume Disc
C. Digital Versatile Disc
D. Digital Visualization Disc

43. Assertion (A): Sustainable development is critical to well being of human society.

Reason (R): Environmentally sound policies do not harm the environment or deplete the natural resources.

Choose the correct code:

A. Both (A) and (R) are correct and (R) is the correct explanation of (A).

B. Both (A) and (R) are correct, but (R) is not the correct explanation of (A).

C. (A) is true, but (R) is false.

D. (A) is false, but (R) is true.

44. The dominant source of pollution due to oxides of nitrogen (NO_X) in urban areas is

A. road transport

B. commercial sector

C. energy use in industry

D. power plants

45. Which of the following is **not** a water-brone disease?

A. Typhoid B. Hepatitis

C. Cholera D. Dengue

46. Indian government's target for power production from small hydro projects by the year 2022 is

A. 1 Giga-Watt B. 5 Giga-Watt

C. 10 Giga-Watt D. 15 Giga-Watt

47. In which country, the recent international agreement on phasing out Hydro Fluoro Carbons (HFCs) was signed?

A. Rwanda B. Morocco

C. South Africa D. Algeria

48. Which of the following natural hazards is **not** hydro-meteorological?

A. Snow avalanche B. Sea erosion

C. Tropical cyclone D. Tsunami

49. Which of the following are the demerits of globalisation of higher education?

(*a*) Exposure to global curriculum

(*b*) Promotion of elitism in education

(*c*) Commodification of higher education

(*d*) Increase in the cost of education

Select the correct answer from the codes given below:

Codes:

A. (*a*) and (*d*) B. (*a*), (*c*) and (*d*)

C. (*b*), (*c*) and (*d*) D. (*a*), (*b*), (*c*) and (*d*)

50. Which of the following statements are correct about Deemed Universities?

(*a*) The Governor of the State is the chancellor of Deemed Universities.

(*b*) They can design their own syllabus and course work.

(*c*) They can frame their own guidelines regarding admission and fees.

(*d*) They can grant degrees.

Select the correct answer from the codes given below:

Codes:

A. (*a*), (*b*) and (*c*) B. (*b*), (*c*) and (*d*)

C. (*a*), (*c*) and (*d*) D. (*a*), (*b*), (*c*) and (*d*)

51. The purpose of value education is best served by focussing on

A. Cultural practices prevailing in the society.

B. Norms of conduct laid down by a social group.

C. Concern for human values.

D. Religious and moral practices and instructions.

52. Which of the following statements are correct?

(*a*) Rajya Sabha is a Permanent House which can be dissolved only during national emergency.

(*b*) Rajya Sabha does not represent the local interests of the States.

(*c*) Members of the Rajya Sabha are not bound to vote at the dictates of the states they represent.

(*d*) No Union territory has a representative in the Rajya Sabha.

Select the correct answer from the codes given below:

Codes:

A. (*a*) and (*d*) B. (*b*) and (*c*)

C. (*b*), (*c*) and (*d*) D. (*a*), (*b*), (*c*) and (*d*)

53. Which of the following are not necessarily the immediate consequences of the proclamation of the President's Rule in a State?

(*a*) Dissolution of the State Assembly.

(*b*) Removal of the Council of Ministers in the State.

(*c*) Takeover of the State administration by the Union Government.

(*d*) Appointment of a new Chief Secretary.

Select the correct answer from the codes given below:

Codes:

A. (*a*) and (*d*) B. (*a*), (*b*) and (*c*)
C. (*a*), (*b*), (*c*) and (*d*) D. (*b*) and (*c*)

54. Instead of holding the office during the pleasure of the President who among the following hold(s) office during good behaviour?

(*a*) Governor of a State
(*b*) Attorney General of India
(*c*) Judges of the High Court
(*d*) Administrator of a Union Territory

Select the correct answer from the codes given below:

Codes:

A. (*a*) only B. (*c*) only
C. (*a*) and (*c*) D. (*a*), (*b*), (*c*) and (*d*)

55. Which of the following set of statements represents acceptable propositions in respect of teaching-learning relationships ? Choose the correct code to indicate your answer.

(*i*) When students fail in a test, it is the teacher who fails.
(*ii*) Every teaching must aim at ensuring learning.
(*iii*) There can be teaching without learning taking place.
(*iv*) There can be no learning without teaching.
(*v*) A teacher teaches but learns also.
(*vi*) Real learning implies rote learning.

Codes:

A. (*ii*), (*iii*), (*iv*) and (*v*)
B. (*i*), (*ii*), (*iii*) and (*v*)
C. (*iii*), (*iv*), (*v*) and (*vi*)
D. (*i*), (*ii*), (*v*) and (*vi*)

56. Assertion (A): Learning is a life long process.

Reason (R) : Learning to be useful must be linked with life processes.

Choose the correct answer from the following code:

A. Both (A) and (R) are true and (R) is the correct explanation of (A).
B. Both (A) and (R) are true, but (R) is not the correct explanation of (A).
C. (A) is true, but (R) is false.
D. (A) is false, but (R) is true.

57. Effectiveness of teaching has to be judged in terms of

A. Course coverage
B. Students' interest
C. Learning outcomes of students
D. Use of teaching aids in the classroom

58. In which teaching method learner's participation is made optimal and proactive ?

A. Discussion method
B. Buzz session method
C. Brainstorming session method
D. Project method

59. One of the most powerful factors affecting teaching effectiveness is related to the

A. Social system of the country
B. Economic status of the society
C. Prevailing political system
D. Educational system

60. Assertion (A): Formative evaluation tends to accelerate the pace of learning.

Reason (R): As against summative evaluation, formative evaluation is highly reliable.

Choose the correct answer from the following code :

A. Both (A) and (R) are true and (R) is the correct explanation of (A).
B. Both (A) and (R) are true, but (R) is not the correct explanation of (A).
C. (A) is true, but (R) is false.
D. (A) is false, but (R) is true.

ANSWERS

1	**2**	**3**	**4**	**5**	**6**	**7**	**8**	**9**	**10**
C	B	C	B	C	A	B	B	D	C
11	**12**	**13**	**14**	**15**	**16**	**17**	**18**	**19**	**20**
D	B	D	C	C	B	D	A	C	B

21	22	23	24	25	26	27	28	29	30
D	D	D	A	A	C	C	B	D	B
31	**32**	**33**	**34**	**35**	**36**	**37**	**38**	**39**	**40**
A	C	D	A	B	B	B	B	C	B
41	**42**	**43**	**44**	**45**	**46**	**47**	**48**	**49**	**50**
C	C	B	A	D	B	A	D	C	B
51	**52**	**53**	**54**	**55**	**56**	**57**	**58**	**59**	**60**
C	B	A	B	B	A	C	D	D	C

EXPLANATORY ANSWERS

1. **Action Research:** Action research is focused on immediate application, not on the development of theory or on general application. It emphasises on a problem here and now in a local setting. Its findings are to be evaluated in terms of local applicability, not universal validity. "Its purpose is to improve school practices and to improve those who try to improve the practices, to combine the research processes, habits of thinking, ability to work harmoniously with others, and professional spirit".

In the field of action research a teacher conducts action research to improve his own teaching. A school administrator conducts action research to improve his administrative behaviour. In action research, the teacher is deliberately more scientific and careful in diagnosing the problem, in collecting facts, in designing hypotheses in experiments with tentative practices and actions, and in evaluating results of the actions taken. He tries to keep experimental approach towards problem solving in close touch with reality. The action-research may be individual or co-operative. But it is found that ultimately utilitarian considerations infiltrate into the high level investigations and pollute the spirit of pure research.

2. Action research is a process by which change and understanding can be pursued at the same time. The action learning process involves a sequence of steps: plan, act, observe and reflect. This sequence should be repeated as many times as necessary to deal with a particular problem.

Action research, therefore, is practical and it involves the actual workings of people in their workplace, learning from their results so that future problem solving is made more effective.

3. The various steps of research are:

- formulation of the problem
- literature study
- aims, objectives and formulation of the hypothesis
- research design (methods)
- research techniques
- sampling
- collection of data
- data analysis
- the writing and critical evaluation of reports.

5. **Ethical Issues in Data Analysis and Interpretation**

Data analysis is making sense of the data and interpreting them appropriately so as to not mislead readers. The ethical issue is not about a researcher's honest error or honest differences of data interpretation; rather, it is in regard to the intent to deceive others or misrepresent one's work. Examples of such misconduct include using inappropriate statistical techniques or other methods of measurement to enhance the significance of your research or interpreting your results in a way that supports your opinions and biases. These are ethical issues of fabrication and falsification of data.

Fabrication is making up data or results, and *falsification* is changing data or results to deliberately distort them and then including them in your research report.

13. Understanding the process: Important element for effective communication is the need to understand how the process of communication works, *i.e.*, the principles and tools of communication. To appreciate the various steps involved in communication in terms of encoding, decoding, transmission, comprehension, feedback, etc., it is necessary to have a good understanding of the mode, channels, types, instruments, mothods and barriers relating to communication and the factors affecting it. Good communicators like good artists, use their tools effectively.

14. Most people believe that nonverbal communication is more reliable than verbal communication in expressing true feelings. This is especially the case when verbal and nonverbal messages are inconsistent. If you say you feel fine, but you are slumping and the corners of your mouth are turned down, others probably will not believe your verbal message.

The fact that people tend to believe nonverbal behaviours doesn't mean that nonverbal behaviours actually are honest or that we can interpret them reliably. It's possible for people to manipulate nonverbal communication, just as we manipulate our verbal communication. Politicians are coached not only in how to speak but also in how to use nonverbal communication to bolster images.

16. Communication is receptive or expressive. Receptive communication is the ability to understand or comprehend communication. Expressive communication means being able to put thoughts into words and sentences. Generally, receptive communication is in advance of expressive communication. Both receptive and expressive communication are supported by a Total Communication Environment.

18. Classroom communication; the process by which someone who has a purpose to accomplish, say a teacher, tries to convey something to get someone else, say a student, to act for the achievement of the purpose. Communication involves both exchanging information and transmitting meaning.

19.

1	4	27	16	?	36	343
↓	↓	↓	↓	↓	↓	↓
1^3	2^2	3^3	4^2	5^3	6^2	7^3

Hence, 125 will come at the place of question mark.

20. YEB WFD UHG SKI QOL

(+3, +2, +1, +2, +3; −2, −2, −2, −2)

Hence, QOL will come at the place of question mark.

21.

A	M	N	S	I	P	E	O	C
↓	↓	↓	↓	↓	↓	↓	↓	↓
C	I	P	O	A	N	M	E	S
C	O	M	P	A	N	I	E	S
↓	↓	↓	↓	↓	↓	↓	↓	↓
S	E	I	N	C	P	A	M	O

Hence, code of COMPANIES will be SEINCPAMO.

22. Continuous data: The data which can take any value between two whole numbers are called continuous data. For example,

Weight of students of a class: 42 kg, 45.030 kg, 47.250 kg, 55 kg

Height of students : 145 cm, 151.50 cm, 147.25 cm, 155.49 cm

Measurement of rainfall on differenct days: 30 mm, 32 mm, 35.23 mm, 34.50 mm

Temperature on different days : 25°C, 23.5°C, 32.4°C, 28.7°C.

23. 1 glass + 1 pencil box + 1 cup = 21 ...(*i*)

1 glass + 2 pencil box + 1 cup = 28 ...(*ii*)

2 glass + 2 pencil box + 1 cup = 35 ...(*iii*)

Eqns. (*ii*) – (*i*) gives

Cost of 1 pencil box = 28 – 21 = ₹ 7

Eqns. (*iii*) – (*ii*) gives

Cost of 1 glass = 35 – 28 = ₹ 7

Cost of 1 glass + 1 pencil box + 1 cup = ₹ 21

7 + 7 + 1 cup = 21

Cost of 1 cup = 21 – 14 = ₹ 7

∴ Cost of 10 cups = ₹ 7 × 10

= ₹ 70.

24. Except Lucknow, other three are situated on the bank of river Ganga.

25. Aristotle identified two fundamental forms of reasoning: inductive and deductive. With either form, there are premises that lead to a conclusion. If the conclusion follows necessarily from the premises and contains no new information, the reasoning is deductive. For example, start with the premise that all lawsuits for personal injury are barred unless filed within three years of the injury. If, as a second premise, it is established that John Jones's lawsuit was filed four years after his injury, it follows necessarily that John Jones's lawsuit is time barred. This argument is based on deductive reasoning. If the premises are true, the conclusion is always true. Thus, in a deductive argument the focus is always on the premises. Once the premises are established as true, the argument is won.

In inductive arguments, focus on the inference. When a conclusion relies upon an inference and contains new information not found in the premises, the reasoning is inductive. For example, if premises were established that the defendant slurred his words, stumbled as he walked, and smelled of alcohol, you might reasonably infer the conclusion that the defendant was drunk. This is inductive reasoning. In an inductive argument the conclusion is, at best, probable. The conclusion is not always true when the premises are true. The probability of the conclusion depends on the strength of the inference from the premises, Thus, when dealing with inductive reasoning, pay special attention to the inductive leap or inference by which the conclusion follows from the premises.

27. **Analogical reasoning** is simply reasoning from an analogy. In other words, it is making an argument by comparing two cases. When using analogical reasoning, it is important that the cases are comparable. Remember, although two cases or situations may be very similar, they are never identical. To remedy this situation, once again we suggest using inoculation. You should point out the differences and minimize them. Recently, a small business owner argued in front of the city council that the town should not support a smoking ban in restaurants. He believed that decisions about smoking should be left to the individual business owner. He based his argument on an analogy comparing the limitation of civil liberties when the Nazis first came to power in Germany with the restriction of civil liberties that this ban represented. He stressed that a ban on smoking was among the Nazis' new laws. He also pointed out that he wasn't trying to compare those that supported the ban to Nazis but that the restrictions were similar, His argument was partially persuasive as he was a nonsmoker who had made the choice as a business owner not to allow smoking in his establishment.

31. $$\text{Required \%} = \frac{78}{173} \times 100 = \frac{7800}{173} = 45\% \text{ (Approx.)}$$

32. 2014 45 - 46 - 78

2015 44 - 51 - 78

33. Revenue in 2015 = 44 + 51 + 78

= 173 lakh

Revenue in 2014 = 45 + 46 + 78

= 169 lakh

Difference = 173 – 169 = 4 lakh

∴ Revenue in 2016 = 173 + 4 = 177 lakh.

37. Hexadecimal number 11 to decimal

$(11)_{16} = 1 \times 16^1 + 1 \times 16^0$.

Obviously this will be much bigger than decimal number 11. So first statement (S1) is wrong. In second statement, we've to find the decimal value of $(0.101)_2$

So,

$$1 \times 2^{-1} + 0 \times 2^{-2} + 1 \times 2^{-3}$$
$$= 0.5 + 0 + 0.125$$
$$= 0.625$$

Hence, second statement (S2) is right.

39.

Cache memory	It's extremely fast compared to main memory (RAM).
CPU registers	They're part of the Control unit and ALU rather than the memory. Hence their contents can be handled much faster than any content of memory.
Secondary storage	Operating speed is slower than of main memory (RAM).

So, accordingly speed wise: CPU registers > Cache > RAM > secondary memory.

41. **Mail Merge:** The process of merging information into a main document from a data source, such as an address book or database, to create customized documents, such as form letters or mailing labels.

42. **Digital Versatile Disc (DVD):** Also referred to as digital video *disc*. For some people, the *acronym* itself has become its name. Although it has the same dimensions of a *compact disc,* it has higher capacities. A DVD is double-sided; a CD is single-sided.

45. **Vector-borne diseases:** Flies are common culprits that breed diseases. Flies may sit on dirt and garbage when pathogens stick to their bodies. If food is left uncovered, the flies carrying germs sit on it and contaminate it. Drinking water may get contaminated by sewage. Consuming such contaminated food and water causes diseases. Insects like flies and mosquitoes are vectors or carriers of various diseases like malaria and dengue. Malaria is actually caused by a pathogen called *Plasmodium* which is transmitted by the female *Anopheles* mosquito. Dengue is caused by the dengue virus and spread by female *Aedes* mosquito.

48. **Hydro-meteorological hazards:** These hazards are of atmospheric, hydrological or oceanographic nature. Hydro-meteorological hazards include: floods, debris and mud floods; tropical cyclones, storm surges, thunder/hailstorms, rain and wind storms, blizzards and other severe storms, drought, desertification, wild land fires, temperature extremes, sand or dust storms; permafrost and snow or ice avalanches. Hydro-meteorological hazards can be single, sequential or combined in their origin and effects.

50. Deemed University is a status granted to high performing institutes and departments of various universities by the Ministry of Human Resource Development on the advice of the University Grants Commission (UGC).

The Deemed University status allows not just full autonomy in setting course work and syllabus, but also allows it to set its own guidelines for the admissions and fees.

Parent universities may award degrees but cannot control the administration of these Deemed Universities, many of whom also award degrees under their own name.

Most Deemed Universities are affiliated to the UGC or the All India Council of Technical Education and are known and recognized for their quality education.

51. Mere academic knowledge without deep rooting in human values will only give rise to personalities who may become rich in material possessions, but will remain poor in self-understanding, peace and social concern. Emphasizing value education Swami Vivekananda said,

"Excess of knowledge and power, without Values, make human beings devils."

Value education is important to help everyone in improving the value system that he/she holds and put hem to use. Once, everyone has understood their values in life they can examine and control the various choice they make in their life. Thus, value education is always essential to shape one's life and to give him an opportunity of performing himself on the global stage. Value education teaches us that how we do things is more important to our well-being than what we do.

54. The executive holds office during the pleasure of the President. This is true of the civil servants and the Armed Forces. Even for Governors. But the judges are not subject to the doctrine of pleasure. They hold office during good behaviour. The doctrine of pleasure is destructive of independence.

56. With the changing world and globalization, the learning needs of the society around us are also changing. The society is no longer the traditional learning society but has emerged as a "lifelong learning society". The world today realizes the fact that learning occurs at all stages of life, in different forms and in variety of arenas. Learning never ceases and continues till death, hence the concept of 'cradle-to-grave' for lifelong learning gains prominence in the present day world and work environment. Thus we can say that the present society around us is a knowledge society; it is a human society in which thrust is on knowledge for justice, solidarity, democracy and peace. This is a society in which knowledge is a force for changing society.

Lifelong education covers "formal, non-formal and informal patterns of learning throughout the life cycle of an individual for the conscious and continuous enhancement of the quality of life, his own and that of society". Lifelong learning is the provision or use of both formal and informal learning opportunities throughout people's lives in order to foster the continuous development and improvement of the knowledge and skills needed for employment and personal fulfillment.

57. Teaching effectiveness is a complex and multifactorial concept that involves the teaching – learning dynamics between faculty and students and assessment of students' learning outcomes. To achieve excellence in teaching, faculty analyze feedback from a variety of resources to improve effectiveness, adjust teaching methods according to diverse needs of learners, evaluate teaching effectiveness using valid and reliable instruments, and mentor novice educators to the academic role.

58. In project work-student has an important role to play starting from planning stage to reporting stage. It provides him experiential learning.

Previous Years' Paper (Solved)

UGC-NET (JRF) EXAM JULY, 2016*

PAPER–I

Note :
- This paper contains **Sixty (60)** multiple choice questions, each question carrying **two (2)** marks.
- Candidate is expected to answer any **Fifty (50)** questions.
- In case more than **Fifty (50)** questions are attempted, only the first **Fifty (50)** questions will be evaluated.

1. Select the alternative which consists of positive factors contributing to effectiveness of teaching :

List of factors :

(*a*) Teacher's knowledge of the subject.

(*b*) Teacher's socio-economic background.

(*c*) Communication skill of the teacher.

(*d*) Teacher's ability to please the students.

(*e*) Teacher's personal contact with students.

(*f*) Teacher's competence in managing and monitoring the classroom transactions.

Codes :

A. (*b*), (*c*) and (*d*) B. (*c*), (*d*) and (*f*)

C. (*b*), (*d*) and (*e*) D. (*a*), (*c*) and (*f*)

2. The use of teaching aids is justified on the grounds of :

A. attracting students' attention in the classroom.

B. minimising indiscipline problems in the classroom.

C. optimising learning outcomes of students.

D. effective engagement of students in learning tasks.

3. Assertion (A) : The purpose of higher education is to promote critical and creative thinking abilities among students.

Reason (R) : These abilities ensure job placements.

Choose the correct answer from the following code :

A. Both (A) and (R) are true and (R) is the correct explanation of (A).

B. Both (A) and (R) are true, but (R) is not the correct explanation of (A).

C. (A) is true, but (R) is false.

D. (A) is false, but (R) is true.

4. Match the items of the first set with that of the second set in respect of evaluation system. Choose the correct code :

Set–I	Set–II
(*a*) Formative evaluation	1. Evaluating cognitive and co-cognitive aspects with regularity
(*b*) Summative evaluation	2. Tests and their interpretations based on a group and certain yardsticks
(*c*) Continuous and comprehensive evaluation	3. Grading the final learning outcomes
(*d*) Norm and criterion referenced tests	4. Quizzes and discussions

Codes :

	(*a*)	(*b*)	(*c*)	(*d*)
A.	4	3	1	2
B.	1	2	3	4
C.	3	4	2	1
D.	1	3	4	2

* *Exam held on 10 July, 2016.*

5. A researcher intends to explore the effect of possible factors for the organization of effective mid-day meal interventions. Which research method will be most appropriate for this study?
A. Historical method
B. Descriptive survey method
C. Experimental method
D. Ex-post-facto method

6. Which of the following is an initial mandatory requirement for pursuing research?
A. Developing a research design
B. Formulating a research question
C. Deciding about the data analysis procedure
D. Formulating a research hypothesis

7. The format of thesis writing is the same as in :
A. preparation of a research paper/article
B. writing of seminar presentation
C. a research dissertation
D. presenting a workshop / conference paper

8. In qualitative research paradigm, which of the following features may be considered critical?
A. Data collection with standardised research tools.
B. Sampling design with probability sample techniques.
C. Data collection with bottom-up empirical evidences.
D. Data gathering to take place with top-down systematic evidences.

9. From the following list of statements identify the set which has negative implications for 'research ethics' :
(*i*) A researcher critically looks at the findings of another research.
(*ii*) Related studies are cited without proper references.
(*iii*) Research findings are made the basis for policy making.
(*iv*) Conduct of practitioner is screened in terms of reported research evidences.
(*v*) A research study is replicated with a view to verify the evidences from other researches.
(*vi*) Both policy making and policy implementing processes are regulated in terms of preliminary studies.

Codes :
A. (*i*), (*ii*) and (*iii*)
B. (*ii*), (*iii*) and (*iv*)
C. (*ii*), (*iv*) and (*vi*)
D. (*i*), (*iii*) and (*v*)

10. In a research on the effect of child-rearing practices on stress-proneness of children in completing school projects, the hypothesis formulated is that 'child rearing practices do influence stress-proneness'. At the data-analysis stage a null hypothesis is advanced to find out the tenability of research hypothesis. On the basis of the evidence available, the null hypothesis is rejected at 0.01 level of significance. What decision may be warranted in respect of the research hypothesis?
A. The research hypothesis will also be rejected.
B. The research hypothesis will be accepted.
C. Both the research hypothesis and the null hypothesis will be rejected.
D. No decision can be taken in respect of the research hypothesis.

Directions (Qs. Nos. 11-16) : *Read the following passage carefully and answer the questions.*

In terms of labour, for decades the relatively low cost and high quality of Japanese workers conferred considerable competitive advantage across numerous durable goods and consumer-electronics industries (*e.g.*, Machinery, automobiles, televisions, radios). Then labour-based advantages shifted to South Korea, then to Malaysia, Mexico and other nations. Today, China appears to be capitalizing best on the basis of labour. Japanese firms still remain competitive in markets for such durable goods, electronics and other products, but the labour force is no longer sufficient for competitive advantage over manufacturers in other industrializing nations. Such shifting of labour-based advantage is clearly not limited to manufacturing industries. Today, a huge number of IT and service jobs are moving from Europe and North America to India, Singapore, and like countries with relatively well-educated, low-cost workforces possessing technical skills. However, as educational levels and technical skills continue to rise in other countries, India, Singapore, and like nations enjoying labour-based competitive advantage today are likely to find such advantage cannot be sustained through emergence of new competitors.

In terms of capital, for centuries the days of gold coins and later even paper money restricted financial flows. Subsequently regional concentrations were formed where large banks, industries and markets coalesced. But today capital flows internationally at rapid speed. Global commerce no longer requires regional interactions among business players. Regional capital concentrations in places such as New York, London and Tokyo still persist, of course, but the capital concentrated there is no longer sufficient for competitive advantage over other capitalists distributed worldwide. Only if an organization is able to combine, integrate and apply its resources (*e.g.* Land, labour, capital, IT) in an effective manner that is not readily imitable by competitors can such an organization enjoy competitive advantage sustainable overtime.

In a knowledge-based theory of the firm, this idea is extended to view organizational knowledge as a resource with atleast the same level of power and importance as the traditional economic inputs. An organization with superior knowledge can achieve competitive advantage in markets that appreciate the application of such knowledge. Semiconductors, genetic engineering, pharmaceuticals, software, military warfare, and like knowledge-intensive competitive arenas provide both time-proven and current examples. Consider semiconductors (*e.g.* computer chips), which are made principally of sand and common metals. These ubiquitous and powerful electronic devices are designed within common office buildings, using commercially available tools, and fabricated within factories in many industrialized nations. Hence, land is not the key competitive resource in the semiconductor industry.

Based on the passage answer the following questions :

11. Which country enjoyed competitive advantages in automobile industry for decades?

A. South Korea B. Japan

C. Mexico D. Malaysia

12. Why labour based competitive advantages of India and Singapore cannot be sustained in IT and service sectors?

A. Due to diminishing levels of skill.

B. Due to capital-intensive technology making inroads.

C. Because of new competitors.

D. Because of shifting of labour-based advantage in manufacturing industries.

13. How can an organisation enjoy competitive advantage sustainable overtime?

A. Through regional capital flows.

B. Through regional interactions among business players.

C. By making large banks, industries and markets coalesced.

D. By effective use of various instrumentalities.

14. What is required to ensure competitive advantages in specific markets?

A. Access to capital

B. Common office buildings

C. Superior knowledge

D. Common metals

15. The passage also mentions about the trend of :

A. Global financial flow

B. Absence of competition in manufacturing industry

C. Regionalisation of capitalists

D. Organizational incompatibility

16. What does the author lay stress on in the passage?

A. International commerce

B. Labour-intensive industries

C. Capital resource management

D. Knowledge-driven competitive advantage

17. Imagine you are working in an educational institution where people are of equal status. Which method of communication is best suited and normally employed in such a context?

A. Horizontal communication
B. Vertical communication
C. Corporate communication
D. Cross communication

18. Identify the important element a teacher has to take cognizance of while addressing students in a classroom.

A. Avoidance of proximity
B. Voice modulation
C. Repetitive pause
D. Fixed posture

19. What are the barriers to effective communication?

A. Moralising, being judgemental and comments of consolation.
B. Dialogue, summary and self-review.
C. Use of simple words, cool reaction and defensive attitude.
D. Personal statements, eye contact and simple narration.

20. The choice of communication partners is influenced by factors of :

A. Proximity, utility, loneliness
B. Utility, secrecy, dissonance
C. Secrecy, dissonance, deception
D. Dissimilarity, dissonance, deviance

21. As a teacher, select the best option to ensure your effective presence in the classroom.

A. Use of peer command
B. Making aggressive statements
C. Adoption of well-established posture
D. Being authoritarian

22. Every communicator has to experience :

A. Manipulated emotions
B. Anticipatory excitement
C. The issue of homophiles
D. Status dislocation

23. In certain code, SELECTION is coded as QCJCARGML. The code of AMERICANS will be :

A. YKCPGAYLQ　　B. BNFSJDBMR
C. QLYAGPCKY　　D. YQKLCYPAG

24. In the series
3, 11, 23, 39, 59, ...
The next term will be :

A. 63　　B. 73
C. 83　　D. 93

25. Two railway tickets from city A to B and three tickets from city A to C cost ₹ 177. Three tickets from city A to B and two tickets from city A to C cost ₹ 173. The fare for city B from city A will be ₹ :

A. 25　　B. 27
C. 30　　D. 33

26. A person walks 10 m infront and 10 m to the right. Then every time turning to his left, he walks 5, 15 and 15 m respectively. How far is he now from his starting point?

A. 20 m　　B. 15 m
C. 10 m　　D. 5 m

27. A is sister of B. F is daughter of G. C is mother of B. D is father of C. E is mother of D. A is related to D as :

A. Grand daughter　　B. Daughter
C. Daughter-in-law　　D. Sister

28. In the series
AB, EDC, FGHI, ...?...., OPQRST, the missing term is :

A. JKLMN　　B. JMKNL
C. NMLKJ　　D. NMKLJ

29. Among the following propositions two are related in such a way that one is the denial of the other. Which are those propositions? Select the correct code :

Propositions :

(*a*) All women are equal to men
(*b*) Some women are equal to men
(*c*) Some women are not equal to men
(*d*) No women are equal to men

Codes :

A. (*a*) and (*b*)
B. (*a*) and (*d*)
C. (*c*) and (*d*)
D. (*a*) and (*c*)

30. If the proposition 'All thieves are poor' is false, which of the following propositions can be claimed certainly to be true?

Propositions :

A. Some thieves are poor.

B. Some thieves are not poor.

C. No thief is poor.

D. No poor person is a thief.

31. Consider the following statement and select the correct code stating the nature of the argument involved in it :

To suppose that the earth is the only populated world in the infinite space is as absurd as to assert that in an entire field of millet only one grain will grow.

A. Astronomical B. Anthropological

C. Deductive D. Analogical

32. Select the code which is not correct about Venn diagram :

A. Venn diagram represents propositions as well as classes.

B. It can provide clear method of notation.

C. It can be either valid or invalid.

D. It can provide the direct method of testing the validity.

33. Select the code which is not correct in the context of deductive argument with two premises :

A. An argument with one true premise, one false premise and a false conclusion may be valid.

B. An argument with two true premises and a false conclusion may be valid.

C. An argument with one true premise, one false premise and a true conclusion may be valid.

D. An argument with two false premises and a false conclusion may be valid.

34. Given below are two premises and four conclusions are drawn from them (taking singly or together). Select the code that states the conclusions validly drawn.

Premises :

(*i*) All religious persons are emotional.

(*ii*) Ram is a religious person.

Conclusions :

(*a*) Ram is emotional.

(*b*) All emotional persons are religious.

(*c*) Ram is not a non-religious person.

(*d*) Some religious persons are not emotional.

Codes :

A. (*a*), (*b*), (*c*) and (*d*)

B. (*a*) only

C. (*a*) and (*c*) only

D. (*b*) and (*c*) only

Directions (Qs. Nos. 35-37) : *The following table shows the percentage profit (%) earned by two companies A and B during the years 2011-15. Answer these questions based on the data contained in the table :*

Profit earned by two companies

Year	Percentage Profit (%)	
	A	B
2011	20	30
2012	35	40
2013	45	35
2014	40	50
2015	25	35

Where, per cent (%) Profit

$$= \frac{\text{Income} - \text{Expenditure}}{\text{Expenditure}} \times 100$$

35. If the total expenditure of the two companies was ₹ 9 lakh in the year 2012 and the expenditure of A and B were in the ratio 2 : 1, then what was the income of the company A in that year?

A. ₹ 9.2 lakh B. ₹ 8.1 lakh

C. ₹ 7.2 lakh D. ₹ 6.0 lakh

36. What is the average percentage profit earned by the company B?

A. 35% B. 42%

C. 38% D. 40%

37. In which year, the percentage profit earned by the company B is less than that of company A?

A. 2012 B. 2013

C. 2014 D. 2015

Directions (Qs. Nos. 38-40) : *The following table shows the number of people in different age groups who responded to a survey about their favourite style of music. Use this information to answer the questions that follow, to the nearest whole percentage :*

Style of Music ↓ / Age →	Number of people (Years) 15-20	(Years) 21-30	(Years) 31+
Classical	6	4	17
Pop	7	5	5
Rock	6	12	14
Jazz	1	4	11
Blues	2	3	15
Hip-Hop	9	3	4
Ambient	2	2	2

38. Approximately what percentage of the total sample were aged 21-30?
A. 31% B. 23%
C. 25% D. 14%

39. Approximately what percentage of the total sample indicates that Hip-Hop is their favourite style of music?
A. 6% B. 8%
C. 14% D. 12%

40. What percentage of respondents aged 31+ indicated a favourite style other than classical music?
A. 64% B. 60%
C. 75% D. 50%

41. The statement "the study, design, development, implementation, support or management of computer-based information systems, particularly software applications and computer Hardware" refers to :
A. Information Technology (IT)
B. Information and Collaborative Technology (ICT)
C. Information and Data Technology (IDT)
D. Artificial Intelligence (AI)

42. If the binary equivalent of the decimal number 48 is 110000, then the binary equivalent of the decimal number 51 is given by :
A. 110011 B. 110010
C. 110001 D. 110100

43. The process of copying files to a CD-ROM is known as :
A. Burning B. Zipping
C. Digitizing D. Ripping

44. An unsolicited e-mail message sent to many recipients at once is a :
A. Worm B. Virus
C. Threat D. Spam

45. _________ is a type of memory circuitry that holds the computer's start-up routine.
A. RIM (Read Initial Memory)
B. RAM (Random Access Memory)
C. ROM (Read Only Memory)
D. Cache Memory

46. An ASCII is a character-encoding scheme that is employed by personal computers in order to represent various characters, numbers and control keys that the computer user selects on the keyboard. ASCII is an acronym for :
A. American Standard Code for Information Interchange
B. American Standard Code for Intelligent Information
C. American Standard Code for Information Integrity
D. American Standard Code for Isolated Information

47. Identify the air pollutant in urban areas which irritates eyes and also respiratory tract of human beings.
A. Particulate matter B. Oxides of nitrogen
C. Surface ozone D. Carbon monoxide

48. Which of the following is the largest source of water pollution in major rivers of India?
A. Untreated sewage
B. Agriculture run-off
C. Unregulated small scale industries
D. Religious practices

49. Sustainable development goals have specific targets to be achieved by :

A. 2022 B. 2030
C. 2040 D. 2050

50. Indian government's target of producing power from biomass by the year 2022, is :

A. 50 MW B. 25 MW
C. 15 MW D. 10 MW

51. **Assertion (A) :** Conserving our soil resources is critical to human survival.

Reason (R) : Soil is home to many micro-organisms and contains minerals.

Choose the correct code :

A. Both (A) and (R) are correct and (R) is the correct explanation of (A).
B. Both (A) and (R) are correct, but (R) is not the correct explanation of (A).
C. (A) is true and (R) is false.
D. (A) is false and (R) is true.

52. World Meteorological Organisation's (WMO) objective has been to reduce the number of deaths due to hydrometeorological disasters over the decade 2010-2019 by (with reference to the decade 1994-2003) :

A. 25% B. 50%
C. 75% D. 80%

53. Which of the following core values among the institutions of higher education are promoted by the NAAC (National Assessment and Accreditation Council)?

(*a*) Contributing to national development.
(*b*) Fostering global competencies among the students.
(*c*) Inculcating a value system among students and teachers.
(*d*) Promoting the optimum utilization of the infrastructure.

Select the correct answer from the codes given below :

Codes :

A. (*b*), (*c*) and (*d*)
B. (*a*), (*b*) and (*c*)
C. (*a*), (*c*) and (*d*)
D. (*a*), (*b*), (*c*) and (*d*)

54. The best way for providing value education is through :

A. discussions on scriptural texts
B. lectures / discourses on values
C. seminars / symposia on values
D. mentoring / reflective sessions on values

55. The National Judicial Appointments Commission (NJAC) has been declared unconstitutional by :

A. The Supreme Court of India
B. The High Court
C. The High Court and the Supreme Court both
D. The President of India

56. Which of the following statements about the Indian political system is/are correct?

(*a*) The President is both Head of the State and Head of the Government.
(*b*) Parliament is Supreme.
(*c*) The Supreme Court is the guardian of the Constitution.
(*d*) The Directive Principles of State Policy are justiciable.

Select the correct answer from the codes given below :

A. (*a*), (*b*), (*c*) and (*d*) B. (*b*), (*c*) and (*d*)
C. (*b*) and (*c*) D. (*c*) only

57. Which of the following are the fundamental duties?

(*a*) To respect the National Flag.
(*b*) To protect and improve the natural environment.
(*c*) For a parent to provide opportunities for education to his/her child.
(*d*) To protect monuments and places of national importance.

Select the correct answer from the codes given:

Codes :

A. (*a*), (*b*) and (*c*) B. (*a*), (*b*) and (*d*)
C. (*a*), (*c*) and (*d*) D. (*a*), (*b*), (*c*) and (*d*)

58. Which of the following statements are correct in respect of NITI Aayog?

(*a*) It is a constitutional body.
(*b*) It is a statutory body.

(*c*) It is neither a constitutional body nor a statutory body.

(*d*) It is a think-tank.

Select the correct answer from the codes given below :

A. (*a*) and (*d*) B. (*b*) and (*d*)

C. (*c*) and (*d*) D. (*b*), (*c*) and (*d*)

59. A college level assistant professor has planned his/her lectures with an intent to develop cognitive dimensions of students centered on skills of analysis and synthesis. Below, given are two sets of items Set–I consisting of levels of cognitive interchange and Set–II comprising basic requirements for promoting them. Match the two sets and indicate your answer by choosing the correct alternative from the code:

Set–I (Levels of Cognitive Interchange)	***Set–II (Basic requirements for promoting cognitive interchange)***
(*a*) Memory level	1. Giving opportunity for discriminating examples and non-examples of a point.
(*b*) Understanding level	2. Recording the important points made during the presentations.
(*c*) Reflective level	3. Asking the students to discuss various items of information.
	4. Critically analyzing the points to be made and discussed.

Codes :

	(*a*)	(*b*)	(*c*)
A.	2	4	1
B.	3	4	2
C.	2	1	4
D.	1	2	3

60. Which set of learner characteristics may be considered helpful in designing effective teaching-learning systems? Select the correct alternative from the codes given below :

(*i*) Prior experience of learners in respect of the subject.

(*ii*) Interpersonal relationships of learner's family friends.

(*iii*) Ability of the learners in respect of the subject.

(*iv*) Student's language background.

(*v*) Interest of students in following the prescribed dress code.

(*vi*) Motivational-orientation of the students.

Codes :

A. (*i*), (*ii*), (*iii*) and (*iv*)

B. (*i*), (*iii*), (*iv*) and (*vi*)

C. (*ii*), (*iii*), (*iv*) and (*v*)

D. (*iii*), (*iv*), (*v*) and (*vi*)

ANSWERS

1	**2**	**3**	**4**	**5**	**6**	**7**	**8**	**9**	**10**
D	C	B	A	D	B	C	C	C	B
11	**12**	**13**	**14**	**15**	**16**	**17**	**18**	**19**	**20**
B	C	D	C	A	D	A	B	A	A
21	**22**	**23**	**24**	**25**	**26**	**27**	**28**	**29**	**30**
C	B	A	C	D	D	A	C	D	B
31	**32**	**33**	**34**	**35**	**36**	**37**	**38**	**39**	**40**
D	C	B	C	B	C	B	C	D	C
41	**42**	**43**	**44**	**45**	**46**	**47**	**48**	**49**	**50**
A	A	A	D	C	A	C	A	B	D
51	**52**	**53**	**54**	**55**	**56**	**57**	**58**	**59**	**60**
B	B	B	D	A	D	A	C	C	B

EXPLANATORY ANSWERS

7. Documentation is important in writing a research paper, thesis and dissertation to determine if a researcher has read and used several research works and other materials as reference. A research paper, thesis and dissertation is worthless without documentation to serve as proof of the research.

Generally speaking, a research paper, thesis or dissertation is *scientific* if it has several documented materials. But it is *unscientific* if the writer does not explain the relationships of the documented materials to his study and most of the writings of his research paper, thesis or dissertation are documented materials where he has no ideas of his own.

17. Horizontal communication is the transmission of information between people, divisions, departments or units within the same level of organizational hierarchy. You can distinguish it from vertical communication, which is the transmission of information between different levels of the organizational hierarchy. Horizontal communication is often referred to as 'lateral communication'.

Horizontal communication presents some distinct advantages. It decreases misunderstanding between departments working on the same project, thereby increasing efficiency and productivity. It may result in better implementation of top-level decisions because employees on lower levels are permitted to coordinate directly with each other in the implementation of the decision made at the top.

23. SELECTION is coded as

S E L E C T I O N
-2| -2| -2| -2| -2| -2| -2| -2| -2|
Q C J C A R G M L

∴ AMERICANS will be coded as

A M E R I C A N S .
-2| -2| -2| -2| -2| -2| -2| -2| -2|
Y K C P G A Y L Q

24. In the series

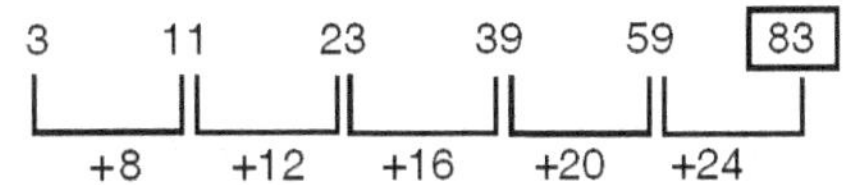

Hence, the next term will be 83.

25. Let fare of A to B = ₹ x

and fare of A to C = ₹ y

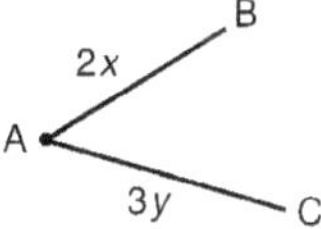

According to the question,

$2x + 3y =$ ₹ 177 ... (i)] × 3

$3x + 2y =$ ₹ 173 ... (ii)] × 2

$6x + 9y = 531$

$6x + 4y = 346$

$- \quad - \qquad -$

$5y = 185 \Rightarrow y = 37$

Putting the value of y in (i)

$2x + 3 \times 37 = 177$

$\Rightarrow \quad 2x = 177 - 111$

$\Rightarrow \quad 2x = 66$

$\Rightarrow \quad x = 33$

∴ Fare of A to B = ₹ 33

Hence, the fare for city B from A will be ₹ 33.

27.

(–) E
|
D (+)
|
(–) C और G (?)
| |
(–) A — B (?) P (–)

Relation between A to D is Grand daughter.

28. AB, EDC, FGHI, NMLKJ, OPQRST

Hence, the missing term is **NMLKJ**.

32. The Venn diagrams constitute an *iconic* representation of the standard form categorical propositions, in which spatial inclusions and exclusions correspond to the nonspatial inclusions and exclusions of classes. They provide an exceptionally clear method of notation. They also provide the basis for the simplest and most direct method of testing the validity of categorical syllogisms.

34.

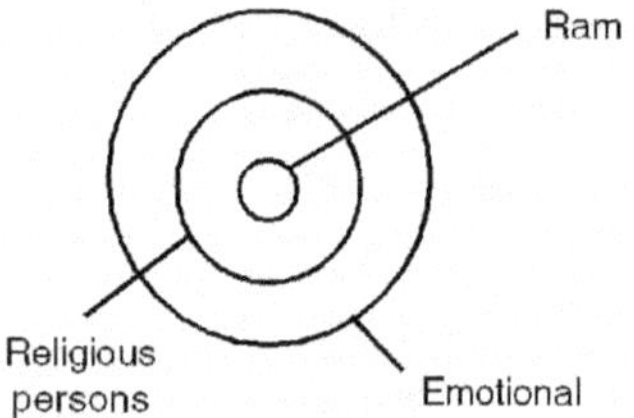

Hence, Ram is emotional and also Ram is not a non-religious person.

35. In 2012, Total expenditure = ₹ 9 lakh

$\therefore$ Expenditure of A = $\frac{2}{3} \times 9 = 6$ lakh

Expenditure of B = $\frac{1}{3} \times 9 = 3$ lakh

Let income of Company A = ₹ x

$$35\% = \left(\frac{x - 6 \text{ lakh}}{6}\right) \times 100$$

$$\frac{35}{100} = \frac{(x-6)}{6}$$

$$\Rightarrow \quad \frac{35 \times 6}{100} = (x - 6)$$

$$\Rightarrow \quad \frac{21}{10} = (x - 6)$$

$$\Rightarrow \quad 10x - 60 = 21$$

$$\Rightarrow \quad 10x = 81$$

$$\Rightarrow \quad x = \frac{81}{10} \text{ lakh} = 8.1 \text{ lakh}$$

$\therefore$ Income of company A = 8.1 lakh.

36. Total % profit of Company B

= (30 + 40 + 35 + 50 + 35) = 190

Required average = $\frac{190}{5} = 38\%$.

37. Required year is 2013, the percentage profit earned by the company B is less than that of company A.

38. Total no. of people = 134

No. of people (21 – 30) years = 33

$$\text{Required } \% = \frac{33}{134} \times 100$$

$$= 25\% \text{ (Approx.).}$$

39. $$\text{Required } \% = \frac{16}{134} \times 100$$

$$= \frac{800}{67} = 12\% \text{ (Approx.).}$$

40. $$\text{Required } \% = \frac{68}{134} \times 100$$

$$= 50\% \text{ (Approx.).}$$

41. Information Technology (IT), as defined by the Information Technology Association of America (ITAA), is "the study, design, development, implementation, support or management of computer-based information systems, particularly software applications and computer hardware". IT deals with the use of electronic computers and computer software to convert, store, protect, process, transmit, and securely retrieve information. Information Technology (IT) is a general term that describes any technology that helps to produce, manipulate, store, communicate, and/or disseminate information.

42. Decimal to Binary Conversion

2	51	1
2	25	1
2	12	0
2	6	0
2	3	1
	1	

$\therefore \quad (51)_{10} = (110011)_2$.

43. Copying files to a CD or DVD is often called "burning". To burn to one of these optical disc drives you need a disc of the appropriate type. Disc types you're likely to encounter include:

- CD-R (a recordable disc that you can only write data to once)
- CD-RW (a rewritable disc that you can erase and burn again)
- DVD-R and DVD+R
- DVD-RW and DVD+RW.

44. Spam, an unsolicited e-mail message sent to many recipients at once, is commonly known as Internet junk mail. The content of spam ranges from selling a product or service, to promoting a business opportunity, to advertising offensive material. It is strongly advised not to reply to spam messages for any reason if you want to keep your personal data private.

45. ROM (read-only memory) is a type of memory circuitry that holds the computer's startup routine. ROM is housed in a single integrated circuitusually a fairly large, caterpillar-like DIP package—which is plugged into the system board.

46. ASCII is an acronym of "American Standard Code for Information Interchange". The ASCII coding system is an agreement made by organizations working in the computing business. As its name implies, the coding system was developed in the United States where the commercial use of computers began.

47. Ozone, nitrogen oxide and organic compounds (PAN, $CH_2 = O$, $CH_2 = CHCHO$) are main constituents of photochemical smog each of which produce hazardous effects.

- Aldehydes and PAN components of smog cause irritation to eyes and affect the respiratory tract of human beings.
- Ozone causes cracks in rubber materials and is also harmful to fabric, crops and ornamental plants.
- The toxic nature of photochemical smog cause coughing, wheezing, bronchial constrictions and irritation to respiratory mucous system.
- The highly toxic PAN attacks newly grown leaves and causes bronzing and glazing of their surfaces.
- The brownish colour of photochemical smog due to NO_2 reduces visibility. NO_2 also produces throat and eye irritation and leads to several chronic disease of throat, eyes, lungs and heart.

48. Water pollution is a major environmental issue in India. The largest source of water pollution in India is untreated sewage. Other sources of pollution include agricultural runoff and unregulated small scale industry. Most rivers, lakes and surface water in India are polluted.

A 2007 study found that discharge of untreated sewage is the single most important source of pollution of surface and groundwater in India. There is a large gap between generation and treatment of domestic waste water in India. The problem is not only that India lacks sufficient treatment capacity but also that the sewage treatment plants that exist do not operate and are not maintained.

49. In September, 2015 the UN General Assembly adopted the 17 Sustainable Development Goals (the SDGs), with 169 specific targets, to guide the world's development agenda through 2030. One of the goals is to "Ensure availability and sustainable management of water and sanitation for all", and one of the six targets to be achieved under this is "By 2030, implement integrated water resources management at all levels, including through transboundary cooperation as appropriate".

55. The National Judicial Appointments Commission (NJAC) is unconstitutional, ruled the Supreme Court of India. The verdict effectively rejects a major law passed by Parliament last year, which was subsequently ratified by 20 state Assemblies, and restores the collegium system of appointing judges.

56. The Supreme Court of India is the guardian of the Constitution. There are two points of significance of the Supreme Court's rule as the protector and guardian of the Constitution.

- First, as the highest Federal Court, it is within the power and authority of the Supreme Court to settle any dispute regarding division of powers between the Union and the States.
- Secondly, it is in the Supreme Court's authority to safeguard the fundamental rights of the citizens.

In order to discharge these two functions it is sometimes necessary for the Supreme Court to examine or review the legality of the laws enacted by both the Union and the State Governments. This is known as the power of Judicial Review. Indian Supreme Court enjoys limited power of Judicial Review.

57. Fundamental Duties

The Forty-second Constitution Amendment Act has inserted Part IVA with Art. 51A having a set of Fundamental Duties. It says that it shall be the duty of every citizen of India:

(*a*) to abide by the Constitution and respect its ideals and institutions, the National Flag and the National Anthem;

(*b*) to cherish and follow the noble ideals which inspired our national struggle for freedom;

(*c*) to uphold and protect the sovereignty, unity and integrity of India;

(*d*) to defend the country and render national service when called upon to do so;

(*e*) to promote harmony and the spirit of common brotherhood amongst all the people of India transcending religious, linguistic and regional or sectional diversities; to renounce practices derogatory to the dignity of women;

(*f*) to value and preserve the rich heritage of our composite culture;

(*g*) to protect and improve the natural environment including forests, lakes, rivers and wildlife and to have compassion for living creatures;

(*h*) to develop the scientific temper, humanism and the spirit of inquiry and reform;

(*i*) to safeguard public property and to abjure violence;

(*j*) to strive for excellence in all spheres of individual and collective activity so that the nation constantly rises to higher levels of endeavour and achievement.

(*k*) to provide as a parent or a guardian opportunities for education to his/her child or ward between the age of 6 to 14 years.

58. NITI Aayog is a Think tank for Government policy formulation. NITI Aayog too is a non-Constitutional, non-statutory body formed by a cabinet resolution. It is not accountable to parliament, and if line-ministries fail to achieve targets, NITI Aayog cannot punish them.

Previous Years' Paper (Solved)

UGC-NET (JRF) Exam December, 2015

PAPER–I

Note : This paper consists **Sixty (60)** multiple-choice type of questions, out of which the candidate would be required to answer **any Fifty (50)** questions. In the event of candidate attempting more than **Fifty (50)** questions, the **first Fifty (50)** questions attempted by the Candidate would be evaluated.

1. Greater the handicap of the students coming to the educational institutions, greater the demand on the:

A. Family B. Society
C. Teacher D. State

2. What are the characteristics of Continuous and Comprehensive Evaluation?

(*a*) It increases the workload on students by taking multiple tests.
(*b*) It replaces marks with grades.
(*c*) It evaluates every aspect of the student.
(*d*) It helps in reducing examination phobia.

Select the **correct** answer from the codes given below:

A. (*a*), (*b*), (*c*) and (*d*) B. (*b*) and (*d*)
C. (*a*), (*b*) and (*c*) D. (*b*), (*c*) and (*d*)

3. Which of the following attributes denote great strengths of a teacher?

(*a*) Full-time active involvement in the institutional management
(*b*) Setting examples
(*c*) Willingness to put assumptions to the test
(*d*) Acknowledging mistakes

Select the **correct** answer from the codes given below:

A. (*a*), (*b*) and (*d*) B. (*b*), (*c*) and (*d*)
C. (*a*), (*c*) and (*d*) D. (*a*), (*b*), (*c*) and (*d*)

4. Which one of the following statements is **correct** in the context of multiple - choice type questions?

A. They are more objective than true-false type questions.
B. They are less objective than essay type questions.
C. They are more subjective than short-answer type questions.
D. They are more subjective than true-false type questions.

5. As Chairman of an independent commission on education, Jacques Delors report to UNESCO was titled:

A. International Commission on Education Report
B. Millennium Development Report
C. Learning : The Treasure Within
D. World Declaration on Education for All

6. What are required for good teaching?

(*a*) Diagnosis (*b*) Remedy
(*c*) Direction (*d*) Feedback

Select the **correct** answer from the codes given below:

A. (*a*), (*b*), (*c*) and (*d*)
B. (*a*) and (*b*)
C. (*b*), (*c*) and (*d*)
D. (*c*) and (*d*)

7. Which of the following statements is **not** true in the context of participatory research?

A. It recognizes knowledge as power.
B. It emphasises on people as experts.
C. It is a collective process of enquiry.
D. Its sole purpose is production of knowledge.

8. Which of the following statements is **true** in the context of the testing of a hypothesis?
A. It is only the alternative hypothesis, that can be tested
B. It is only the null hypothesis, that can be tested
C. Both, the alternative and the null hypotheses can be tested
D. Both, the alternative and the null hypotheses cannot be tested

9. Which of the following are the basic rules of APA style of referencing format?
(*a*) Italicize titles of shorter works such as journal articles or essays
(*b*) Invert authors' names (last name first)
(*c*) Italicize titles of longer works such as books and journals
(*d*) Alphabetically index reference list
Select the **correct** answer from the codes given below:
A. (*a*) and (*b*)
B. (*b*), (*c*) and (*d*)
C. (*c*) and (*d*)
D. (*a*), (*b*), (*c*) and (*d*)

10. Which of the following are the characteristics of a seminar?
(*a*) It is a form of academic instruction
(*b*) It involves questioning, discussion and debates
(*c*) It involves large groups of individuals
(*d*) It needs involvement of skilled persons
Select the **correct** answer from the codes given below:
A. (*b*) and (*c*)
B. (*b*) and (*d*)
C. (*b*), (*c*) and (*d*)
D. (*a*), (*b*) and (*d*)

11. A researcher is interested in studying the prospects of a particular political party in an urban area. What tool should he prefer for the study?
A. Rating scale
B. Interview
C. Questionnaire
D. Schedule

12. Ethical norms in research do **not** involve guidelines for:
A. Thesis format
B. Copyright
C. Patenting policy
D. Data sharing policies

Direction (Qs. 13 to 17): *Read the following passage carefully and answer the question.*

I did that thing recently where you have to sign a big card - which is a horror unto itself, especially as the keeper of the Big Card was leaning over me at the time. Suddenly I was on the spot, a rabbit in the headlights, torn between doing a fun message or some sort of in-joke or a drawing. Instead overwhelmed by the myriad options available to me, I decided to just write : "Good luck, best, Joel".

It was then that I realised, to my horror, that I had forgotten how to write. My entire existence is "tap letters into computer". My shopping lists are hidden in the notes function of my phone. If I need to remember something I send an e-mail to myself. A pen is something I chew when I'm struggling to think. Paper is something I pile beneath my laptop to make it a more comfortable height for me to type on.

A poll of 1,000 teens by the stationers, Bic found that one in 10 don't own a pen, a third have never written a letter, and half of 13 to 19 years - old have never been forced to sit down and write a thank you letter. More than 80% have never written a love letter, 56% don't have letter paper at home. And a quarter have never known the unique torture of writing a birthday card. The most a teen ever has to use a pen is on an exam paper.

Bic, have you heard of mobile phones? Have you heard of e-mail, facebook and snap chatting? This is the future. Pens are dead. Paper is dead. Handwriting is a relic.

"Handwriting is one of the most creative outlets we have and should be given the same importance as other art forms such as sketching, painting or photography."

Answer the following questions:

13. When confronted with signing a big card, the author felt like "a rabbit in the headlight". What does this phrase mean?
A. A state of confusion
B. A state of pleasure
C. A state of anxiety
D. A state of pain

14. According to the author, which one is **not** the most creative outlet of pursuit?
A. Handwriting B. Photography
C. Sketching D. Reading

15. The entire existence of the author revolves round:
(*a*) Computer
(*b*) Mobile phone
(*c*) Typewriter
Identify the **correct** answer from the codes given below:
A. (*b*) only B. (*a*) and (*b*) only
C. (*a*), (*b*) and (*c*) D. (*b*) and (*c*) only

16. How many teens, as per the Bic survey, do **not** own a pen?
A. 800 B. 560
C. 500 D. 100

17. What is the main concern of the author?
A. That the teens use social networks for communication
B. That the teens use mobile phones
C. That the teens use computer
D. That the teens have forgotten the art of handwriting

18. The main objectives of student evaluation of teachers are:
(*a*) To gather information about student weaknesses.
(*b*) To make teachers take teaching seriously.
(*c*) To help teachers adopt innovative methods of teaching.
(*d*) To identify the areas of further improvement in teacher traits.
Identify the **correct** answer from the codes given below:
A. (*a*) and (*b*) only B. (*b*), (*c*) and (*d*) only
C. (*a*), (*b*) and (*c*) only D. (*a*) only

19. Using the central point of the classroom communication as the beginning of a dynamic pattern of ideas is referred to as:
A. Systemisation
B. Problem - orientation
C. Idea protocol
D. Mind mapping

20. Aspects of the voice, other than the speech are known as:
A. Physical language B. Personal language
C. Para language D. Delivery language

21. Every type of communication is affected by its:
A. Reception B. Transmission
C. Non-regulation D. Context

22. Attitudes, actions and appearances in the context of classroom communication are considered as:
A. Verbal B. Non-verbal
C. Impersonal D. Irrational

23. Most often, the teacher - student communication is:
A. Spurious B. Critical
C. Utilitarian D. Confrontational

24. In a classroom, a communicator's trust level is determined by:
A. the use of hyperbole
B. the change of voice level
C. the use of abstract concepts
D. eye contact

25. The next term in the series
2, 5, 10, 17, 26, 37, ___?___ is :
A. 50 B. 57
C. 62 D. 72

26. A group of 210 students appeared in some test. The mean of $\frac{1}{3}$rd of students is found to be 60. The mean of the remaining students is found to be 78. The mean of the whole group will be :
A. 80 B. 76
C. 74 D. 72

27. Anil after travelling 6 km towards East from his house realized that he has travelled in a wrong direction. He turned and travelled 12 km towards West, turned right and travelled 8 km to reach his office. The straight distance of the office from his house is:
A. 20 km B. 14 km
C. 12 km D. 10 km

28. The next term in the series:
B2E, D5H, F12K, H27N, __?__ is:
A. J56I B. I62Q
C. Q62J D. J58Q

29. A party was held in which a grandmother, father, mother, four sons, their wives and one son and two daughters to each of the sons were present. The number of females present in the party is:
A. 12 B. 14
C. 18 D. 24

30. P and Q are brothers. R and S are sisters. The son of P is brother of S. Q is related to R as:
A. Son B. Brother
C. Uncle D. Father

31. Consider the argument given below:
'Pre - employment testing of teachers is quite fair because doctors, architects and engineers who are now employed had to face such a testing.'
What type of argument it is ?
A. Deductive B. Analogical
C. Psychological D. Biological

32. Among the following propositions two are related in such a way that they can both be true although they cannot both be false. Which are those propositions? Select the **correct** code.
Propositions:
(*a*) Some priests are cunning.
(*b*) No priest is cunning.
(*c*) All priests are cunning.
(*d*) Some priests are not cunning.
Codes:
A. (*a*) and (*b*) B. (*c*) and (*d*)
C. (*a*) and (*c*) D. (*a*) and (*d*)

33. A Cluster of propositions with a structure that exhibits some inference is called:
A. An inference B. An argument
C. An explanation D. A valid argument

34. Consider the following **assertion (A)** and **reason (R)** and select the **correct** code given below :
Assertion (A): No man is perfect.
Reason (R): Some men are not perfect.
A. Both (A) and (R) are true but (R) does not provide sufficient reason for (A)
B. Both (A) and (R) are true and (R) provides sufficient reason for (A)
C. (A) is true but (R) is false
D. (A) is false but (R) is true

35. A definition that has a meaning that is deliberately assigned to some symbol is called:
A. Lexical B. Precising
C. Stipulative D. Persuasive

36. If the proposition 'No men are honest' is taken to be false which of the following proposition/ propositions can be claimed certainly to be true?
Propositions:
A. All men are honest
B. Some men are honest
C. Some men are not honest
D. No honest person is man

Given below in the table is the decadal data of Population and Electrical Power Production of a country.

Year	*Population (million)*	*Electrical Power Production (GW)**
1951	20	10
1961	21	20
1971	24	25
1981	27	40
1991	30	50
2001	32	80
2011	35	100
	* 1 GW = 1000 million watt	

Directions (Qs. 37 to 42): *Based on the above table answer the questions.*

37. Which decade registered the maximum growth rate (%) of population?
A. 1961-71 B. 1971-81
C. 1991-2001 D. 2001-2011

38. Average decadal growth rate (%) of population is:
A. ~ 12.21% B. ~ 9.82%
C. ~ 6.73% D. ~ 5%

39. Based on the average decadal growth rate, what will be the population in the year 2021?
A. 40.34 million B. 38.49 million
C. 37.28 million D. 36.62 million

40. In the year 1951, what was the power availability per person?
A. 100 W B. 200 W
C. 400 W D. 500 W

41. In which decade, the average power availability per person was maximum?
A. 1981-1991 B. 1991-2001
C. 2001-2011 D. 1971-1981

42. By what percentage (%) the power production increased from 1951 to 2011?
A. 100% B. 300%
C. 600% D. 900%

43. NMEICT stands for:
A. National Mission on Education through ICT
B. National Mission on E-governance through ICT
C. National Mission on E-commerce through ICT
D. National Mission on E-learning through ICT

44. Which of the following is an instant messaging application?
(*a*) WhatsApp (*b*) Google Talk
(*c*) Viber
Select the **correct** answer from the codes given below:
A. (*a*) and (*b*) only B. (*b*) and (*c*) only
C. (*a*) only D. (*a*), (*b*) and (*c*)

45. In a Computer a byte generally consists of:
A. 4 bits B. 8 bits
C. 16 bits D. 10 bits

46. Which of the following is **not** an input device?
A. Microphone B. Keyboard
C. Joystick D. Monitor

47. Which of the following is an open source software?
A. MS Word B. Windows
C. Mozilla Firefox D. Acrobat Reader

48. Which of the following enables us to send the same letter to different persons in MS Word?
A. Mail join B. Mail copy
C. Mail insert D. Mail merge

49. Inside rural homes, the source/sources of Nitrogen Oxide Pollution may be:
(*a*) Unvented gas stoves
(*b*) Wood stoves
(*c*) Kerosene heaters
Choose the **correct** code:
A. (*a*) and (*b*) only
B. (*b*) and (*c*) only
C. (*b*) only
D. (*a*), (*b*) and (*c*)

50. Which of the following pollutants can cause cancer in humans?
A. Pesticides B. Mercury
C. Lead D. Ozone

51. **Assertion (A):** People population control measures do not necessarily help in checking environmental degradation.
Reason (R): The relationship between population growth and environmental degradation is rather complex.
Choose the **correct** answer from the following:
A. Both (A) and (R) are true and (R) is the correct explanation of (A)
B. Both (A) and (R) are true but (R) is not the correct explanation of (A)
C. (A) is true but (R) is false
D. (A) is false but (R) is true

52. Which of the following phenomena is **not** a natural hazard?
A. Wildfire
B. Lightning
C. Landslide
D. Chemical contamination

53. As part of National Climate Change Policy, Indian government is planning to raise the installed capacity of renewable energy by the year 2030 to:
A. 175 GW B. 200 GW
C. 250 GW D. 350 GW

54. At present, in terms of per capita energy consumption (kWh/year), identify the **correct** sequence.

A. Brazil > Russia > China > India
B. Russia > China > India > Brazil
C. Russia > China > Brazil > India
D. China > Russia > Brazil > India

55. Which of the following are the objectives of Rashtriya Uchchatar Shiksha Abhiyan (RUSA)?

(*a*) To improve the overall quality of state institutions.
(*b*) To ensure adequate availability of quality faculty.
(*c*) To create new institutions through upgradation of existing autonomous colleges.
(*d*) To downgrade universities with poor infrastructure into autonomous colleges.
Select the **correct** answer from the codes given below :

A. (*a*), (*b*), (*c*) and (*d*) B. (*a*), (*b*) and (*c*)
C. (*a*), (*c*) and (*d*) D. (*a*), (*b*) and (*d*)

56. The grounds on which discrimination in admission to educational institutions is constitutionally prohibited are:

(*a*) Religion
(*b*) Sex
(*c*) Place of birth
(*d*) Nationality

Select the **correct** answer from the codes given below:

A. (*b*), (*c*) and (*d*) B. (*a*), (*b*) and (*c*)
C. (*a*), (*b*) and (*d*) D. (*a*), (*b*), (*c*) and (*d*)

57. Which of the following statements are **correct** about Lok Sabha?

(*a*) The Constitution puts a limit on the size of the Lok Sabha.
(*b*) The size and shape of the Parliamentary Constituencies is determined by the Election Commission.
(*c*) First - past - the Post electoral system is followed.
(*d*) The Speaker of Lok Sabha does not have a casting vote in case of an equality of votes.

Select the **correct** answer from the codes given below:

A. (*a*) and (*c*)
B. (*a*), (*b*) and (*c*)
C. (*a*), (*c*) and (*d*)
D. (*a*), (*b*), (*c*) and (*d*)

58. Public Order as an item in the Constitution figures in:

A. the Union List
B. the State List
C. the Concurrent List
D. the Residuary Powers

59. The term of office of the Advocate General of a State is:

A. 4 years
B. 5 years
C. 6 years or 65 years of age whichever is earlier
D. not fixed

60. Which among the following States has the highest number of seats in the Lok Sabha?

A. Maharashtra B. Rajasthan
C. Tamil Nadu D. West Bengal

ANSWERS

1	**2**	**3**	**4**	**5**	**6**	**7**	**8**	**9**	**10**
C	D	B	A	C	A	D	B	B	D
11	**12**	**13**	**14**	**15**	**16**	**17**	**18**	**19**	**20**
C	A	A	D	B	D	D	B	D	C
21	**22**	**23**	**24**	**25**	**26**	**27**	**28**	**29**	**30**
D	B	C	D	A	D	D	D	B	C

31	32	33	34	35	36	37	38	39	40
B	D	B	A	C	B	A	B	B	D
41	**42**	**43**	**44**	**45**	**46**	**47**	**48**	**49**	**50**
C	D	A	D	B	D	C	D	D	A
51	**52**	**53**	**54**	**55**	**56**	**57**	**58**	**59**	**60**
A	D	D	C	B	B	A	B	D	A

SOME SELECTED EXPLANATORY ANSWERS

5. Jacques Delors is the chairman of the International Commission on Education for the Twenty-first Century. The result of three years of research and debate by an international panel of 14 specialists on how education should confront the complex challenges of the next century, the 266-page report is being published simultaneously in English and French.

Entitled "Learning: the Treasure Within," the report revolves around six main lines of enquiry which will guide UNESCO's future education policies and those of its 184 Member States. The lines focus on the relationship between education and the six subject areas of development, science, citizenship, culture, social cohesion, and work.

20. **Paralanguage** is a component of meta-communication that may modify or nuance meaning, or convey emotion, such as prosody, pitch, volume, intonation etc. It is sometimes defined as relating to nonphonemic properties only.

The paralinguistic properties of speech play an important role in human communication. There are no utterances or speech signals that lack paralinguistic properties, since speech requires the presence of a voice that can be modulated. This voice must have some properties, and all the properties of a voice as such are paralinguistic.

21. Each context has an influence on the communication process. Contexts can overlap, creating an even more dynamic process. You have been communicating in many of these contexts across your lifetime, and you'll be able to apply what you've learned through experience in each context to business communication.

25.

28.

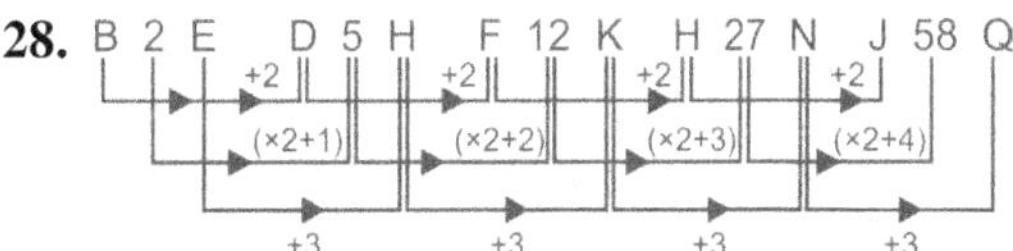

33. **Argument:** An argument is any group of propositions of which one is claimed to follow from the others, which are regarded as providing support or grounds for the truth of that one.

35. A definition that has a meaning which is deliberately assigned to some symbol is called stipulative. One who introduces a new symbol is free to assign, or stipulate, whatever meaning he cares to. Even an old term in a new context may also have its present meaning stipulated. What are here called *stipulative* definitions are sometimes referred to as *nominal* or *verbal* definitions.

37. Growth rate (%) of population in decade

1961-71 :

$$\left(\frac{24-21}{21}\right)\times 100 = \frac{100}{7} = 14.285\%$$

1971-81 :

$$\left(\frac{27-24}{24}\right)\times 100 = \frac{3}{24}\times 100 = 12.5\%$$

1991-2001 :

$$\left(\frac{32-30}{30}\right)\times 100 = \frac{2}{30}\times 100 = 6.67\%$$

2001-2011 :

$$\left(\frac{35-32}{32}\right)\times 100 = \frac{2}{32}\times 100 = 9.375\%$$

$\therefore$ Maximum growth rate (%) of population registered on 1961-71.

38. Average decadal growth rate (%) of population

$$= \frac{5+14.28+12.5+11.11+6.67+9.38}{6}$$

= 9.82%.

39. Projected Population in 2021

$$= 35+\frac{35\times 9.82}{100}$$

= 35 + 3.4

= 38.4 million.

40. Power availabilty per person in year 1951

$$= \frac{10\times 1000}{20} = 500 \text{ W}.$$

41. Average Power availability per person in decade

1981-91 : $\dfrac{(40+50)\times 1000}{(27+30)} \cong 1579$ W

1991-2001 : $\dfrac{(50+80)\times 1000}{(30+32)} \cong 2097$ W

2001-2011 : $\dfrac{(80+100)\times 1000}{(32+35)} \cong 2686.5$ W

1971-1981 : $\dfrac{(25+40)\times 1000}{(24+27)} \cong 1274.5$ W

So, Average Power availability per person was maximum in 2001-2011.

42. Percentage (%) increase in power production from 1951 to 2011

$$= \left(\frac{100-10}{10}\right)\times 100$$

= 900%.

43. National Mission on Education through Information and Communication Technology is abbreviated as NMEICT .

45. The byte is a unit of digital information that most commonly consists of eight bits. Historically, the byte was the number of bits used to encode a single character of text in a computer and for this reason it is the smallest addressable unit of memory in many computer architectures.

50. Pesticides are the only toxic substances released intentionally into our environment to kill living things. Pesticides are used in our schools, parks, and public lands. Pesticides are sprayed on agricultural fields and wood lots. Pesticides can be found in our air, our food, our soil, our water and even in our breast milk.

Pesticides can cause many types of cancer in humans. Some of the most prevalent forms include leukemia, non-Hodgkins lymphoma, brain, bone, breast, ovarian, prostate, testicular and liver cancers.

Previous Years' Paper (Solved)

UGC-NET (JRF) EXAM JUNE, 2015*

PAPER–I

Note . This paper contains **Sixty (60)** multiple choice questions, each question carrying **two (2)** marks. Candidate is expected to answer any **Fifty (50)** questions. In case more than **Fifty (50)** questions are attempted, only the first **Fifty (50)** questions will be evaluated.

1. Which of the following is the highest level of cognitive ability?

A. Knowing B. Understanding
C. Analysing D. Evaluating

2. Which of the following factors does **not** impact teaching?

A. Teacher's knowledge
B. Class-room activities that encourage learning
C. Socio-economic background of teachers and students
D. Learning through experience

3. Which of the following statements about teaching aids are correct?

(*a*) They help in retaining concepts for longer duration.
(*b*) They help students learn better.
(*c*) They make teaching learning process interesting.
(*d*) They enhance rote learning.

Select the correct answer from the codes given below:

A. (*a*), (*b*), (*c*) and (*d*) B. (*a*), (*b*) and (*c*)
C. (*b*), (*c*) and (*d*) D. (*a*), (*b*) and (*d*)

4. Techniques used by a teacher to teach include:

(*a*) Lecture
(*b*) Interactive lecture
(*c*) Group work
(*d*) Self study

Select the correct answer from the codes given below :

A. (*a*), (*b*) and (*c*) B. (*a*), (*b*), (*c*) and (*d*)
C. (*b*), (*c*) and (*d*) D. (*a*), (*b*) and (*d*)

5. Achievement tests are commonly used for the purpose of :

A. Making selections for a specific job
B. Selecting candidates for a course
C. Identifying strengths and weaknesses of learners
D. Assessing the amount of learning after teaching

6. A good teacher is one who:

A. gives useful information
B. explains concepts and principles
C. gives printed notes to students
D. inspires students to learn

7. Which of the following statements regarding the meaning of research are correct?

(*a*) Research refers to a series of systematic activity or activities undertaken to find out the solution of a problem.
(*b*) It is a systematic, logical and an unbiased process wherein verification of hypothesis, data analysis, interpretation and formation of principles can be done.
(*c*) It is an intellectual enquiry or quest towards truth.
(*d*) It leads to enhancement of knowledge.

Select the correct answer from the codes given below :

A. (*a*), (*b*) and (*c*) B. (*b*), (*c*) and (*d*)
C. (*a*), (*c*) and (*d*) D. (*a*), (*b*), (*c*) and (*d*)

* Held on 28/06/2005

8. A good thesis writing should involve:

(*a*) reduction of punctuation and grammatical errors to a minimum.

(*b*) careful checking of references.

(*c*) consistency in the way the thesis is written.

(*d*) a clear and well written abstract.

Select the correct answer from the codes given below:

A. (*a*), (*b*), (*c*) and (*d*) B. (*a*), (*b*) and (*c*)

C. (*a*), (*b*) and (*d*) D. (*b*), (*c*) and (*d*)

9. Jean Piaget gave a theory of cognitive development of humans on the basis of his:

A. Fundamental Research

B. Applied Research

C. Action Research

D. Evaluation Research

10. "Male and female students perform equally well in a numerical aptitude test." This statement indicates a :

A. research hypothesis

B. null hypothesis

C. directional hypothesis

D. statistical hypothesis

11. The conclusions/findings of which type of research cannot be generalized to other situations?

A. Historical Research

B. Descriptive Research

C. Experimental Research

D. Causal Comparative Research

12. Which of the following steps are required to design a questionnaire?

(*a*) Writing primary and secondary aims of the study.

(*b*) Review of the current literature.

(*c*) Prepare a draft of questionnaire.

(*d*) Revision of the draft.

Select the correct answer from the codes given below:

A. (*a*), (*b*) and (*c*) B. (*a*), (*c*) and (*d*)

C. (*b*), (*c*) and (*d*) D. (*a*), (*b*), (*c*) and (*d*)

Directions (Qs. 13-18): *Read the following passage carefully and answer the questions given below:*

Story telling is not in our genes. Neither it is an evolutionary history. It is the essence of what makes us Human.

Human beings progress by telling stories. One event can result in a great variety of stories being told about it. Sometimes those stories differ greatly. Which stories are picked up and repeated and which ones are dropped and forgotten often determines how we progress. Our history, knowledge and understanding are all the collections of the few stories that survive. This includes the stories that we tell each other about the future. And how the future will turn out depends partly, possibly largely, on which stories we collectively choose to believe.

Some stories are designed to spread fear and concern. This is because some story-tellers feel that there is a need to raise some tensions. Some stories are frightening, they are like totemic warnings: "Fail to act now and we are all doomed." Then there are stories that indicate that all will be fine so long as we leave everything upto a few especially able adults. Currently, this trend is being led by those who call themselves "rational optimists". They tend to claim that it is human nature to compete and to succeed and also to profit at the expense of others. The rational optimists however, do not realize how humanity has progressed overtime through amiable social networks and how large groups work in less selfishness and in the process accommodate rich and poor, high and low alike. This aspect in story-telling is considered by the 'Practical Possibles', who sit between those who say all is fine and cheerful and be individualistic in your approach to a successful future, and those who ordain pessimism and fear that we are doomed.

What the future holds for us is which stories we hold on to and how we act on them.

13. Our knowledge is a collection of:

A. all stories that we have heard during our life-time

B. some stories that we remember
C. a few stories that survive
D. some important stories

14. Story telling is:
A. an art
B. a science
C. in our genes
D. the essence of what makes us human

15. How the future will turn out to be, depends upon the stories?
A. We collectively choose to believe in
B. Which are repeatedly narrated
C. Designed to spread fear and tension
D. Designed to make prophecy

16. Rational optimists:
(*a*) Look for opportunities
(*b*) Are sensible and cheerful
(*c*) Are selfishly driven

Identify the correct answer from the codes given below:
A. (*a*), (*b*) and (*c*) B. (*a*) only
C. (*a*) and (*b*) only D. (*b*) and (*c*) only

17. Humans become less selfish when:
A. they work in large groups
B. they listen to frightening stories
C. they listen to cheerful stories
D. they work in solitude

18. 'Practical Possibles' are the ones who:
A. follow Midway Path
B. are doom-mongers
C. are self-centred
D. are cheerful and carefree

19. Effectiveness of communication can be traced from which of the following?
(*a*) Attitude surveys
(*b*) Performance records
(*c*) Students attendance
(*d*) Selection of communication channel

Select the correct answer from the codes given below:
A. (*a*), (*b*), (*c*) and (*d*) B. (*a*), (*b*) and (*c*)
C. (*b*), (*c*) and (*d*) D. (*a*), (*b*) and (*d*)

20. **Assertion (A):** Formal communication tends to be fast and flexible.

Reason (R): Formal communication is a systematic and orderly flow of information.
A. Both **(A)** and **(R)** are correct and **(R)** is correct explanation of **(A)**
B. Both **(A)** and **(R)** are correct, but **(R)** is not correct explanation of **(A)**
C. **(A)** is correct, but **(R)** is false
D. **(A)** is false, but **(R)** is correct

21. Which of the following are the characteristic features of communication?
(*a*) Communication involves exchange of ideas, facts and opinions.
(*b*) Communication involves both information and understanding.
(*c*) Communication is a continuous process.
(*d*) Communication is a circular process.

Select the correct answer from the codes given below:
A. (*a*), (*b*) and (*c*) B. (*a*), (*b*) and (*d*)
C. (*b*), (*c*) and (*d*) D. (*a*), (*b*), (*c*) and (*d*)

22. The term 'grapevine' is also known as :
A. Downward communication
B. Informal communication
C. Upward communication
D. Horizontal communication

23. Which of the following is **not** a principle of effective communication?
A. Persuasive and convincing dialogue
B. Participation of the audience
C. One-way transfer of information
D. Strategic use of grapevine

24. In communication, the language is:
A. The verbal code
B. Intrapersonal
C. The symbolic code
D. The non-verbal code

25. The next term in the series is:

2, 5, 9, 19, 37, ?
A. 73 B. 75
C. 78 D. 80

26. In certain code MATHURA is coded as JXQEROX. The code of HOTELS will be :

A. LEQIBP   B. ELQBIP
C. LEBIQP   D. ELIPQB

27. One day Prakash left home and walked 10 km towards south, turned right and walked 5 km, turned right and walked 10 km and turned left and walked 10 km. How many km will he have to walk to reach his home straight?

A. 10   B. 20
C. 15   D. 30

28. A girl introduced a boy as the son of the daughter of the father of her uncle. The boy is related to the girl as :

A. Brother   B. Uncle
C. Nephew   D. Son

29. In an examination 10,000 students appeared. The result revealed the number of students who have:

passed in all five subjects = 5583
passed in three subjects only = 1400
passed in two subjects only = 1200
passed in one subject only = 735
failed in English only = 75
failed in Physics only = 145
failed in Chemistry only = 140
failed in Mathematics only = 200
failed in Bio-science only = 157

The number of students passed in at least four subjects is:

A. 6300   B. 6900
C. 7300   D. 7900

30. At present a person is 4 times older than his son and is 3 years older than his wife. After 3 years the age of the son will be 15 years. The age of the person's wife after 5 years will be:

A. 42   B. 48
C. 45   D. 50

31. If we want to seek new knowledge of facts about the world, we must rely on reason of the type:

A. Inductive   B. Deductive
C. Demonstrative   D. Physiological

32. A deductive argument is invalid if :

A. Its premises and conclusions are all false
B. Its premises are true but its conclusion is false
C. Its premises are false but its conclusion is true
D. Its premises and conclusions are all true

33. Inductive reasoning is grounded on:

A. Integrity of nature
B. Unity of nature
C. Uniformity of nature
D. Harmony of nature

34. Among the following statements **two** are contradictory to each other. Select the correct code that represents them:

Statements:

(*a*) All poets are philosophers.
(*b*) Some poets are philosophers.
(*c*) Some poets are not philosophers.
(*d*) No philosopher is a poet.

Codes:

A. (*a*) and (*b*)   B. (*a*) and (*d*)
C. (*a*) and (*c*)   D. (*b*) and (*c*)

35. Which of the codes given below contains only the **correct** statements? Select the code:

Statements:

(*a*) Venn diagram represents the arguments graphically.
(*b*) Venn diagram can enhance our understanding.
(*c*) Venn diagram may be called valid or invalid.
(*d*) Venn diagram is clear method of notation.

Codes:

A. (*a*), (*b*) and (*c*)
B. (*a*), (*b*) and (*d*)
C. (*b*), (*c*) and (*d*)
D. (*a*), (*c*) and (*d*)

36. When the purpose of a definition is to explain the use or to eliminate ambiguity the definition is called:

A. Stipulative   B. Theoretical
C. Lexical   D. Persuasive

Direction (Qs. 37-42): *Answer the question based on the tabulated data given below:*

A company has 20 employees with their age (in years) and salary (in thousand rupees per month) mentioned against each of them:

S.No.	Age (in years)	Salary (in thousand rupees per month)
1.	44	35
2.	32	20
3.	54	45
4.	42	35
5.	31	20
6.	53	60
7.	42	50
8.	51	55
9.	34	25
10.	41	30
11.	33	30
12.	31	35
13.	30	35
14.	37	40
15.	44	45
16.	36	35
17.	34	35
18.	49	50
19.	43	45
20.	45	50

37. Classify the data of age of each employee in class interval of 5 years. Which class interval of 5 years has the maximum average salary?
A. 35-40 years B. 40-45 years
C. 45-50 years D. 50-55 years

38. What is the frequency (%) in the class interval of 30-35 years?
A. 20% B. 25%
C. 30% D. 35%

39. What is the average age of the employees?
A. 40.3 years B. 38.6 years
C. 47.2 years D. 45.3 years

40. What is the fraction (%) of employees getting salary ≥ 40,000 per month?
A. 45% B. 50%
C. 35% D. 32%

41. What is the average salary (in thousand per month) in the age group 40-50 years?
A. 35 B. 42.5
C. 40.5 D. 36.5

42. What is the fraction of employees getting salary less than the average salary of all the employees?
A. 45% B. 50%
C. 55% D. 47%

43. Encoding or scrambling data for transmission across a network is known as :
A. Protection B. Detection
C. Encryption D. Decryption

44. Which of the following is **not** an output device?
A. Printer B. Speaker
C. Monitor D. Keyboard

45. Which of the following represents one billion characters ?
A. Kilobyte B. Megabyte
C. Gigabyte D. Terabyte

46. Which of the following is **not** open source software?
A. Internet explorer
B. Fedora Linux
C. Open office
D. Apache HTTP server

47. Which one of the following represents the binary equivalent of the decimal number 25?
A. 10101 B. 01101
C. 11001 D. 11011

48. Which is an instant messenger that is used for chatting?
A. Altavista B. MAC
C. Microsoft Office D. Google Talk

49. In which of the countries per capita use of water is maximum?
A. USA B. European Union
C. China D. India

50. India's contribution to total global carbon dioxide emissions is about:
A. ~ 3% B. ~ 6%
C. ~ 10% D. ~ 15%

51. Two earthquakes A and B happen to be of magnitude 5 and 6 respectively on Richter Scale. The ratio of the energies released E_B/E_A will be approximately:

A. ~8 B. ~16
C. ~32 D. ~64

52. Which of the following combinations represent renewable natural resources?

A. Fertile soil, fresh water and natural gas
B. Clean air, phosphates and biological diversity
C. Fishes, fertile soil and fresh water
D. Oil, forests and tides

53. In the recently launched Air Quality Index in India, which of the following pollutants is **not** included?

A. Carbon monoxide
B. Fine particulate matter
C. Ozone
D. Chlorofluorocarbons

54. The factors which are most important in determining the impact of anthropogenic activities on environment are :

A. Population, affluence per person, land available per person
B. Population, affluence per person and the technology used for exploiting resources
C. Atmospheric conditions, population and forest cover
D. Population, forest cover and land available per person

55. The session of the Parliament is summoned by:

A. The President
B. The Prime Minister
C. The Speaker of the Lok Sabha
D. The Speaker of the Lok Sabha and the Chairman of the Rajya Sabha

56. Civil Service Day is celebrated in India on:

A. 21st April B. 24th April
C. 21st June D. 7th July

57. The South Asia University is situated in the city of :

A. Colombo B. Dhaka
C. New Delhi D. Kathmandu

58. The University Grants Commission was established with which of the following aims?

(*a*) Promotion of research and development in higher education
(*b*) Identifying and sustaining institutions of potential learning
(*c*) Capacity building of teachers
(*d*) Providing autonomy to each and every higher educational institution in India.

Select the correct answer from the codes given below :

A. (*a*), (*b*), (*c*) and (*d*) B. (*a*), (*b*) and (*c*)
C. (*b*), (*c*) and (*d*) D. (*a*), (*b*) and (*d*)

59. The Gross Enrolment Ratio (GER) in institutions of higher education in India at present (2015) is about:

A. 8 per cent B. 12 per cent
C. 19 per cent D. 23 per cent

60. The total number of central universities in India in April 2015 was:

A. 08 B. 14
C. 27 D. 43

ANSWERS

1	2	3	4	5	6	7	8	9	10
D	C	B	A	D	D	D	A	A	B
11	**12**	**13**	**14**	**15**	**16**	**17**	**18**	**19**	**20**
A	D	C	D	A	A	A	A	B	D
21	**22**	**23**	**24**	**25**	**26**	**27**	**28**	**29**	**30**
D	B	C	A	B	B	C	A	A	D

31	32	33	34	35	36	37	38	39	40
A	B	C	C	B	C	D	D	A	A
41	**42**	**43**	**44**	**45**	**46**	**47**	**48**	**49**	**50**
B	C	C	D	C	A	C	D	B	B
51	**52**	**53**	**54**	**55**	**56**	**57**	**58**	**59**	**60**
C	C	D	B	A	A	C	B	C	D

SOME SELECTED EXPLANATORY ANSWERS

1. Bloom identified six levels within the cognitive domain, from the simple recall or recognition of facts, as the lowest level, through increasingly more complex and abstract mental levels, to the highest order which is classified as evaluation.

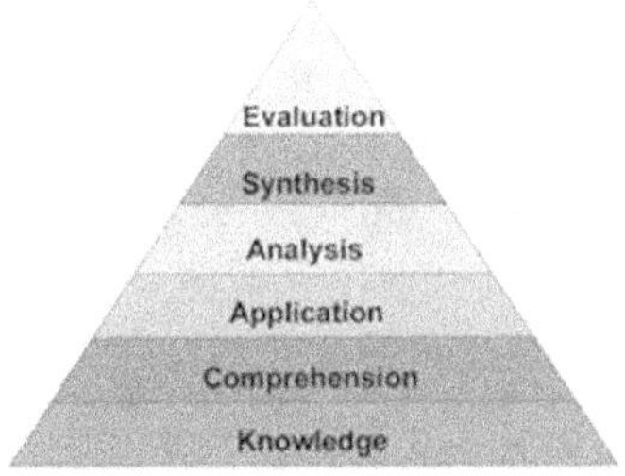

Evaluation is concerned with the ability to judge the value of material (statement, novel, poem, research report) for a given purpose. The judgements are to be based on definite criteria. These may be internal criteria (organization) or external criteria (relevance to the purpose) and the student may determine the criteria or be given them. Learning outcomes in this area are highest in the cognitive hierarchy because they contain elements of all the other categories, plus conscious value judgements based on clearly defined criteria.

5. An **achievement test** is a test of developed skill or knowledge. It is the assessment of the amount of the learning after teaching. The most common type of achievement test is a standardized test developed to measure skills and knowledge learned in a given grade level, usually through planned instruction, such as training or classroom instruction. Achievement tests are often contrasted with tests that measure aptitude, a more general and stable cognitive trait.

6. It is not an exaggeration to say that a great teacher can change a student's life. As some of the most influential role models for developing students, teachers are responsible for more than just academic enrichment. If you want to be a great educator, you must connect with your pupils and reach them on multiple levels, because the best teachers are committed to their students' well-being both inside and outside the classroom.

Inspiring students is integral to ensuring their success and encouraging them to fulfil their potential. Students who are inspired by their teachers can accomplish amazing things, and that motivation almost always stays with them. Inspiration can also take many forms, from helping a pupil through the academic year and their short-term goals, to guiding them towards their future career. Years after graduation, many working professionals will still cite a particular teacher as the one who fostered their love of what they currently do and attribute their accomplishments to that educator.

9. **Piaget's theory of cognitive development** is a comprehensive theory about the nature and development of human intelligence. Piaget believed that one's childhood plays a vital and active role in a person's development. Piaget's idea is primarily known as a developmental stage theory. It is based on his fundamental research.

To Piaget, cognitive development was a progressive reorganization of mental processes resulting from biological maturation and environmental experience.

10. In inferential statistics the **null hypothesis** usually refers to a general statement or default position that there is no relationship between two measured phenomena, or no difference among groups.

For example "Male and female students perform equally well in a numerical aptitude test".

19. Communication is an exchange of feelings, ideas, and information, whether by speaking, writing, signals, or behaviours. Effective communication is an essential component of organizational success at all levels.

It can be traced out by following points:

(a) Attitude surveys

(b) Performance records

(c) Students attendance

20. Formal communication refers to the communication transmitted through the officially established chain of command in the organisation structure. The organisation structure reflecting superior subordinate relationships determines the flow of formal communication. Formal communication, according to the direction or flow may be of three types-(a) upward, (b) downward, and (c) horizontal. Formal communication is generally in writing and includes transmission of orders, instructions and decisions. Speed of communication is abit slow and time consuming. By Nature, it is systematic and orderly flow of information.

22. Informal communication is also known as grapevine communication because there is no definite route of communication for sharing information.

In this form of communication, information converges a long way by passing from one person to another person leaving no indication from which point it started. This is quite similar to the vine of grapes. It is also difficult to find out the beginning and the end of the grapevine.

23. One-way communication is a misnomer. The one-way process is not communication; it is simply the dispensing of information to another person, incormation that may or may not be received in the form intended. It is not a way of effective communication because the one-way posture inhibits interchange, and limits feedback.

24. Verbal means "consisting of words". Therefore, a verbal code is a set of rules about the use of words in the creation of messages. It is language we use for communication. Words can obviously be either spoken or written. Verbal codes, then, include both oral (spoken) language and non-oral (written) language.

25.

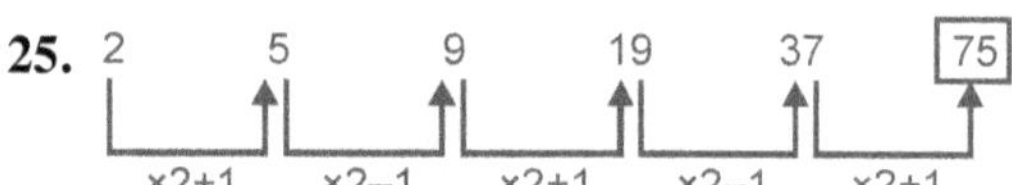

Hence, the next term in the series is 75.

26. M A T H U R A
–3↓ –3↓ –3↓ –3↓ –3↓ –3↓ –3↓
J X Q E R O X

Similarly,

H O T E L S
–3↓ –3↓ –3↓ –3↓ –3↓ –3↓
E L Q B I P

27.

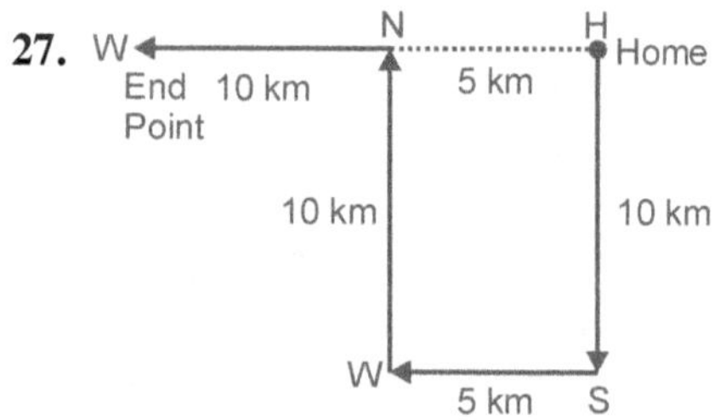

He has to walk 15 km to reach his home straight.

28. 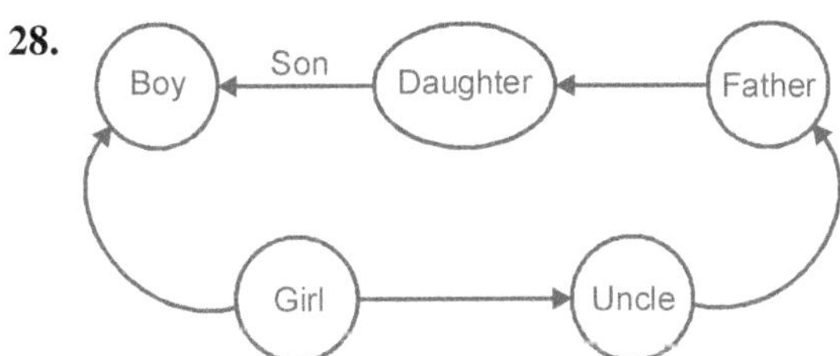

Hence the relation between boy and girl is brother and sister.

∴ The boy is related to the girl as brother.

29. Required no. of Students passed in at least four subjects is 5583 + 717 = 6300.

30. Let present age of son = x years

Present age of father = $4x$ years

Wife's present age = $4x - 3$ years

According to the question,

$$x + 3 = 15 \Rightarrow x = 12$$

Wife's present age = $4 \times 12 - 3 = 45$ years

After 5 years wife's age = 45 + 5 = 50 years.

31. Inductive reasoning is one in which the premises seek to supply strong evidence for the truth of the conclusion. While the conclusion of a deductive argument is certain, the truth of the conclusion of an inductive argument is *probable*, based upon the evidence given.

Inductive reasoning is also known as hypothesis construction because any conclusions made are based on current knowledge and predictions. As with deductive arguments, biases can distort the proper application of inductive argument, thereby preventing the reasoner from forming the most logical conclusion based on the clues. Examples of these biases include the availability heuristic, confirmation bias, and the predictable-world bias.

32. An argument is said to be deductive if its conclusion is claimed to *necessarily* follow from its premises. That is, if it is claimed that since the premises are true or acceptable, the conclusion must also be true or acceptable, then the argument is deductive. We can also define deduction by saying that in a deductive argument, the logical relation between the premises and the conclusion is claimed to be 100% supporting.

36. A lexical definition simply reports the way in which a term is already used within a language community. The goal here is to inform someone else of the accepted meaning of the term, so the definition is more or less correct depending upon the accuracy with which it captures that usage. In these pages, my definitions of technical terms of logic are lexical because they are intended to inform you about the way in which these terms are actually employed within the discipline of logic.

37. 35-40 years:

Average Salary

$$= \frac{40+35}{2} = \frac{75}{2} = 37.5 \text{ thousand/month}$$

40-45 years:

$$\text{Average} = \frac{35+35+50+30+45+45}{6}$$

$$= \frac{240}{6} = 40 \text{ thousand/month}$$

45-50 years:

$$\text{Average} = \frac{50+50}{2} = \frac{100}{2}$$

$$= 50 \text{ thousand/month}$$

50-55 years:

$$\text{Average} = \frac{45+60+55}{3} = \frac{160}{3}$$

$$= 53.3 \text{ thousand/month}$$

Hence, the 50-55 class interval has the maximum average salary.

38. Required % = $\frac{7}{20} \times 100 = 35\%$.

39. Total age of 20 employees

= 424 + 382 = 806 years

$$\text{Average} = \frac{806}{20} = 40.3 \text{ years.}$$

40. Required % = $\frac{9}{20} \times 100 = 45\%$.

41. 40-50 years:

Total salary = 35 + 35 + 50 + 30 + 45 + 50 + 45 + 50

= 340 thousand

Required average salary = $\frac{340}{8} = 42.5$.

42. Total salary of 20 workers

= (375 + 400) thousand = 775 thousand

Average salary = $\frac{775}{20} = 38.75$ thousand

Required% = $\frac{11}{20} \times 100 = 55\%$.

43. *Encryption* involves scrambling and perhaps compressing the data prior to transmission; the receiving device is provided with the necessary logic to decrypt and decompress the trasmitted information. Encryption generally resides in firmware included in stand-alone devices, although it can be built into virtually any device. Encryption logic, for example, often is incorporated into routers, which can encrypt data on a packet-by-packet basis. Encryption comes in two basic flavors: private key and public key. *Private key* is a symmetric encryption method that uses the same key to encrypt and decrypt data and requires that the key be kept secret. *Public key* is an asymmetric encryption method with two keys—an encryption (encoding) key that can be used by all authorized network users and a decryption (decoding) key that is kept secret.

44. A computer **keyboard** is one of the primary input devices used with a computer that looks similar to those found on electric typewriters, but with some additional keys. Keyboards allow you to input letters, numbers, and other symbols into a computer that often function as commands.

45. A Gigabyte is approximately 1,000 Megabytes or 1 billion characters. A Gigabyte is still a very common term used these days when referring to disk space or drive storage. 1 Gigabyte of data is almost twice the amount of data that a CD-ROM can hold. But it's about one thousand times the capacity of a 3-1/2 floppy disk. 1 Gigabyte could hold the contents of about 10 yards of books on a shelf. 100 Gigabytes could hold the entire library floor of academic journals.

46. Open source software (OSS) as "software for which the human-readable source code is available for use, study, re-use, modification, enhancement, and re-distribution by the users of that software".

The Internet Explorer Developer Relations Team at Microsoft have hinted at the possibility that the browser may one day become "Open Source".

"Open Source" is a term referring to software that whose source code is available for modification or enhancement by anyone. All other major web browsers (Mozilla Firefox, Google Chrome, Opera and Safari are based on open-source components). Presently, Internet Explorer is the only one of the big 5 browsers to remain entirely "closed source".

47.

2	25	1
2	12	0
2	6	0
2	3	1
	1	

$\therefore \ (25)_{10} = (11001)_2$.

48. Google Talk is an instant messaging service that provides both text and voice communication. The instant messaging service is colloquially known as "gtalk", "gchat", or "gmessage" to its users, although Google does not endorse those names.

50. Carbon dioxide (CO_2) emissions from fossil fuel burning and cement production increased by 2.3% in 2013, with a total of 9.9 ± 0.5 GtC (billion tonnes of carbon) (36 $GtCO_2$) emitted to the atmosphere, 61% above 1990 emissions (the Kyoto Protocol reference year).

India and China are among the world's biggest contributors to fossil fuel emissions with India's carbon dioxide discharge increasing by a whopping ~ 6 per cent.

52. **Renewable Resources:** These are the resources that are replenished through rapid natural cycles. Common examples of such resources are:

(*i*) Oxygen in the air, which is replenished through photosynthesis.

(*ii*) Fresh water, which is replenished through the water cycle.

(*iii*) All biological products (food, fishes, timber, etc.,) which are replenished through natural cycles of growth and reproduction.

(*iv*) Solar energy is also considered as renewable as on a human time scale and it is inexhaustible. It is expected that sun will last at least 6.5 billion years.

(*v*) Some other renewable resources that can be renewed (hours to several decades) through natural processes include forests, grassland grasses, wild animals, fishes, fresh air & water and fertile soil. However, potentially renewable resources can be depleted when resources utilization rate exceeds the natural replacement rate.

53. The Centre for Science and Environment (CSE), which has been demanding adoption of an **Air Quality Index** (AQI) for "an important step forward for building awareness and protecting public health".

There are six AQI categories, namely: Good, Satisfactory, Moderately polluted, Poor, Very poor and Severe.

The index considers eight pollutants — PM10, PM2.5, NO_2, SO_2, CO, O_3, NH_3 and Pb (CFC is not included). The likely health implications of the six categories would also be provided with a colour code. CSE said that with this step, India has joined the global league of countries like the US, China, Mexico and France that have implemented smog alert systems.

55. A **joint session** or **joint convention** is, most broadly, when two normally-separate decision-making groups meet together, often in a special session or other extraordinary meeting, for a specific purpose.

Most often it refers to when both houses of a bicameral legislature sit together. A joint session typically occurs to receive foreign or domestic diplomats or leaders, or to allow both houses to consider bills together.

In India, if a bill has been rejected by any house of the parliament and if more than six months have elapsed, the President may summon a joint session for purpose of passing the bill. The bill is passed by a simple majority of a joint sitting. Since the lower house (Lok Sabha) has more than twice the members of the upper house (Rajya Sabha), a group commanding a majority in the lower house of the Government of India can pass such a bill even if it was previously rejected by the upper house.

So far, only three bills - the Dowry Prohibition Act, 1960, the Banking Service Commission Repeal Bill, 1977, and the Prevention of Terrorism Act, 2002 - have been passed at joint sessions.

56. The **Civil Services of India** refer to the civil service and the permanent bureaucracy of the Government of India. The civil service system is the backbone of the administrative machinery of the country.

Every year, on the 21st of April, the "Civil Service Day" is observed by all Civil Services to re-dedicate and re-commit themselves to the cause of the people. It provides a unique opportunity for introspection as also chalking out future strategies to deal with the challenges being posed by the changing times.

57. **South Asian University** (SAU) is an International University sponsored by the eight

Member States of the South Asian Association for Regional Cooperation (SAARC). The eight countries are : Afghanistan, Bangladesh, Bhutan, India, Maldives, Nepal, Pakistan and Sri Lanka. South Asian University started admitting students in 2010, at a temporary campus at Akbar Bhawan, India. Its permanent campus will be at Maidan Garhi in South Delhi, India, next to Indira Gandhi National Open University (IGNOU). First academic session of the university started in August 2010 with two post-graduate academic programmes, in economics and computer sciences. As of 2014 SAU offered Master's and MPhil/PhD programs in applied mathematics, biotechnology, computer science, development economics, international relations, law and sociology. The degrees of the university are recognized by all the member nations of the SAARC according to an inter-governmental agreement signed by the foreign ministers of the 8 countries.

59. The UGC had chalked out several plans to increase gross enrolment ratio (GER) of students (in the age group of 18 to 22) in higher education. He was optimistic of increasing the GER from the present 19 per cent to 30 per cent by the end of the 12th Five Year Plan (2012-17). The enrolment of candidates for degree courses would be increased from the present 20 million to 29 million by the end of 12th Plan period. The number of students enrolled in distance education would go up from 4.6 million to 6.3 million by 2017.

60. A **Central University** or a **Union University** in India is established by Act of Parliament and are under the purview of the Department of Higher Education in the Union Human Resource Development Ministry. In general, universities in India are recognised by the University Grants Commission (UGC), which draws its power from the *University Grants Commission Act, 1956.* In addition, 15 Professional Councils are established, controlling different aspects of accreditation and coordination. Central universities, in addition, are covered by the *Central Universities Act, 2009*, which regulates their purpose, powers governance etc., and established 12 new universities.

The number of central universities published by the UGC includes 43 central universities as on April 2015.

Previous Years' Paper (Solved)

CBSE-NET (JRF) EXAM DECEMBER, 2014*

PAPER–I

Note : This paper contains **Sixty (60)** multiple choice questions, each question carrying **two (2)** marks. Candidate is expected to answer any **Fifty (50)** questions. In case more than **Fifty (50)** questions are attempted, only the first **Fifty (50)** questions will be evaluated.

1. Namita and Samita are brilliant and studious. Anita and Karabi are obedient and irregular. Babita and Namita are irregular but brilliant. Samita and Kabita are regular and obedient. Who among them is/are brilliant, obedient, regular and studious?

A. Samita alone B. Namita and Samita
C. Kabita alone D. Anita alone

2. Warrior is related to sword, carpenter is related to saw, farmer is related to plough. In the same way, the author is related to

A. Book B. Fame
C. Reader D. Pen

3. Given below is a diagram of three circles A, B and C over-lapping each other. The circle A represents the class of honest people, the circle B represents the class of sincere people and circle C represents the class of politicians. p, q, r, s, U, X, Y represent different regions. Select the code that represents the region indicating the class of honest politicians who are not sincere.

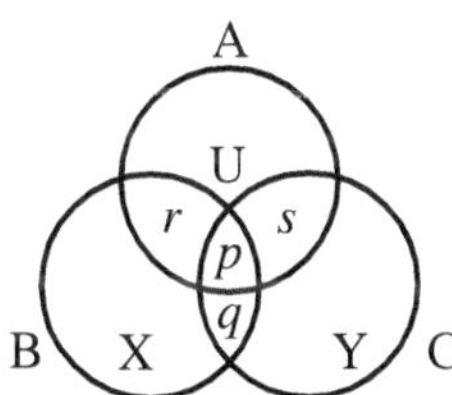

Codes:

A. X B. q
C. p D. s

4. "A man ought no more to value himself for being wiser than a woman if he owes his advantage to a better education, than he ought to boast of his courage for beating a man when his hands were tied."
The above passage is an instance of

A. Deductive argument
B. Hypothetical argument
C. Analogical argument
D. Factual argument

5. By which of the following proposition, the proposition 'wise men are hardly afraid of death' is contradicted?

A. Some wise men are afraid of death
B. All wise men are afraid of death
C. No wise men is afraid of death
D. Some wise men are not afraid of death

6. When in a group of propositions, one proposition is claimed to follow from the others, that group of propositions is called

A. An argument B. A valid argument
C. An explanation D. An invalid argument

Directions (Qs. 7 to 12): *For a country CO_2 emissions (million metric tons) from various sectors are given in the following table. Answer the questions based on the data given:*

CO_2 emissions (million metric tons)					
Sector / Year	Power	Industry	Commercial	Agriculture	Domestic
2005	500	200	150	80	100
2006	600	300	200	90	110
2007	650	320	250	100	120
2008	700	400	300	150	150
2009	800	450	320	200	180

* Held on 28-12-2014

7. Which sector has recorded maximum growth in CO_2 emissions during 2005 to 2009?
A. Power
B. Industry
C. Commercial
D. Agriculture

8. By what percentage (%), the total emissions of CO_2 have increased from 2005 to 2009?
A. ~89.32%
B. ~57.62%
C. ~40.32%
D. ~113.12%

9. What is the average annual growth rate of CO_2 emissions in power sector?
A. ~12.57% B. ~16.87%
C. ~30.81% D. ~50.25%

10. What is the percentage contribution of power sector to total CO_2 emissions in the year 2008?
A. ~30.82% B. ~41.18%
C. ~51.38% D. ~60.25%

11. In which year, the contribution (%) of industry to total sectoral CO_2 emissions was minimum?
A. 2005 B. 2006
C. 2007 D. 2009

12. What is the percentage (%) growth of CO_2 emissions from power sector during 2005 to 2009?
A. 60 B. 50
C. 40 D. 80

13. Which one of the following is not a search engine?
A. Google B. Chrome
C. Yahoo D. Bing

14. CSS stands for
A. Cascading Style Sheets
B. Collecting Style Sheets
C. Comparative Style Sheets
D. Comprehensive Style Sheets

15. MOOC stands for
A. Media Online Open Course
B. Massachusetts Open Online Course
C. Massive Open Online Course
D. Myrind Open Online Course

16. Binary equivalent of decimal number 35 is
A. 100011 B. 110001
C. 110101 D. 101011

17. gif, jpg, bmp, png are used as extensions for files which store
A. audio data
B. image data
C. video data
D. text data

18. Symbols A-F are used in which one of the following?
A. Binary number system
B. Decimal number system
C. Hexadecimal number system
D. Octal number system

19. One of the anthropogenic sources of gaseous pollutants chlorofluorocarbons (CFCs) in air is
A. Cement industry
B. Fertiliser industry
C. Foam industry
D. Pesticide industry

20. In terms of total CO_2 emissions from a country, identity the correct sequence:
A. U.S.A. > China > India > Russia
B. China > U.S.A. > India > Russia
C. China > U.S.A. > Russia > India
D. U.S.A. > China > Russia > India

21. Match List-I and List-II and identify the correct code:

List-I	**List-II**
(*a*) World Health Day	(*i*) 16th September
(*b*) World Population Day	(*ii*) 1st December
(*c*) World Ozone Day	(*iii*) 11th July
(*d*) World AIDS Day	(*iv*) 7th April

Codes:

	(*a*)	(*b*)	(*c*)	(*d*)
A.	(*i*)	(*ii*)	(*iii*)	(*iv*)
B.	(*iv*)	(*iii*)	(*i*)	(*ii*)
C.	(*ii*)	(*iii*)	(*iv*)	(*i*)
D.	(*iii*)	(*iv*)	(*ii*)	(*i*)

22. Which of the anthropogenic activity accounts for more than $\frac{2}{3}$rd of global water consumption?

A. Agriculture

B. Hydropower generation

C. Industry

D. Domestic and Municipal usage

23. Which of the following is ***not*** a renewable natural resource?

A. Clean air B. Fresh water

C. Fertile soil D. Salt

24. The maximum number of fake institutions/ universities as identified by the UGC in the year 2014 are in the State/Union territory of

A. Bihar B. Uttar Pradesh

C. Tamil Nadu D. Delhi

25. Which of the following institutions are empowered to confer or grant degrees under the UGC Act, 1956?

1. A university established by an Act of Parliament.
2. A university established by an Act of Legislature.
3. A university/institution established by a linguistic minority.
4. An institution which is a deemed to be university.

Select the correct answer from the codes given below:

A. 1 and 2 B. 1, 2 and 3

C. 1, 2 and 4 D. 1, 2, 3 and 4

26. Which of the following are the tools of good governance?

1. Social Audit
2. Separation of Powers
3. Citizen's Charter
4. Right to Information

Select the correct answer from the codes given below:

A. 1, 3 and 4

B. 2, 3 and 4

C. 1 and 4

D. 1, 2, 3 and 4

27. The cyclone 'Hudhud' hit the coast of which State?

A. Andhra Pradesh

B. Karnataka

C. Kerala

D. Gujarat

28. The interval between two sessions of parliament must not exceed

A. 3 months B. 6 months

C. 4 months D. 100 days

29. Right to Privacy as a Fundamental Right is implied in

A. Right to Freedom

B. Right to Life and Personal Liberty

C. Right to Equality

D. Right against Exploitation

30. Which of the following organizations deals with 'capacity building program' on Educational Planning?

A. NCERT B. UGC

C. NAAC D. NUEPA

31. Which of the following powers, the President has in relation to Lok Sabha?

1. Summoning
2. Adjournment – sine die
3. Prorogation
4. Dissolution

Select the correct answer from the codes given below:

A. 1 and 4 B. 1, 2 and 3

C. 1, 3 and 4 D. 1, 2, 3 and 4

32. Which of the following is not a prescribed level of teaching?

A. Memory

B. Understanding

C. Reflective

D. Differentiation

33. Maximum participation of students during teaching is possible through

A. Lecture method

B. Demonstration method

C. Inductive method

D. Textbook method

34. Diagnostic evaluation ascertains
A. Students performance at the beginning of instructions
B. Learning progress and failures during instructions
C. Degree of achievement of instructions at the end
D. Causes and remedies of persistent learning problems during instructions

35. Instructional aids are used by the teacher to
A. glorify the class
B. attract the students
C. clarify the concepts
D. ensure discipline

36. Attitude of the teacher that affects teaching pertains to
A. Affective domain
B. Cognitive domain
C. Connative domain
D. Psychomotor domain

37. "Education is the manifestation of perfection already in man" was stated by
A. M.K. Gandhi
B. R.N. Tagore
C. Swami Vivekanand
D. Sri Aurobindo

38. When academicians are called to deliver lecture or presentation to an audience on certain topics or a set of topics of educational nature, it is called
A. Training Program B. Seminar
C. Workshop D. Symposium

39. The core elements of a dissertation are
A. Introduction; Data Collection; Data Analysis; Conclusions and Recommendations
B. Executive Summary; Literature review; Data gathered; Conclusions; Bibliography
C. Research Plan; Research Data; Analysis; References
D. Introduction; Literature Review; Research Methodology; Results; Discussion and Conclusion

40. What is a Research Design?
A. A way of conducting research that is not grounded in theory
B. The choice between using qualitative or quantitative methods
C. The style in which you present your research findings e.g. a graph
D. A framework for every stage of the collection and analysis of data

41. 'Sampling Cases' means
A. Sampling using a sampling frame
B. Identifying people who are suitable for research
C. Literally the researcher's brief case
D. Sampling of people, newspapers, television programmes etc.

42. The frequency distribution of a research data which is symmetrical in shape similar to a normal distribution but center peak is much higher, is
A. Skewed B. Mesokurtic
C. Leptokurtic D. Platykurtic

43. When planning to do as social research, it is better to
A. approach the topic with an open mind
B. do a pilot study before getting stuck into it
C. be familiar with literature on the topic
D. forget about theory because this is a very practical

44. In the classroom, the teacher sends the message either as words or images. The students are really
A. Encoders B. Decoders
C. Agitators D. Propagators

45. Media is known as
A. First Estate B. Second Estate
C. Third Estate D. Fourth Estate

46. The mode of communication that involves a single source transmitting information to a large number of receivers simultaneously, is called
A. Group Communication

B. Mass Communication
C. Intrapersonal Communication
D. Interpersonal Communication

47. A smart classroom is a teaching space which has
(*i*) Smart portion with a touch panel control system
(*ii*) PC/Laptop connection and DVD/VCR player
(*iii*) Document camera and specialized software
(*iv*) Projector and screen
Select the correct answer from the codes given below:
A. (*i*) and (*ii*) only
B. (*ii*) and (*iv*) only
C. (*i*), (*ii*) and (*iii*) only
D. (*i*), (*ii*), (*iii*) and (*iv*)

48. The term 'Yellow Journalism' refers to
A. sensational news about terrorism and violence
B. sensationalism and exaggeration to attract readers/viewers
C. sensational news about arts and culture
D. sensational news prints in yellow paper

49. The next term in the series:
2, 7, 28, 63, 126, ...
is
A. 215 B. 245
C. 276 D. 296

50. The next term in the series:
AB, ED, IH, NM, ...
is
A. TS B. ST
C. TU D. SU

51. If STREAMERS is coded as UVTGALDQR, then KNOWLEDGE will be coded as
A. MQPYLCDFD B. MPQYLDCFD
C. PMYQLDFCD D. YMQPLDDFC

52. A is brother of B. B is the brother of C. C is the husband of D. E is the father of A. D is related to E as
A. Daughter B. Daughter-in-law
C. Sister-in-law D. Sister

53. Two numbers are in the ratio 3 : 5. If 9 is subtracted from the numbers, the ratio becomes 12 : 23. The numbers are
A. 30, 50 B. 36, 60
C. 33, 55 D. 42, 70

54. The mean of the ages of father and his son is 27 years. After 18 years, father will be twice as old as his son. Their present ages are
A. 42, 12 B. 40, 14
C. 30, 24 D. 36, 18

55. Digital Empowerment means
(*i*) Universal digit literacy.
(*ii*) Universal access to all digital resources.
(*iii*) Collaborative digital platform for participative governance.
(*iv*) Probability of all entitlements for individuals through cloud.
Choose the correct answer from the codes given below:
A. (*i*) and (*ii*) only
B. (*ii*) and (*iii*) only
C. (*i*), (*ii*) and (*iii*) only
D. (*i*), (*ii*), (*iii*) and (*iv*)

Directions (Qs. 56 to 60): *Read the following passage carefully and answer questions.*

The literary distaste for politics, however, seems to be focused not so much on the largely murky practice of politics in itself as a subject of literary representation but rather more on how it is often depicted in literature, *i.e.,* on the very politics of such representation. A political novel often turns out to be not merely a novel about politics but a novel with a politics of its own, for it seeks not merely to show us how things are but has fairly definite ideas about how things should be, and precisely what one should think and do in order to make things move in that desired direction. In short, it seeks to convert and enlist the reader to a particular cause or ideology: it often is (in an only too familiar phrase) not literature but propaganda. This is said to violate the very spirit of literature which is to broaden our understanding of the world and the range of our sympathies rather than to narrow them down through partisan commitment. As John Keats said, 'We hate poetry that has a palpable design upon us'.

Another reason why politics does not seem amenable to the highest kind of literary representation seems to arise from the fact that politics by its very nature is constituted of ideas and ideologies. If political situations do not lend themselves to happy literary treatment, political ideas present perhaps an even greater problem in this regard. Literature, it is argued, is about human experiences rather than about intellectual abstractions; it deals in what is called the 'felt reality' of human flesh and blood, and in sap and savour (*rasa*) rather than in arid and lifeless ideas. In an extensive discussion of the matter in her book *Ideas and the Novel,* the American novelist Mary McCarthy observed that 'ideas are still today felt to be unsightly in the novel' though that was not so in 'former days', *i.e.*, in the 18th and 19th centuries. Her formulation of the precise nature of the incompatibility between ideas on the one hand and the novel no the other betrays perhaps a divided conscience in the matter and a sense of dilemma shared by many writers and readers: 'An idea cannot have loose ends, but a novel. I almost think, needs them. Nevertheless, there is enough in common for the novelists to feel .... the attraction of ideas while taking up arms against them – most often with weapons of mockery.'

56. A political novel reveals
   A. Reality of the things
   B. Writer's perception
   C. Particular ideology of the readers
   D. The spirit of literature

57. The constructs of politics by its nature is
   A. Prevalent political situation
   B. Ideas and Ideologies
   C. Political propaganda
   D. Understanding of human nature

58. Literature deals with
   A. Human experiences in politics
   B. Intellectual abstractions
   C. Dry and empty ideas
   D. Felt reality of human life

59. The observation of the novelist, Mary McCarthy reveals
   A. unseen felt ideas of today in the novel
   B. dichotomy of conscience on political ideas and novels
   C. compatibility between idea and novel
   D. endless ideas and novels

60. According to the passage, a political novel often turns out to be a
   A. Literary distaste for politics
   B. Literary representation of politics
   C. Novel with its own politics
   D. Depiction of murky practice of politics

ANSWERS

1	2	3	4	5	6	7	8	9	10
A	D	D	C	B	A	D	A	A	B
11	**12**	**13**	**14**	**15**	**16**	**17**	**18**	**19**	**20**
A	A	B	A	C	A	B	C	C	B
21	**22**	**23**	**24**	**25**	**26**	**27**	**28**	**29**	**30**
B	A	D	B	C	A	A	B	B	D
31	**32**	**33**	**34**	**35**	**36**	**37**	**38**	**39**	**40**
C	D	B	D	C	A	C	B	D	D
41	**42**	**43**	**44**	**45**	**46**	**47**	**48**	**49**	**50**
D	C	C	B	D	B	D	B	A	A
51	**52**	**53**	**54**	**55**	**56**	**57**	**58**	**59**	**60**
B	B	C	A	D	B	B	D	A	C

SOME SELECTED EXPLANATORY ANSWERS

3. Elements of A = u, r, p, s (honest)
Elements of B = x, r, p, q (sincere)
Elements of C = p, q, s, y (politician)
Hence (honest and politician but not sincere) p, q, s are sincere.
$\therefore$ Required code is S which is in A and C.

7. Power 800 – 500 = 300

$$\% = \frac{300}{500} \times 100 = 60\%$$

Industry 450 – 200 = 250

$$\% = \frac{250}{200} \times 100 = 125\%$$

Commercial 320 – 150 = 170

$$\% = \frac{170}{150} \times 100$$

$$= \frac{340}{3} = 113\%$$

Agriculture 200 – 80 = 120

$$\% = \frac{120}{80} \times 100 = 150\%$$

Domestic 180 – 100 = 80

$$\% = \frac{80}{100} \times 100 = 80\%$$

Hence, maximum growth in CO_2 is Agriculture.

8. Total emissions of CO_2 in 2005
= 500 + 200 + 150 + 80 + 100
= 1030
Total emissions of CO_2 in 2009
= 800 + 450 + 320 + 200 + 180
= 1950
increased = 1950 – 1030 = 920

$$\% \text{ increased} = \frac{920}{1030} \times 100 = 89.32\%.$$

9. In power sector 2005 to 2006

$$= \frac{100}{500} \times 100 = 20\%$$

$$\text{In 2006 to 2007} = \frac{50}{600} \times 100 = 8.33\%$$

$$\text{In 2007 to 2008} = \frac{50}{650} \times 100 = 7.69\%$$

$$\text{In 2008 to 2009} = \frac{100}{700} \times 100 = 14.28\%$$

Average Annual growth rate

$$= \frac{50.30}{4} = 12.57\%.$$

10. $\text{Required \% in 2008} = \frac{700}{1700} \times 100$

$$= \frac{700}{17} = 41.18\%.$$

11. Required year = 2005.

12. Growth of CO_2 from power sector during 2005 to 2009
= 800 – 500 = 300

$$\% \text{ growth} = \frac{300}{500} \times 100 = 60\%.$$

49. 2 7 28 63 126 215
↓ ↓ ↓ ↓ ↓
$2^3 - 1$ $3^3 - 1$ $4^3 - 1$ $5^3 - 1$ $6^3 - 1$
Hence, the next term in the series will be 215.

53. Let the numbers are $3x$ and $5x$
According to the question,

$$\frac{3x-9}{5x-9} = \frac{12}{23}$$

$\Rightarrow$ $69x - 207 = 60x - 108$
$\Rightarrow$ $9x = 99$
$\Rightarrow$ $x = 11$
$\therefore$ Numbers are 33 and 55.

54. Let present age of father = x years
and present age of son = y years

$$x + y = 2 \times 27 = 54$$

$$\Rightarrow \quad x = 54 - y$$

After 18 years, father's age = $(x + 18)$ years
After 18 years, son's age = $(y + 18)$ years
According to the question,

$$x + 18 = 2\,(y + 18)$$

$$\Rightarrow \quad x + 18 = 2y + 36$$

$$\Rightarrow \quad x - 2y = 18$$

$$\Rightarrow \quad 54 - y - 2y = 18$$

$$\Rightarrow \quad -3y = -\,36$$

$$\Rightarrow \quad y = 12$$

$$x = 54 - 12 = 42$$

Hence, present age of father
= 42 years
and present age of son
= 12 years.

16. Remainder

$$35 \div 2 = 17 + 1$$

$$17 \div 2 = 8 + 1$$

$$8 \div 2 = 4 + 0$$

$$4 \div 2 = 2 + 0$$

$$2 \div 2 = 1 + 0$$

$$1 \div 2 = 0 + 1$$

$$\therefore \quad 35 = 100011$$

Hence, binary equivalent of decimal number
35 = 100011.

Previous Years' Paper (Solved)

UGC-NET (JRF) EXAM JUNE, 2014*

PAPER–I

Note : This paper contains **Sixty (60)** multiple-choice questions, each question carrying **two (2)** marks. Candidate is expected to answer any **fifty (50)** questions. In case more than **fifty (50)** questions are attempted, only the first **fifty (50)** questions will be evaluated.

1. "If a large diamond is cut up into little bits, it will lose its value just as an army is divided up into small units of soldiers, it loses its strength."

The argument put above may be called as

A. Analogical B. Deductive

C. Statistical D. Causal

2. Given below are some characteristics of logical argument. Select the code which expresses a characteristic which is not of inductive in character.

A. The conclusion is claimed to follow from its premises.

B. The conclusion is based on causal relation.

C. The conclusion conclusively follows from its premises.

D. The conclusion is based on observation and experiment.

3. If two propositions having the same subject and predicate terms can both be true but can not both be false, the relation between those two propositions is called

A. contradictory B. contrary

C. subcontrary D. subaltern

4. One writes all numbers from 50 to 99 without the digits 2 and 7. How many numbers have been written?

A. 32 B. 36

C. 40 D. 38

5. Given below is a diagram of three circles A, B and C enter-related with each other. The circle A represents the class of Indians, the circle B represents the class of scientists and circle C represents the class of politicians. p, q, r, s ... represent different regions. Select the code containing the region that indicates the class of Indian scientists who are not politicians.

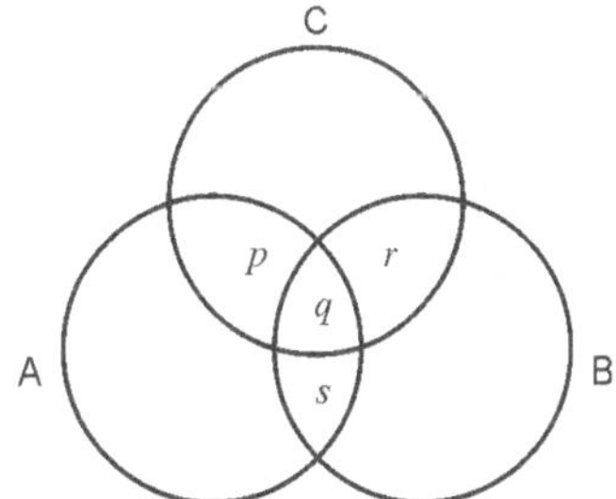

Codes :

A. q and s only B. s only

C. s and r only D. p, q and s only

6. Given below are two premises and four conclusions drawn from those premises. Select the code that expresses conclusion drawn validly from the premises (separately or jointly).

Premises :

(*a*) All dogs are mammals

(*b*) No cats are dogs

Conclusions :

(*i*) No cats are mammals

(*ii*) Some cats are mammals

(*iii*) No dogs are cats

(*iv*) No dogs are non-mammals

Codes :

A. (*i*) only B. (*i*) and (*ii*)

C. (*iii*) and (*iv*) D. (*ii*) and (*iii*)

* Held on 29-06-2014

Read the following table carefully. Based upon this table answer questions from 7 to 11 :

Net area under irrigation by sources in a country

(in Thousand Hectares)

Year	Govern-ment canals	Private canals	Tanks	Tube-wells & other wells	Other Sources	Total
1997-98	17117	211	2593	32090	3102	55173
1998-99	17093	212	2792	33988	3326	57411
1999-00	16842	194	2535	34623	2915	57109
2000-01	15748	203	2449	33796	2880	55076
2001-02	15031	209	2179	34906	4347	56672
2002-03	13863	206	1802	34250	3657	53778
2003-04	14444	206	1908	35779	4281	56618
2004-05	14696	206	1727	34785	7453	58867
2005-06	15268	207	2034	35372	7314	60196

7. Find out the source of Irrigation that has registered the maximum improvement in terms of percentage of Net irrigated area during 2002-03 and 2003-04.
A. Government canals
B. Tanks
C. Tube-wells and other wells
D. Other sources

8. In which of the following years, Net irrigation by tanks increased at the highest rate?
A. 1998-99 B. 2000-01
C. 2003-04 D. 2005-06

9. Identify the source of Irrigation that has recorded the maximum incidence of negative growth in terms of Net irrigated area during the years given in the table.
A. Government canals
B. Private canals
C. Tube-wells and other wells
D. Other sources

10. In which of the following years, share of the tube-wells and other wells in the total net irrigated area was the highest?
A. 1998-99 B. 2000-01
C. 2002-03 D. 2004-05

11. Which of the following sources of Irrigation has registered the largest percentage of decline in Net area under irrigation during 1997-98 and 2005-06?
A. Government canals
B. Private canals
C. Tanks
D. Other sources

12. Which one of the following is not a/an image/ graphic file format?
A. PNG B. GIF
C. BMP D. GUI

13. The first web browser is
A. Internet Explorer B. Netscape
C. World Wide Web D. Firefox

14. When a computer is booting, BIOS is loaded to the memory by
A. RAM B. ROM
C. CD-ROM D. TCP

15. Which one of the following is not the same as the other three?
A. MAC address B. Hardware address
C. Physical address D. IP address

16. Identify the IP address from the following:
A. 300 · 215 · 317 · 3
B. 302 · 215 @ 417 · 5
C. 202 · 50 · 20 · 148
D. 202 - 50 - 20 - 148

17. The acronym FIP stands for
A. File Transfer Protocol
B. Fast Transfer Protocol
C. File Tracking Protocol
D. File Transfer Procedure

18. Which of the following cities has been worst affected by urban smog in recent times?
A. Paris B. London
C. Los Angeles D. Beijing

19. The primary source of organic pollution in fresh water bodies is
A. run-off urban areas
B. run-off from agricultural forms
C. sewage effluents
D. industrial effluents

20. 'Lahar' is a natural disaster involving
A. eruption of large amount of material
B. strong winds
C. strong water waves
D. strong winds and water waves

21. The population of India is about 1.2 billion. Take the average consumption of energy per person per year in India as 30 Mega Joules. If this consumption is met by carbon based fuels and the rate of carbon emissions per kilojoule is 15 × 106 kgs, the total carbon emissions per year from India will be

A. 54 million metric tons
B. 540 million metric tons
C. 5400 million metric tons
D. 2400 million metric tons

22. The National Disaster Management Authority functions under the Union Ministry of

A. Environment
B. Water Resources
C. Home Affairs
D. Defence

23. Match List-I and List-II and select the correct answer from the codes given below:

List-I	***List-II***
(*a*) Flood	1. Lack of rainfall of sufficient duration
(*b*) Drought	2. Tremors produced by the passage of vibratory waves through the rocks of the earth
(*c*) Earthquake	3. A vent through which molted substances come out
(*d*) Volcano	4. Excess rain and uneven distribution of water

Codes :

	(*a*)	(*b*)	(*c*)	(*d*)
A.	4	1	2	3
B.	2	3	4	1
C.	3	4	2	1
D.	4	3	1	2

24. Which one of the following greenhouse gases has the shortest residence time in the atmosphere?

A. Chlorofluorocarbon
B. Carbon dioxide
C. Methane
D. Nitrous oxide

25. In order to avoid catastrophic consequences of climate change, there is general agreement among the countries of the world to limit the rise in average surface temperature of earth compared to that of pre-industrial times by

A. 1.5 °C to 2 °C
B. 2.0 °C to 3.5 °C
C. 0.5 °C to 1.0 °C
D. 0.25 °C to 0.5 °C

26. Who among the following is the de facto executive head of the Planning Commission?

A. Chairman
B. Deputy Chairman
C. Minister of State for Planning
D. Member Secretary

27. Education as a subject of legislation figures in the

A. Union List   B. State List
C. Concurrent List   D. Residuary Powers

28. Which of the following are Central Universities?

1. Pondicherry University
2. Vishwa Bharati
3. H.N.B. Garhwal University
4. Kurukshetra University

Select the correct answer from the code given below:

Codes:

A. 1, 2 and 3   B. 1, 3 and 4
C. 2, 3 and 4   D. 1, 2 and 4

29. Consider the following statements and select the correct answer from the code given below:

(*i*) Rajasthan receives the highest solar radiation in the country.
(*ii*) India has the fifth largest installed wind power in the world.
(*iii*) The maximum amount of wind power is contributed by Tamil Nadu.
(*iv*) The primary source of uranium in India is Jaduguda.

Codes :

A. (*i*) and (*ii*)   B. (*i*), (*ii*) and (*iii*)
C. (*ii*) and (*iii*)   D. (*i*) and (*iv*)

30. Which of the following universities has adopted the meta university concept?
A. Assam University
B. Delhi University
C. Hyderabad University
D. Pondicherry University

31. Which of the following statements are correct about a Central University?
1. Central University is established under an Act of Parliament
2. The President of India acts as the visitor of the University.
3. The President has the power to nominate some members to the Executive Committee or the Board of Management of the University.
4. The President occasionally presides over the meetings of the Executive Committee or Court.

Select the correct answer from the code given below:

A. 1, 2 and 4 B. 1, 3 and 4
C. 1, 2 and 3 B. 1, 2, 3 and 4

32. Consider the statement which is followed by two arguments (*i*) and (*ii*).

Statement : India should have a very strong and powerful Lokpal.

Arguments : (*i*) Yes, it will go a long in eliminating corruption in bureaucracy.
(*ii*) No, it will discourage honest officers from making quick decisions.

Codes:
A. Only argument (*i*) is strong.
B. Only argument (*ii*) is strong.
C. Both the arguments are strong.
D. Neither of the arguments is strong.

33. Which one of the following is the best method of teaching?
A. Lecture B. Discussion
C. Demonstration D. Narration

34. Dyslexia is associated with
A. mental disorder
B. behavioural disorder
C. reading disorder
D. writing disorder

35. The e-content generation for under-graduate courses has been assigned by the Ministry of Human Resource Development to
A. INFLIBNET
B. Consortium for Educational Communication.
C. National Knowledge Commission
D. Indira Gandhi National Open University

36. Classroom communication is normally considered as
A. effective B. cognitive
C. affective D. selective

37. Which one of the following is considered a sign of motivated teaching?
A. Students asking questions
B. Maximum attendance of the students
C. Pin drop silence in the classroom
D. Students taking notes

38. In a thesis, figures and tables are included in
A. the appendix
B. a separate chapter
C. the concluding chapter
D. the text itself

39. A thesis statement is
A. an observation B. a fact
C. an assertion D. a discussion

40. The research approach of Max Weber to understand how people create meanings in natural settings is identified as
A. positive paradigm
B. critical paradigm
C. natural paradigm
D. interpretative paradigm

41. Which one of the following is a non-probability sampling?
A. Simple random B. Purposive
C. Systematic D. Stratified

42. Identify the category of evaluation that assesses the learning progress to provide continuous feedback to the students during instruction.
A. Placement B. Diagnostic
C. Formative D. Summative

43. The research stream of immediate application is

A. Conceptual research
B. Action research
C. Fundamental research
D. Empirical research

44. Who among the following, propounded the concept of paradigm?

A. Peter Haggett
B. Von Thunen
C. Thomas Kuhn
D. John K. Wright

Read the following passage carefully and answer questions 45 to 49:

Traditional Indian Values must be viewed both from the angle of the individual and from that of the geographically delimited agglomeration of peoples or groups enjoying a common system of leadership which we call the 'State'. The Indian 'State's' special feature is the peaceful, or perhaps mostly peaceful, co-existence of social groups of various historical provenances which mutually adhere in a geographical, economic, and political sense, without ever assimilating to each other in social terms, in ways of thinking, or even in language. Modern Indian law will determine certain rules, especially in relation to the regime of the family, upon the basis of how the loin-cloth is tied, or how the turban is worn, for this may identify the litigants as members of a regional group, and therefore as participants in its traditional law, though their ancestors left the region three or four centuries earlier. The use of the word 'State' above must not mislead us. There was no such thing as a conflict between the individual and the State, atleast before foreign governments became established, just as there was no concept of state 'sovereignty' or of any church-and-state dichotomy.

Modern Indian 'secularism' has an admittedly peculiar feature : It requires the state to make a fair distribution of attention and support amongst all religions. These blessed aspects of India's famed tolerance (Indian kings so rarely persecuted religious groups that the exceptions prove the rule) at once struck Portuguese and other European visitors to the West Coast of India in the sixteenth century, and the impression made upon them in this and other ways gave rise, at one remove, to the basic constitution of Thomas More's Utopia. There is little about modern India that strikes one at once as Utopian : but the insistence upon the inculcation of norms, and the absence of bigotry and institutionalized exploitation of human or natural resources, are two very different features which link the realities of India and her tradition with the essence of all Utopians.

45. The author uses the world 'State' to highlight.

A. Antagonistic relationship between the state and the individual throughout the period of history.
B. Absence of conflict between the state and the individuals upto a point in time.
C. The concept of state sovereignty.
D. Dependence on religion.

46. Which one is the peculiar feature of modern Indian 'Secularism'?

A. No discrimination on religious considerations
B. Total indifference to religion.
C. No space for social identity
D. Disregard for social law

47. The basic construction of Thomas More's Utopia was inspired by

A. Indian tradition of religious tolerance.
B. Persecution of religious groups by Indian rulers.
C. Social inequality in India.
D. European perception of Indian State.

48. What is the striking feature of modern India?

A. A replica of Utopian State
B. Uniform laws
C. Adherence to traditional values
D. Absence of Bigotry

49. Which of the following is a special feature of the Indian State?

A. Peaceful co-existence of people under a common system of leadership.
B. Peaceful co-existence of social groups of different historical provenances attached to each other in a geographical, economic and political sense.
C. Social integration of all groups.
D. Cultural assimilation of all social groups.

50. The Telephone Model of Communication was first developed in the area of

A. Technological theory
B. Dispersion theory
C. Minimal effects theory
D. Information theory

51. The Dada Saheb Phalke Award for 2013 has been conferred on

A. Karan Johar B. Amir Khan
C. Asha Bhonsle D. Gulzar

52. Photographs are not easy to

A. publish B. secure
C. decode D. change

53. The grains that appear on a television set when operated are also referred to as

A. sparks B. green dots
C. snow D. rain drops

54. In circular communication, the encoder becomes a decoder when there is

A. noise B. audience
C. criticality D. feedback

55. Break-down in verbal communication is described as

A. Short circuit B. Contradiction
C. Unevenness D. Entropy

56. In certain coding method, the word QUESTION is encoded as DOMESTIC. In this coding, what is the code word for the word RESPONSE?

A. OMESUCEM B. OMESICSM
C. OMESICEM D. OMESISCM

57. If the series, 4, 5, 8, 13, 14, 17, 22, ... is continued in the same pattern, which one of the following is not a term of this series?

A. 31 B. 32
C. 33 D. 35

58. Complete the series BB, FE, II, ML, PP, ... by choosing one of the following option given:

A. TS B. ST
C. RS D. SR

59. A man started walking from his house towards south. After walking 6 km, he turned to his left and walked 5 km. Then he walked further 3 km after turning left. He then turned to his left and continued his walk for 9 km. How far is he away from his house?

A. 3 km B. 4 km
C. 5 km D. 6 km

60. In a post-office, stamps of three different denominations of ₹ 7, ₹ 8, ₹ 10 are available. The exact amount for which one cannot buy stamps is

A. 19 B. 20
C. 23 D. 29

ANSWERS

1	2	3	4	5	6	7	8	9	10
A	B	D	A	B	C	D	D	A	C
11	**12**	**13**	**14**	**15**	**16**	**17**	**18**	**19**	**20**
A	D	C	B	D	C	A	D	C	A
21	**22**	**23**	**24**	**25**	**26**	**27**	**28**	**29**	**30**
C	C	A	C	A	B	C	A	B	B
31	**32**	**33**	**34**	**35**	**36**	**37**	**38**	**39**	**40**
C	A	C	C	B	B	A	D	D	D
41	**42**	**43**	**44**	**45**	**46**	**47**	**48**	**49**	**50**
B	C	B	C	B	A	A	A	B	B
51	**52**	**53**	**54**	**55**	**56**	**57**	**58**	**59**	**60**
D	C	C	D	C	C	C	A	C	A

SOME SELECTED EXPLANATORY ANSWERS

4. 50 51 (52) 53 54 55 56 (57) 58 59
60 61 (62) 63 64 65 66 (67) 68 69
(70) (71) (72) (73) (74) (75) (76) (77) (78) (79)
80 81 (82) 83 84 85 86 (87) 88 89
90 91 (92) 93 94 95 96 (97) 98 99

$\therefore$ 50 – 18 = 32

He has written 32 numbers.

5.

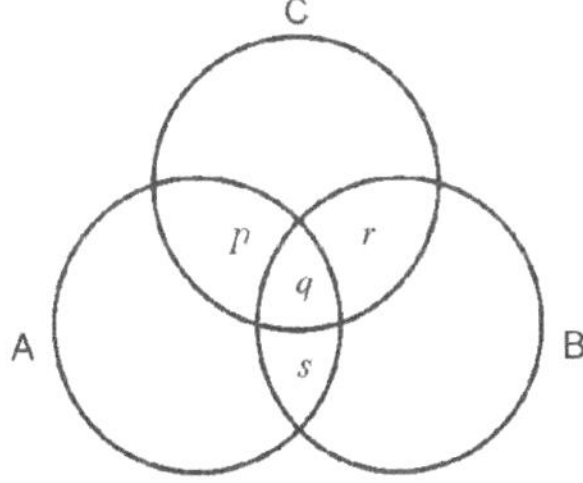

⊙ A represents – Indians
⊙ B represents – Scientists
⊙ C represents – Politicians
p, *q*, *r*, *s*.... represents different regions
Required code is (B) *s* only.

6.

or

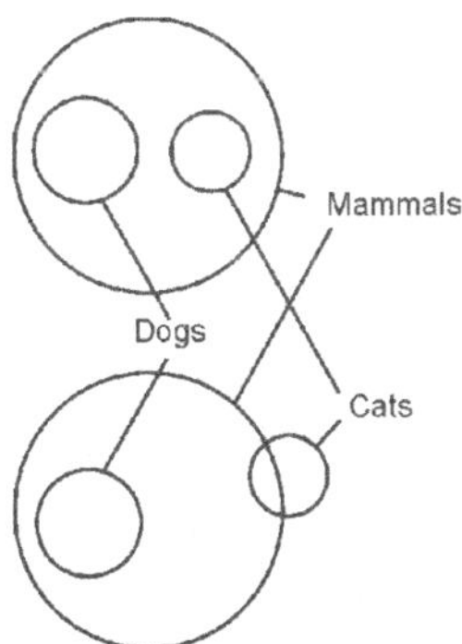

As from premise-II,
No cats are dogs,
So, No dogs are cats.
Again from premise-I
All dogs are mammals
So, No dogs are non-mammals.

7. A. Government canals

$= 14444 - 13863 = 581$

$$\% = \frac{581}{13863} \times 100 = \frac{58100}{13863} = 4\%$$

B. Tanks $= 1908 - 1802 = 106$

$$\% = \frac{106}{1802} \times 100 = \frac{10600}{1802} = 5.9\%$$

C. Tube-wells and other wells

$= 35779 - 34250 = 1529$

$$\% = \frac{1529}{34250} \times 100 = \frac{152900}{34250} = 4\%$$

D. Other sources

$= 4281 - 3657 = 624$

$$\% = \frac{624}{3657} \times 100 = \frac{62400}{3657} = 17\%$$

Clearly (D) gives maximum.
Hence, correct answer is (D).

8. A. 1998-99 $\Rightarrow 2792 - 2593 = 199$

$$\% = \frac{199}{2593} \times 100 = \frac{19900}{2593} = 7\%$$

B. 2000-01 $\Rightarrow 2449 - 2535 = -86$

negative sign shows not increase.

C. 2003-04 $\Rightarrow 1908 - 1802 = 106$

$$\% = \frac{106}{1802} \times 100 = \frac{10600}{1802} = 5.8\%$$

D. 2005-06 $\Rightarrow 2034 - 1727 = 307$

$$\% = \frac{307}{1727} \times 100 = \frac{30700}{1727} = 17\%$$

Hence, 2005-06 net irrigation by tanks increases at the highest rate.

9. Required answer is (A) Government canals.

10. Required year is 2002-03.

11. Required Sources of irrigation is Government canals.

16. The correct format to write IP address is to use dots between each set of digits.

17. FTP stands for file transfer protocol and is a method by which you can transfer files from one computer to another.

18. Beijing along with Tianjin and Hebei province & central and western Shandong province is affected by the worst urban smog in recent times. Bejing has a four-tier alert system, using blue, yellow, orrange and red to indicate the air pollution level. A red alert indicates the most serious air pollution (AQI above 300) for 3 consecutive days. An orange alert indicates heavy to serious air pollution (AQI between 200 and 300) alternately for 3 consecutive days. A yellow alert means severe pollution for 1 day or heavy pollution for 3 consecutive days.

19. The main source of freshwater pollution can be attributed to discharge of untreated waste mainly sewage effluents.

20. Lahar is a natural disaster that involves eruption of large amount of material from volcano. The material flows down from a volcano, typically along a river valley is known as lahar.

56.

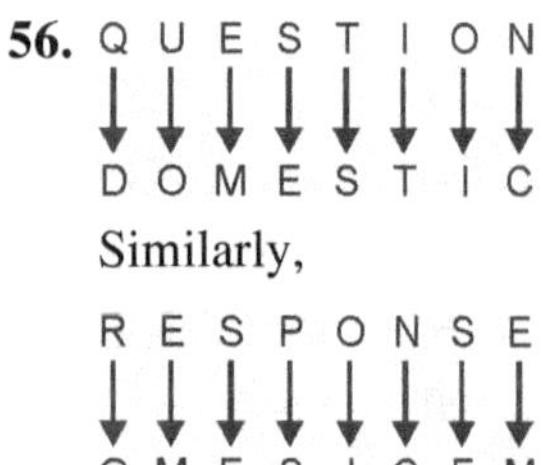

57.

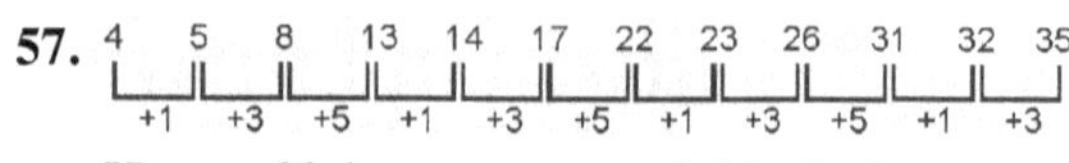

Hence, 33 is not a term of this Series.

58.

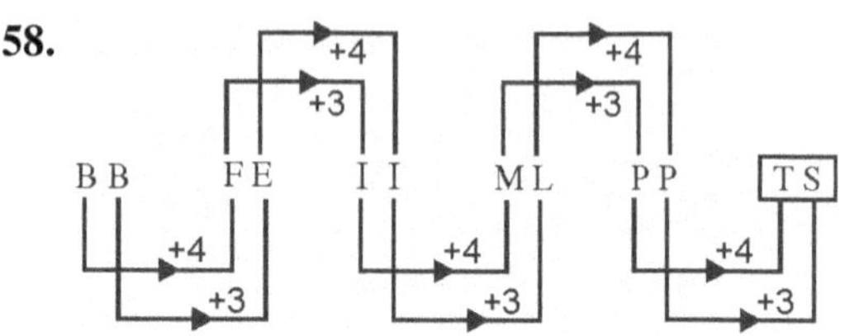

59.

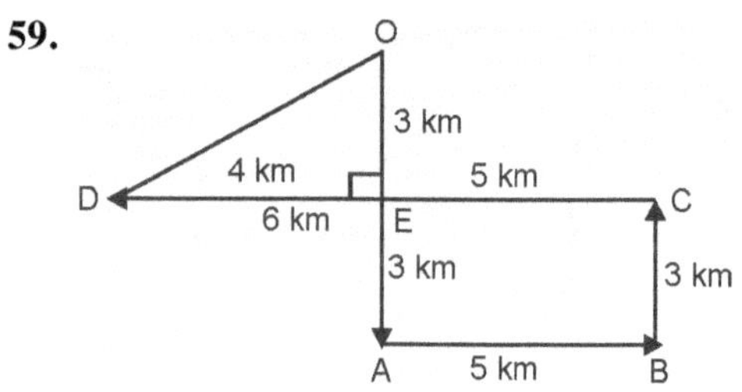

In ΔOED,

$$(OD)^2 = (4)^2 + (3)^2$$
$$= 16 + 9 = 25$$

$\therefore \quad OD = \sqrt{25} = 5$ km.

Hence, he is 5 km away from his house.

60. B. $20 = 10 \times 2 = 20$

C. $23 = 8 \times 2 + 7 \times 1$
$= 16 + 7 = 23$

D. $29 = 7 \times 3 + 8 \times 1$
$= 21 + 8 = 29$

A. $19 = 7 \times 2 + 5 = 8 \times 2 + 3$
$= 10 \times 1 + 8 \times 1 + 1$
$= 10 \times 1 + 7 \times 1 + 2$

Hence, the exact amount for which one can not buy stamps is 19.

Previous Years' Paper (Solved)

UGC-NET (JRF) Exam December, 2013

PAPER–I

Note: *This paper contains* ***Sixty (60)*** *multiple choice questions, each question carrying* ***two (2)*** *marks. Attempt any* ***Fifty (50)*** *questions.*

1. Which is the main objective of research ?
   A. To review the literature
   B. To summarize what is already known
   C. To get an academic degree
   D. To discover new facts or to make fresh interpretation of known facts

2. Sampling error decreases with the
   A. decrease in sample size
   B. increase in sample size
   C. process of randomization
   D. process of analysis

3. The principles of fundamental research are used in
   A. action research
   B. applied research
   C. philosophical research
   D. historical research

4. Users who use media for their own ends are identified as
   A. Passive audience
   B. Active audience
   C. Positive audience
   D. Negative audience

5. Classroom communication can be described as
   A. Exploration
   B. Institutionalisation
   C. Unsignified narration
   D. Discourse

6. Ideological codes shape our collective
   A. Productions B. Perceptions
   C. Consumptions D. Creations

7. In communication, myths have power, but are
   A. uncultural. B. insignificant.
   C. imprecise. D. unpreferred.

8. The first multi-lingual news agency of India was
   A. Samachar
   B. API
   C. Hindustan Samachar
   D. Samachar Bharati

9. Organisational communication can also be equated with
   A. intra-personal communication.
   B. inter-personal communication.
   C. group communication.
   D. mass communication.

10. If two propositions having the same subject and predicate terms are such that one is the denial of the other, the relationship between them is called
   A. Contradictory B. Contrary
   C. Sub-contrary D. Sub-alternation

11. Ananya and Krishna can speak and follow English. Bulbul can write and speak Hindi as Archana does. Archana talks with Ananya also in Bengali. Krishna can not follow Bengali. Bulbul talks with Ananya in Hindi. Who can speak and follow English, Hindi and Bengali?
   A. Archana B. Bulbul
   C. Ananya D. Krishna

12. A stipulative definition may be said to be
   A. Always true
   B. Always false
   C. Sometimes true, sometimes false
   D. Neither true nor false

13. When the conclusion of an argument follows from its premise/premises conclusively, the argument is called

A. Circular argument
B. Inductive argument
C. Deductive argument
D. Analogical argument

14. Saturn and Mars are planets like the earth. They borrow light from the Sun and moves around the Sun as the Earth does. So those planets are inhabited by various orders of creatures as the earth is. What type of argument is contained in the above passage ?

A. Deductive B. Astrological
C. Analogical D. Mathematical

15. Given below are two premises. Four conclusions are drawn from those two premises in four codes. Select the code that states the conclusion validly drawn.

Premises:

(*i*) All saints are religious. (major)
(*ii*) Some honest persons are saints. (minor)

Codes:

A. All saints are honest.
B. Some saints are honest.
C. Some honest persons are religious.
D. All religious persons are honest.

Following table provides details about the Foreign Tourist Arrivals (FTAs) in India from different regions of the world in different years. Study the table carefully and answer questions from 16 to 19 based on this table.

Region	**Number of Foreign Tourist Arrivals**		
	2007	**2008**	**2009**
Western Europe	1686083	1799525	1610086
North America	1007276	1027297	1024469
South Asia	982428	1051846	982633
South East Asia	303475	332925	348495
East Asia	352037	355230	318292
West Asia	171661	215542	201110
Total FTAs in India	5081504	5282603	5108579

16. Find out the region that contributed around 20 per cent of the total foreign tourist arrivals in India in 2009.

A. Western Europe B. North America
C. South Asia D. South East Asia

17. Which of the following regions has recorded the highest negative growth rate of foreign tourist arrivals in India in 2009?

A. Western Europe B. North America
C. South Asia D. West Asia

18. Find out the region that has been showing declining trend in terms of share of foreign tourist arrivals in India in 2008 and 2009.

A. Western Europe B. South East Asia
C. East Asia D. West Asia

19. Identify the region that has shown hyper growth rate of foreign tourist arrivals than the growth rate of the total FTAs in India in 2008.

A. Western Europe B. North America
C. South Asia D. East Asia

20. The post-industrial society is designated as

A. Information society
B. Technology society
C. Mediated society
D. Non-agricultural society

21. The initial efforts for internet based communication was for

A. Commercial communication
B. Military purposes
C. Personal interaction
D. Political campaigns

22. Internal communication within institutions is done through

A. LAN B. WAN
C. EBB D. MMS

23. Virtual reality provides

A. Sharp pictures
B. Individual audio
C. Participatory experience
D. Preview of new films

24. The first virtual university of India came up in

A. Andhra Pradesh B. Maharashtra
C. Uttar Pradesh D. Tamil Nadu

25. Arrange the following books in chronological order in which they appeared. Use the code given below :

(*i*) Limits to Growth
(*ii*) Silent Spring
(*iii*) Our Common Future
(*iv*) Resourceful Earth

Codes:

A. (*i*), (*iii*), (*iv*), (*ii*)
B. (*ii*), (*iii*), (*i*), (*iv*)
C. (*ii*), (*i*), (*iii*), (*iv*)
D. (*i*), (*ii*), (*iii*), (*iv*)

26. Which one of the following continents is at a greater risk of desertification?

A. Africa B. Asia
C. South America D. North America

27. "Women are closer to nature than men." What kind of perspective is this?

A. Realist B. Essentialist
C. Feminist D. Deep ecology

28. Which one of the following is not a matter a global concern in the removal of tropical forests?

A. Their ability to absorb the chemicals that contribute to depletion of ozone layer.
B. Their role in maintaining the oxygen and carbon balance of the earth.
C. Their ability to regulate surface and air temperatures, moisture content and reflectivity.
D. Their contribution to the biological diversity of the planet.

29. The most comprehensive approach to address the problems of man-environment interaction is one of the following:

A. Natural Resource Conservation Approach
B. Urban-industrial Growth Oriented Approach
C. Rural-agricultural Growth Oriented Approach
D. Watershed Development Approach

30. The major source of the pollutant gas, carbon mono-oxide (CO), in urban areas is

A. Thermal power sector
B. Transport sector
C. Industrial sector
D. Domestic sector

31. In a fuel cell driven vehicle, the energy is obtained from the combustion of

A. Methane B. Hydrogen
C. LPG D. CNG

32. Which one of the following Councils has been disbanded in 2013?

A. Distance Education Council (DEC)
B. National Council for Teacher Education (NCTE)
C. National Council of Educational Research and Training (NCERT)
D. National Assessment and Accreditation Council (NAAC)

33. Which of the following statements are correct about the National Assessment and Accreditation Council?

1. It is an autonomous institution.
2. It is tasked with the responsibility of assessing and accrediting institutions of higher education.
3. It is located in Delhi.
4. It has regional offices.

Select the correct answer from the codes given below:

Codes:

A. 1 and 3 B. 1 and 2
C. 1, 2 and 4 D. 2, 3 and 4

34. The power of the Supreme Court of India to decide disputes between two or more States falls under its

A. Advisory Jurisdiction
B. Appellate Jurisdiction
C. Original Jurisdiction
D. Writ Jurisdiction

35. Which of the following statements are correct?

1. There are seven Union Territories in India.
2. Two Union Territories have Legislative Assemblies
3. One Union Territory has a High Court.
4. One Union Territory is the capital of two States.

Select the correct answer from the codes given below :

A. 1 and 3 only B. 2 and 4 only
C. 2, 3 and 4 only D. 1, 2, 3 and 4

36. Which of the following statements are correct about the Central Information Commission?

1. The Central Information Commission is a statutory body.
2. The Chief Information Commissioner and other Information Commissioners are appointed by the President of India.
3. The Commission can impose a penalty upto a maximum of ₹ 25,000/-
4. It can punish an errant officer.

Select the correct answer from the codes given below:

Codes:

A. 1 and 2 only B. 1, 2 and 4
C. 1, 2 and 3 D. 2, 3 and 4

37. Who among the following conducted the CNN-IBN – The Hindu 2013 Election Tracker Survey across 267 constituencies in 18 States?

A. The Centre for the Study of Developing Societies (CSDS)
B. The Association for Democratic Reforms (ADR)
C. CNN and IBN
D. CNN, IBN and The Hindu

38. In certain code TEACHER is written as VGCEJGT. The code of CHILDREN will be

A. EKNJFTGP B. EJKNFTGP
C. KNJFGTP D. None of these

39. A person has to buy both apples and mangoes. The cost of one apple is ₹ 7/- whereas that of a mango is ₹ 5/-. If the person has ₹ 38, the number of apples he can buy is

A. 1 B. 2
C. 3 D. 4

40. A man pointing to a lady said, "The son of her only brother is the brother of my wife". The lady is related to the man as

A. Mother's sister
B. Grand mother
C. Mother-in-law
D. Sister of Father-in-law

41. In this series
6, 4, 1, 2, 2, 8, 7, 4, 2, 1, 5, 3, 8, 6, 2, 2, 7, 1, 4, 1, 3, 5, 8, 6,
how many pairs of successive numbers have a difference of 2 each ?

A. 4 B. 5
C. 6 D. 8

42. The mean marks obtained by a class of 40 students is 65. The mean marks of half of the students is found to be 45. The mean marks of the remaining students is

A. 85 B. 60
C. 70 D. 65

43. Anil is twice as old as Sunita. Three years ago, he was three times as old as Sunita. The present age of Anil is

A. 6 years B. 8 years
C. 12 years D. 16 years

44. Which of the following is a social network?

A. amazon.com B. eBay
C. gmail.com D. Twitter

45. The population information is called parameter while the corresponding sample information is known as

A. Universe B. Inference
C. Sampling design D. Statistics

Read the following passage carefully and answer questions 46 to 51 :

Heritage conservation practices improved worldwide after the International Centre for the Study of the Preservation and Restoration of Cultural Property (ICCROM) was established with UNESCO's assistance in 1959. The inter-governmental organisation with 126 member states has done a commendable job by training more than 4,000 professionals, providing practice standards, and sharing technical expertise. In this golden jubilee year, as we acknowledge its key role in global conservation, an assessment of international practices would be meaningful to the Indian conservation movement. Consistent investment, rigorous attention, and dedicated research and dissemination are some of the positive lessons to imbibe. Countries such as Italy have demonstrated that prioritising heritage with significant budget provision pays. On the other hand, India, which is no less endowed in terms of cultural capital, has a long way to go. Surveys indicate that in addition to the 6,600 protected monuments, there are over 60,000 equally valuable heritage structures that await attention. Besides the small group in the service of Archaeological Survey of India, there are only about 150 trained conservation professionals. In order to overcome this severe shortage the emphasis has been on setting up dedicated labs and training institutions. It would make much better sense for conservation to be made part of mainstream research and engineering institutes, as has been done in Europe. Increasing funding and building institutions are the relatively easy part. The real challenge is to redefine international approaches to address local contexts. Conservation cannot limit itself to enhancing the art-historical value of the heritage structures, which international charters perhaps overemphasise. The effort has to be broad-based : It must also serve as a means to improving the quality of life in the area where the heritage structures are located. The first task therefore is to integrate conservation efforts with sound development plans that take care of people living in the heritage vicinity. Unlike in western countries, many traditional building crafts survive in India, and conservation practices offer an avenue to support them. This has been acknowledged by the Indian National Trust for Art and Cultural Heritage charter for conservation but is yet to receive substantial state support. More strength for heritage conservation can be mobilised by aligning it with the green building movement. Heritage structures are essentially eco-friendly and conservation could become a vital part of the sustainable building practices campaign in future.

46. The outlook for conservation heritage changed

A. after the establishment of the International Centre for the Study of the Preservation and Restoration of Cultural Property.

B. after training the specialists in the field.

C. after extending UNESCO's assistance to the educational institutions.

D. after ASI's measures to protect the monuments.

47. The inter-government organization was appreciated because of

A. increasing number of members to 126.

B. imparting training to professionals and sharing technical expertise.

C. consistent investment in conservation.

D. its proactive role in renovation and restoration.

48. Indian conservation movement will be successful if there would be

A. Financial support from the Government of India.

B. Non-governmental organisations role and participation in the conservation movement.

C. consistent investment, rigorous attention, and dedicated research and dissemination of awareness for conservation.

D. Archaeological Survey of India's meaningful assistance.

49. As per the surveys of historical monuments in India, there is very small number of protected monuments. As per given the total number of monuments and enlisted number of protected monuments, percentage comes to

A. 10 per cent B. 11 per cent

C. 12 per cent D. 13 per cent

50. What should India learn from Europe to conserve our cultural heritage ?

(*i*) There should be significant budget provision to conserve our cultural heritage.

(*ii*) Establish dedicated labs and training institutions.

(*iii*) Force the government to provide sufficient funds.

(*iv*) Conservation should be made part of mainstream research and engineering institutes.

Choose correct answer from the codes given below :

A. (*i*), (*ii*), (*iii*), (*iv*) B. (*i*), (*ii*), (*iv*)

(C. (*i*), (*ii*) D. (*i*), (*iii*), (*iv*)

51. INTACH is known for its contribution for conservation of our cultural heritage. The full form of INTACH is

A. International Trust for Art and Cultural Heritage
B. Intra-national Trust for Art and Cultural Heritage
C. Integrated Trust for Art and Cultural Heritage
D. Indian National Trust for Art and Cultural Heritage

52. While delivering lecture if there is some disturbance in the class, a teacher should

A. keep quiet for a while and then continue.
B. punish those causing disturbance.
C. motivate to teach those causing disturbance.
D. not bother of what is happening in the class.

53. Effective teaching is a function of

A. Teacher's satisfaction.
B. Teacher's honesty and commitment.
C. Teacher's making students learn and understand.
D. Teacher's liking for professional excellence.

54. The most appropriate meaning of learning is

A. Acquisition of skills
B. Modification of behaviour
C. Personal adjustment
D. Inculcation of knowledge

55. Arrange the following teaching process in order :

(*i*) Relate the present knowledge with previous one
(*ii*) Evaluation
(*iii*) Reteaching
(*iv*) Formulating instructional objectives
(*v*) Presentation of instructional materials

A. (*i*), (*ii*), (*iii*), (*iv*), (*v*)
B. (*ii*), (*i*), (*iii*), (*iv*), (*v*)
C. (*v*), (*iv*), (*iii*), (*i*), (*ii*)
D. (*iv*), (*i*), (*v*), (*ii*), (*iii*)

56. CIET stands for

A. Centre for Integrated Education and Technology
B. Central Institute for Engineering and Technology
C. Central Institute for Education Technology
D. Centre for Integrated Evaluation Techniques.

57. Teacher's role at higher education level is to

A. provide information to students.
B. promote self learning in students.
C. encourage healthy competition among students.
D. help students to solve their problems.

58. The Verstehen School of Understanding was popularised by

A. German Social Scientists
B. American Philosophers
C. British Academicians
D. Italian Political Analysts

59. The sequential operations in scientific research are

A. Co-variation, Elimination of Spurious Relations, Generalisation, Theorisation
B. Generalisation, Co-variation, Theorisation, Elimination of Spurious Relations
C. Theorisation, Generalisation, Elimination of Spurious Relations, Co-variation
D. Elimination of Spurious Relations, Theorisation, Generalisation, Co-variation.

60. In sampling, the lottery method is used for

A. Interpretation
B. Theorisation
C. Conceptualisation
D. Randomisation

ANSWERS

1	2	3	4	5	6	7	8	9	10
D	B	B	B	D	B	C	C	C	A
11	**12**	**13**	**14**	**15**	**16**	**17**	**18**	**19**	**20**
C	D	C	C	C	B	D	A	C	A
21	**22**	**23**	**24**	**25**	**26**	**27**	**28**	**29**	**30**
B	A	C	D	C	A	B	A	D	B
31	**32**	**33**	**34**	**35**	**36**	**37**	**38**	**39**	**40**
B	A	B	C	D	C	A	B	D	D
41	**42**	**43**	**44**	**45**	**46**	**47**	**48**	**49**	**50**
C	A	C	D	D	A	B	C	B	B
51	**52**	**53**	**54**	**55**	**56**	**57**	**58**	**59**	**60**
D	C	C	B	D	C	B	A	A	D

SOME SELECTED EXPLANATORY ANSWERS

11.

Language:	Hindi	English	Bengali
Name:	Bulbul	Ananya	Archana
	Archana	Krishna	Ananya
	Ananya		

Hence, Ananya can speak & follow English, Hindi and Bengali.

15.

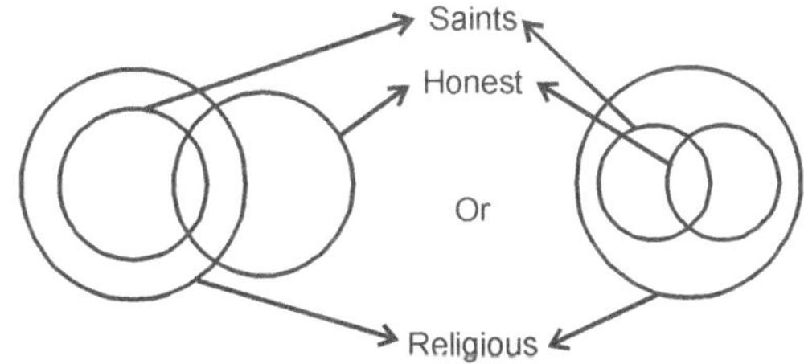

Here, there is no premises given to whether some or all saints are honests.

Hence, clear validly drawn is some honest persons are religious.

16. FTA contribution (in per cent) by different region in year 2009.

$$\text{Western Europe} = \frac{1610086}{5108579} \times 100 = 31.5\%$$

$$\text{North America} = \frac{1024469}{5108579} \times 100 = 20\%$$

$$\text{South Asia} = \frac{982633}{5108579} \times 100 = 19.23\%$$

$$\text{South East Asia} = \frac{348495}{5108579} \times 100 = 6.82\%$$

Hence, North America's contribution is around 20% of the total FTAs.

22. LAN — Local Area Network

This is an interconnection technique use to connect different PC installed within a small area like institutions.

24. The government of Tamil Nadu established the Tamil Virtual University (TVU) on 17 February 2001 as a Society. The university provides internet-based educational resources and opportunities for the Tamil diaspora as well as for others interested in learning the Tamil language and acquiring knowledge of the history, art, literature and culture of the Tamils.

30. Transport contributes to ambient air pollution, one of the most serious poblic health problems.

The main source of ambient air pollution is the combustion of fossil fuels by both stationary and mobile sources. The transportation sector is in general responsible for a significant share of the ambient air pollution in urban areas by emission of carbon monoxide. Ambient air quality problems tend to be most severe in urban areas where both population and pollution sources, particularly automobiles and industry, are most concentrated.

31. A hydrogen vehicle is a vehicle that uses hydrogen as its onboard fuel for motive power. Hydrogen vehicles include hydrogen fueled space rockets, as well as automobiles and other transportation vehicles. The power plants of such vehicles convert the chemical energy of hydrogen to mechanical energy either by burning hydrogen in an internal combustion engine, or by reacting hydrogen with oxygen in a fuel cell to run electric motors. Widespread use of hydrogen for fueling transportation is a key element of a proposed hydrogen economy.

38. 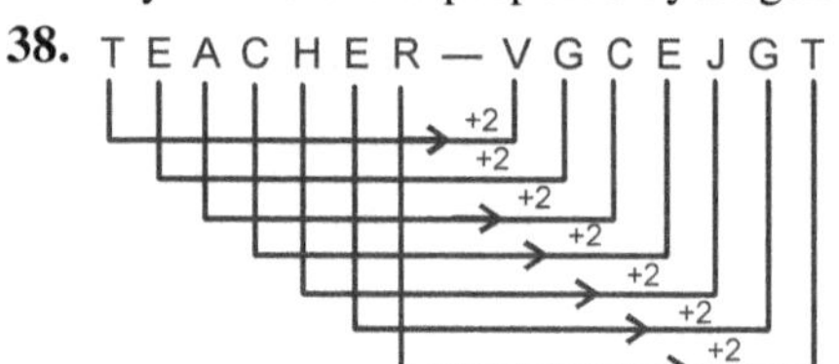

Similarly,

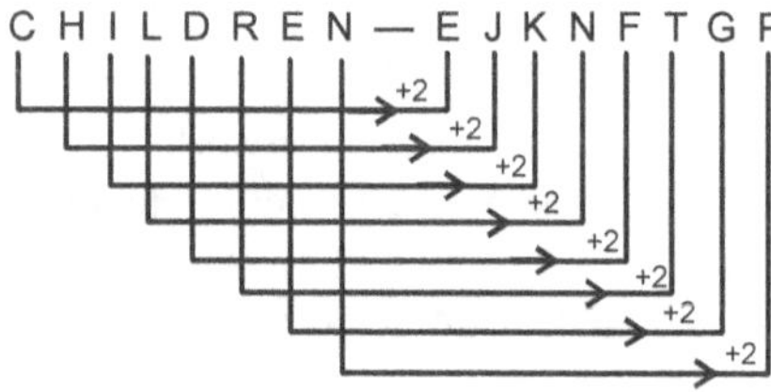

39. Let number of apples and mangoes bought by man is x and y respectively.

then,

$$7x + 5y = 38$$

for x, y an integer number, this is satisfied for $x = 4$, $y = 2$

Hence, number of apples = 4

41. Such pairs are (6, 4), (4, 2), (5, 3), (8, 6), (3, 5), (8, 6).

42. Total marks obtained by 40 students

$$= 65 \times 40 = 2600$$

Total marks obtained by 20 students

$$= 45 \times 20 = 900$$

Marks obtained by remaining 20 students

$$= 2600 - 900 = 1700$$

So, Average of marks obtained by remaining

$$20 \text{ students} = \frac{1700}{20} = 85.$$

43. Let Sunita's age is x yrs.

Then Anil's age is $2x$ yrs.

According to the question,

$$2x - 3 = 3(x - 3)$$

$$2x - 3 = 3x - 9$$

$$x = 6 \text{ yrs}$$

Hence, Anil's present age = $2x$ = 12 yrs.

44. amazon.com and gmail.com are websites used for mailing services. eBay is marketing site used for online sale/purchase while Twitter is a social networking site.

Previous Years' Paper (Solved)

UGC-NET (JRF) EXAM JUNE, 2013

PAPER–I

Note: *This paper contains **Sixty (60)** objective type questions, each question carrying **two (2)** marks. Attempt all the questions.*

1. Which one of the following references is written as per Modern Language Association (MLA) format?

A. Hall, Donald. Fundamentals of Electronics, New Delhi : Prentice Hall of India, 2005

B. Hall, Donald, Fundamentals of Electronics, New Delhi : Prentice Hall of India, 2005

C. Hall, Donald, Fundamentals of Electronics, New Delhi – Prentice Hall of India, 2005

D. Hall, Donald. Fundamentals of Electronics. New Delhi : Prentice Hall of India, 2005

2. A workshop is

A. a conference for discussion on a topic.

B. a meeting for discussion on a topic.

C. a class at a college or a university in which a teacher and the students discuss a topic.

D. a brief intensive course for a small group emphasizing the development of a skill or technique for solving a specific problem.

3. A working hypothesis is

A. a proven hypothesis for an argument.

B. not required to be tested.

C. a provisionally accepted hypothesis for further research.

D. a scientific theory.

Read the following passage carefully and answer the questions (4 to 9) :

The Taj Mahal has become one of the world's best known monuments. This domed white marble structure is situated on a high plinth at the southern end of a four-quartered garden, evoking the gardens of paradise, enclosed within walls measuring 305 by 549 metres. Outside the walls, in an area known as Mumtazabad, were living quarters for attendants, markets, serais and other structures built by local merchants and nobles. The tomb complex and the other imperial structures of Mumtazabad were maintained by the income of thirty villages given specifically for the tomb's support. The name Taj Mahal is unknown in Mughal chronicles, but it is used by contemporary Europeans in India, suggesting that this was the tomb's popular name. In contemporary texts, it is generally called simply the Illuminated Tomb (Rauza-i-Munavvara).

Mumtaz Mahal died shortly after delivering her fourteenth child in 1631. The Mughal court was then residing in Burhanpur. Her remains were temporarily buried by the griefstricken emperor in a spacious garden known as Zainabad on the bank of the river Tapti. Six months later her body was transported to Agra, where it was interred in land chosen for the mausoleum. This land, situated south of the Mughal city on the bank of the Jamuna, had belonged to the Kachhwaha rajas since the time of Raja Man Singh and was purchased from the current raja, Jai Singh. Although contemporary chronicles indicate Jai Singh's willing cooperation in this exchange, extant *farmans* (imperial commands) indicate that the final price was not settled until almost two years after the mausoleum's commencement. Jai Singh's further cooperation was insured by imperial orders issued between 1632 and 1637 demanding that he provide stone masons and carts to transport marble from the mines at Makrana, within his "ancestral domain", to Agra where both the Taj Mahal and Shah Jahan's additions to the Agra fort were constructed concurrently.

Work on the mausoleum was commenced early in 1632. Inscriptional evidence indicates much of the tomb was completed by 1636. By 1643, when Shah Jahan most lavishly celebrated the 'Urs ceremony for Mumtaz Mahal', the entire complex was virtually complete.

4. Marble stone used for the construction of the Taj Mahal was brought from the ancestral domain of Raja Jai Singh. The name of the place where mines of marble is
A. Burhanpur B. Makrana
C. Amber D. Jaipur

5. The popular name Taj Mahal was given by
A. Shah Jahan
B. Tourists
C. Public
D. European travellers

6. Point out the true statement from the following:
A. Marble was not used for the construction of the Taj Mahal.
B. Red sand stone is non-visible in the Taj Mahal complex.
C. The Taj Mahal is surrounded by a four-quartered garden known as Chahr Bagh.
D. The Taj Mahal was constructed to celebrate the 'Urs ceremony for Mumtaz Mahal'.

7. In the contemporary texts the Taj Mahal is known
A. Mumtazabad
B. Mumtaz Mahal
C. Zainabad
D. Rauza-i-Munavvara

8. The construction of the Taj Mahal was completed between the period
A. 1632 – 1636 A.D. B. 1630 – 1643 A.D.
C. 1632 – 1643 A.D. D. 1636 – 1643 A.D.

9. The documents indicating the ownership of land, where the Taj Mahal was built, known as
A. Farman
B. Sale Deed
C. Sale-Purchase Deed
D. None of the above

10. In the process of communication, which one of the following is in the chronological order?
A. Communicator, Medium, Receiver, Effect, Message
B. Medium, Communicator, Message, Receiver, Effect
C. Communicator, Message, Medium, Receiver, Effect
D. Message, Communicator, Medium, Receiver, Effect

11. Bengal Gazette, the first Newspaper in India was started in 1780 by
A. Dr. Annie Besant
B. James Augustus Hicky
C. Lord Cripson
D. A.O. Hume

12. Press censorship in India was imposed during the tenure of the Prime Minister
A. Rajeev Gandhi B. Narasimha Rao
C. Indira Gandhi D. Deve Gowda

13. Communication via New media such as computers, teleshopping, internet and mobile telephony is termed as
A. Entertainment
B. Interactive communication
C. Developmental communication
D. Communitarian

14. Classroom communication of a teacher rests on the principle of
A. Infotainment B. Edutainment
C. Entertainment D. Enlightenment

15. ________ is important when a teacher communicates with his/her student.
A. Sympathy B. Empathy
C. Apathy D. Antipathy

16. In a certain code GALIB is represented by HBMJC. TIGER will be represented by
A. UJHFS B. UHJSF
C. JHUSF D. HUJSF

17. In a certain cricket tournament 45 matches were played. Each team played once against each of the other teams. The number of teams participated in the tournament is
A. 8 B. 10
C. 12 D. 14

18. The missing number in the series 40, 120, 60, 180, 90,?, 135 is

A. 110 B. 270
C. 105 D. 210

19. The odd numbers from 1 to 45 which are exactly divisible by 3 are arranged in an ascending order. The number at 6th position is

A. 18 B. 24
C. 33 D. 36

20. The mean of four numbers a, b, c, d is 100. If c = 70, then the mean of the remaining numbers is

A. 30 B. $\frac{85}{2}$
C. $\frac{170}{3}$ D. 110

21. If the radius of a circle is increased by 50%, the perimeter of the circle will increase by

A. 20% B. 30%
C. 40% D. 50%

22. If the statement 'some men are honest' is false, which among the following statements will be true.

Choose the correct code given below :

(*i*) All men are honest.
(*ii*) No men are honest.
(*iii*) Some men are not honest.
(*iv*) All men are dishonest.

Codes :

A. (*i*), (*ii*) and (*iii*)
B. (*ii*), (*iii*) and (*iv*)
C. (*i*), (*iii*) and (*iv*)
D. (*ii*), (*i*) and (*iv*)

23. Choose the proper alternative given in the codes to replace the question mark.

Bee – Honey, Cow – Milk, Teacher – ?

A. Intelligence B. Marks
C. Lessons D. Wisdom

24. P is the father of R and S is the son of Q and T is the brother of P. If R is the sister of S, how is Q related to T?

A. Wife B. Sister-in-law
C. Brother-in-law D. Daughter-in-law

25. A definition put forward to resolve a dispute by influencing attitudes or stirring emotions is called

A. Lexical B. Persuasive
C. Stipulative D. Precisions

26. Which of the codes given below contains only the correct statements?

Statements :

(*i*) Venn diagram is a clear method of notation.
(*ii*) Venn diagram is the most direct method of testing the validity of categorical syllogisms.
(*iii*) In Venn diagram method the premises and the conclusion of a categorical syllogism is diagrammed.
(*iv*) In Venn diagram method the three overlapping circles are drawn for testing a categorical syllogism.

Codes :

A. (*i*), (*ii*) & (*iii*) B. (*i*), (*ii*) & (*iv*)
C. (*ii*), (*iii*) & (*iv*) D. (*i*), (*iii*) & (*iv*)

27. Inductive reasoning presupposes

A. unity in human nature
B. integrity in human nature
C. uniformity in human nature
D. harmony in human nature

Read the table below and based on this table answer questions from 28 to 33 :

Area under Major Horticulture Crops

(in lakh hectares)

Year	*Fruits*	*Vegetables*	*Flowers*	*Total Horticulture Area*
2005–06	53	72	1	187
2006–07	56	75	1	194
2007–08	58	78	2	202
2008–09	61	79	2	207
2009–10	63	79	2	209

28. Which of the following two years have recorded the highest rate of increase in area under the total horticulture?

A. 2005–06 & 2006–07
B. 2006–07 & 2008–09
C. 2007–08 & 2008–09
D. 2006–07 & 2007–08

29. Shares of the area under flowers, vegetables and fruits in the area under total horticulture are respectively :
A. 1, 38 and 30 percent
B. 30, 38 and 1 percent
C. 38, 30 and 1 percent
D. 35, 36 and 2 percent

30. Which of the following has recorded the highest rate of increase in area during 2005–06 to 2009–10?
A. Fruits B. Vegetables
C. Flowers D. Total horticulture

31. Find out the horticultural crop that has recorded an increase of area by around 10 percent from 2005–06 to 2009–10
A. Fruits B. Vegetables
C. Flowers D. Total horticulture

32. What has been the share of area under fruits, vegetables and flowers in the area under total horticulture in 2007–08?
A. 53 percent B. 68 percent
C. 79 percent D. 100 percent

33. In which year, area under fruits has recorded the highest rate of increase?
A. 2006–07 B. 2007–08
C. 2008–09 D. 2009–10

34. 'www' stands for
A. work with web B. word wide web
C. world wide web D. worth while web

35. A hard disk is divided into tracks which is further subdivided into
A. Clusters B. Sectors
C. Vectors D. Heads

36. A computer program that translates a program statement by statement into machine language is called a/an
A. Compiler B. Simulator
C. Translator D. Interpreter

37. A Gigabyte is equal to
A. 1024 Megabytes B. 1024 Kilobytes
C. 1024 Terabytes D. 1024 Bytes

38. A Compiler is a software which converts
A. characters to bits
B. high level language to machine language
C. machine language to high level language
D. words to bits

39. Virtual memory is
A. an extremely large main memory.
B. an extremely large secondary memory.
C. an illusion of extremely large main memory.
D. a type of memory used in super computers.

40. The phrase 'tragedy of commons' is in the context of
A. tragic event related to damage caused by release of poisonous gases.
B. tragic conditions of poor people.
C. degradation of renewable free access resources.
D. climate change.

41. Kyoto Protocol is related to
A. Ozone depletion B. Hazardous waste
C. Climate change D. Nuclear energy

42. Which of the following is a source of emissions leading to the eventual formation of surface ozone as a pollutant?
A. Transport sector
B. Refrigeration and Airconditioning
C. Wetlands
D. Fertilizers

43. The smog in cities in India mainly consists of
A. Oxides of sulphur
B. Oxides of nitrogen and unburnt hydrocarbons
C. Carbon monoxide and SPM
D. Oxides of sulphur and ozone

44. Which of the following types of natural hazards have the highest potential to cause damage to humans?
A. Earthquakes
B. Forest fires
C. Volcanic eruptions
D. Droughts and Floods

45. The percentage share of renewable energy sources in the power production in India is around
A. 2–3% B. 22–25%
C. 10–12% D. $< 1\%$

46. In which of the following categories the enrolment of students in higher education in 2010–11 was beyond the percentage of seats reserved?

A. OBC students
B. SC students
C. ST students
D. Woman students

47. Which one of the following statements is not correct about the University Grants Commission (UGC)?

A. It was established in 1956 by an Act of Parliament.
B. It is tasked with promoting and coordinating higher education.
C. It receives Plan and Non-plan funds from the Central Government.
D. It receives funds from State Governments in respect of State Universities.

48. Consider the statement which is followed by two arguments (I) and (II) :

Statement : Should India switch over to a two party system?

Arguments : (I) Yes, it will lead to stability of Government.

(II) No, it will limit the choice of voters.

A. Only argument (I) is strong.
B. Only argument (II) is strong.
C. Both the arguments are strong.
D. Neither of the arguments is strong.

49. Consider the statement which is followed by two arguments (I) and (II) :

Statement : Should persons with criminal background be banned from contesting elections?

Arguments : (I) Yes, it will decriminalise politics.

(II) No, it will encourage the ruling party to file frivolous cases against their political opponents.

A. Only argument (I) is strong.
B. Only argument (II) is strong.
C. Both the arguments are strong.
D. Neither of the arguments is strong.

50. Which of the following statement(s) is/are correct about a Judge of the Supreme Court of India?

1. A Judge of the Supreme Court is appointed by the President of India.
2. He holds office during the pleasure of the President.
3. He can be suspended, pending an inquiry.
4. He can be removed for proven misbehaviour or incapacity.

Select the correct answer from the codes given below :

Codes :

A. 1, 2 and 3 B. 1, 3 and 4
C. 1 and 3 D. 1 and 4

51. In the warrant of precedence, the Speaker of the Lok Sabha comes next only to

A. The President
B. The Vice-President
C. The Prime Minister
D. The Cabinet Ministers

52. The black-board can be utilised best by a teacher for

A. putting the matter of teaching in black and white
B. making the students attentive
C. writing the important and notable points
D. highlighting the teacher himself

53. Nowadays the most effective mode of learning is

A. self study
B. face-to-face learning
C. e-learning
D. blended learning

54. At the primary school stage, most of the teachers should be women because they

A. can teach children better than men.
B. know basic content better than men.
C. are available on lower salaries.
D. can deal with children with love and affection.

55. Which one is the highest order of learning?

A. Chain learning
B. Problem-solving learning
C. Stimulus-response learning
D. Conditioned-reflex learning

56. A person can enjoy teaching as a profession when he

A. has control over students.
B. commands respect from students.
C. is more qualified than his colleagues.
D. is very close to higher authorities.

57. "A diagram speaks more than 1000 words." The statement means that the teacher should

A. use diagrams in teaching.
B. speak more and more in the class.
C. use teaching aids in the class.
D. not speak too much in the class.

58. A research paper

A. is a compilation of information on a topic.
B. contains original research as deemed by the author.
C. contains peer-reviewed original research or evaluation of research conducted by others.
D. can be published in more than one journal.

59. Which one of the following belongs to the category of good "research ethics"?

A. Publishing the same paper in two research journals without telling the editors.
B. Conducting a review of the literature that acknowledges the contributions of other people in the relevant field or relevant prior work.
C. Trimming outliers from a data set without discussing your reasons in a research paper.
D. Including a colleague as an author on a research paper in return for a favour even though the colleague did not make a serious contribution to the paper.

60. Which of the following sampling methods is not based on probability?

A. Simple Random Sampling
B. Stratified Sampling
C. Quota Sampling
D. Cluster Sampling

ANSWERS

1	2	3	4	5	6	7	8	9	10
D	D	C	B	D	C	D	C	A	C
11	**12**	**13**	**14**	**15**	**16**	**17**	**18**	**19**	**20**
B	C	B	B	B	A	B	B	C	D
21	**22**	**23**	**24**	**25**	**26**	**27**	**28**	**29**	**30**
D	B	D	B	B	B	C	D	A	C
31	**32**	**33**	**34**	**35**	**36**	**37**	**38**	**39**	**40**
B	B	A	C	B	D	A	B	C	C
41	**42**	**43**	**44**	**45**	**46**	**47**	**48**	**49**	**50**
C	A	B	D	C	A	D	C	A	D
51	**52**	**53**	**54**	**55**	**56**	**57**	**58**	**59**	**60**
C	C	D	D	D	B	C	C	B	C

SOME SELECTED EXPLANATORY ANSWERS

16. 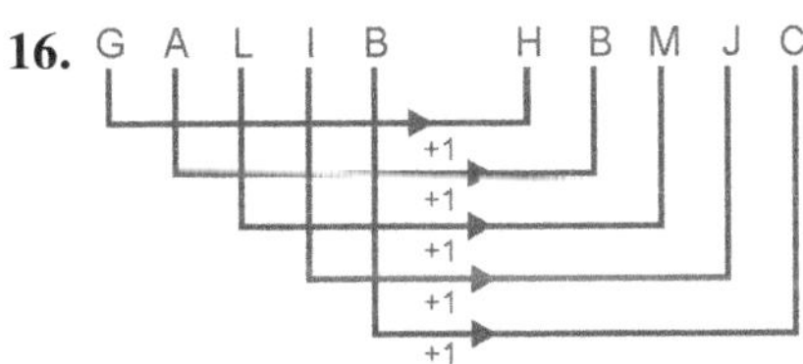

Similarly,

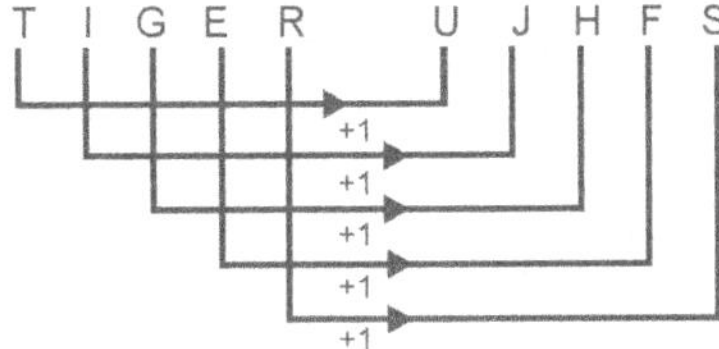

17. Let number of teams participated in the tournament are n

then, number of game played by,

first team $= (n - 1)$

Second team $= (n - 2)$

....

....

....

$(n - 1)^{th}$ team $= 1$

According to the question,

$(n - 1) + (n - 2) + (n - 3) + ... + 1 = 45$

This is equivalent to, Selection of two teams out of n teams ${}^{n}c_2$

$$\therefore \quad {}^{n}c_2 = 45$$

$$\frac{n(n-1)}{2} = 45$$

or, $$n(n - 1) = 90$$

$$n^2 - n - 90 = 0$$

$$(n - 10)(n + 9) = 0$$

$$\Rightarrow \quad n = 10.$$

18. 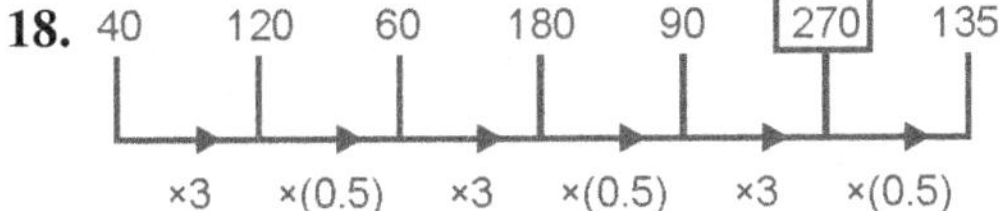

19. Odd numbers from 1 to 45 which are exactly divisible by 3 are following.

3, 9, 15, 21, ..., 45

This is an arithmetic series with first term $a = 3$, and common difference $d = 6$

Sixth term of this series

$$t_6 = a + (6 - 1).d$$
$$= 3 + 5 \times 6 = 33.$$

20. Mean of four numbers $\frac{a+b+c+d}{4} = 100$

or, $a + b + c + d = 400$

or, $a + b + 70 + d = 400$

$a + b + d = 400 - 70 = 330$

Mean $= \frac{a+b+d}{3} = \frac{330}{3}$

$= 110.$

21. Perimeter of circle $(p) = 2\pi r$

when radius (r) increased by 50%

$$r' = r + \frac{r \times 50}{100} = \frac{3r}{2}$$

New Perimeter $(p') = 2\pi\, r'$

$= 3\pi r$

Increase in perimeter

$$p' - p = 3\pi r - 2\pi r = \pi r$$

Percentage increment $= \frac{\pi r}{2\pi r} \times 100 = 50\%.$

23. Bee give us honey and Cow gives milk, similarly from teacher we get wisdom.

24. 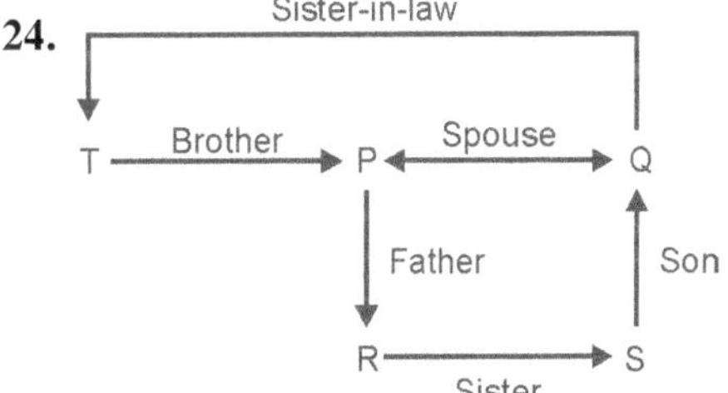

28. Increase in total horticulture area

from 2005-06 & 2006-07

194 − 187 = 7 Lakh hect.

from 2006-07 & 2007-08

202 − 194 = 8 Lakh hect.

from 2007-08 & 2008-09

207 − 202 = 5 Lakh hect.

from 2006-07 & 2008-09

207 − 194 = 13 Lakh hect.

Hence, highest rate of increase is registered in 2006-07 & 2007-08.

29. Total horticultural area

= 187 + 194 + 202 + 207 + 209 = 999 lakh hect.

Total flowers area

= 1 + 1 + 2 + 2 + 2 = 8 lakh hect.

Percentage area under flowers

$$= \frac{8}{999} \times 100 \cong 0.8\%$$

Total area under Vegetation

= 72 + 75 +78 + 79 + 79 = 383 Lakh hect.

Percentage area under vegetation

$$= \frac{383}{999} \times 100 \cong 38.3\%$$

Total area under Fruits

= 53 + 56 + 58 + 61 + 63 = 291 Lakh hect.

Percentage area under fruits

$$= \frac{291}{999} \times 100 \cong 29.1\%$$

Hence, Correct option is (A).

30. Increase in area under

Fruits = 63 − 53 = 10 lakh hect.

Rate of increase $= \frac{10}{5} = 2$ lakh hect

Increase in area under

Vegetables = 79 − 72 = 7 lakh hect.

Rate of increase $= \frac{7}{5} = 1.4$ lakh hect.

Increase in area under flowers

= 2 − 1 = 1 Lakh hect.

Rate of increase $= \frac{1}{5} = 0.2$ lakh hect.

Increase in area under total horticulture

= 209 − 187 = 22 lakh hect.

Rate of increase $= \frac{22}{5} = 4.4$ lakh hect.

Hence correct option is (D).

31. Percentage increase in area under

$$\text{fruits} = \frac{63-53}{53} \times 100 = 18.89\% \cong 20\%$$

$$\text{Vegetables} = \frac{79-72}{72} \times 100 = 9.77\% \cong 10\%$$

$$\text{Flowers} = \frac{2-1}{1} \times 100 = 100\%$$

Total horticulture

$$= \frac{209-187}{187} \times 100$$

$$= 11.7\% \cong 12\%$$

Hence, correct option is (B).

32. Area under fruits, vegetables and flowers in year 2007 − 08

= 58 + 78 + 2 = 138 lakh hect.

Area under horticulture in year 2007 − 08

= 202 lakh hect.

Percentage of area $= \frac{138}{202} \times 100 = 68.33\%$.

33. Rate of increase of area under flowers

in year 2006-07 $= \frac{56-53}{1} = 3$

in year 2007-08 $= \frac{58-56}{1} = 2$

in year 2008-09 $= \frac{61-58}{1} = 3$

in year 2009-10 $= \frac{63-61}{1} = 2.$

Previous Years' Paper (Solved)

UGC-NET (JRF) Exam December, 2012

PAPER–I

Note : This paper contains **sixty (60)** multiple-choice questions, each question carrying **two (2)** marks. Candidate is expected to answer any **fifty (50)** questions. In case more than **fifty (50)** questions are attempted, only the first **fifty (50)** questions will be evaluated.

1. The English word 'Communication' is derived from the words:
A. Communis and Communicare
B. Communist and Commune
C. Communism and Communalism
D. Communion and Common sense

2. Chinese Cultural Revolution leader Mao Zedong used a type of communication to talk to the masses is known as:
A. Mass line communication
B. Group communication
C. Participatory communication
D. Dialogue communication

3. Conversing with the spirits and ancestors is termed as:
A. Transpersonal communication
B. Intrapersonal communication
C. Interpersonal communication
D. Face-to-face communication

4. The largest circulated daily newspaper among the following is:
A. The Times of India
B. The Indian Express
C. The Hindu
D. The Deccan Herald

5. The Pioneer of the silent feature film in India was:
A. K.A. Abbas B. Satyajit Ray
C. B.R. Chopra D. Dada Sahib Phalke

6. Classroom communication of a teacher rests on the principle of:
A. Infotainment B. Edutainment
C. Entertainment D. Power equation

7. The missing number in the series :
0, 6, 24, 60, 120, ?, 336, is:
A. 240 B. 220
C. 280 D. 210

8. A group of 7 members having a majority of boys is to be formed out of 6 boys and 4 girls. The number of ways the group can be formed is:
A. 80 B. 100
C. 90 D. 110

9. The number of observations in a group is 40. The average of the first 10 members is 4.5 and the average of the remaining 30 members is 3.5. The average of the whole group is:
A. 4 B. 15/2
C. 15/4 D. 6

10. If MOHAN is represented by the code KMFYL, then COUNT will be represented by:
A. AMSLR B. MSLAR
C. MASRL D. SAMLR

11. The sum of the ages of two persons A and B is 50. 5 years ago, the ratio of their ages was 5/3. The present age of A and B are:
A. 30, 20 B. 35, 15
C. 38, 12 D. 40, 10

12. Let a means minus (–), b means multiplied by (×), C means divided by (÷) and D means plus (+). The value of 90 D 9 a 29 C 10 b 2 is:
A. 8 B. 10
C. 12 D. 14

13. Consider the Assertion-I and Assertion-II and select the right code given below :
Assertion-I : Even Bank-lockers are not safe. Thieves can break them and take away your

wealth. But thieves can not go to heaven. So you should keep your wealth in heaven.

Assertion-II : The difference of skin-colour of beings is because of the distance from the sun and not because of some permanent traits. Skin-colour is the result of body's reaction to the sun and its rays.

Codes :

A. Both the assertions-I and II are forms of argument.
B. The assertion-I is an argument but the assertion-II is not.
C. The assertion-II is an argument but the assertion-I is not.
D. Both the assertions are explanations of facts.

14. By which of the following proposition, the proposition 'some men are not honest' is contradicted?

A. All men are honest
C. Some men are honest
B. No men are honest
D. All of the above

15. A stipulative definition is:

A. always true
B. always false
C. sometimes true sometimes false
D. neither true nor false

16. Choose the appropriate alternative given in the codes to replace the question mark.

Examiner – Examinee, Pleader – Client, Preceptor – ?

A. Customer B. Path-finder
C. Perceiver D. Disciple

17. If the statement 'most of the students are obedient' is taken to be true, which one of the following pair of statements can be claimed to be true?

I. All obedient persons are students.
II. All students are obedient.
III. Some students are obedient.
IV. Some students are not disobedient.

Codes:

A. I & II B. II & III
C. III & IV D. II & IV

18. Choose the right code :

A deductive argument claims that :

I. The conclusion does not claim something more than that which is contained in the premises.
II. The conclusion is supported by the premise/premises conclusively.
III. If the conclusion is false, then premise/premises may be either true or false.
IV. If premise/combination of premises is true, then conclusion must be true.

Codes:

A. I and II B. I and III
C. II and III D. All of the above

Direction (Qs. 19 to 24): *On the basis of the data given in the following table, give answers to questions.*

Government Expenditures on Social Services

(As per cent of total expenditure)

S.I. No.	Items	2007-08	2008-09	2009-10	2010-11
	Social Services	11.06	12.94	13.06	14.02
(a)	Education, sports & youth affairs	4.02	4.04	3.96	4.46
(b)	Health & family welfare	2.05	1.91	1.90	2.03
(c)	Water supply, housing, etc,	2.02	2.31	2.20	2.27
(d)	Information & broadcasting	0.22	0.22	0.20	0.22
(e)	Welfare to SC/ST & OBC	0.36	0.35	0.41	0.63
(f)	Labour and employment	0.27	0.27	0.22	0.25
(g)	Social welfare & nutrition	0.82	0.72	0.79	1.06
(h)	North-eastern areas	0.00	1.56	1.50	1.75
(i)	Other social services	1.29	1.55	1.87	1.34
	Total Government expenditure	100.00	100.00	100.00	100.00

19. How many activities in the social services are there where the expenditure has been less than 5 per cent of the total expenditures incurred on the social services in 2008-09?
A. One B. Three
C. Five D. All of the above

20. In which year, the expenditures on the social services have increased at the highest rate?
A. 2007-08 B. 2008-09
C. 2009-10 D. 2010-11

21. Which of the following activities remains almost stagnant in terms of share of expenditures?
A. North-eastern areas
B. Welfare to SC/ST & OBC
C. Information & broadcasting
D. Social welfare and nutrition

22. Which of the following item's expenditure share is almost equal to the remaining three items in the given years?
A. Information & broadcasting
B. Welfare to SC/ST and OBC
C. Labour and employment
D. Social welfare & nutrition

23. Which of the following items of social services has registered the highest rate of increase in expenditures during 2007-08 to 2010-11?
A. Education, sports & youth affairs
B. Welfare to SC/ST & OBC
C. Social welfare & nutrition
D. Overall social services

24. Which of the following items has registered the highest rate of decline in terms of expenditure during 2007-08 to 2009-10?
A. Labour and employment
B. Health & family welfare
C. Social welfare & nutrition
D. Education, sports & youth affairs

25. ALU stands for:
A. American Logic Unit
B. Alternate Local Unit
C. Alternating Logic Unit
D. Arithmetic Logic Unit

26. A Personal Computer uses a number of chips mounted on a circuit board called:
A. Microprocessor B. System Board
C. Daughter Board D. Mother Board

27. Computer Virus is a:
A. Hardware B. Bacteria
C. Software D. None of these

28. Which one of the following is correct?
A. $(17)_{10} = (17)_{16}$
B. $(17)_{10} = (17)_8$
C. $(17)_{10} = (10111)_2$
D. $(17)_{10} = (10001)_2$

29. The file extension of MS-Word document in Office 2007 is ....
A. .pdf B. .doc
C. .docx D. .txt

30. .... is a protocol used by e-mail clients to download e-mails to your computer.
A. TCP B. FTP
C. SMTP D. POP

31. Which of the following is a source of methane?
A. Wetlands
B. Foam Industry
C. Thermal Power Plants
D. Cement Industry

32. 'Minamata disaster' in Japan was caused by pollution due to:
A. Lead B. Mercury
C. Cadmium D. Zinc

33. Biomagnification means increase in the:
A. concentration of pollutants in living organisms
B. number of species
C. size of living organisms
D. biomass

34. Nagoya Protocol is related to:
A. Climate change B. Ozone depletion
C. Hazardous waste D. Biodiversity

35. The second most important source after fossil fuels contributing to India's energy needs is:
A. Solar energy C. Nuclear energy
B. Hydropower D. Wind energy

36. In case of earthquakes, an increase of magnitude 1 on Richter Scale implies:

A. a ten-fold increase in the amplitude of seismic waves.

B. a ten-fold increase in the energy of the seismic waves.

C. two-fold increase in the amplitude of seismic waves.

D. two-fold increase in the energy of seismic waves.

37. Which of the following is not a measure of Human Development Index?

A. Literacy Rate B. Gross Enrolment

C. Sex Ratio D. Life Expectancy

38. India has the highest number of students in colleges after:

A. the U.K.

B. the U.S.A.

C. Australia

D. Canada

39. Which of the following statement(s) is/are not correct about the Attorney General of India?

1. The President appoints a person, who is qualified to be a Judge of a High Court, to be the Attorney General of India.
2. He has the right of audience in all the Courts of the country.
3. He has the right to take part in the proceedings of the Lok Sabha and the Rajya Sabha.
4. He has a fixed tenure.

Select the correct answer from the codes given below :

Codes:

A. 1 and 4 B. 2, 3 and 4

C. 3 and 4 D. 3 only

40. Which of the following prefix President Pranab Mukherjee desires to be discontinued while interacting with Indian dignitaries as well as in official notings?

1. His Excellency 2. Mahamahim

3. Hon'ble 4. Shri/Smt.

Select the correct answer from the codes given below:

Codes:

A. 1 and 3 B. 2 and 3

C. 1 and 2 D. 1, 2 and 3

41. Which of the following can be done under conditions of financial emergency?

1. State Legislative Assemblies can be abolished.
2. Central Government can acquire control over the budget and expenditure of States.
3. Salaries of the Judges of the High Courts and the Supreme Court can be reduced.
4. Right to Constitutional Remedies can be suspended.

Select the correct answer from the codes given below :

Codes :

A. 1, 2 and 3 B. 2, 3 and 4

C. 1 and 2 D. 2 and 3

42. Match List-I with List-II and select the correct answer from the codes given below :

List-I	List-II
(a) Poverty Reduction Programme	(i) Mid-day Meals
(b) Human Development Scheme	(ii) Indira Awas Yojna (IAY)
(c) Social Assistance Scheme	(iii) National Old Age Pension (NOAP)
(d) Minimum Need Scheme	(iv) MNREGA

Codes :

	(a)	(b)	(c)	(d)
A.	(iv)	(i)	(iii)	(ii)
B.	(ii)	(iii)	(iv)	(ii)
C.	(iii)	(iv)	(i)	(ii)
D.	(iv)	(iii)	(ii)	(i)

43. For an efficient and durable learning, learner should have:

A. ability to learn only

B. requisite level of motivation only

C. opportunities to learn only

D. desired level of ability and motivation

44. Classroom communication must be:

A. Teacher centric B. Student centric

C. General centric D. Textbook centric

45. The best method of teaching is to:
A. impart information
B. ask students to read books
C. suggest good reference material
D. initiate a discussion and participate in it

46. Interaction inside the classroom should generate:
A. Argument B. Information
C. Ideas D. Controversy

47. "Spare the rod and spoil the child", gives the message that:
A. punishment in the class should be banned.
B. corporal punishment is not acceptable.
C. undesirable behaviour must be punished.
D. children should be beaten with rods.

48. The type of communication that the teacher has in the classroom, is termed as:
A. Interpersonal
B. Mass communication
C. Group communication
D. Face-to-face communication

49. Which one of the following is an indication of the quality of a research journal?
A. Impact factor B. h-index
C. g-index D. i10-index

50. Good 'research ethics' means:
A. Not disclosing the holdings of shares/ stocks in a company that sponsors your research.
B. Assigning a particular research problem to one Ph.D./research student only.
C. Discussing with your colleagues confidential data from a research paper that you are reviewing for an academic journal.
D. Submitting the same research manuscript for publishing in more than one journal.

51. Which of the following sampling methods is based on probability?
A. Convenience sampling
B. Quota sampling
C. Judgement sampling
D. Stratified sampling

52. Which one of the following references is written according to American Psychological Association (APA) format?
A. Sharma, V. (2010). Fundamentals of Computer Science.
New Delhi : Tata McGraw Hill
B. Sharma, V. 2010. Fundamentals of Computer Science.
New Delhi : Tata McGraw Hill
C. Sharma. V. 2010. Fundamentals of Computer Science,
New Delhi : Tata McGraw Hill
D. Sharma, V. (2010), Fundamentals of Computer Science,
New Delhi : Tata McGraw Hill

53. Arrange the following steps of research in correct sequence:
1. Identification of research problem
2. Listing of research objectives
3. Collection of data
4. Methodology
5. Data analysis
6. Results and discussion
A. 1 – 2 – 3 – 4 – 5 – 6
B. 1 – 2 – 4 – 3 – 5 – 6
C. 2 – 1 – 3 – 4 – 5 – 6
D. 2 – 1 – 4 – 3 – 5 – 6

54. Identify the **incorrect** statement :
A. A hypothesis is made on the basis of limited evidence as a starting point for further investigations.
B. A hypothesis is a basis for reasoning without any assumption of its truth.
C. Hypothesis is a proposed explanation for a phenomenon.
D. Scientific hypothesis is a scientific theory.

Directions (Qs. 50 to 60) : *Read the following passage carefully and answer the questions:*

The popular view of towns and cities in developing countries and of urbanization process is that despite the benefits and comforts it brings, the emergence of such cities connotes environmental degradation, generation of slums and squatters, urban poverty, unemployment, crimes, lawlessness, traffic chaos etc. But what is the reality? Given the unprecedental increase in urban population over the last 50 years from 300 million in 1950 to 2 billion in 2000 in developing countries, the wonder really is how well the world has coped, and not how badly.

In general, the urban quality of life has improved in terms of availability of water and sanitation, power, health and education, communication and transport. By way of illustration, a large number of urban residents have been provided with improved water in urban areas in Asia's largest countries such as China, India, Indonesia and Philippines. Despite that, the access to improved water in terms of percentage of total urban population seems to have declined during the last decade of 20th century, though in absolute numbers, millions of additional urbanites, have been provided improved services. These countries have made significant progress in the provision of sanitation services too, together, providing for an additional population of more than 293 million citizens within a decade (1990-2000). These improvements must be viewed against the backdrop of rapidly increasing urban population, fiscal crunch and strained human resources and efficient and quality-oriented public management.

55. The popular view about the process of urbanization in developing countries is:
A. Positive B. Negative
C. Neutral D. Unspecified

56. The average annual increase in the number of urbanites in developing countries, from 1950 to 2000 A.D. was close to:
A. 30 million B. 40 million
C. 50 million D. 60 million

57. The reality of urbanization is reflected in:
A. How well the situation has been managed.
B. How badly the situation has gone out of control.
C. How fast has been tempo of urbanization.
D. How fast the environment has degraded.

58. Which one of the following is not considered as an indicator of urban quality of life?
A. Tempo of urbanization
B. Provision of basic services
C. Access to social amenities
D. All of the above

59. The author in this passage has tried to focus on
A. Extension of Knowledge
B. Generation of Environmental Consciousness
C. Analytical Reasoning
D. Descriptive Statement

60. In the above passage, the author intends to state:
A. The hazards of the urban life
B. The sufferings of the urban life
C. The awareness of human progress
D. The limits to growth

ANSWERS

1	2	3	4	5	6	7	8	9	10
A	A	A	A	D	B	D	B	C	A
11	12	13	14	15	16	17	18	19	20
A	*	B	A	D	D	C	A	D	B
21	22	23	24	25	26	27	28	29	30
C	D	B	A	D	D	C	D	C	D
31	32	33	34	35	36	37	38	39	40
A	B	A	D	C	A	C	B	A	C
41	42	43	44	45	46	47	48	49	50
D	A	D	B	D	C	C	C	A	B
51	52	53	54	55	56	57	58	59	60
D	A	B	D	B	A	A	A	C	D

SOME SELECTED EXPLANATORY ANSWERS

7. 0, 6, 24, 60, 120, x, 336.

Let missing term is x

Now,

$$\frac{0}{6}, \frac{6}{24}, \frac{24}{60}, \frac{60}{120}, \frac{120}{x}, \frac{x}{336}$$

$$= 0, \frac{1}{4}, \frac{2}{5}, \frac{3}{6}, \frac{120}{x}, \frac{x}{336}$$

From the pattern

$\frac{120}{x}$ should be $\frac{4}{7}$

so, $\frac{120}{x} = \frac{4}{7}$ or, $x = 210$.

8. The group must formed by 4, 5 or 6 boys and 3, 2 or 1 girls

the required number of ways

when group formed by 4 boys and 3 girls

Number of ways for this selection

$$^6C_4 \times {}^4C_3$$

when group formed by 5 boys and 2 girls

Number of ways for this selection

$$^6C_5 \times {}^4C_2$$

when group formed by 6 boys and 1 girl

the number of ways for this selection

$$^6C_6 \times {}^4C_1$$

total number of ways

$= {}^6C_4 \times {}^4C_3 + {}^6C_5 \times {}^4C_2 + {}^6C_6 \times {}^4C_1$

$= 15 \times 4 + 6 \times 6 + 1 \times 4$

$= 60 + 36 + 4 = 100.$

9. Observation of first 10 members

$= 4.5 \times 10 = 45$

observation of last 30 members

$= 3.5 \times 30 = 105$

total observation done by 40 members

$= 45 + 105 = 150$

Average observation $= \frac{150}{40} = \frac{15}{4}$.

11. Let present age of A is x and B is y.

According to the question

$$x + y = 50 \qquad ...(i)$$

5 years ago, ratio of their age

$$\frac{x-5}{y-5} = \frac{5}{3}$$

$$3(x - 5) = 5(y - 5)$$

or, $\quad 3x - 5y = -10 \qquad ...(ii)$

from (i) and (ii)

$$8x = 250 - 10$$

$$x = \frac{240}{8} = 30$$

$$y = 20$$

Present Age of A = 30 years

Present Age of B = 20 years.

28. $(10001)_2 = 1 \times 2^4 + 0 \times 2^3 + 0 \times 2^2 + 0 \times 2^1 + 1 \times 2^0$

$= 16 + 0 + 0 + 0 + 1 = 17$

so, $(17)^{10} = (10001)_2$.

Previous Years' Paper (Solved)

UGC-NET (JRF) EXAM JUNE, 2012

PAPER–I

Note : This paper contains **sixty (60)** multiple-choice questions, each question carrying **two (2)** marks. Candidate is expected to answer any **fifty (50)** questions. In case more than **fifty (50)** questions are attempted, only the first **fifty (50)** questions will be evaluated.

1. Video-Conferencing can be classified as one of the following types of communication:
(A) Visual one way
(B) Audio-Visual one way
(C) Audio-Visual two way
(D) Visual two way

2. MC National University of Journalism and Communication is located at:
(A) Lucknow (B) Bhopal
(C) Chennai (D) Mumbai

3. All India Radio (A.I.R.) for broadcasting was named in the year:
(A) 1926 (B) 1936
(C) 1946 (D) 1956

4. In India for broadcasting TV programmes which system is followed?
(A) NTCS (B) PAL
(C) NTSE (D) SECAM

5. The term 'DAVP' stands for:
(A) Directorate of Advertising & Vocal Publicity
(B) Division of Audio-Visual Publicity
(C) Department of Audio-Visual Publicity
(D) Directorate of Advertising & Visual Publicity

6. The term "TRP" is associated with TV shows stands for:
(A) Total Rating Points
(B) Time Rating Points
(C) Thematic Rating Points
(D) Television Rating Points

7. Which is the number that comes next in the following sequence?
2, 6, 12, 20, 30, 42, 56, _____
(A) 60 (B) 64
(C) 72 (D) 70

8. Find the next letter for the series YVSP ....
(A) N (B) M
(C) O (D) L

9. Given that in a code language, '645' means 'day is warm'; '42' means 'warm spring' and '634' means 'spring is sunny'; which digit represents 'sunny'?
(A) 3 (B) 2
(C) 4 (D) 5

10. The basis of the following classification is: 'first President of India', 'author of *Godan*', 'books in my library', 'blue things' and 'students who work hard'
(A) Common names
(B) Proper names
(C) Descriptive phrases
(D) Indefinite description

11. In the expression 'Nothing is larger than itself' the relation 'is larger than' is:
(A) antisymmetric

(B) asymmetrical
(C) intransitive
(D) irreflexive

12. **Assertion (A) :** There are more laws on the books today than ever before, and more crimes being committed than ever before.
Reason (R) : Because to reduce crime we must eliminate the laws.
Choose the correct answer from below:
(A) (A) is true, (R) is doubtful and (R) is not the correct explanation of (A).
(B) (A) is false, (R) is true and (R) is the correct explanation of (A).
(C) (A) is doubtful, (R) is doubtful and (R) is not the correct explanation of (A).
(D) (A) is doubtful, (R) is true and (R) is not the correct explanation of (A).

13. If the proposition "All men are not mortal" is true then which of the following inferences is correct? Choose from the code given below:
1. "All men are mortal" is true.
2. "Some men are mortal" is false.
3. "No men are mortal" is doubtful.
4. "All men are mortal" is false.

Code :
(A) 1, 2 and 3 (B) 2, 3 and 4
(C) 1, 3 and 4 (D) 1 and 3

14. Determine the nature of the following definition:
"Abortion" means the ruthless murdering of innocent beings.
(A) Lexical (B) Persuasive
(C) Stipulative (D) Theoretical

15. Which one of the following is **not** an argument?
(A) Devadutt does not eat in the day so he must be eating at night.
(B) If Devadutt is growing fat and if he does not eat during the day, he will be eating at night.
(C) Devadutt eats in the night so he does not eat during the day.
(D) Since Devadutt does not eat in the day, he must be eating in the night.

16. Venn diagram is a kind of diagram to:
(A) represent and assess the validity of elementary inferences of syllogistic form.
(B) represent but not assess the validity of elementary inferences of syllogistic form.
(C) represent and assess the truth of elementary inferences of syllogistic form.
(D) assess but not represent the truth of elementary inferences of syllogistic form.

17. Reasoning by analogy leads to:
(A) certainty
(B) definite conclusion
(C) predictive conjecture
(D) surety

18. Which of the following statements are false? Choose from the code given below:
1. Inductive arguments always proceed from the particular to the general.
2. A cogent argument must be inductively strong.
3. A valid argument may have a false premise and a false conclusion.
4. An argument may legitimately be spoken of as 'true' or 'false'.

Code :
(A) 2, 3 and 4 (B) 1 and 3
(C) 2 and 4 (D) 1 and 2

19. Six persons A, B, C, D, E and F are standing in a circle. B is between F and C, A is between E and D, F is to the left of D. Who is between A and F?
(A) B (B) C
(C) D (D) E

20. The price of petrol increases by 25%. By what percentage must a customer reduce the consumption so that the earlier bill on the petrol does not alter?
(A) 20% (B) 25%
(C) 30% (D) 33.33%

21. If Ram knows that y is an integer greater than 2 and less than 7 and Hari knows that y is an integer greater than 5 and less than 10, then they may correctly conclude that
(A) y can be exactly determined
(B) y may be either of two values

(C) y may be any of three values
(D) there is no value of y satisfying these conditions

22. Four pipes can fill a reservoir in 15, 20, 30 and 60 hours respectively. The first one was opened at 6 AM, second at 7 AM, third at 8 AM and the fourth at 9 AM. When will the reservoir be filled?
(A) 11 AM (B) 12 Noon
(C) 1 PM (D) 1:30 PM

The total electricity generation in a country is 97 GW. The contribution of various energy sources is indicated in percentage terms in the Pie Chart given below:

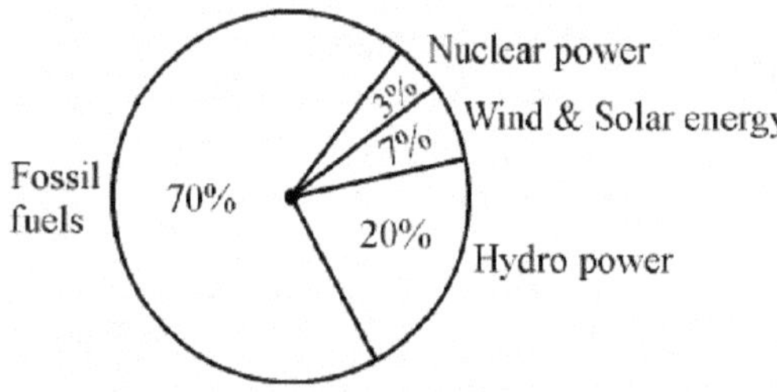

23. What is the contribution of wind and solar power in absolute terms in the electricity generation?
(A) 6.79 GW (B) 19.4 GW
(C) 9.7 GW (D) 29.1 GW

24. What is the contribution of renewable energy sources in absolute terms in the electricity generation?
(A) 29.1 GW (B) 26.19 GW
(C) 67.9 GW (D) 97 GW

25. TCP/IP is necessary if one is to connect to the:
(A) Phone lines
(B) LAN
(C) Internet
(D) Server

26. Each character on the keyboard of computer has an ASCII value which stands for:
(A) American Stock Code for Information Interchange
(B) American Standard Code for Information Interchange
(C) African Standard Code for Information Interchange
(D) Adaptable Standard Code for Information Change

27. Which of the following is not a programming language?
(A) Pascal
(B) Microsoft Office
(C) Java
(D) C++

28. Minimum number of bits required to store any 3 digit decimal number is equal to:
(A) 3 (B) 5
(C) 8 (D) 10

29. Internet explorer is a type of
(A) Operating System
(B) Compiler
(C) Browser
(D) IP address

30. POP3 and IMAP are e-mail accounts in which:
(A) One automatically gets one's mail everyday
(B) One has to be connected to the server to read or write one's mail
(C) One only has to be connected to the server to send and receive e-mail
(D) One does not need any telephone lines

31. Irritation in eyes is caused by the pollutant:
(A) Sulphur di-oxide
(B) Ozone
(C) PAN
(D) Nitrous oxide

32. Which is the source of chlorofluorocarbons?
(A) Thermal power plants
(B) Automobiles
(C) Refrigeration and Airconditioning
(D) Fertilizers

33. Which of the following is not a renewable natural resource?
(A) Clean air (B) Fertile soil
(C) Fresh water (D) Salt

34. Which of the following parameters is not used as a pollution indicator in water?

(A) Total dissolved solids
(B) Coliform count
(C) Dissolved oxygen
(D) Density

35. S and P waves are associated with:
(A) floods
(B) wind energy
(C) earthquakes
(D) tidal energy

36. Match Lists I and II and select the correct answer from the codes given below:

List-I	***List-II***
(i) Ozone hole	*(a)* Tsunami
(ii) Greenhouse effect	*(b)* UV radiations
(iii) Natural hazards	*(c)* Methane
(iv) Sustainable development	*(d)* Eco-centrism

Codes :

	(i)	*(ii)*	*(iii)*	*(iv)*
(A)	*(b)*	*(c)*	*(a)*	*(d)*
(B)	*(c)*	*(b)*	*(a)*	*(d)*
(C)	*(d)*	*(c)*	*(a)*	*(b)*
(D)	*(d)*	*(b)*	*(c)*	*(a)*

37. Indian Institute of Advanced Study is located at:
(A) Dharmshala
(B) Shimla
(C) Solan
(D) Chandigarh

38. Indicate the number of Regional Offices of National Council of Teacher Education.
(A) 04 (B) 05
(C) 06 (D) 08

39. Which of the following rights was considered the "Heart and Soul" of the Indian Constitution by Dr. B.R. Ambedkar?
(A) Freedom of Speech
(B) Right to Equality
(C) Right to Freedom of Religion
(D) Right to Constitutional Remedies

40. Who among the following created the office of the District Collector in India?
(A) Lord Cornwallis
(B) Warren Hastings
(C) The Royal Commission on Decentralisation
(D) Sir Charles Metcalf

41. The Fundamental Duties of a citizen include:
1. Respect for the Constitution, the National Flag and the National Anthem
2. To develop the scientific temper.
3. Respect for the Government.
4. To protect Wildlife.

Choose the correct answer from the codes given below:
Codes :
(A) 1, 2 and 3 (B) 1, 2 and 4
(C) 2, 3 and 4 (D) 1, 3, 4 and 2

42. The President of India takes oath:
(A) to uphold the sovereignty and integrity of India.
(B) to bear true faith and allegiance to the Constitution of India.
(C) to uphold the Constitution and Laws of the country.
(D) to preserve, protect and defend the Constitution and the law of the country.

43. If you get an opportunity to teach a visually challenged student along with normal students, what type of treatment would you like to give him in the class?
(A) Not giving extra attention because majority may suffer.
(B) Take care of him sympathetically in the class-room.
(C) You will think that blindness is his destiny and hence you cannot do anything.
(D) Arrange a seat in the front row and try to teach at a pace convenient to him.

44. Which of the following is not a characteristic of a good achievement test?
(A) Reliability (B) Objectivity
(C) Ambiguity (D) Validity

45. Which of the following does not belong to a projected aid?
(A) Overhead projector
(B) Blackboard

(C) Epidiascope
(D) Slide projector

46. For a teacher, which of the following methods would be correct for writing on the blackboard?
(A) Writing fast and as clearly as possible.
(B) Writing the matter first and then asking students to read it.
(C) Asking a question to students and then writing the answer as stated by them.
(D) Writing the important points as clearly as possible.

47. A teacher can be successful if he/she:
(A) helps students in becoming better citizens
(B) imparts subject knowledge to students
(C) prepares students to pass the examination
(D) presents the subject matter in a well organized manner

48. Dynamic approach to teaching means:
(A) Teaching should be forceful and effective
(B) Teachers should be energetic and dynamic
(C) The topics of teaching should not be static, but dynamic
(D) The students should be required to learn through activities

49. The research that aims at immediate application is:
(A) Action Research
(B) Empirical Research
(C) Conceptual Research
(D) Fundamental Research

50. When two or more successive footnotes refer to the same work which one of the following expressions is used?
(A) ibid (B) et.al
(C) op.cit : (D) loc.cit.

51. Nine year olds are taller than seven year olds. This is an example of a reference drawn from:
(A) Vertical study
(B) Cross-sectional study
(C) Time series study
(D) Experimental study

52. Conferences are meant for:
(A) Multiple target groups
(B) Group discussions
(C) Show-casing new Research
(D) All the above

53. Ex Post Facto research means:
(A) The research is carried out after the incident
(B) The research is carried out prior to the incident
(C) The research is carried out along with the happening of an incident.
(D) The research is carried out keeping in mind the possibilities of an incident.

54. Research ethics do not include:
(A) Honesty (B) Subjectivity
(C) Integrity (D) Objectivity

Directions (Qs. 55 to 60): *Read the following passage carefully and answer the questions:*

James Madison said, "A people who mean to be their own governors must arm themselves with power that knowledge gives." In India, the Official Secrets Act, 1923 was a convenient smokescreen to deny members of the public access to information. Public functioning has traditionally been shrouded in secrecy. But in a democracy in which people govern themselves, it is necessary to have more openness. In the maturing of our democracy, right to information is a major step forward; it enables citizens to participate fully in the decision-making process that affects their lives so profoundly. It is in this context that the address of the Prime Minister in the Lok Sabha is significant. He said, "I would only like to see that everyone, particularly our civil servants, should see the Bill in a positive spirit; not as a draconian law for paralyzing Government, but as an instrument for improving Government-Citizen interface resulting in a friendly, caring and effective Government functioning for the good of our People." He further said, "This is an innovative Bill, where there will be scope to review its functioning as we gain experience. Therefore, this is a piece of legislation, whose working will be kept under constant reviews."

The Commission, in its Report, has dealt with the application of the Right to Information in Executive, Legislature and Judiciary. The judiciary could be a pioneer in implementing the Act in letter and spirit because much of the work that the Judiciary does is open to public scrutiny, Government of India has sanctioned an e-governance project in the Judiciary for about ₹ 700 crores which would bring about systematic classification, standardization and categorization of records. This would help the judiciary to fulfil its mandate under the Act. Similar capacity building would be required in all other public authorities. The transformation from non-transparency to transparency and public accountability is the responsibility of all three organs of State.

55. A person gets power:
(A) by acquiring knowledge
(B) from the Official Secrets Act, 1923
(C) through openings
(D) by denying public information

56. Right to Information is a major step forward to:
(A) enable citizens to participate fully in the decision-making process
(B) to make the people aware of the Act
(C) to gain knowledge of administration
(D) to make the people Government friendly

57. The Prime Minister considered the Bill:
(A) to provide power to the civil servants
(B) as an instrument for improving Government-citizen interface resulting in a friendly, caring and effective Government
(C) a draconian law against the officials
(D) to check the harassment of the people

58. The Commission made the Bill effective by:
(A) extending power to the executive authorities
(B) combining the executive and legislative power
(C) recognizing Judiciary a pioneer in implementing the act in letter and spirit
(D) educating the people before its implementation

59. The Prime Minister considered the Bill innovative and hoped that
(A) It could be reviewed based on the experience gained on its functioning.
(B) The civil servants would see the Bill in a positive spirit.
(C) It would not be considered as a draconian law for paralyzing Government
(D) All the above

60. The transparency and public accountability is the responsibility of three organs of the State. These three organs are:
(A) Lok Sabha, Rajya Sabha and Judiciary
(B) Lok Sabha, Rajya Sabha and Executive
(C) Judiciary, Legislature and the Commission
(D) Legislature, Executive and Judiciary

ANSWERS

1	2	3	4	5	6	7	8	9	10
(C)	(B)	(B)	(B)	(D)	(A)	(C)	(B)	(A)	(C)
11	**12**	**13**	**14**	**15**	**16**	**17**	**18**	**19**	**20**
(D)	(A)	(B)	(B)	(B)	(A)	(C)	(C)	(C)	(A)
21	**22**	**23**	**24**	**25**	**26**	**27**	**28**	**29**	**30**
(A)	(C)	(A)	(B)	(C)	(B)	(B)	(D)	(C)	(C)
31	**32**	**33**	**34**	**35**	**36**	**37**	**38**	**39**	**40**
(C)	(C)	(D)	(D)	(C)	(A)	(B)	(A)	(D)	(B)
41	**42**	**43**	**44**	**45**	**46**	**47**	**48**	**49**	**50**
(B)	(D)	(D)	(C)	(B)	(D)	(A)	(D)	(A)	(A)
51	**52**	**53**	**54**	**55**	**56**	**57**	**58**	**59**	**60**
(B)	(D)	(A)	(B)	(A)	(A)	(B)	(C)	(D)	(D)

SOME SELECTED EXPLANATORY ANSWERS

1. Video-conferencing is the conduct of a video-conference by a set of tele-communication technologies which allow two or more locations to communicate by simultaneous two-way video and audio transmissions. It has also been called visual collaboration and is a type of groupware.

2. Makhanlal Chaturvedi National University of Journalism and Communication, officially known as MC Rashtriya Patrakarita Vishwa-vidyalaya is a government University located in Bhopal, Madhya Pradesh. It was set up by the Act 15 of 1990 of the Madhya Pradesh Legislative Assembly. This University was formally inaugurated by Dr. Shankar Dayal Sharma, the then Vice President of India, on 16th January, 1990.

3. In June 1923, the Radio Club of Bombay made the first ever broadcast in the country. This was followed by the setting up of the Calcutta Radio Club five month later. The first radio station of the Indian Broadcasting Company (IBC) at Bombay (now Mumbai), formally inaugurated by the then Viceroy of India, Lord Irwin, on January 23, 1927, heralded the beginning of organised broadcasting in India. Interestingly, this was the year in which the British Broadcasting Corporation (BBC) was formed. The IBC was liquidated in 1930.

4. PAL (Phase Alternating Line) is a analogue television colour encoding system used in broadcast television systems in many countries. Other common analogue television systems are NTSC (National Television System Committee) and SECAM (Sequential Couleur Avec Memoire).

North America, most of South America, Japan, South Korea and Taiwan adopted NTSC. Most of Western Europe, India, Iceland, Australia, parts of Africa and the Middle East, and a few countries in South America adopted PAL. SECAM was mainly adopted in France, Eastern Europe and parts of Africa.

5. The Directorate of Advertising & Visual Publicity (DAVP) is the nodal agency to undertake multi-media advertising and publicity for various Ministries and Departments of Governments of India. Some of the Autonomous Bodies also route their advertisements through DAVP. As a service agency, it endeavours to Communicate at grass roots level on behalf of various Central Government Ministries.

7.

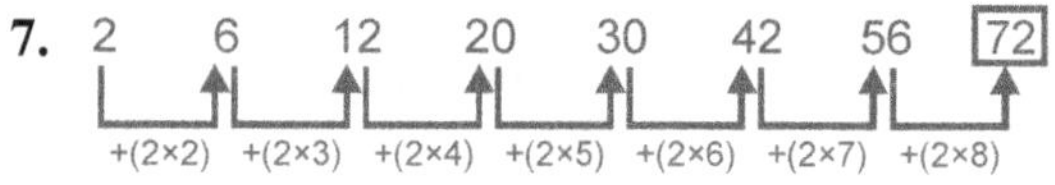

8.

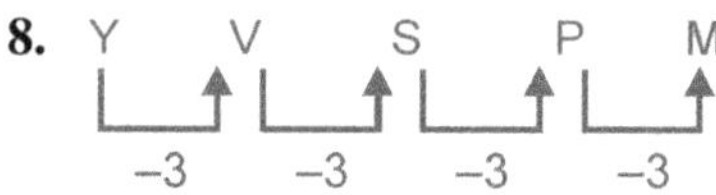

14. **Persuasive Definitions:** The purpose of a persuasive definition is to convince us to believe that something is the case and to get us to act accordingly. Frequently definitions of words like "freedom," "democracy," and "communism," are of this type. (E.g., taxation is the means by which bureaucrats rip off the people who have elected them.) While these sorts of definitions might be emotionally useful, we should avoid them when we are attempting to be logical.

Theoretical Definitions: Theoretical definitions are designed to explain a theory. Whether they are correct or not will depend, largely, on whether the theory they are an integral part of is correct. Newton's famous formula "F = ma" (*i.e.*, Force = mass x acceleration), provides a good example of such a definition.

Stipulative Definitions: Stipulative definitions are frequently provided when we need to refer to a complex idea, but there simply is no word for that idea. A word is selected and assigned a meaning without any pretense that this is what that word really means. (E.g., by "a blue number" we mean any number greater than 17 but less than 36.)

Lexical Definitions: Unlike stipulative definitions, lexical definitions do attempt to capture the real meaning of a word and so can be either correct or incorrect. When we tell someone that "intractable" means not easily governed, or obstinate, this is the kind of definition we are providing. Roughly, lexical definitions are the kinds of definitions found in dictionaries.

20. Let the price of petrol be ₹ 100 per litre. Let the user use 1 litre of petrol. Therefore, his expense on petrol = 100 × 1 = ₹ 100
Now, the price of petrol increases by 25%.
Therefore, the new price of petrol = ₹ 125.
As he has to maintain his expenditure on petrol constant, he will be spending only ₹ 100 on petrol.
Let 'x' be the number of litres of petrol he will use at the new price.
Therefore,

$$125 \times x = 100$$

$$\Rightarrow x = \frac{100}{125} = \frac{4}{5} = 0.8 \text{ litres}$$

He has cut down his petrol consumption by

$$0.2 \text{ litres} = \frac{0.2}{1} \times 100 = 20\%.$$

22. Upto 9 A.M. 1st pipe has worked for 3 hrs; 2nd pipe for 2 hrs. and 3rd pipe for 1 hr.

∴ Part filled up to 9 A.M.

$$= 3 \times \frac{1}{15} + 2 \times \frac{1}{20} + \frac{1}{30}$$

$$= \frac{1}{5} + \frac{1}{10} + \frac{1}{30}$$

$$= \frac{1}{3}$$

$$\text{Unfilled part at 9 A.M.} = 1 - \frac{1}{3} = \frac{2}{3}$$

From 9 A.M. onwards all four pipes are functioning.
Part filled (by all four pipes) in 1 hr.

$$= \frac{1}{15} + \frac{1}{20} + \frac{1}{30} + \frac{1}{60} = \frac{1}{6}$$

∴ $\frac{2}{3}$ of reservoir will be filled up in

$$6 \times \frac{2}{3} = 4 \text{ hr.}$$

Counting 4 hrs. from 9 A.M. reservoir will be full at 1.00 P.M.

23. Contribution of wind and solar power in absolute terms = $97 \times \frac{7}{100}$ = 6.79 GW.

24. Contribution of renewable energy sources in absolute terms = $\frac{97 \times 27}{100}$ = 26.19 GW.

25. TCP/IP is the communication protocol for communication between computers on the Internet.
TCP/IP stands for **T**ransmission **C**ontrol **P**rotocol/**I**nternet **P**rotocol.
TCP/IP defines how electronic devices (like computers) should be connected to the Internet, and how data should be transmitted between them.

26. ASCII stands for the "American Standard Code for Information Interchange". It was designed in the early 60's, as a standard character-set for computers and hardware devices like teleprinters and tapedrives.
ASCII is a 7-bit character set containing 128 characters.
It contains the numbers from 0-9, the uppercase and lowercase English letters from A to Z, and some special characters.
The character-sets used in modern computers, HTML, and Internet are all based on ASCII.

29. Internet Explorer is a free web browser from Microsoft.
Internet Explorer was released in 1995 and is one of the most popular browsers today.

30. POP3 stands for a Post Office Protocol version 3. The POP3 protocol is designed to allow the users to retrieve e-mail messages when they are connected to the e-mail server (via Internet, Ethernet or VPN network connection). Once the e-mail messages are downloaded from the server they can be modified, read and manipulated offline.

The IMAP (Internet Message Access Protocol) is a newer and modern alternative to the POP3 protocol. Unlike it, the IMAP allows the users to work with their messages in both online and offline modes. The IMAP-capable e-mail client programs retrieve the messages' headers from the server and can store local copies of the messages in a local (temporary) cache. All the messages are left on the server until they are deleted by the user. This mechanism allows multiple e-mail clients to access a single mailbox and is often used for corporate/ business e-mails (*e.g.* sales@company-domain.com).

31. Peroxyacyl nitrates (PANs) are powerful respiratory and eye irritants present in photochemical smog.

35. There are two types of seismic waves, *body waves* and *surface waves*. Body waves travel through the interior of the Earth, while surface waves travel only within the top surface layers. Most earthquakes take place at depths of less than 80 km below the Earth's surface. There are two types of body waves, *P waves* and *S waves*. P waves bunch together and then spread apart when they move. It is a bit like the movement of an inch worm or a slinky. S waves are like rolling ocean waves or like when you snap a rope. The oscillations are in a waveform.

37. The Indian Institute of Advanced Study (IIAS) is a prestigious research institute based in Shimla. It was set up by the Ministry of Education, Government of India in 1964 and it started functioning from October 20, 1965. The building that houses the Institute was originally built as a home for Lord Dufferin, Viceroy of India from 1884-1888 and was called the Viceregal Lodge. It housed all the subsequent viceroys and governors general of India. It occupied the Observatory Hill, one of the seven hills that Shimla is built upon.

38. NCTE has 4 Regional offices which are as follows:

1. Eastern Regional Committee (ERC) located at Bhubaneshwar.
2. Southern Regional Committee (SRC) located at Bangalore.
3. Western Regional Committee (WRC) located at Bhopal.
4. Northern Regional Committee (NRC) located at Jaipur.

39. Right to Constitutional Remedies (Article 32) was regarded as the heart and soul of the Indian Constitution by Dr. B.R. Ambedkar.

45. **Non-projected Aids:** Visual instructional devices which are simply presented without any projection equipment are non-projected aids. **Examples:** blackboard, chart, etc.

Projected Aids: Visual instructional devices which are shown with a projector are called projected aids. **Examples:** slides, filmstrip, silent films, cartoons, etc. projected through an opaque projector (epidiascope), or an over head projector.

50. Ibid is a contraction of *ibidem*, a Latin word meaning "the same place." This term is most commonly used for footnoting in scholarly texts, allowing the author to say "ibid" instead of citing a lengthy title. In legal texts, people may use "id," a shortening of "idem," a word which means "as mentioned previously."

53. *Ex-post facto* research is systematic empirical inquiry in which the scientist does not have direct control of independent variables because their manifestations have already occurred or because they are inherently not manipulated.

Previous Years' Paper (Solved)

UGC-NET (JRF) EXAM DECEMBER, 2011

PAPER–I

Note : This paper contains **Sixty (60)** multiple-choice questions, each question carrying **two (2)** marks. Candidate is expected to answer any **Fifty (50)** questions. In case more than **Fifty (50)** questions are attempted, only the first **Fifty (50)** questions will be evaluated.

1. Photo bleeding means
A. Photo cropping
B. Photo placement
C. Photo cutting
D. Photo colour adjustment

2. While designing communication strategy feed-forward studies are conducted by
A. Audience B. Communicator
C. Satellite D. Media

3. In which language the newspapers have highest circulation ?
A. English B. Hindi
C. Bengali D. Tamil

4. Aspect ratio of TV Screen is
A. 4 : 3 B. 3 : 4
C. 2 : 3 D. 2 : 4

5. Communication with oneself is known as
A. Organisational Communication
B. Grapewine Communication
C. Interpersonal Communication
D. Intrapersonal Communication

6. The term 'SITE' stands for
A. Satellite Indian Television Experiment
B. Satellite International Television Experiment
C. Satellite Instructional Television Experiment
D. Satellite Instructional Teachers Education

7. What is the number that comes next in the sequence ?
2, 5, 9, 19, 37, ___
A. 76 B. 74
C. 75 D. 50

8. Find the next letter for the series MPSV.....
A. X B. Y
C. Z D. A

9. If '367' means 'I am happy'; '748' means 'you are sad' and '469' means 'happy and sad' in a given code, then which of the following represents 'and' in that code ?
A. 3 B. 6
C. 9 D. 4

10. The basis of the following classification is 'animal', 'man', 'house', 'book', and 'student':
A. Definite descriptions
B. Proper names
C. Descriptive phrases
D. Common names

11. **Assertion (A) :** The coin when flipped next time will come up tails.

Reason (R) : Because the coin was flipped five times in a row, and each time it came up heads.
Choose the correct answer from below :
A. Both (A) and (R) are true, and (R) is the correct explanation of (A).

B. Both (A) and (R) are false, and (R) is the correct explanation of (A).
C. (A) is doubtful, (R) is true, and (R) is not the correct explanation of (A).
D. (A) is doubtful, (R) is false, and (R) is the correct explanation of (A).

12. The relation 'is a sister of ' is
A. non-symmetrical
B. symmetrical
C. asymmetrical
D. transitive

13. If the proposition "Vegetarians are not meat eaters" is false, then which of the following inferences is correct ? Choose from the codes given below :
1. "Some vegetarians are meat eaters" is true.
2. "All vegetarians are meat eaters" is doubtful.
3. "Some vegetarians are not meat eaters" is true.
4. "Some vegetarians are not meat eaters" is doubtful.

Codes:
A. 1, 2 and 3 B. 2, 3 and 4
C. 1, 3 and 4 D. 1, 2 and 4

14. Determine the nature of the following definition :

'Poor' means having an annual income of ₹ 10,000.
A. persuasive B. precising
C. lexical D. stipulative

15. Which one of the following is not an argument ?
A. If today is Tuesday, tomorrow will bc Wednesday.
B. Since today is Tuesday, tomorrow will be Wednesday.
C. Ram insulted me so I punched him in the nose.
D. Ram is not at home, so he must have gone to town.

16. Venn diagram is a kind of diagram to
A. represent and assess the truth of elementary inferences with the help of Boolean Algebra of classes.
B. represent and assess the validity of elementary inferences with the help of Boolean Algebra of classes.
C. represent but not assess the validity of elementary inferences with the help of Boolean Algebra of classes.
D. assess but not represent the validity of elementary inferences with the help of Boolean Algebra of classes.

17. Inductive logic studies the way in which a premise may
A. support and entail a conclusion
B. not support but entail a conclusion
C. neither support nor entail a conclusion
D. support a conclusion without entailing it

18. Which of the following statements are true ? Choose from the codes given below.
1. Some arguments, while not completely valid, are almost valid.
2. A sound argument may be invalid.
3. A cogent argument may have a probably false conclusion.
4. A statement may be true or false.

Codes:
A. 1 and 2 B. 1, 3 and 4
C. 4 alone D. 3 and 4

19. If the side of the square increases by 40%, then the area of the square increases by
A. 60 % B. 40 %
C. 196 % D. 96 %

20. There are 10 lamps in a hall. Each one of them can be switched on independently. The number of ways in which hall can be illuminated is
A. 10^2 B. 1023
C. 2^{10} D. 10 !

21. How many numbers between 100 and 300 begin or end with 2 ?
A. 100 B. 110
C. 120 D. 180

22. In a college having 300 students, every student reads 5 newspapers and every newspaper is read by 60 students. The number of newspapers required is

A. at least 30 B. at most 20
C. exactly 25 D. exactly 5

The total CO_2 emissions from various sectors are 5 mmt. In the Pie Chart given below, the percentage contribution to CO_2 emissions from various sectors is indicated.

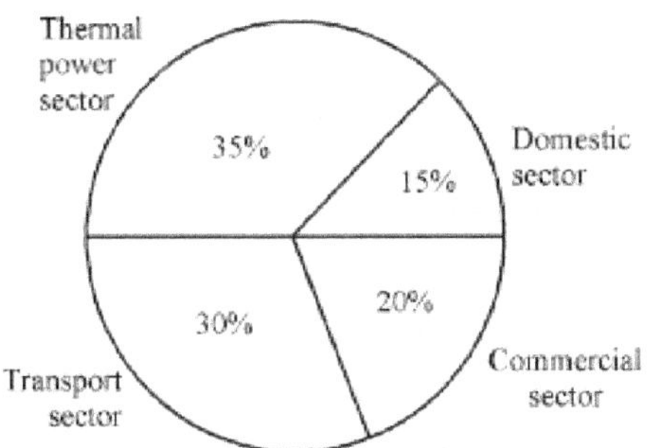

23. What is the absolute CO_2 emission from domestic sector ?
A. 1.5 mmt B. 2.5 mmt
C. 1.75 mmt D. 0.75 mmt

24. What is the absolute CO_2 emission for combined thermal power and transport sectors?
A. 3.25 mmt B. 1.5 mmt
C. 2.5 mmt D. 4 mmt

25. Which of the following operating system is used on mobile phones?
A. Windows Vista B. Android
C. Windows XP D. All of the above

26. If $(y)_x$ represents a number y in base x, then which of the following numbers is smallest of all?
A. $(1111)_2$ B. $(1111)_8$
C. $(1111)_{10}$ D. $(1111)_{16}$

27. High level programming language can be converted to machine language using which of the following?
A. Oracle B. Compiler
C. Mat lab D. Assembler

28. HTML is used to create
A. machine language program
B. high level program
C. web page
D. web server

29. The term DNS stands for
A. Domain Name System
B. Defense Nuclear System
C. Downloadable New Software
D. Dependent Name Server

30. IPv4 and IPv6 are addresses used to identify computers on the internet. Find the correct statement out of the following :
A. Number of bits required for IPv4 address is more than number of bits required for IPv6 address.
B. Number of bits required for IPv4 address is same as number of bits required for IPv6 address.
C. Number of bits required for IPv4 address is less than number of bits required for IPv6 address.
D. Number of bits required for IPv4 address is 64.

31. Which of the following pollutants affects the respiratory tract in humans?
A. Carbon monoxide
B. Nitric oxide
C. Sulphur di-oxide
D. Aerosols

32. Which of the following pollutants is not emitted from the transport sector?
A. Oxides of nitrogen
B. Chlorofluorocarbons
C. Carbon monoxide
D. Poly aromatic hydrocarbons

33. Which of the following sources of energy has the maximum potential in India?
A. Solar energy
B. Wind energy
C. Ocean thermal energy
D. Tidal energy

34. Which of the following is not a source of pollution in soil ?
A. Transport sector
B. Agriculture sector
C. Thermal power plants
D. Hydropower plants

35. Which of the following is ***not*** a natural hazard?

A. Earthquake B. Tsunami
C. Flash floods D. Nuclear accident

36. Ecological footprint represents

A. area of productive land and water to meet the resources requirement
B. energy consumption
C. CO_2 emissions per person
D. forest cover

37. The aim of value education to inculcate in students is

A. the moral values
B. the social values
C. the political values
D. the economic values

38. Indicate the number of Regional Offices of University Grants Commission of India.

A. 10 B. 07
C. 08 D. 09

39. One-rupee currency note in India bears the signature of

A. The President of India
B. Finance Minister of India
C. Governor, Reserve Bank of India
D. Finance Secretary of Government of India

40. Match the List – I with the List – II and select the correct answer from the codes given below:

List – I (Commissions and Committees)	**List – II (Year)**
(*a*) First Administrative Reforms Commission	(*i*) 2005
(*b*) Paul H. Appleby Committee I	(*ii*) 1962
(*c*) K. Santhanam Committee	(*iii*) 1966
(*d*) Second Administrative Reforms Commission	(*iv*) 1953

Codes :

	(*a*)	(*b*)	(*c*)	(*d*)
A.	(i)	(iii)	(ii)	(iv)
B.	(iii)	(iv)	(ii)	(i)
C.	(iv)	(ii)	(iii)	(i)
D.	(ii)	(i)	(iv)	(iii)

41. Constitutionally the registration and recognition of political parties is the function performed by

A. The State Election Commission of respective States
B. The Law Ministry of Government of India
C. The Election Commission of India
D. Election Department of the State Governments

42. The members of Gram Sabha are

A. Sarpanch, Upsarpanch and all elected Panchas
B. Sarpanch, Upsarpanch and Village level worker
C. Sarpanch, Gram Sevak and elected Panchas
D. Registered voters of Village Panchayat

43. By which of the following methods the true evaluation of the students is possible?

A. Evaluation at the end of the course.
B. Evaluation twice in a year.
C. Continuous evaluation.
D. Formative evaluation.

44. Suppose a student wants to share his problems with his teacher and he visits the teacher's house for the purpose, the teacher should

A. contact the student's parents and solve his problem.
B. suggest him that he should never visit his house.
C. suggest him to meet the principal and solve the problem.
D. extend reasonable help and boost his morale.

45. When some students are deliberately attempting to disturb the discipline of the class by making mischief, what will be your role as a teacher?

A. Expelling those students.
B. Isolate those students.
C. Reform the group with your authority.
D. Giving them an opportunity for introspection and improve their behaviour.

46. Which of the following belongs to a projected aid?

A. Blackboard B. Diorama
C. Epidiascope D. Globe

47. A teacher is said to be fluent in asking questions, if he can ask

A. meaningful questions
B. as many questions as possible
C. maximum number of questions in a fixed time
D. many meaningful questions in a fixed time

48. Which of the following qualities is most essential for a teacher ?

A. He should be a learned person.
B. He should be a well dressed person.
C. He should have patience.
D. He should be an expert in his subject.

49. A hypothesis is a

A. law B. canon
C. postulate D. supposition

50. Suppose you want to investigate the working efficiency of nationalised bank in India, which one of the following would you follow?

A. Area Sampling
B. Multi-stage Sampling
C. Sequential Sampling
D. Quota Sampling

51. Controlled group condition is applied in

A. Survey Research
B. Historical Research
C. Experimental Research
D. Descriptive Research

52. Workshops are meant for

A. giving lectures
B. multiplc target groups
C. showcase new theories
D. hands on training/experience

53. Which one of the following is a research tool?

A. Graph B. Illustration
C. Questionnaire D. Diagram

54. Research is not considered ethical if it

A. tries to prove a particular point.
B. does not ensure privacy and anonymity of the respondent.
C. does not investigate the data scientifically.
D. is not of a very high standard.

Directions (Qs. 55 to 60): *Read the following passage carefully and answer the questions.*

The catalytic fact of the twentieth century is uncontrollable development, consumerist society, political materialism, and spiritual devaluation. This inordinate development has led to the transcendental 'second reality' of sacred perception that biologically transcendence is a part of human life. As the century closes, it dawns with imperative vigour that the 'first reality' of enlightened rationalism and the 'second reality' of the Beyond have to be harmonised in a worthy state of man. The *de facto* values describe what we are, they portray the 'is' of our ethic, they are *est* values (Latin *est* means is). The ideal values tell us what we ought to be, they are *esto* values (Latin *esto* 'ought to be'). Both have to be in the ebb and flow of consciousness. The ever new science and technology and the ever-perennial faith are two modes of one certainty, that is the wholeness of man, his courage to be, his share in Being.

The materialistic foundations of science have crumbled down. Science itself has proved that matter is energy, processes are as valid as facts, and affirmed the non-materiality of the universe. The encounter of the 'two cultures', the scientific and the humane, will restore the normal vision, and will be the bedrock of a 'science of understanding' in the new century. It will give new meaning to the ancient perception that quantity (measure) and quality (value) coexist at the root of nature. Human endeavours cannot afford to be humanistically irresponsible.

55. The problem raised in the passage reflects overall on

A. Consumerism
B. Materialism
C. Spiritual devaluation
D. Inordinate development

56. The '*de facto*' values in the passage means

A. What is B. What ought to be
C. What can be D. Where it is

57. According to the passage, the 'first reality' constitutes
A. Economic prosperity
B. Political development
C. Sacred perception of life
D. Enlightened rationalism

58. Encounter of the 'two cultures', the scientific and the human implies
A. Restoration of normal vision
B. Universe is both material and non-material
C. Man is superior to nature
D. Co-existence of quantity and quality in nature

59. The contents of the passage are
A. Descriptive B. Prescriptive
C. Axiomatic D. Optional

60. The passage indicates that science has proved that
A. universe is material
B. matter is energy
C. nature has abundance
D. humans are irresponsible

ANSWERS

1	2	3	4	5	6	7	8	9	10
A	B	B	A	D	C	C	B	C	D
11	**12**	**13**	**14**	**15**	**16**	**17**	**18**	**19**	**20**
C	B	A	B	A	B	D	D	D	B
21	**22**	**23**	**24**	**25**	**26**	**27**	**28**	**29**	**30**
B	C	D	A	B	A	B	C	A	C
31	**32**	**33**	**34**	**35**	**36**	**37**	**38**	**39**	**40**
A	B	B	D	D	A	A	B	D	B
41	**42**	**43**	**44**	**45**	**46**	**47**	**48**	**49**	**50**
C	D	D	D	D	C	D	C	D	B
51	**52**	**53**	**54**	**55**	**56**	**57**	**58**	**59**	**60**
C	D	C	B	C	A	D	A	A	B

SOME SELECTED EXPLANATORY ANSWERS

7.
$$2 \times 2 + 1 = 5$$
$$5 \times 2 - 1 = 9$$
$$9 \times 2 + 1 = 19$$
$$19 \times 2 - 1 = 37$$
$$\therefore \quad 37 \times 2 + 1 = \boxed{75}$$

8. 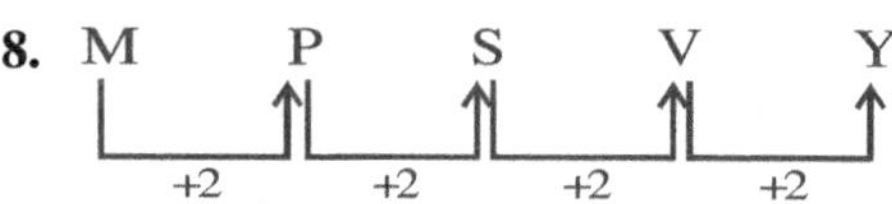

9.
I am happy = 367 ...(1)
You are sad = 748 ...(2)
Happy and sad = 469 ...(3)
From (1) and (3)
Happy = 6
and from (2) and (3)
Sad = 4
$\therefore$ and = 9

19. Let the side of the square be 100 m.
$\therefore$ Area = side^2 = 10000 m^2
After increase, side of the square = 100 + 40
= 140 cm

$\therefore$ Area = 140 × 140 = 19600 cm^2

$\therefore$ Percentage increase = $\frac{19600-10000}{10000}\times 100$

$= \frac{9600 \times 100}{10000} = 96\%$

21. The required numbers are—
Numbers from 200 to 299
And 102, 112, 122, 132, 142, 152, 162, 172, 182, 192
Hence total required number = 100 + 10
= 110

22. Here we suppose group of 5 students as 1 unit.

so, number of units = $\frac{300}{60} = 5$ units

Now, each unit requires sets of papers

Total requirement = 5 × 5 = $\boxed{25}$

23. Domestic sector emission = $5\times\frac{15}{100}$

= 0.75 mmt.

24. Combined % of emission of CO_2 from thermal and transport sector = 30 + 35 = 65%

Required emission = $5\times\frac{65}{100}$ = 3.25 mmt.

26. $(1111)_2 = 2^3 + 2^2 + 2^1 + 2^0 = \boxed{15}$

Previous Years' Paper (Solved)

UGC-NET (JRF) EXAM JUNE, 2011

PAPER–I

Note : This paper contains **sixty (60)** multiple-choice questions, each question carrying **two (2)** marks. Candidate is expected to answer any **fifty (50)** questions. In case more than **fifty (50)** questions are attempted, only the first **fifty (50)** questions will be evaluated.

1. A research paper is a brief report of research work based on
A. Primary Data only
B. Secondary Data only
C. Both Primary and Secondary Data
D. None of the above

2. Newton gave three basic laws of motion. This research is categorized as
A. Descriptive Research
B. Sample Survey
C. Fundamental Research
D. Applied Research

3. A group of experts in a specific area of knowledge assembled at a place and prepared a syllabus for a new course. The process may be termed as
A. Seminar B. Workshop
C. Conference D. Symposium

4. In the process of conducting research "Formulation of Hypothesis" is followed by
A. Statement of Objectives
B. Analysis of Data
C. Selection of Research Tools
D. Collection of Data

Read the following passage carefully and answer questions from 5 to 10:

All historians are interpreters of text if they be private letters, Government records or parish birthlists or whatever. For most kinds of historians, these are only the necessary means to understanding something other than the texts themselves, such as a political action or a historical trend, whereas for the intellectual historian, a full understanding of his chosen texts is itself the aim of his enquiries. Of course, the intellectual history is particularly prone to draw on the focus of other disciplines that are habitually interpreting texts for purposes of their own, probing the reasoning that ostensibly connects premises and conclusions. Furthermore, the boundaries with adjacent subdisciplines are shifting and indistinct : the history of art and the history of science both claim a certain autonomy, partly just because they require specialised technical skills, but both can also be seen as part of a wider intellectual history, as is evident when one considers, for example, the common stock of knowledge about cosmological beliefs or moral ideals of a period.

Like all historians, the intellectual historian is a consumer rather than a producer of 'methods'. His distinctiveness lies in which aspect of the past he is trying to illuminate, not in having exclusive possession of either a corpus of evidence or a body of techniques. That being said, it does seem that the label 'intellectual history' attracts a disproportionate share of misunderstanding.

It is alleged that intellectual history is the history of something that never really mattered. The long dominance of the historical profession by political historians bred a kind of philistinism, an unspoken belief that power and its exercise was 'what mattered'. The prejudice was reinforced by the assertion that political action was never really the outcome of principles or ideas that were 'more flapdoodle'. The legacy of this precept is still discernible in the tendency to require ideas to have 'licensed' the political class before they can be deemed worthy of intellectual attention, as if there were some reasons why the history of art or science, of philosophy or literature, were somehow of interest and significance than the history of Parties or Parliaments. Perhaps in recent years the mirror-image of this philistinism has been more common in the claim that ideas of any one is of systematic expression or sophistication do not matter, as if they were only held by a minority.

Answer the following questions :

5. An intellectual historian aims to fully understand
A. the chosen texts of his own
B. political actions
C. historical trends
D. his enquiries

6. Intellectual historians do not claim exclusive possession of
A. conclusions
B. any corpus of evidence
C. distinctiveness
D. habitual interpretation

7. The misconceptions about intellectual history stem from
A. a body of techniques
B. the common stock of knowledge
C. the dominance of political historians
D. cosmological beliefs

8. What is philistinism?
A. Reinforcement of prejudice
B. Fabrication of reasons
C. The hold of land-owning classes
D. Belief that power and its exercise matter

9. Knowledge of cosmological beliefs or moral ideas of a period can be drawn as part of
A. literary criticism
B. history of science
C. history of philosophy
D. intellectual history

10. The claim that ideas of any one is of systematic expression do not matter, as if they were held by a minority, is
A. to have a licensed political class
B. political action
C. a philosophy of literature
D. the mirror-image of philistinism

11. Public communication tends to occur within a more
A. complex structure
B. political structure
C. convenient structure
D. formal structure

12. Transforming thoughts, ideas and messages into verbal and non-verbal signs is referred to as
A. channelisation B. mediation
C. encoding D. decoding

13. Effective communication needs a supportive
A. economic environment
B. political environment
C. social environment
D. multi-cultural environment

14. A major barrier in the transmission of cognitive data in the process of communication is an individual's
A. personality C. expectation
B. social status D. coding ability

15. When communicated, institutionalised stereotypes become
A. myths B. reasons
C. experiences D. convictions

16. In mass communication, selective perception is dependent on the receiver's
A. competence B. pre-disposition
C. receptivity D. ethnicity

17. Determine the relationship between the pair of words NUMERATOR : DENOMINATOR and then select the pair of words from the following which have a similar relationship :
A. fraction : decimal
B. divisor : quotient
C. top : bottom
D. dividend : divisor

18. Find the wrong number in the sequence 125, 127, 130, 135, 142, 153, 165
A. 130 B. 142
C. 153 D. 165

19. If HOBBY is coded as IOBY and LOBBY is coded as MOBY; then BOBBY is coded as
A. BOBY B. COBY
C. DOBY D. OOBY

20. The letters in the first set have certain relationship. On the basis of this relationship, make the right choice for the second set : K/T : 11/20 : : J/R : ?
A. 10/8 B. 10/18
C. 11/19 D. 10/19

21. If A = 5, B = 6, C = 7, D = 8 and so on, what do the following numbers stand for?
17, 19, 20, 9, 8
A. Plane B. Moped
C. Motor D. Tonga

22. The price of oil is increased by 25%. If the expenditure is not allowed to increase, the ratio between the reduction in consumption and the original consumption is
A. 1 : 3 B. 1 : 4
C. 1 : 5 D. 1 : 6

23. How many 8's are there in the following sequence which are preceded by 5 but not immediately followed by 3?
5 8 3 7 5 8 6 3 8 5 4 5 8 4 7 6
5 5 8 3 5 8 7 5 8 2 8 5
A. 4 B. 5
C. 7 D. 3

24. If a rectangle were called a circle, a circle a point, a point a triangle and a triangle a square, the shape of a wheel is
A. Rectangle B. Circle
C. Point D. Triangle

25. Which one of the following methods is best suited for mapping the distribution of different crops as provided in the standard classification of crops in India?
A. Pie diagram
B. Chorochromatic technique
C. Isopleth technique
D. Dot method

26. Which one of the following does not come under the methods of data classification?
A. Qualitative B. Normative
C. Spatial D. Quantitative

27. Which one of the following is not a source of data?
A. Administrative records
B. Population census
C. GIS
D. Sample survey

28. If the statement 'some men are cruel' is false, which of the following statements/statement are/is true?
(*i*) All men are cruel.
(*ii*) No men are cruel.
(*iii*) Some men are not cruel.
A. (*i*) and (*iii*) B. (*i*) and (*ii*)
C. (*ii*) and (*iii*) D. (*iii*) only

29. The octal number system consists of the following symbols:
A. 0 – 7 B. 0 – 9
C. 0 – 9, A – F D. None of the above

30. The binary equivalent of $(-19)_{10}$ in signed magnitude system is
A. 11101100 B. 11101101
C. 10010011 D. None of these

31. DNS in internet technology stands for
A. Dynamic Name System
B. Domain Name System
C. Distributed Name System
D. None of these

32. HTML stands for
A. Hyper Text Markup Language
B. Hyper Text Manipulation Language
C. Hyper Text Managing Links
D. Hyper Text Manipulating Links

33. Which of the following is type of LAN?
A. Ethernet B. Token Ring
C. FDDI D. All of the above

34. Which of the following statements is true?
A. Smart cards do not require an operating system.
B. Smart cards and PCs use some operating system.

C. COS is smart card operating system.
D. The communication between reader and card is in full duplex mode.

35. The Ganga Action Plan was initiated during the year

A. 1986 C. 1988
B. 1990 D. 1992

36. Identify the correct sequence of energy sources in order of their share in the power sector in India:

A. Thermal > nuclear > hydro > wind
B. Thermal > hydro > nuclear > wind
C. Hydro > nuclear > thermal > wind
D. Nuclear > hydro > wind > thermal

37. Chromium as a contaminant in drinking water in excess of permissible levels, causes

A. Skeletal damage
B. Gastrointestinal problem
C. Dermal and nervous problems
D. Liver/Kidney problems

38. The main precursors of winter smog are

A. N_2O and hydrocarbons
B. NO_x and hydrocarbons
C. SO_2 and hydrocarbons
D. SO_2 and ozone

39. Flash floods are caused when

A. the atmosphere is convectively unstable and there is considerable vertical wind-shear
B. the atmosphere is stable
C. the atmosphere is convectively unstable with no vertical windshear
D. winds are catabatic

40. In mega cities of India, the dominant source of air pollution is

A. transport sector
B. thermal power
C. municipal waste
D. commercial sector

41. The first Open University in India was set up in the State of

A. Andhra Pradesh
B. Delhi
C. Himachal Pradesh
D. Tamil Nadu

42. Most of the Universities in India are funded by

A. the Central Government
B. the State Governments
C. the University Grants Commission
D. Private bodies and Individuals

43. Which of the following organizations looks after the quality of Technical and Management education in India?

A. NCTE
B. MCI
C. AICTE
D. CSIR

44. Consider the following statements :
Identify the statement which implies natural justice.

A. The principle of natural justice is followed by the Courts.
B. Justice delayed is justice denied.
C. Natural justice is an inalienable right of a citizen
D. A reasonable opportunity of being heard must be given.

45. The President of India is

A. the Head of State
B. the Head of Government
C. both A and B
D. None of the above

46. Who among the following holds office during the pleasure of the President of India?

A. Chief Election Commissioner
B. Comptroller and Auditor General of India
C. Chairman of the Union Public Service Commission
D. Governor of a State

Questions 47 to 49 are based upon the following diagram in which there are three interlocking circles A, P and S where A stands for Artists, circle P for Professors and circle S for Sportspersons.

Different regions in the figure are lettered from a to f :

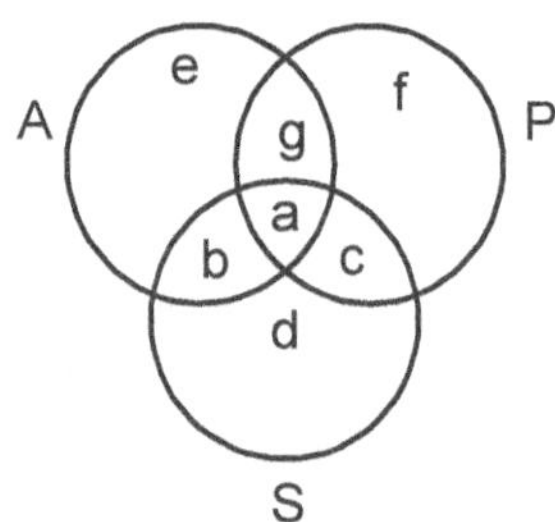

47. The region which represents artists who are neither sportsmen nor professors.

A. d B. e
C. b D. g

48. The region which represents professors, who are both artists and sportspersons.

A. a B. c
C. d D. g

49. The region which represents professors, who are also sportspersons, but not artists.

A. e B. f
C. c D. g

Questions 50 to 52 are based on the following data :

Measurements of some variable X were made at an interval of 1 minute from 10 A.M. to 10:20 A.M. The data, thus, obtained is as follows :

X : 60, 62, 65, 64, 63, 61, 66, 65, 70, 68
63, 62, 64, 69, 65, 64, 66, 67, 66, 64

50. The value of X, which is exceeded 10% of the time in the duration of measurement, is

A. 69 B. 68
C. 67 D. 66

51. The value of X, which is exceeded 90% of the time in the duration of measurement, is

A. 63 B. 62
C. 61 D. 60

52. The value of X, which is exceeded 50% of the time in the duration of measurement, is

A. 66 B. 65
C. 64 D. 63

53. For maintaining an effective discipline in the class, the teacher should

A. Allow students to do what they like.
B. Deal with the students strictly.
C. Give the students some problem to solve.
D. Deal with them politely and firmly.

54. An effective teaching aid is one which

A. is colourful and good looking
B. activates all faculties
C. is visible to all students
D. easy to prepare and use

55. Those teachers are popular among students who

A. develop intimacy with them
B. help them solve their problems
C. award good grades
D. take classes on extra tuition fee

56. The essence of an effective classroom environment is

A. a variety of teaching aids
B. lively student-teacher interaction
C. pin-drop silence
D. strict discipline

57. On the first day of his class, if a teacher is asked by the students to introduce himself, he should

A. ask them to meet after the class
B. tell them about himself in brief
C. ignore the demand and start teaching
D. scold the student for this unwanted demand

58. Moral values can be effectively inculcated among the students when the teacher

A. frequently talks about values
B. himself practices them
C. tells stories of great persons
D. talks of Gods and Goddesses

59. The essential qualities of a researcher are

A. spirit of free enquiry
B. reliance on observation and evidence

C. systematization or theorizing of knowledge
D. All of the above

60. Research is conducted to
I. Generate new knowledge
II. Not to develop a theory
III. Obtain research degree
IV. Reinterpret existing knowledge

Which of the above are correct?
A. I, III & II B. III, II & IV
C. II, I & III D. I, III & IV

ANSWERS

1	**2**	**3**	**4**	**5**	**6**	**7**	**8**	**9**	**10**
C	C	B	C	A	B	C	D	D	D
11	**12**	**13**	**14**	**15**	**16**	**17**	**18**	**19**	**20**
D	C	D	C	D	B	D	D	B	B
21	**22**	**23**	**24**	**25**	**26**	**27**	**28**	**29**	**30**
B	C	A	C	A	B	A	B	A	D
31	**32**	**33**	**34**	**35**	**36**	**37**	**38**	**39**	**40**
B	A	D	C	A	B	D	C	A	A
41	**42**	**43**	**44**	**45**	**46**	**47**	**48**	**49**	**50**
A	C	C	D	B	D	B	A	C	C
51	**52**	**53**	**54**	**55**	**56**	**57**	**58**	**59**	**60**
B	D	D	B	B	B	B	B	D	D

SOME SELECTED EXPLANATORY ANSWERS

18.

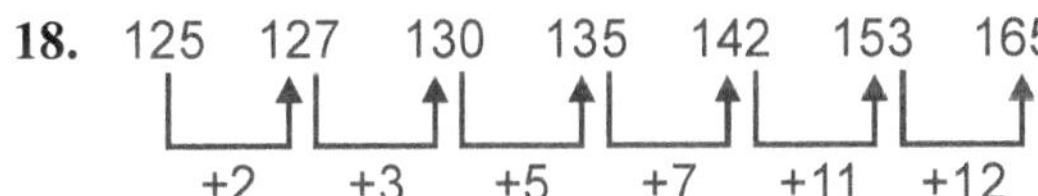

Except 12, all others are odd numbers.

19.

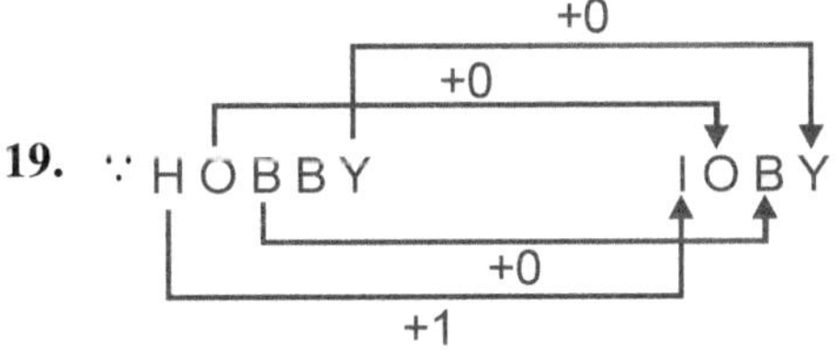

and

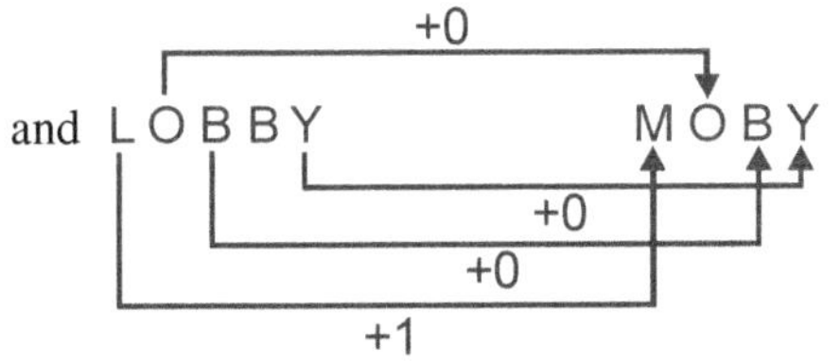

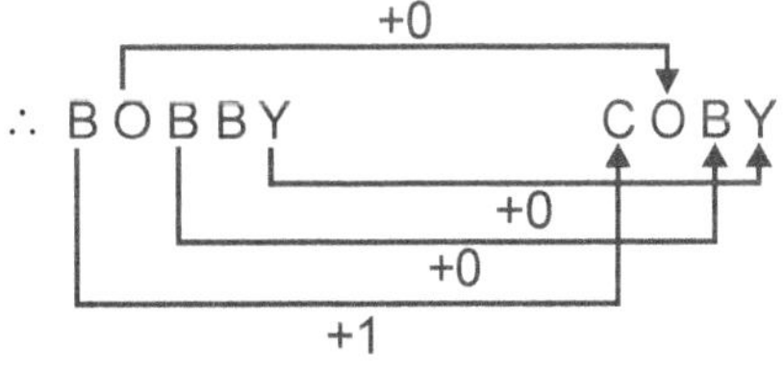

20.

A	B	C	D	E	F	G	H	I	J
1	2	3	4	5	6	7	8	9	10
K	L	M	N	O	P	Q	R	S	T
11	12	13	14	15	16	17	18	19	20
U	V	W	X	Y	Z				
21	22	23	24	25	26				

∵ K → 11
and T → 20
∴ J → 10
R → 18

21. ∵ A = 5, B = 6, C = 7, D = 8,
∴ E = 9, F = 10, G = 11, H = 12, I = 13,

J = 14, K = 15, L = 16, M = 17, N = 18, O = 19, P = 20, Q = 21, R = 22, S = 23 ....

Therefore, 17 = M
19 = O
20 = P
9 = E
8 = D

23. There are four 8's in the sequence which are preceded by 5 but not immediately followed by 3.

24. Since

□ → ○ → · → △ → □

Rectangle circle point triangle square

∴ The shape of a wheel is Point.

29. An octal number is a number that consists of any of the following eight symbols – 0, 1, 2, 3, 4, 5, 6 and 7.

Hints : 47 to 49

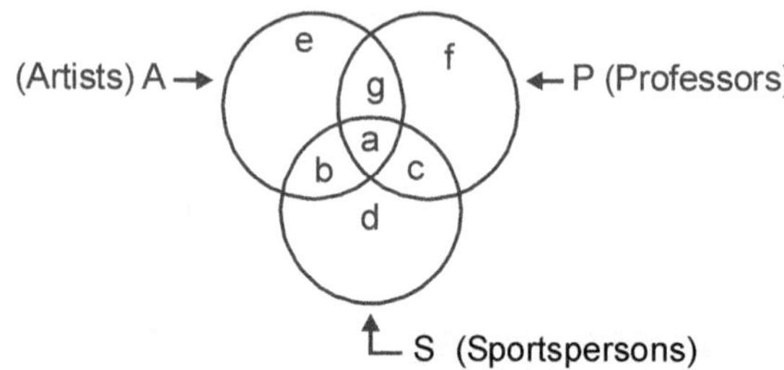

47. 'e' represents artists who are neither sportsmen nor professors.

48. 'a' represents professors, who are both artists and sportspersons.

49. 'c' represents professors, who are also sports persons but not artists.

Previous Years' Paper (Solved)

UGC-NET (JRF) EXAM DECEMBER, 2010

PAPER–I

Note : This paper contains **sixty** (60) multiple-choice questions, each question carrying **two** (2) marks. Candidate is expected to answer any **fifty** (50) questions. In case more than **fifty** **(50)** questions are attempted, only the first **fifty** **(50)** questions will be evaluated.

1. Which of the following variables cannot be expressed in quantitative terms?
A. Socio-economic Status
B. Marital Status
C. Numerical Aptitude
D. Professional Attitude

2. A doctor studies the relative effectiveness of two drugs of dengue fever. His research would be classified as
A. Descriptive Survey
B. Experimental Research
C. Case Study
D. Ethnography

3. The term 'phenomenology' is associated with the process of
A. Qualitative Research
B. Analysis of Variance
C. Correlational Study
D. Probability Sampling

4. The 'Sociogram' technique is used to study
A. Vocational Interest
B. Professional Competence
C. Human Relations
D. Achievement Motivation

Read the following passage carefully and answer questions from 5 to 10.

It should be remembered that the nationalist movement in India, like all nationalist movements, was essentially a bourgeois movement. It represented the natural historical stage of development, and to consider it or to criticise it as a working-class movement is wrong. Gandhi represented that movement and the Indian masses in relation to that movement to a supreme degree, and he became the voice of Indian people to that extent. The main contribution of Gandhi to India and the Indian masses has been through the powerful movements which he launched through the National Congress. Through nation-wide action he sought to mould the millions, and largely succeeded in doing so, and changing them from a demoralised, timid and hopeless mass, bullied and crushed by every dominant interest, and incapable of resistance, into a people with self-respect and self-reliance, resisting tyranny, and capable of united action and sacrifice for a larger cause.

Gandhi made people think of political and economic issues and every village and every bazaar hummed with argument and debate on the new ideas and hopes that filled the people. That was an amazing psychological change. The time was ripe for it, of course, and circumstances and world conditions worked for this change. But a great leader is necessary to take advantage of circumstances and conditions. Gandhi was that leader, and he released many of the bonds that imprisoned and disabled our minds, and none of us who experienced it can ever forget that great feeling of release and exhilaration that came over the Indian people.

Gandhi has played a revolutionary role in India of the greatest importance because he knew how to make the most of the objective conditions and could reach the heart of the masses, while groups with a more advanced ideology functioned largely in the air because they did not fit in with those conditions and could therefore not evoke any substantial response from the masses.

It is perfectly true that Gandhi, functioning in the nationalist plane, does not think in terms of the conflict of classes, and tries to compose their differences. But the action he has indulged and taught the people has inevitably raised mass consciousness tremendously and made social issues vital. Gandhi and the Congress must be judged by the policies they pursue and the action they indulge in. But behind this, personality counts and colours those policies and activities. In the case of very exceptional person like Gandhi the question of personality becomes especially important in order to understand and appraise him. To us he has represented the spirit and honour of India, the yearning of her sorrowing millions to be rid of their innumerable burdens, and an insult to him by the British Government or others has been an insult to India and her people.

5. Which one of the following is true of the given passage?
A. The passage is a critique of Gandhi's role in Indian movement for independence.
B. The passage hails the role of Gandhi in India's freedom movement.
C. The author is neutral on Gandhi's role in India's freedom movement.
D. It is an account of Indian National Congress's support to the working-class movement.

6. The change that the Gandhian movement brought among the Indian masses was
A. Physical B. Cultural
C. Technological D. Psychological

7. To consider the nationalist movement or to criticise it as a working-class movement was wrong because it was a
A. historical movement
B. voice of the Indian people
C. bourgeois movement
D. movement represented by Gandhi

8. Gandhi played a revolutionary role in India because he could
A. preach morality
B. reach the heart of Indians
C. see the conflict of classes
D. lead the Indian National Congress

9. Groups with advanced ideology functioned in the air as they did not fit in with
A. objective conditions of masses
B. the Gandhian ideology
C. the class consciousness of the people
D. the differences among masses

10. The author concludes the passage by
A. criticising the Indian masses
B. the Gandhian movement
C. pointing out the importance of the personality of Gandhi
D. identifying the sorrows of millions of Indians

11. Media that exist in an interconnected series of communication – points are referred to as
A. Networked media
B. Connective media
C. Nodal media
D. Multimedia

12. The information function of mass communication is described as
A. diffusion B. publicity
C. surveillance D. diversion

13. An example of asynchronous medium is
A. Radio B. Television
C. Film D. Newspaper

14. In communication, connotative words are
A. explicit C. abstract
B. simple D. cultural

15. A message beneath a message is labelled as
A. embedded text B. internal text
C. inter-text D. sub-text

16. In analog mass communication, stories are
A. static B. dynamic
C. interactive D. exploratory

17. Determine the relationship between the pair of words ALWAYS : NEVER and then select from the following pair of words which have a similar relationship

A. often : rarely
B. frequently : occasionally
C. constantly : frequently
D. intermittently : casually

18. Find the wrong number in the sequence

52, 51, 48, 43, 34, 27, 16

A. 27 B. 34
C. 43 D. 48

19. In a certain code, PAN is written as 31 and PAR as 35, then PAT is written in the same code as

A. 30 B. 37
C. 39 D. 41

20. The letters in the first set have certain relationship. On the basis of this relationship, make the right choice for the second set :

AF : IK : : LQ : ?

A. MO B. NP
C. OR D. TV

21. If 5472 = 9, 6342 = 6, 7584 = 6, what is 9236?

A. 2 B. 3
C. 4 D. 5

22. In an examination, 35% of the total students failed in Hindi, 45% failed in English and 20% in both. The percentage of those who passed in both subjects is

A. 10 B. 20
C. 30 D. 40

23. Two statements I and II given below are followed by two conclusions (a) and (b). Supposing the statements are true, which of the following conclusions can logically follow?

Statements :

I. Some flowers are red.
II. Some flowers are blue.

Conclusions :

(a) Some flowers are neither red nor blue.
(b) Some flowers are both red and blue.

A. Only (a) follows.
B. Only (b) follows.
C. Both (a) and (b) follows.
D. Neither (a) nor (b) follows.

24. If the statement 'all students are intelligent' is true, which of the following statements are false?

(*i*) No students are intelligent.
(*ii*) Some students are intelligent.
(*iii*) Some students are not intelligent.

A. (*i*) and (*ii*)
B. (*i*) and (*iii*)
C. (*ii*) and (*iii*)
D. (*i*) only

25. A reasoning where we start with certain particular statements and conclude with a universal statement is called

A. Deductive Reasoning
B. Inductive Reasoning
C. Abnormal Reasoning
D. Transcendental Reasoning

26. What is the smallest number of ducks that could swim in this formation — two ducks in front of a duck, two ducks behind a duck and a duck between two ducks?

(a) 5 (b) 7
(c) 4 (d) 3

27. Mr. A, Miss B, Mr. C and Miss D are sitting around a table and discussing their trades.

(*i*) Mr. A sits opposite to the cook.
(*ii*) Miss B sits right to the barber.
(*iii*) The washerman sits right to the barber.
(*iv*) Miss D sits opposite to Mr. C.

What are the trades of A and B?

(a) Tailor and barber
(b) Barber and cook
(c) Tailor and cook
(d) Tailor and washerman

28. Which one of the following methods serve to measure correlation between two variables?

(a) Scatter Diagram
(b) Frequency Distrubution
(c) Two-way table
(d) Coefficient of Rank Correlation

29. Which one of the following is not an Internet Service Provider (ISP)?
(a) MTNL (b) BSNL
(c) ERNET India (d) Infotech India Ltd.

30. The hexadecimal number system consists of the symbols
(a) 0 – 7 (b) 0 – 9, A – F
(c) 0 – 7, A – F (d) None of these

31. The binary equivalent of $(-15)_{10}$ is (2's complement system is used)
A. 11110001 B. 11110000
C. 10001111 D. None of these

32. 1 GB is equal to
A. 2^{30} bits B. 2^{30} bytes
C. 2^{20} bits D. 2^{20} bytes

33. The set of computer programs that manage the hardware/software of a computer is called
A. Compiler system
B. Operation system
C. Operating system
D. None of these

34. S/MIME in Internet technology stands for
A. Secure Multipurpose Internet Mail Extension
B. Secure Multimedia Internet Mail Extension
C. Simple Multipurpose Internet Mail Extension
D. Simple Multimedia Internet Mail Extension

35. Which of the following is **not** covered in 8 missions under the Climate Action Plan of Government of India?
A. Solar power
C. Waste to energy conversion
B. Afforestation
D. Nuclear energy

36. The concentration of Total Dissolved Solids (TDS) in drinking water should not exceed
A. 500 mg/L B. 400 mg/L
C. 300 mg/L D. 200 mg/L

37. 'Chipko movement was first started by
A. Arundhati Roy
B. Medha Patkar
C. Ila Bhatt
D. Sunderlal Bahuguna

38. The constitutents of photochemical smog responsible for eye irritation are
A. SO_2 and O_3
B. SO_2 and NO_2
C. HCHO and PAN
D. SO_2 and SPM

39. **Assertion (A) :** Some carbonaceous aerosols may be carcinogenic.

Reason (R) : They may contain polycyclic aromatic hydrocarbons (PAHs).
A. Both (A) and (R) are correct and (R) is the correct explanation of (A).
B. Both (A) and (R) are correct but (R) is not the correct explanation of (A).
C. (A) is correct, but (R) is false.
D. (A) is false, but (R) is correct.

40. Volcanic eruptions affect
A. atmosphere and hydrosphere
B. hydrosphere and biosphere
C. lithosphere, biosphere and atmosphere
D. lithosphere, hydrosphere and atmosphere

41. India's first Defence University is in the State of
A. Haryana B. Andhra Pradesh
C. Uttar Pradesh D. Punjab

42. Most of the Universities in India
A. conduct teaching and research only
B. affiliate colleges and conduct examinations
C. conduct teaching/research and examinations
D. promote research only

43. Which one of the following is not a Constitutional Body?
A. Election Commission
B. Finance Commission
C. Union Public Service Commission
D. Planning Commission

44. Which one of the following statements is not correct?
A. Indian Parliament is supreme.
B. The Supreme Court of India has the power of judicial review.

C. There is a division of powers between the Centre and the States.
D. There is a Council of Ministers to aid and advise the President.

45. Which one of the following statements reflects the republic character of Indian democracy?
A. Written constitution
B. No State religion
C. Devolution of power to local Government institutions
D. Elected President and directly or indirectly elected Parliament

46. Who among the following appointed by the Governor can be removed by only the President of India?
A. Chief Minister of a State
B. A member of the State Public Service Commission
C. Advocate-General
D. Vice-Chancellor of a State University

47. If two small circles represent the class of the 'men' and the class of the 'plants and the big circle represents 'mortality', which one of the following figures represent the proposition 'All men are mortal.'?

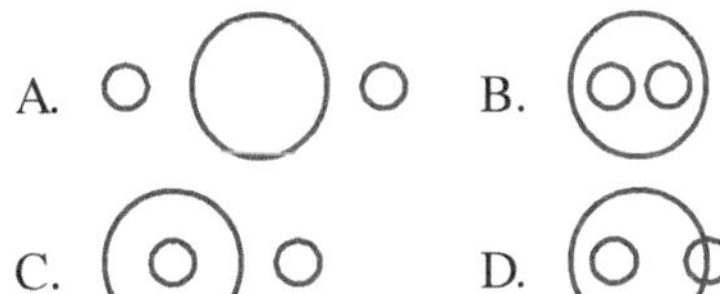

The following table presents the production of electronic items (TVs and LCDs) in a factory during the period from 2006 to 2010. Study the table carefully and answer the questions from **48** to **52** :

Year	2006	2007	2008	2009	2010
TVs	6000	9000	13000	11000	8000
LCDs	7000	9400	9000	10000	12000

48. In which year, the total production of electronic items is maximum?
A. 2006 B. 2007
C. 2008 D. 2010

49. What is the difference between averages of production of LCDs and TVs from 2006 to 2008?
A. 3000 B. 2867
C. 3015 D. None of these

50. What is the year in which production of TVs is half the production of LCDs in the year 2010?
(a) 2007 (b) 2006
(c) 2009 (d) 2008

51. What is the ratio of production of LCDs in the years 2008 and 2010?
A. 4 : 3 B. 3 : 4
C. 1 : 3 D. 2 : 3

52. What is the ratio of production of TVs in the years 2006 and 2007?
A. 6 : 7 B. 7 : 6
C. 2 : 3 D. 3 : 2

53. Some students in a class exhibit great curiosity for learning. It may be because such children
A. Are gifted
B. Come from rich families
C. Show artificial behaviour
D. Create indiscipline in the class

54. The most important quality of a good teacher is
A. Sound knowledge of subject matter
B. Good communication skills
C. Concern for students' welfare
D. Effective leadership qualities

55. Which one of the following is appropriate in respect of teacher-student relationship?
A. Very informal and intimate
B. Limited to classroom only
C. Cordial and respectful
D. Indifferent

56. The academic performance of students can be improved if parents are encouraged to
A. supervise the work of their wards
B. arrange for extra tuition
C. remain unconcerned about it
D. interact with teachers frequently

57. In a lively classroom situation, there is likely to be
A. occasional roars of laughter
B. complete silence
C. frequent teacher-student dialogue
D. loud discussion among students

58. If a parent approaches the teacher to do some favour to his/her ward in the examination, the teacher should
A. try to help him
B. ask him not to talk in those terms
C. refulse politely and firmly
D. ask him rudely to go away

59. Which of the following phrases is not relevant to describe the meaning of research as a process?
A. Systematic Activity
B. Objective Observation
C. Trial and Error
D. Problem Solving

60. Which of the following is not an example of a continuous variable?
A. Family size
B. Intelligence
C. Height
D. Attitude

ANSWERS

1	**2**	**3**	**4**	**5**	**6**	**7**	**8**	**9**	**10**
D	B	A	C	B	D	C	B	A	C
11	**12**	**13**	**14**	**15**	**16**	**17**	**18**	**19**	**20**
A	C	D	D	D	A	A	B	B	D
21	**22**	**23**	**24**	**25**	**26**	**27**	**28**	**29**	**30**
A	B	C	D	B	A	C	D	D	B
31	**32**	**33**	**34**	**35**	**36**	**37**	**38**	**39**	**40**
D	B	C	A	D	A	D	B	A	D
41	**42**	**43**	**44**	**45**	**46**	**47**	**48**	**49**	**50**
A	C	D	B	D	B	C	C	D	B
51	**52**	**53**	**54**	**55**	**56**	**57**	**58**	**59**	**60**
B	C	A	B	C	D	C	C	C	C

SOME SELECTED EXPLANATORY ANSWERS

18. 52 51 48 43 34 27 16

Differences: 1 3 5 9 7 11

Only 9 is divisible by 3 and rest are not divisible by any number.

19. $\because$

A	B	C	D	E	F	G	H	I
1	2	3	4	5	6	7	8	9
J	K	L	M	N	O	P	Q	R
10	11	12	13	14	15	16	17	18

S	T	U	V	W	X	Y	Z
19	20	21	22	23	24	25	26

$\because$ PAN $\Rightarrow$ $16 + 1 + 14 = 31$

PAR $\Rightarrow$ $16 + 1 + 18 = 35$

$\therefore$ PAT $\Rightarrow$ $16 + 1 + 20 = \boxed{37}$.

21. $\because$ $5472 \Rightarrow 5 + 4 + 7 + 2 = 18 \Rightarrow 1 + 8 = 9$

$6342 \Rightarrow 6 + 3 + 4 + 2 = 15 \Rightarrow 1 + 5 = 6$

$7584 \Rightarrow 7 + 5 + 8 + 4 = 24 \Rightarrow 2 + 4 = 6$

$\therefore$ $9236 \Rightarrow 9 + 2 + 3 + 6 = 20 \Rightarrow 2 + 0 = 2$

Previous Paper (Solved)

UGC-NET (JRF) EXAM JUNE, 2010

PAPER–I

Note : This paper contains **sixty** (60) multiple-choice questions, each question carrying **two** (2) marks. Candidate is expected to answer any **fifty** (50) questions. In case more than 50 questions are attempted, only the first 50 questions will be evaluated.

1. Which one of the following is the most important quality of a good teacher ?
A. Punctuality and sincerity
B. Content mastery
C. Content mastery and reactive
D. Content mastery and sociable

2. The primary responsibility for the teacher's adjustment lies with
A. The children
B. The principal
C. The teacher himself
D. The community

3. As per the NCTE norms, what should be the staff strength for a unit of 100 students at B.Ed, level ?
A. 1 + 7 B. 1 + 9
C. 1 + 10 D. 1 + 5

4. Research has shown that the most frequent symptom of nervous instability among teachers is
A. Digestive upsets
B. Explosive behaviour
C. Fatigue
D. Worry

5. Which one of the following statements is correct ?
A. Syllabus is an annexure to the curriculum.
B. Curriculum is the same in all educational institutions.
C. Curriculum includes both formal, and informal education.
D. Curriculum does not include methods of evaluation.

6. A successful teacher is one who is
A. Compassionate and disciplinarian
B. Quite and reactive
C. Tolerant and dominating
D. Passive and active

Read the following passage carefully and answer the questions 7 to 12.

The phrase "What is it like ?" stands for a fundamental thought process. How does one go about observing and reporting on things and events that occupy segments of earth space ? Of all the infinite variety of phenomena on the face of the earth, how does one decide what phenomena to observe ? There is no such thing as a complete description of the earth or any part of it, for every microscopic point on the earth's surface differs from every other such point. Experience shows that the things observed are already familiar, because they are like phenomena that occur at home or because they resemble the abstract images and models developed in the human mind.

How are abstract images formed ? Humans alone among the animals possess language; their words symbolize not only specific things but also mental images of classes of things. People can remember what they have seen or experienced because they attach a word symbol to them.

During the long record of our efforts to gain more and more knowledge about the face of the earth as the human habitat, there has been a continuing interplay between things and events. The direct observation through the senses is described as a percept; the mental image is described as a concept. Percepts are what some people describe as reality, in contrast to mental images, which are theoretical, implying that they are not real.

The relation of Percept to Concept is not as simple as the definition implies. It is now quite clear that people of different cultures or even individuals in the same culture develop different mental images of reality and what they perceive is a reflection of these preconceptions. The direct observation of things and events on the face of the earth is so clearly a function of the mental images of the mind of the observer that the whole idea of reality must be reconsidered.

Concepts determine what the observer perceives, yet concepts are derived from the generalizations of previous percepts. What happens is that the educated observer is taught to accept a set of concepts and then sharpens or changes these concepts during a professional career. In any one field of scholarship, professional opinion at one time determines what concepts and procedures are acceptable, and these form a kind of model of scholarly behaviour.

7. The problem raised in the passage reflects on
A. thought process
B. human behaviour
C. cultural perceptions
D. professional opinion

8. According to the passage, human beings have mostly in mind
A. Observation of things
B. Preparation of mental images
C. Expression through language
D. To gain knowledge

9. Concept means
A. A mental image
B. A reality
C. An idea expressed in language form
D. All the above

10. The relation of Percept to Concept is
A. Positive B. Negative
C. Reflective D. Absolute

11. In the passage, the earth is taken as
A. The Globe
B. The Human Habitat
C. A Celestial Body
D. A Planet

12. Percept means
A. Direct observation through the senses
B. A conceived idea
C. Ends of a spectrum
D. An abstract image

13. Action research means
A. A longitudinal research
B. An applied research
C. A research initiated to solve an immediate problem
D. A research with socio-economic objective

14. Research is
A. Searching again and again
B. Finding solution to any problem
C. Working in a scientific way to search for truth of any problem
D. None of the above

15. A common test in research demands much priority on
A. Reliability B. Useability
C. Objectivity D. All of the above

16. Which of the following is the first step in starting the research process ?
A. Searching sources of information to locate problem.
B. Survey of related literature
C. Identification of problem
D. Searching for solutions to the problem

17. If a researcher conducts a research on finding out which administrative style contributes more to institutional effectiveness ? This will be an example of
A. Basic Research
B. Action Research
C. Applied Research
D. None of the above

18. Normal Probability Curve should be
A. Positively skewed
B. Negatively skewed
C. Leptokurtic skewed
D. Zero skewed

19. In communication, a major barrier to reception of messages is
A. audience attitude
B. audience knowledge
C. audience education
D. audience income

20. Post-modernism is associated with
A. newspapers B. magazines
C. radio D. television

21. Didactic communication is
A. intra-personal B. inter-personal
C. organisational D. relational

22. In communication, the language is
A. the non-verbal code
B. the verbal code
C. the symbolic code
D. the iconic code

23. Identify the correct sequence of the following:
A. Source, channel, message, receiver
B. Source, receiver, channel, message
C. Source, message, receiver, channel
D. Source, message, channel, receiver

24. **Assertion** A.: Mass media promote a culture of violence in the society.

Reason (R) : Because violence sells in the market as people themselves are violent in character.
A. Both A. and (R) are true and (R) is the correct explanation of A..
B. Both A. and (R) are true, but (R) is not the correct explanation of A..
C. A. is true, but (R) is false.
D. Both A. and (R) are false.

25. When an error of 1% is made in the length of a square, the percentage error in the area of a square will be
A. 0 B. 1/2
C. 1 D. 2

26. On January 12, 1980, it was a Saturday. The day of the week on January 12, 1979 was
A. Thursday B. Friday
C. Saturday D. Sunday

27. If water is called food, food is called tree, tree is called earth, earth is called world, which of the following grows a fruit ?
A. Water B. Tree
C. World D. Earth

28. E is the son of A, D is the son of B, E is married to C, C is the daughter of B. How is D related to E ?
A. Brother B. Uncle
C. Father-in-law D. Brother-in-law

29. If INSURANCE is coded as ECNARUSNI, how HINDRANCE will be coded ?
A. CADNHIWCE B. HANODEINR
C. AENIRHDCN D. ECNARDNIH

30. Find the next number in the following series: 2, 5, 10, 17, 26, 37, 50, ?
A. 63 B. 65
C. 67 D. 69

31. Which of the following is an example of circular argument ?
A. God created man in his image and man created God in his own image.
B. God is the source of a scripture and the scripture is the source of our knowledge of God.
C. Some of the Indians are great because India is great.
D. Rama is great because he is Rama.

32. Lakshmana is a morally good person because
A. he is religious B. he is educated
C. he is rich D. he is rational

33. Two statements I and II given below are followed by two conclusions (a) and (b). Supposing the statements are true, which of the following conclusions can logically follow ?
I. Some religious people are morally good.
II. Some religious people are rational.

Conclusions :
(a) Rationally religious people are good morally.

(b) Non-rational religious persons are not morally good.

A. Only (a) follows.
B. Only (b) follows.
C. Both (a) and (b) follow.
D. Neither (a) nor (b) follows.

34. Certainty is

A. an objective fact
B. emotionally satisfying
C. logical
D. ontological

Questions from 35 to 36 are based on the following diagram in which there are three intersecting circles I, S and P where circle I stands for Indians, circle S stands for scientists and circle P for politicians. Different regions of the figure are lettered from a to g.

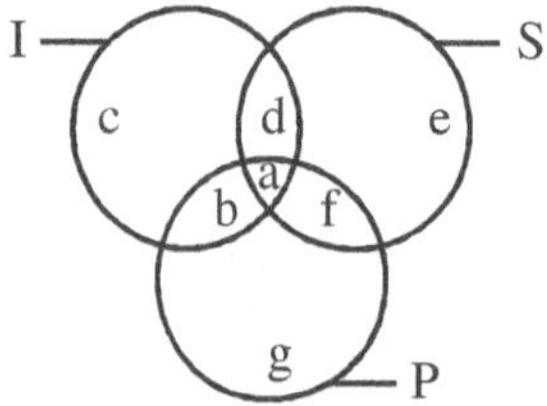

35. The region which represents non-Indian scientists who are politicians.

A. f B. d
C. a D. c

36. The region which represents politicians who are Indians as well as scientists.

A. b B. c
C. a D. d
A. an objective fact

37. The population of a city is plotted as a function of time (years) in graphic form below:

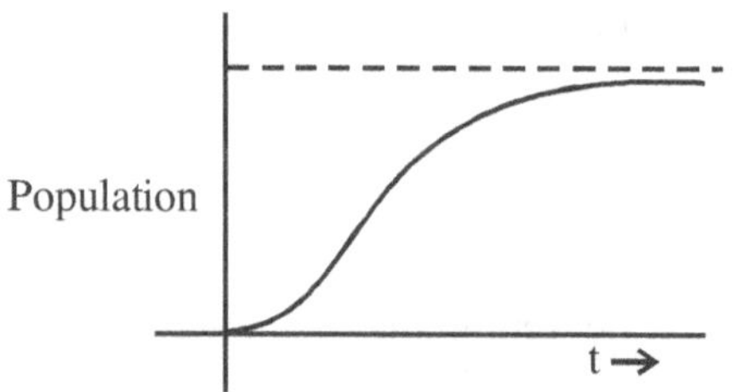

Which of the following inference can be drawn from above plot ?

A. The population increases exponentially. The population increases in parabolic fashion.

The population initially increases in a linear fashion and then stabilizes.

The population initially increases exponentially and then stabilizes.

In the following chart, the price of logs is shown in per cubic metre and that of Plywood and Saw Timber in per tonnes. Study the chart and answer the following questions 38, 39 and 40.

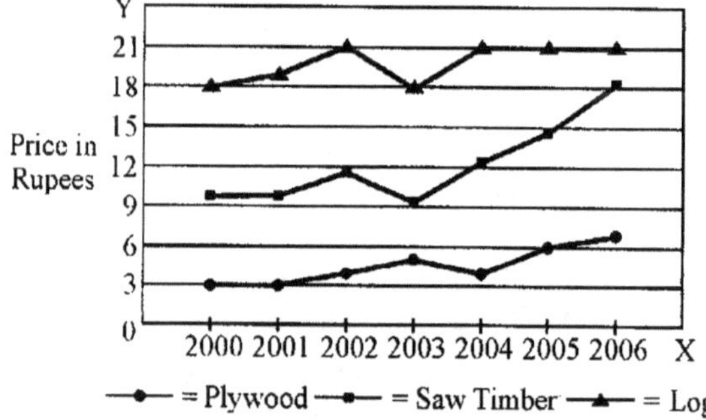

38. Which product shows the maximum percentage increase in price over the period?

A. Saw timber
B. Plywood
C. Log
D. None of the above

39. What is the maximum percentage increase in price per cubic metre of log ?

A. 6 B. 12
C. 18 D. None of these

40. In which year the prices of two products increased and that of the third increased ?

A. 2000 B. 2002
C. 2003 D. 2006

41. Which one of the following is the oldest Archival source of data in India ?

A. National Sample Surveys
B. Agricultural Statistics
C. Census
D. Vital Statistics

42. In a large random data set following normal distribution, the ratio (%) of number of data points which are in the range of (mean ± standard deviation) to the total number of data points, is

A. ~ 50% B. ~ 67%

C. ~ 97% D. ~ 47%

43. Which number system is usually followed in a typical 32-bit computer?

A. 2 B. 8

C. 10 D. 16

44. Which one of the following is an example of Operating System ?

A. Microsoft Word

B. Microsoft Excel

C. Microsoft Access

D. Microsoft Windows

45. Which one of the following represent the binary equivalent of the decimal number 23?

A. 01011 B. 10111

C. 10011 D. None of the above

46. Which one of the following is different from other members?

A. Google B. Windows

C. Linux D. Mac

47. Where does a computer add and compare its data?

A. CPU B. Memory

C. Hard disk D. Floppy disk

48. Computers on an internet are identified by

A. e-mail address

B. street address

C. IP address

D. None of the above

49. The Right to Information Act, 2005 makes the provision of

A. Dissemination of all types of information by all Public authorities to any person.

B. Establishment of Central, State and District Level Information Commissions as an appellate body.

C. Transparency and accountability in Public authorities.

D. All of the above

50. Which type of natural hazards cause maximum damage to property and lives?

A. Hydrological

B. Hydro-meteorological

C. Geological

D. Geo-chemical

51. Dioxins are produced from

A. Wastelands

B. Power plants

C. Sugar factories

D. Combustion of plastics

52. The slogan "A tree for each child" was coined for

A. Social forestry programme

B. Clean Air programme

C. Soil conservation programme

D. Environmental protection programme

53. The main constituents of biogas are

A. Methane and Carbon di-oxide

B. Methane and Nitric oxide

C. Methane, Hydrogen and Nitric oxide

D. Methane and Sulphur di-oxide

54. **Assertion (A):** In the world as a whole, the environment has degraded during past several decades.

Reason (R) : The population of the world has been growing significantly.

A. A. is correct, (R) is correct and (R) is the correct explanation of A..

B. A. is correct, (R) is correct and (R) is not the correct explanation of A..

C. A. is correct, but (R) is false.

D. A. is false, but (R) is correct.

55. Climate change has implications for

1. soil moisture 2. forest fires

3. biodiversity 4. ground water

Identify the correct combination according to the code :

Codes :

A. 1 and 3 B. 1, 2 and 3

C. 1, 3 and 4 D. 1, 2, 3 and 4

56. The accreditation process by National Assessment and Accreditation Council (NAAC) differs from that of National Board of Accreditation (NBA) in terms of

A. Disciplines covered by both being the same, there is duplication of efforts.

B. One has institutional grading approach and the other has programme grading approach.

C. Once get accredited by NBA or NAAC, the institution is free from renewal of grading, which is not a progressive decision.

D. This accreditation amounts to approval of minimum standards in the quality of education in the institution concerned.

57. Which option is not correct ?

A. Most of the educational institutions of National repute in scientific and technical sphere fall under 64th entry of Union list.

B. Education, in general, is the subject of concurrent list since 42nd Constitutional Amendment Act 1976.

C. Central Advisory Board on Education (CABE) was first established in 1920.

D. India had implemented the right to Free and Compulsory Primary Education in 2002 through 86th Constitutional Amendment.

58. Which statement is not correct about the "National Education Day" of India ?

A. It is celebrated on 5th September every year.

B. It is celebrated on 11th November every year.

C. It is celebrated in the memory of India's first Union Minister of Education, Dr. Abul Kalam Azad.

D. It is being celebrated since 2008.

59. Match List-I with List-II and select the correct answer from the codes given below:

List -1 (Articles of the Constitution)	**List - II (Institutions)**
(a) Article 280	(i) Administrative Tribunals
(b) Article 324	(ii) Election Commission of India
(c) Article 323	(iii) Finance Commission at Union level
(d) Article 315	(iv) Union Public Service Commission

Codes :

	(a)	*(b)*	*(c)*	*(d)*
A.	*(i)*	*(ii)*	*(iii)*	*(iv)*
B.	*(iii)*	*(ii)*	*(i)*	*(iv)*
C.	*(ii)*	*(iii)*	*(iv)*	*(i)*
D.	*(ii)*	*(iv)*	*(iii)*	*(i)*

60. Deemed Universities declared by UGC under Section 3 of the UGC Act 1956, are not permitted to

A. offer programmes in higher education and issue degrees.

B. give affiliation to any institute of higher education.

C. open off-campus and off-shore campus anywhere in the country and overseas respectively without the permission of the UGC.

D. offer distance education programmes without the approval of the Distance Education Council.

ANSWERS

1	2	3	4	5	6	7	8	9	10
B	C	C	B	C	A	C	A	A	C
11	**12**	**13**	**14**	**15**	**16**	**17**	**18**	**19**	**20**
B	A	C	C	D	C	C	D	C	D
21	**22**	**23**	**24**	**25**	**26**	**27**	**28**	**29**	**30**
B	B	D	D	D	B	C	D	D	B

31	32	33	34	35	36	37	38	39	40
B	A	D	C	A	C	D	C	D	B
41	**42**	**43**	**44**	**45**	**46**	**47**	**48**	**49**	**50**
C	B	A	D	B	B	A	C	D	C
51	**52**	**53**	**54**	**55**	**56**	**57**	**58**	**59**	**60**
D	D	A	B	D	C	A	A	B	B

SOME SELECTED EXPLANATORY ANSWERS

29. Since,

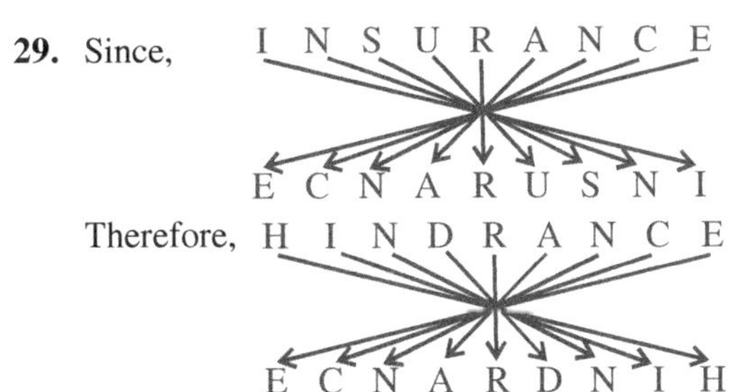

30.

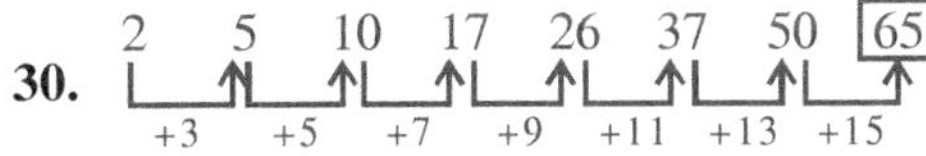

48. Computers on an internet are identified by IP address.

53. Main constituents of biogas are: Methane and Carbon di-oxide.

Previous Paper (Solved)

UGC-NET (JRF) EXAM DECEMBER, 2009

PAPER–I

Note : This paper contains **sixty** (60) multiple-choice questions, each question carrying **two** (2) marks. Candidate is expected to answer any **fifty** (50) questions. In case more than 50 questions are attempted, only the first 50 questions will be evaluated.

1. The University which telecasts interaction educational programmes through its own channel is
- A. Osmania University
- B. University of Pune
- C. Annamalai University
- D. Indira Gandhi National University (IGNOU)

2. Which of the following skills are needed for present day teacher to adjust effectively with the classroom teaching?
1. Knowledge of technology
2. Use of technology in teaching learning
3. Knowledge of students' needs
4. Content mastery

A. 1 & 3 B. 2 & 3
C. 2, 3 & 4 D. 2 & 4

3. Who has signed as MOU for Accreditation of Teacher Education Institutions in India?
- A. NAAC and UGC
- B. NCTE and NAAC
- C. UGC and NCTE
- D. NCTE and IGNOU

4. The primary duty of the teacher is to
- A. raise the intellectual standard of the students
- B. improve the physical standard of the students
- C. help all round development of the students
- D. imbibe value system in the students

5. Micro teaching is more effective
- A. during the preparation for teaching-practice
- B. during the teaching-practice
- C. after the teaching-practice
- D. always

6. What quality the students like the most in a teacher ?
- A. Idealist philosophy
- B. Compassion
- C. Discipline
- D. Entertaining

7. A null hypothesis is
- A. when there is no difference between the variables
- B. the same as research hypothesis
- C. subjective in nature
- D. when there is difference between the variables

8. The research which is exploring new facts through the study of the past is called
- A. Philosophical research
- B. Historical research
- C. Mythological research
- D. Content analysis

9. Action research is
- A. An applied research
- B. A research carried out to solve immediate problems
- C. A longitudinal research
- D. Simulative research

10. The process <u>not</u> needed in Experimental Researches is

A. Observation
B. Manipulation
C. Controlling
D. Content Analysis

11. Manipulation is always a part of

A. Historical research
B. Fundamental research
C. Descriptive research
D. Experimental research

12. Which correlation co-efficient best explains the relationship between creativity and intelligence ?

A. 1.00
B. 0.6
C. 0.5
D. 0.3

Read the following passage and answer the Question Nos. 13 to 18 :

The decisive shift in British Policy really came about under mass pressure in the autumn and winter of 1945 to 46 - the months which Perderel Moon while editing Wavell's Journal has perceptively described as 'The Edge of a Volcano'. Very foolishly, the British initially decided to hold public trials of several hundreds of the 20,000 I.N.A. prisoners (as well as dismissing from service and detaining without trial no less than 7,000). They compounded the folly by holding the first trial in the Red Fort, Delhi in November 1945, and putting on the dock together a Hindu, a Muslim and a Sikh (P.K. Sehgal, Shah Nawaz, Gurbaksh Singh Dhillon). Bhulabhai Desai, Tejbahadur Sapru and Nehru appeared for the defence (the latter putting on his barrister's gown after 25 years), and the Muslim League also joined the countrywide protest. On 20 November, an Intelligence Bureau note admitted that "there has seldom been a matter which has attracted so much Indian public interest and, it is safe to say, sympathy ... this particular brand of sympathy cuts across communal barriers.' A journalist (B. Shiva Rao) visiting the Red Fort prisoners on the same day reported that 'There is not the slightest feeling among them of Hindu and Muslim ... A majority of the men now awaiting trial in the Red Fort is Muslim. Some of these men are bitter that Mr. Jinnah is keeping alive a controversy about Pakistan.' The British became extremely nervous about the I.N.A. spirit spreading to the Indian Army, and in January the Punjab Governor reported that a Lahore reception for released I.N.A. prisoners had been attended by Indian soldiers in uniform.

13. Which heading is more appropriate to assign to the above passage ?

A. Wavell's Journal
B. Role of Muslim League
C. I.N.A. Trials
D. Red Fort Prisoners

14. The trial of P.K. Sehgal, Shah Nawaz and Gurbaksh Singh Dhillon symbolises

A. communal harmony
B. threat to all religious persons
C. threat to persons fighting for the freedom
D. British reaction against the natives

15. I.N.A. stands for

A. Indian National Assembly
B. Indian National Association
C. Inter-national Association
D. Indian National Army

16. 'There has seldom been a matter which has attracted so much Indian Public Interest and, it is safe to say, sympathy ... this particular brand of sympathy cuts across communal barriers.' Who sympathises to whom and against whom ?

A. Muslims sympathised with Shah Nawaz against the British
B. Hindus sympathised with P.K. Sehgal against the British
C. Sikhs sympathised with Gurbaksh Singh Dhillon against the British
D. Indians sympathised with the persons who were to be trialled

17. The majority of people waiting for trial outside the Red Fort and criticising Jinnah were the

A. Hindus
B. Muslims
C. Sikhs
D. Hindus and Muslims both

18. The sympathy of Indian soldiers in uniform with the released I.N.A. prisoners at Lahore indicates

A. Feeling of Nationalism and Fraternity
B. Rebellious nature of Indian soldiers
C. Simply to participate in the reception party
D. None of the above

19. The country which has the distinction of having the two largest circulated newspapers in the world is
A. Great Britain B. The United States
C. Japan D. China

20. The chronological order of non-verbal communication is
A. Signs, symbols, codes, colours
B. Symbols, codes, signs, colours
C. Colours, signs, codes, symbols
D. Codes, colours, symbols, signs

21. Which of the following statements is <u>not</u> connected with communication ?
A. Medium is the message.
B. The world is an electronic cocoon.
C. Information is power.
D. Telepathy is technological.

22. Communication becomes circular when
A. the decoder becomes an encoder
B. the feedback is absent
C. the source is credible
D. the channel is clear

23. The site that played a major role during the terrorist attack on Mumbai (26/11) in 2008 was
A. Orkut B. Facebook
C. Amazon.com D. Twitter

24. **Assertion (A):** For an effective classroom communication at times it is desirable to use the projection technology.
Reason (R): Using the projection technology facilitates extensive coverage of course contents.
A. Both A. and (R) are true, and (R) is the correct explanation.
B. Both A. and (R) are true, but (R) is not the correct explanation.
C. A. is true, but (R) is false.
D. A. is false, but (R) is true.

25. January 1, 1995 was a Sunday. What day of the week lies on January 1, 1996 ?
A. Sunday B. Monday
C. Wednesday D. Saturday

26. When an error of 1% is made in the length and breadth of a rectangle, the percentage error (%) in the area of a rectangle will be
A. 0 B. 1
C. 2 D. 4

27. The next number in the series 2, 5, 9, 19, 37, ? will be
A. 74 B. 75
C. 76 D. None of the above

28. There are 10 true-false questions in an examination. Then these questions can be answered in
A. 20 ways B. 100 ways
C. 240 ways D. 1024 ways

29. What will be the next term in the following? DCXW, FEVU, HGTS, ?
A. AKPO B. ABYZ
C. JIRQ D. LMRS

30. Three individuals X, Y, Z hired a car on a sharing basis and paid Rs. 1,040. They used it for 7, 8, 11 hours, respectively. What are the charges paid by Y ?
A. Rs. 290 B. Rs. 320
C. Rs. 360 D. Rs. 440

31. Deductive argument involves
A. sufficient evidence
B. critical thinking
C. seeing logical relations
D. repeated observation

32. Inductive reasoning is based on or presupposes
A. uniformity of nature
B. God created the world
C. unity of nature
D. laws of nature

33. To be critical, thinking must be
A. practical
B. socially relevant
C. individually satisfying
D. analytical

34. Which of the following is an analogous statement ?

A. Man is like God
B. God is great
C. Gandhiji is the Father of the Nation
D. Man is a rational being.

Questions from 35 - 36 are based on the following diagram in which there are three intersecting circles. H representing The Hindu, I representing Indian Express and T representing The Times of India. A total of 50 persons were surveyed and the number in the Venn diagram indicates the number of persons reading the newspapers.

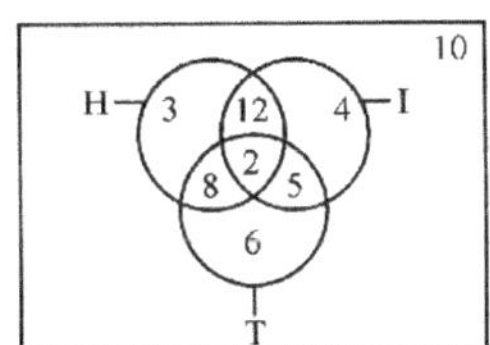

35. How many persons would be reading at least two newspapers ?

A. 23 B. 25
C. 27 D. 29

36. How many persons would be reading almost two newspapers ?

A. 23 B. 25
C. 27 D. 48

37. Which of the following graphs does not represent regular (periodic) behaviour of the variable f(t) ?

1.
2.

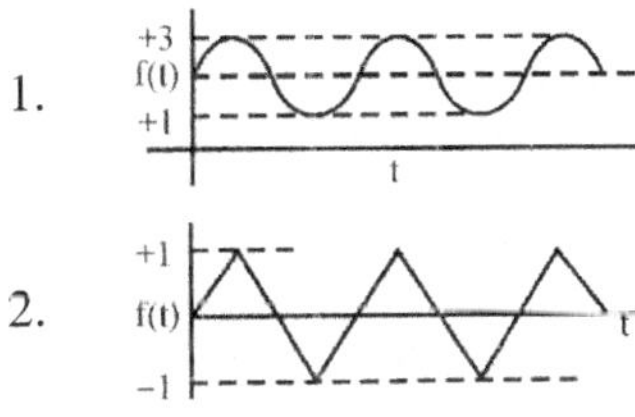

3.

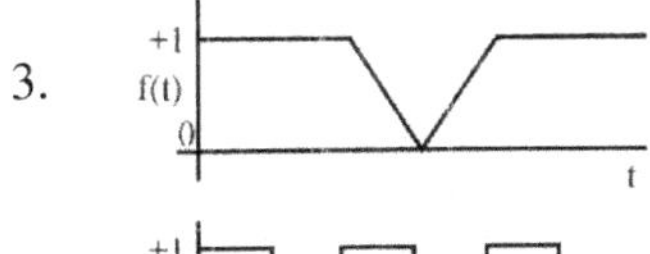

4.

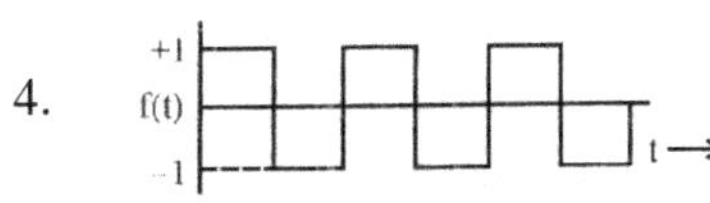

A. 1 B. 2
C. 3 D. 4

Study the following graph and answer the questions 38 to 40.

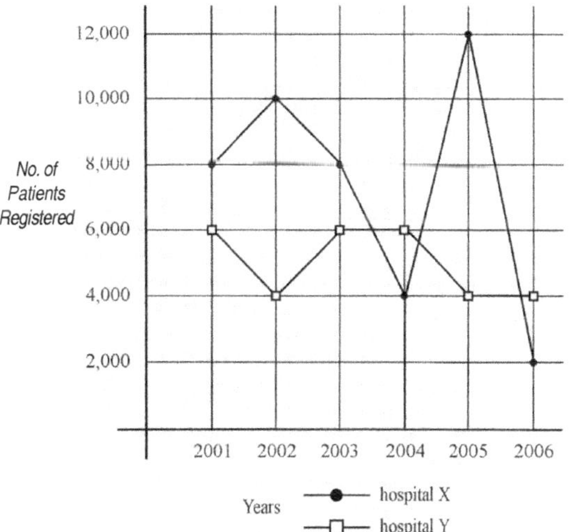

38. In which year total number of patients registered in hospital X and hospital Y was the maximum ?

A. 2003 C. 2005
B. 2004 D. 2006

39. What is the maximum dispersion in the registration of patients in the two hospitals in a year?

A. 8000 C. 4000
B. 6000 D. 2000

40. In which year there was maximum decrease in registration of patients in hospital X ?

A. 2003 B. 2004
C. 2005 D. 2006

41. Which of the following sources of data is not based on primary data collection ?

A. Census of India
B. National Sample Survey
C. Statistical Abstracts of India
D. National Family Health Survey

42. Which of the four data sets have more dispersion ?

A.	88	91	90	92	89	91
B.	0	1	1	0	–1	–2
C.	3	5	2	4	1	5
D.	0	5	8	10	–2	–8

43. Which of the following is not related to information security on the Internet ?
A. Data Encryption
B. Water marking
C. Data Hiding
D. Information Retrieval

44. Which is the largest unit of storage among the following ?
A. Terabyte B. Megabyte
C. Kilobyte D. Gigabyte

45. bit stands for
A. binary information term
C. binary tree
B. binary digit
D. Bivariate Theory

46. Which one of the following is not a linear data structure ?
A. Array B. Binary Tree
C. Queue D. Stack

47. Which one of the following is not a network device ?
A. Router B. Switch
C. Hub D. CPU

48. A compiler is used to convert the following to object code which can be executed
A. High-level language
B. Low-level language
C. Assembly language
D. Natural language

49. The great Indian Bustard bird is found in
A. Thar Desert of Rajasthan
B. Malabar Coast
C. Coastal regions of India
D. Delta regions

50. The Sagarmanthan National Park has been established to preserve the eco-system of which mountain peak ?
A. Kanchenjunga B. Mount Everest
C. Annapurna D. Dhaulavira

51. Maximum soot is released from
A. Petrol vehicles
B. CNG vehicles
C. Diesel vehicles
D. Thermal Power Plants

52. Surface Ozone is produced from
A. Transport sector
B. Cement plants
C. Textile industry
D. Chemical industry

53. Which one of the following non-conventional energy sources can be exploited most economically ?
A. Solar
B. Wind
C. Geo-thermal
D. Ocean Thermal Energy Conversion (OTEC)

54. The most recurring natural hazard in India is
A. Earthquakes B. Floods
C. Landslides D. Volcanoes

55. The recommendation of National Knowledge Commission for the establishment of 1500 Universities is to
A. create more teaching jobs
B. ensure increase in student enrolment in higher education
C. replace or substitute the privately managed higher education institutions by public institutions
D. enable increased movement of students from rural areas to urban areas

56. According to Article 120 of the Constitution of India, the business in Parliament shall be transacted in
A. English only
B. Hindi only
C. English and Hindi both
D. All the languages included in Eighth Schedule of the Constitution

57. Which of the following is more interactive and student centric ?
A. Seminar B. Workshop
C. Lecture D. Group Discussion

58. The Parliament in India is composed of
A. Lok Sabha & Rajya Sabha
B. Lok Sabha, Rajya Sabha & Vice President
C. Lok Sabha, Rajya Sabha & President
D. Lok Sabha, Rajya Sabha with their Secretariats

59. The enrolment in higher education in India is contributed both by Formal System of Education and by System of Distance Education. Distance education contributes

A. 50% of formal system

B. 25% of formal system

C. 10% of the formal system

D. Distance education system's contribution is not taken into account while considering the figures of enrolment in higher education

60. **Assertion A :** The U.G.C. Academic Staff Colleges came into existence to improve the quality of teachers.

Reason (R) : University and college teachers have to undergo both orientation and refresher courses.

A. Both A. and (R) are true and (R) is the correct explanation.

B. Both A. and (R) are correct but (R) is not the correct explanation of A..

C. A. is correct and (R) is false.

D. A. is false and (R) is correct.

ANSWERS

1	**2**	**3**	**4**	**5**	**6**	**7**	**8**	**9**	**10**
D	C	B	C	B	C	A	B	B	B
11	**12**	**13**	**14**	**15**	**16**	**17**	**18**	**19**	**20**
C	B	C	A	D	D	B	A	C	A
21	**22**	**23**	**24**	**25**	**26**	**27**	**28**	**29**	**30**
D	A	A	A	B	C	B	D	C	B
31	**32**	**33**	**34**	**35**	**36**	**37**	**38**	**39**	**40**
C	A	B	A	C	D	C	C	A	D
41	**42**	**43**	**44**	**45**	**46**	**47**	**48**	**49**	**50**
C	D	D	A	B	B	D	A	A	B
51	**52**	**53**	**54**	**55**	**56**	**57**	**58**	**59**	**60**
D	A	A	B	B	C	D	C	B	A

SOME SELECTED EXPLANATORY ANSWERS

27. 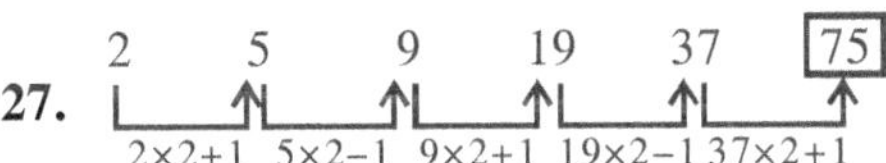

44. Kilobyte < Megabyte < Gigabyte < Terabyte

49. The great Indian Bustard bird is found in Thar Desert.

58. The Parliament in India is composed of Lok Sabha, Rajya Sabha & President.

Previous Paper (Solved)

UGC-NET (JRF) EXAM JUNE, 2008

PAPER–I

Note : This paper contains **fifty** (50) multiple-choice questions, each question carrying **two** (2) marks. Attempt **all** of them.

1. The teacher has been glorified by the phrase "Friend, philosopher and guide" because :
A. He has to play all vital roles in the context of society
B. He transmits the high value of humanity to students
C. He is the great reformer of the society
D. He is a great patriot

2. The most important cause of failure for teacher lies in the area of :
A. inter personal relationship
B. lack of command over the knowledge of the subject
C. verbal ability
D. strict handling of the students

3. A teacher can establish rapport with his students by :
A. becoming a figure of authority
B. impressing students with knowledge and skill
C. playing the role of a guide
D. becoming a friend to the students

4. Education is a powerful instrument of :
A. Social transformation
B. Personal transformation
C. Cultural transformation
D. All the above

5. A teacher's major contribution towards the maximum self-realization of the student is affected through :
A. Constant fulfilment of the students' needs
B. Strict control of class-room activities
C. Sensitivity to students' needs, goals and purposes
D. Strict reinforcement of academic standards

6. Research problem is selected from the stand point of :
A. Researcher's interest
B. Financial support
C. Social relevance
D. Availability of relevant literature

7. Which one is called non-probability sampling?
A. Cluster sampling
B. Quota sampling
C. Systematic sampling
D. Stratified random sampling

8. Formulation of hypothesis may NOT be required in :
A. Survey method
B. Historical studies
C. Experimental studies
D. Normative studies

9. Field-work based research is classified as :
A. Empirical B. Historical
C. Experimental D. Biographical

10. Which of the following sampling method is appropriate to study the prevalence of AIDS amongst male and female in India in 1976, 1986, 1996 and 2006 ?

A. Cluster sampling
B. Systematic sampling
C. Quota sampling
D. Stratified random sampling

Read the following passage and answer the questions 11 to 15 :

The fundamental principle is that Article 14 forbids class legislation but permits reasonable classification for the purpose of legislation which classification must satisfy the twin tests of classification being founded on an intelligible differentia which distinguishes persons or things that are grouped together from those that are left out of the group and that differentia must have a rational nexus to the object sought to be achieved by the Statute in question. The thrust of Article 14 is that the citizen is entitled to equality before law and equal protection of laws. In the very nature of things the society being composed of unequals a welfare State will have to strive by both executive and legislative action to help the less fortunate in society to ameliorate their condition so that the social and economic inequality in the society may be bridged. This would necessitate a legislative application to a group of citizens otherwise unequal and amelioration of whose lot is the object of state affirmative action. In the absence of the doctrine of classification such legislation is likely to flounder on the bed rock of equality enshrined in Article 14. The Court realistically appraising the social and economic inequality and keeping in view the guidelines on which the State action must move as constitutionally laid down in Part IV of the Constitution evolved the doctrine of classification. The doctrine was evolved to sustain a legislation or State action designed to help weaker sections of the society or some such segments of the society in need of succour. Legislative and executive action may accordingly be sustained if it satisfies the twin tests of reasonable classification and the rational principle correlated to the object sought to be achieved.

The concept of equality before the law does not involve the idea of absolute equality among human beings which is a physical impossibility. All that Article 14 guarantees is a similarity of treatment contra-distinguished from identical treatment. Equality before law means that among equals the law should be equal and should be equally administered and that the likes should be treated alike. Equality before the law does not mean that things which are different shall be as though they are the same. It ofcourse means denial of any special privilege by reason of birth, creed or the like. The legislation as well as the executive government, while dealing with diverse problems arising out of an infinite variety of human relations must of necessity have the power of making special laws, to attain any particular object and to achieve that object it must have the power of selection or classification of persons and things upon which such laws are to operate.

11. Right to equality, one of the fundamental rights, is enunciated in the constitution under Part III, Article :
A. 12 B. 13
C. 14 D. 15

12. The main thrust of Right to equality is that it permits :
A. class legislation
B. equality before law and equal protection under the law
C. absolute equality
D. special privilege by reason of birth

13. The social and economic inequality in the society can be bridged by :
A. executive and legislative action
B. universal suffrage
C. identical treatment
D. none of the above

14. The doctrine of classification is evolved to :
A. Help weaker sections of the society
B. Provide absolute equality
C. Provide identical treatment
D. None of the above

15. While dealing with diverse problems arising out of an infinite variety of human relations, the government :
A. must have the power of making special laws

B. must not have any power to make special laws
C. must have power to withdraw equal rights
D. none of the above

16. Communication with oneself is known as :
A. Group communication
B. Grapevine communication
C. Interpersonal communication
D. Intrapersonal communication

17. Which broadcasting system for TV is followed in India ?
A. NTSE B. PAL
C. SECAM D. NTCS

18. All India Radio before 1936 was known as :
A. Indian Radio Broadcasting
B. Broadcasting Service of India
C. Indian State Broadcasting Service
D. All India Broadcasting Service

19. The biggest news agency of India is :
A. PTI B. UNI
C. NANAP D. Samachar Bharati

20. Prasar Bharati was launched in the year :
A. 1995 B. 1997
C. 1999 D. 2001

21. A statistical measure based upon the entire population is called parameter while measure based upon a sample is known as :
A. Sample parameter
B. Inference
C. Statistics
D. None of these

22. The importance of the correlation co-efficient lies in the fact that :
A. There is a linear relationship between the correlated variables.
B. It is one of the most valid measure of statistics.
C. It allows one to determine the degree or strength of the association between two variables.
D. It is a non-parametric method of statistical analysis.

23. The F-test:
A. is essentially a two tailed test.
B. is essentially a one tailed test.
C. can be one tailed as well as two tailed depending on the hypothesis.
D. can never be a one tailed test.

24. What will be the next letter in the following series : DCXW, FEVU, HGTS, _____
A. AKPO B. JBYZ
C. JIRQ D. LMRS

25. The following question is based on the diagram given below. If the two small circles represent formal class-room education and distance education and the big circle stands for university system of education, which figure represents the university systems.

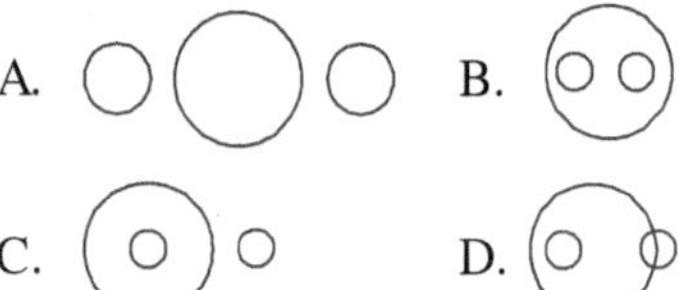

26. The statement, *'To be non-violent is good'* is a :
A. Moral judgement
B. Factual judgement
C. Religious judgement
D. Value judgement

27. **Assertion (A):** Man is a rational being.
Reason (R): Man is a social being.
A. Both A. and **(R)** are true and **(R)** is the correct explanation of A.
B. Both A. and **(R)** are true but **(R)** is not the correct explanation of A.
C. A. is true but **(R)** is false
D. A. is false but **(R)** is true

28. Value Judgements are :
A. Factual Judgements
B. Ordinary Judgements
C. Normative Judgements
D. Expression of public opinion

29. Deductive reasoning proceeds from :
A. general to particular
B. particular to general
C. one general conclusion to another general conclusion
D. one particular conclusion to another particular conclusion

30. AGARTALA is written in code as 14168171, the code for AGRA is :
A. 1641 B. 1416
C. 1441 D. 1461

31. Which one of the following is the most comprehensive source of population data ?
A. National Family Health Surveys
B. National Sample Surveys
C. Census
D. Demographic Health Surveys

32. Which one of the following principles is *not* applicable to sampling ?
A. Sample units must be clearly defined
B. Sample units must be dependent on each other
C. Same units of sample should be used throughout the study
D. Sample units must be chosen in a systematic and objective manner

33. If January 1st, 2007 is Monday, what was the day on 1st January 1995 ?
A. Sunday B. Monday
C. Friday D. Saturday

34. Insert the missing number in the following series :
4 16 8 64 ? 256
A. 16 B. 24
C. 32 D. 20

35. If an article is sold for Rs. 178 at a loss of 11%; what would be its selling price in order to earn a profit of 11% ?
A. Rs. 222.50 B. Rs. 267
C. Rs. 222 D. Rs. 220

36. WYSIWYG - describes the display of a document on screen as it will actually print
A. What you state is what you get
B. What you see is what you get
C. What you save is what you get
D. What you suggest is what you get

37. Which of the following is *not a* Computer language ?
A. PASCAL B. UNIX
C. FORTRAN D. COBOL

38. A key-board has at least :
A. 91 keys B. 101 keys
C. 111 keys D. 121 keys

39. An E-mail address is composed of
A. two parts B. three parts
C. four parts D. five parts

40. Corel Draw is a popular :
A. Illustration programme
B. Programming language
C. Text programme
D. None of the above

41. Human ear is most sensitive to noise in which of the following ranges :
A. 1-2 KHz B. 100 - 500 Hz
C. 10 - 12 KHz D. 13 - 16 KHz

42. Which one of the following units is used to measure intensity of noise ?
A. decible B. Hz
C. Phon D. Watts/m^2

43. If the population growth follows a logistic curve, the maximum sustainable yield :
A. is equal to half the carrying capacity.
B. is equal to the carrying capacity.
C. depends on growth rates.
D. depends on the initial population.

44. Chemical weathering of rocks is largely dependent upon :
A. high temperature
B. strong wind action
C. heavy rainfall
D. glaciation

45. Structure of earth's system consists of the following :

Match *List-I* with *List-II* and give the correct answer.

List-I *(Zone)*	**List-II** *(Chemical Character)*
(a) Atmosphere	(i) Inert gases
(b) Biosphere	(ii) Salt, fresh water, snow and ice
(c) Hydrosphere	(iii) Organic substances, skeleton matter
(d) Lithosphere	(iv) Light silicates

Codes :

	(a)	*(b)*	*(c)*	*(d)*
A.	*(ii)*	*(iii)*	*(i)*	*(iv)*
B.	*(i)*	*(iii)*	*(ii)*	*(iv)*
C.	*(ii)*	*(i)*	*(iii)*	*(iv)*
D.	*(i)*	*(i)*	*(ii)*	*(iv)*

46. NAAC is an autonomous institution under the aegis of :

A. ICSSR B. CSIR
C. AICTE D. UGC

47. National Council for Women's Education was established in :

A. 1958 B. 1976
C. 1989 D. 2000

48. Which one of the following is *not* situated in New Delhi ?

A. Indian Council of Cultural Relations
B. Indian Council of Scientific Research
C. National Council of Educational Research and Training
D. Indian Institute of Advanced Studies

49. Autonomy in higher education implies freedom in :

A. Administration
B. Policy-making
C. Finance
D. Curriculum development

50. Match *List-I* with *List-II* and select the correct answer from the code given below

List-I (Institutions)

(a) Dr. Hari Singh Gour University
(b) S.N.D.T. University
(c) M.S. University
(d) J.N. Vyas University *Codes :*

List-II (Locations)

(i) Mumbai (ii) Baroda
(iii) Jodhpur (iv) Sagar

	(a)	*(b)*	*(c)*	*(d)*
A.	(iv)	(i)	(ii)	(iii)
B.	(i)	(ii)	(iii)	(iv)
C.	(iii)	(i)	(ii)	(iv)
D.	(ii)	(iv)	(i)	(iii)

ANSWERS

1	**2**	**3**	**4**	**5**	**6**	**7**	**8**	**9**	**10**
B	B	B	D	C	C	B	B	A	D
11	**12**	**13**	**14**	**15**	**16**	**17**	**18**	**19**	**20**
C	B	A	A	A	D	B	C	A	B
21	**22**	**23**	**24**	**25**	**26**	**27**	**28**	**29**	**30**
A	C	C	C	B	A	B	C	A	D
31	**32**	**33**	**34**	**35**	**36**	**37**	**38**	**39**	**40**
C	B	D	A	C	B	B	B	A	A
41	**42**	**43**	**44**	**45**	**46**	**47**	**48**	**49**	**50**
B	A	A	C	B	D	A	D	C	A

SOME SELECTED EXPLANATORY ANSWERS

24. D C X W (each pair −1)   H G T S (each pair −1)

F E V U (each pair −1)   ∴ J I R Q (each pair −1)

30. Since,

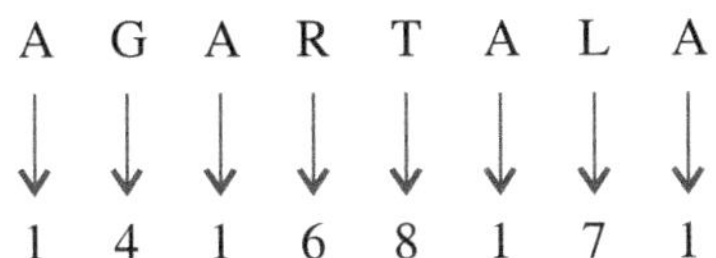

Therefore

A G R A
↓ ↓ ↓ ↓
| 1 4 6 1 |

34. 4 16 8 64 $\boxed{16}$ 256

(16 ×4 → 64, 64 ×4 → 256; 4 ×2 → 8, 8 ×2 → 16)

35. S.P. = 89% of C.P.

$$\Rightarrow \quad 178 = \text{C.P.} \times \frac{89}{100}$$

$$\Rightarrow \quad \text{C.P.} = \frac{100 \times 178}{89} = 200$$

$\therefore$ For 11% Profit, the selling price will be

$$\text{S.P.} = 200 \times \frac{111}{100} = \text{Rs. } 222$$

Previous Paper (Solved)

UGC-NET (JRF) EXAM DECEMBER, 2008

PAPER–I

Note : This paper contains **fifty** (50) multiple-choice questions, each question carrying **two** (2) marks. Attempt **all** of them.

1. According to Swami Vivekananda, teacher's success depends on:
   A. His renunciation of personal gain and service to others
   B. His professional training and creativity
   C. His concentration on his work and duties with a spirit of obedience to God
   D. His mastery on the subject and capacity in controlling the students
2. Which of the following teacher, will be liked most:
   A. A teacher of high idealistic attitude
   B. A loving teacher
   C. A teacher who is disciplined
   D. A teacher who often amuses his students
3. A teacher's most important challenge is:
   A. To make students do their home work
   B. To make teaching-learning process enjoyable
   C. To maintain discipline in the class room
   D. To prepare the question paper
4. Value-education stands for:
   A. making a student healthy
   B. making a student to get a job
   C. inculcation of virtues
   D. all-round development of personality
5. When a normal student behaves in an erratic manner in the class, you would:
   A. pull up the student then and there
   B. talk to the student after the class
   C. ask the student to leave the class
   D. ignore the student
6. The research is always—
   A. verifying the old knowledge
   B. exploring new knowledge
   C. filling the gap between knowledge
   D. all of these
7. The research that applies the laws at the time of field study to draw more and more clear ideas about the problem is:
   A. Applied research
   B. Action research
   C. Experimental research
   D. None of these
8. When a research problem is related to heterogeneous population, the most suitable sampling method is:
   A. Cluster Sampling
   B. Stratified Sampling
   C. Convenient Sampling
   D. Lottery Method
9. The process not needed in experimental research is:
   A. Observation
   B. Manipulation and replication
   C. Controlling
   D. Reference collection
10. A research problem is not feasible only when:
   A. it is researchable

B. it is new and adds something to knowledge
C. it consists of independent and dependent variables
D. it has utility and relevance

Read the following passage carefully and answer the questions 11 to 15 :

Radically changing monsoon patterns, reduction in the winter rice harvest and a quantum increase in respiratory diseases all part of the environmental doomsday scenario which is reportedly playing out in South Asia. According to a United Nations Environment Programme report, a deadly three-kilometer deep blanket of pollution comprising a fearsome, cocktail of ash, acids, aerosols and other particles has enveloped in this region. For India, already struggling to cope with a drought, the implication of this are devastating and further crop failure will amount to a life and death question for many Indians. The increase in premature deaths will have adverse social and economic consequences and a rise in morbidities will place an unbearable burden on our crumbling health system. And there is no one to blame but ourselves. Both official and corporate India has always been allergic to any mention of clean technology. Most mechanical two wheelers roll of the assembly line without proper pollution control system. Little effort is made for R&D on simple technologies, which could make a vital difference to people's lives and the environment.

However, while there is no denying that South Asia must clean up its act, skeptics might question the timing of the haze report. The Kyoto meet on climate change is just two weeks away and the stage is set for the usual battle between the developing world and the West, particularly the Unites States of America. President Mr. Bush has adamantly refused to sign any protocol, which would mean a change in American consumption level. U.N. environment report will likely find a place in the U.S. arsenal as it plants an accusing finger towards controls like India and China. Yet the U.S.A. can hardly deny its own dubious role in the matter of erasing trading quotas.

Richer countries can simply buy up excess credits from poorer countries and continue to pollute. Rather than try to get the better of developing countries, who undoubtedly have taken up environmental shortcuts in their bid to catch up with the West, the USA should take a look at the environmental profigacy, which is going on within. From opening up virgin territories for oil exploration to relaxing the standards for drinking water, Mr. Bush's policies are not exactly beneficial, not even to America's interests. We realize that we are all in this together and that pollution anywhere should be a global concern otherwise there will only be more tunnels at the end of the tunnel.

11. Both official and corporate India is allergic to:
A. Failure of Monsoon
B. Poverty and Inequality
C. Slowdown in Industrial Production
D. Mention of Clean Technology

12. If the rate of premature death increases it will:
A. Exert added burden on the crumbling economy
B. Have adverse social and economic consequences
C. Make positive effect on our effort to control population
D. Have less job aspirants in the society

13. According to the passage, the two wheeler industry is not adequately concerned about:
A. Passenger safety on the roads
B. Life cover insurance of the vehicle owner
C. Pollution control system in the vehicle
D. Rising cost of the two wheelers

14. What could be the reason behind timing of the haze report just before the Kyoto meet ?
A. United Nations is working hand-in-glove with U.S.A.
B. Organizers of the forthcoming meet to teach a lesson to the U.S.A.
C. Drawing attention of the world towards devastating effects of environment degradation.
D. U.S.A. wants to use it as a handle against the developing countries in the forthcoming meet

15. Which of the following is the indication of environmental degradation in South Asia ?
A. Social and economic inequality
B. Crumbling health care system
C. Inadequate pollution control system
D. Radically changing monsoon pattern

16. Community Radio is a type of radio service that caters to the interest of :
A. Local audience B. Education
C. Entertainment D. News

17. Orcut is a part of :
A. Intra personal Communication
B. Mass Communication
C. Group Communication
D. Interpersonal Communication

18. Match **List-I** with **List-II** and select the correct answer using the codes given below:

List - I (Artists)	**List - II (Art)**
(a) Amrita Shergill	(i) Flute
(b) T. Swaminathan Pillai	(ii) Classical Song
(c) Bhimsen Joshi	(iii) Painting
(d) Padma Subramaniyam	(iv) Bharat Natyam

Codes :

	(a)	(b)	(c)	(d)
A.	(iii)	(i)	(ii)	(iv)
B.	(ii)	(iii)	(i)	(iv)
C.	(iv)	(ii)	(iii)	(i)
D.	(i)	(iv)	(ii)	(iii)

19. Which is not correct in latest communication award ?
A. Salman Rushdie – Booker's Prize - July 20, 2008
B. Dilip Sanghavi – Business Standard CEO Award July 22, 2008
C. Tapan Sinha – Dada Saheb Falke Award, July 21, 2008
D. Gautam Ghosh – Osians Lifetime Achievement Award July 11, 2008

20. Firewalls are used to protect a communication network system against:
A. Unauthorized attacks
B. Virus attacks
C. Data-driven attacks
D. Fire-attacks

21. Insert the missing number in the following :

$$\frac{2}{3}, \frac{4}{7}, ?, \frac{11}{21}, \frac{16}{31}$$

A. $\frac{10}{8}$ B. $\frac{6}{10}$
C. $\frac{5}{10}$ D. $\frac{7}{13}$

22. In a certain code, GAMESMAN is written as AGMEMSAN. How would DISCLOSE be written in that code ?
A. IDSCOLSE
B. IDCSOLES
C. IDSCOLES
D. IDSCLOSE

23. The letters in the first set have a certain relationship. On the basis of this relationship mark the right choice for the second set :
AST : BRU : : NQV : ?
A. ORW B. MPU
C. MRW D. OPW

24. On what dates of April 1994 did SUNDAY fall?
A. 2, 9, 16, 23, 30
B. 3, 10, 17, 24
C. 4, 11, 18, 25
D. 1, 8, 15, 22, 29

25. Find out the wrong number in the sequence:
125, 127, 130, 135, 142, 153, 165
A. 130 B. 142
C. 153 D. 165

26. There are five books A, B, C, D and E. The book C lies above D, the book E is below A and B is below E. Which is at the bottom ?
A. E B. B
C. A D. C

27. Logical reasoning is based on:
A. Truth of involved propositions
B. Valid relation among the involved propositions

C. Employment of symbolic language
D. Employment of ordinary language

28. Two propositions with the same subject and predicate terms but different in quality are :
A. Contradictory B. Contrary
C. Subaltern D. Identical

29. The premises of a valid deductive argument:
A. Provide some evidence for its conclusion
B. Provide no evidence for its conclusion
C. Are irrelevant for its conclusion
D. Provide conclusive evidence for its conclusion

30. Syllogistic reasoning is :
A. Deductive
B. Inductive
C. Experimental
D. Hypothetical

Study the following Venn diagram and answer questions nos. 31 to 33.

Three circles representing GRADUATES, CLERKS and GOVERNMENT EMPLOYEES are intersecting. The intersections are marked A, B, C, e, f, g and h. Which part best represents the statements in questions 31 to 33 ?

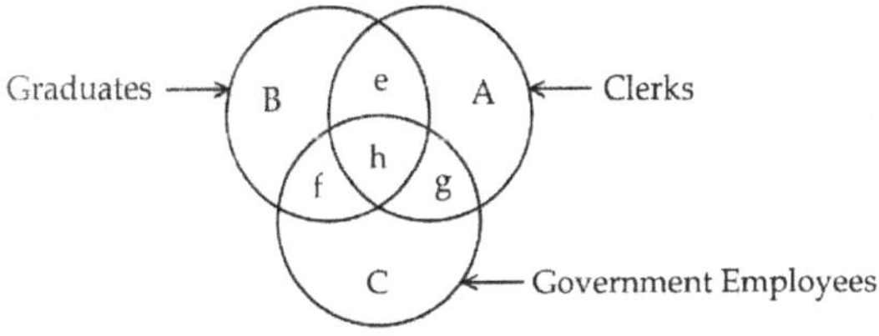

31. Some Graduates are Government employees but not as Clerks.
A. h B. g
C. f D. e

32. Clerks who are graduates as well as government employees :
A. e B. f
C. g D. h

33. Some graduates are Clerks but not Government employees.
A. f B. g
C. h D. e

Study the following graph and answer questions numbered from 34 to 35

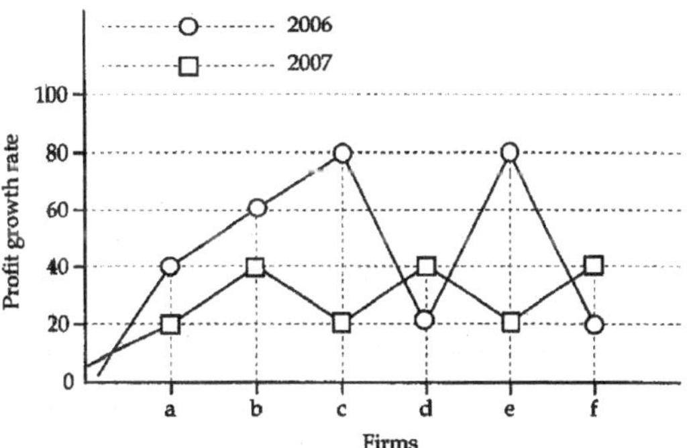

34. Which of the firms got maximum profit growth rate in the year 2006.
A. ab B. ce
C. cd D. ef

35. Which of the firms got maximum profit growth rate in the year 2007.
A. bdf B. acf
C. bed D. ace

36. The accounting software 'Tally' was developed by :
A. HCL B. TCS
C. Infosys D. Wipro

37. Errors in computer programmes are called :
A. Follies B. Mistakes
C. Bugs D. Spam

38. HTML is basically used to design :
A. Web-page
B. Web-site
C. Graphics
D. Tables and Frames

39. 'Micro Processing' is made for :
A. Computer
B. Digital System
C. Calculator
D. Electronic Goods

40. Information, a combination of graphics, text, sound, video and animation is called :
A. Multiprogramme
B. Multifacet

C. Multimedia
D. Multiprocess

41. Which of the following pairs regarding typical composition of hospital wastes is incorrect ?
A. Plastic- 9-12%
B. Metals- 1-2%
C. Ceramic - 8 - 10%
D. Biodegradable - 35 - 40%

42. Fresh water achieves its greatest density at :
A. –4°C B. 0° C
C. 4°C D. –2.5° C

43. Which one of the following is not associated with earthquakes ?
A. Focus B. Epicenter
C. Seismograph D. Swells

44. The tallest trees in the world are found in the region :
A. Equatorial region
B. Temperate region
C. Monsoon region
D. Mediterranean region

45. Match **List-I** with **List-II** and select the correct answer from the codes given below :

List - I (National Parks)	**List - II (States)**
(a) Periyar	(i) Orissa
(b) Nandan Kanan	(ii) Kerala
(c) Corbett National Park	(iii) Rajasthan
(d) Sariska Tiger Reserve	(iv) Uttarakhand

Codes :

	(a)	(b)	(c)	(d)
A.	(ii)	(i)	(iv)	(iii)
B.	(i)	(ii)	(iv)	(iii)
C.	(iii)	(ii)	(i)	(iv)
D.	(i)	(ii)	(iii)	(iv)

46. According to Radhakrishnan Commission, the aim of Higher Education is :
A. To develop the democratic values, peace and harmony
B. To develop great personalities who can give their contributions in politics, administration, industry and commerce
C. Both A. and B.
D. None of these

47. The National Museum at New Delhi is attached to:
A. Delhi University
B. a Deemed University
C. a Subordinate Office of the JNU
D. Part of Ministry of Tourism and Culture

48. Match **List-I** with **List-II** and select the correct answer from the code given below :

List - I (Institutions)	**List - II (Locations)**
(a) National Law Institute	(i) Shimla
(b) Indian Institute of Advanced Studies	(ii) Bhopal
(c) National Judicial Academy	(iii) Hyderabad
(d) National Savings Institute	(iv) Nagpur

Codes :

	(a)	(b)	(c)	(d)
A.	(iii)	(ii)	(iv)	(i)
B.	(i)	(ii)	(iii)	(iv)
C.	(iv)	(iii)	(i)	(ii)
D.	(iii)	(i)	(ii)	(iv)

49. Election of Rural and Urban local bodies are conducted and ultimately supervised by :
A. Election Commission of India
B. State Election Commission
C. District Collector and District Magistrate
D. Concerned Returning Officer

50. Which opinion is not correct ?
A. Education is a subject of concurrent list of VII schedule of Constitution of India
B. University Grants Commission is a statutory body
C. Patent, inventions, design, copyright and trade marks are the subject of concurrent list
D. Indian Council of Social Science Research is a statutory body related to research in social sciences

ANSWERS

1	2	3	4	5	6	7	8	9	10
D	C	B	C	B	D	A	B	D	B
11	**12**	**13**	**14**	**15**	**16**	**17**	**18**	**19**	**20**
D	B	C	C	D	A	D	A	B	A
21	**22**	**23**	**24**	**25**	**26**	**27**	**28**	**29**	**30**
D	A	D	B	D	B	B	A	D	A
31	**32**	**33**	**34**	**35**	**36**	**37**	**38**	**39**	**40**
C	D	D	B	A	B	C	A	A	C
41	**42**	**43**	**44**	**45**	**46**	**47**	**48**	**49**	**50**
D	C	D	B	A	C	D	D	B	C

SOME SELECTED EXPLANATORY ANSWERS

21. Since, $\frac{2}{3} = \frac{2}{2 \times 2 - 1}$

$\frac{4}{7} = \frac{4}{4 \times 2 - 1}$

$\frac{11}{21} = \frac{11}{11 \times 2 - 1}$

and $\frac{16}{31} = \frac{16}{16 \times 2 - 1}$

Therefore $\frac{7}{13} = \frac{7}{7 \times 2 - 1}$

22. Since,

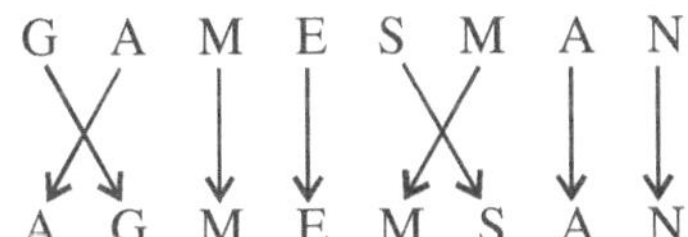

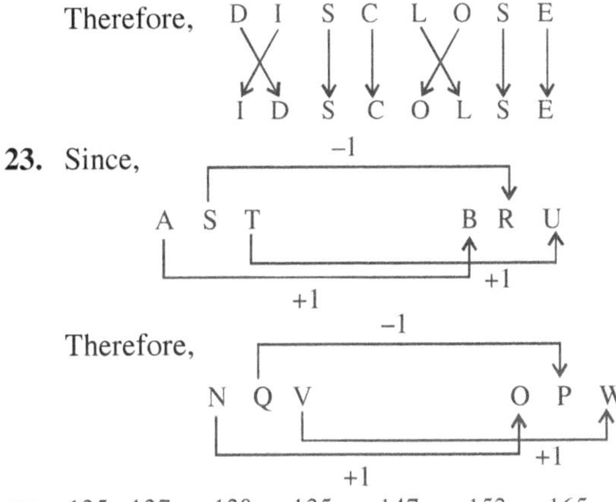

25. 125 127 130 135 147 153 165

+2 +3 +5 +7 +11 +12

Except 12, rest are not divisible by any numbers.

Previous Paper (Solved)

UGC-NET (JRF) EXAM JUNE, 2007

PAPER–I

Note : This paper contains **fifty** (50) multiple-choice questions, each question carrying **two** (2) marks. Attempt **all** of them.

1. Teacher uses visual-aids to make learning:
A. simple
B. more knowledgeable
C. quicker
D. interesting

2. The teacher's role at the higher educational level is to :
A. provide information to students
B. promote self-learning in students
C. encourage healthy competition among students
D. help students to solve their personal problems

3. Which one of the following teachers would you like the most
A. punctual
B. having research aptitude
C. loving and having high idealistic philosophy
D. who often amuses his students

4. Micro teaching is most effective for the student-teacher :
A. during the practice-teaching
B. after the practice-teaching
C. before the practice-teaching
D. none of the above

5. Which is the least important factor in teaching?
A. punishing the students
B. maintaining discipline in the class
C. lecturing in impressive way
D. drawing sketches and diagrams on the black-board

6. To test null hypothesis, a researcher uses :
A. t test
B. ANOVA
C. x^2
D. factorial analysis

7. A research problem is feasible only when :
A. it has utility and relevance
B. it is researchable
C. it is new and adds something to knowledge
D. all the above

8. Bibliography given in a research report :
A. shows vast knowledge of the researcher
B. helps those interested in further research
C. has no relevance to research
D. all the above

9. Fundamental research reflects the ability to :
A. Synthesize new ideals
B. Expound new principles
C. Evaluate the existing material concerning research
D. Study the existing literature regarding various topics

10. The study in which the investigators attempt to trace an effect is known as
A. Survey Research

B. 'Ex-post Facto' Research
C. Historical Research
D. Summative Research

Read the following passage and answer the questions 11 to 15 :

All political systems need to mediate the relationship between private wealth and public power. Those that fail risk a dysfunctional government captured by wealthy interests. Corruption is one symptom of such failure with private willingness-to-pay trumping public goals. Private individuals and business firms pay to get routine services and to get to the head of the bureaucratic queue. They pay to limit their taxes, avoid costly regulations, obtain contracts at inflated prices and get concessions and privatised firms at low prices. If corruption is endemic, public officials - both bureaucrats and elected officials - may redesign programmes and propose public projects with few public benefits and many opportunities for private profit. Ofcourse, corruption, in the sense of bribes, pay-offs and kickbacks, is only one type of government failure. Efforts to promote 'good governance' must be broader than anti-corruption campaigns. Governments may be honest but inefficient because no one has an incentive to work productively, and narrow elites may capture the state and exert excess influence on policy. Bribery may induce the lazy to work hard and permit those not in the inner circle of cronies to obtain benefits. However, even in such cases, corruption cannot be confined to 'functional' areas. It will be a temptation whenever private benefits are positive. It may be a reasonable response to a harsh reality but, over time, it can facilitate a spiral into an even worse situation.

11. The governments which fail to focus on the relationship between private wealth and public power are likely to become :
A. Functional
B. Dysfunctional
C. Normal functioning
D. Good governance

12. One important symptom of bad governance is :
A. Corruption
B. High taxes
C. Complicated rules and regulations
D. High prices

13. When corruption is rampant, public officials always aim at many opportunities for :
A. Public benefits B. Public profit
C. Private profit D. Corporate gains

14. Productivity linked incentives to public/ private officials is one of the indicatives for:
A. Efficient government
B. Bad governance
C. Inefficient government
D. Corruption

15. The spiralling corruption can only be contained by promoting :
A. Private profit
B. Anti-corruption campaign
C. Good governance
D. Pay-offs and kick backs

16. Press Council of India is located at :
A. Chennai B. Mumbai
C. Kolkata D. Delhi

17. Adjusting the photo for publication by cutting is technically known as :
A. Photo cutting
B. Photo bleeding
C. Photo cropping
D. Photo adjustment

18. Feed-back of a message comes from :
A. Satellite B. Media
C. Audience D. Communicator

19. Collection of information in advance before designing communication strategy is known as :
A. Feed-back B. Feed-forward
C. Research study D. Opinion poll

20. The aspect ratio of TV screen is :
A. 4 : 3 B. 4 : 2
C. 3 : 5 D. 2 : 3

21. Which is the number that comes next in the sequence ?
9, 8, 8, 8, 7, 8, 6, __
A. 5 B. 6
C. 8 D. 4

22. If in a certain language PUNCTUAL is coded as 16598623, how would ACTUPULN be coded?

A. 8 3 4 5 3 6 B. 2 9 8 6 1 6 3 5
C. 8 3 4 5 3 0 D. 8 3 4 5 3 9

23. The question to be answered by factorial analysis of the quantitative data does not explain one of the following :

A. Is 'X' related to 'Y' ?
B. How is 'X' related to 'Y' ?
C. How does 'X' affect the dependent variable 'Y' at different levels of another independent variable 'K' or 'M' ?
D. How is 'X' by 'K' related to 'M' ?

24. January 12, 1980 was Saturday, what day was January 12, 1979 :

A. Saturday B. Friday
C. Sunday D. Thursday

25. How many Mondays are there in a particular month of a particular year, if the month ends on Wednesday ?

A. 5 B. 4
C. 3 D. None of the above

26. From the given four statements, select the two which cannot be true but yet both can be false. Choose the right pair :

(i) All men are mortal
(ii) Some men are mortal
(iii) No man is mortal
(iv) Some men are not mortal

A. (i) and (ii) B. (iii) and (iv)
C. (i) and (iii) D. (ii) and (iv)

27. A Syllogism must have :

A. Three terms B. Four terms
C. Six terms D. Five terms

28. Copula is that part of proposition which denotes the relationship between :

A. Subject and predicate
B. Known and unknown
C. Major premise and minor premise
D. Subject and object

29. "E" denotes :

A. Universal Negative Proposition
B. Particular Affirmative Proposition
C. Universal Affirmative Proposition
D. Particular Negative Proposition

30. 'A' is the father of 'C', and 'D' is the son of 'B'. 'E' is the brother of 'A'. If 'C' is the sister of 'D', how is 'B' related to 'E' ?

A. daughter B. husband
C. sister-in-law D. brother-in-law

31. Which of the following methods will you choose to prepare choropleth map of India showing urban density of population :

A. Quartiles B. Quintiles
C. Mean and SD D. Break - point

32. Which of the following methods is best suited to show on a map the types of crops being grown in a region :

A. Choropleth B. Chorochromatic
C. Choroschematic D. Isopleth

33. A ratio represents the relation between :

A. Part and Part
B. Part and Whole
C. Whole and Whole
D. All of the above

34. Out of four numbers, the average of the first three numbers is thrice the fourth number. If the average of the four numbers is 5, the fourth number is :

A. 4.5 B. 5
C. 2 D. 4

35. Circle graphs are used to show :

A. How various sections share in the whole
B. How various parts are related to the whole
C. How one whole is related to other wholes
D. How one part is related to other parts

36. On the keyboard of computer each character has an "ASCII" value which stands for :

A. American Stock Code for Information Interchange
B. American Standard Code for Information Interchange
C. African Standard Code for Information Interchange
D. Adaptable Standard Code for Information Change

37. Which part of the Central Processing Unit (CPU) performs calculation and makes decisions :

A. Arithematic Logic Unit
B. Alternating Logic Unit
C. Alternate Local Unit
D. American Logic Unit

38. "Dpi" stands for :

A. Dots per inch
B. Digits per unit
C. Dots pixel inch
D. Diagrams per inch

39. The process of laying out a document with text, graphics, headlines and photographs is involved in:

A. Deck Top Publishing
B. Desk Top Printing
C. Desk Top Publishing
D. Deck Top Printing

40. Transfer of data from one application to another line is known as :

A. Dynamic Disk Exchange
B. Dodgy Data Exchange
C. Dogmatic Data Exchange
D. Dynamic Data Exchange

41. Tsunami occurs due to :

A. Mild earthquakes and landslides in the oceans
B. Strong earthquakes and landslides in the oceans
C. Strong earthquakes and landslides in mountains
D. Strong earthquakes and landslides in deserts

42. Which of the natural hazards have big effect on Indian people each year ?

A. Cyclones B. Floods
C. Earthquakes D. Landslides

43. Comparative Environment Impact Assessment study is to be conducted for :

A. the whole year
B. three seasons excluding monsoon
C. any three seasons
D. the worst season

44. Sea level rise results primarily due to :

A. Heavy rainfall
B. Melting of glaciers
C. Submarine volcanism
D. Seafloor spreading

45. The plume rise in a coal based power plant depends on :

(i) Buoyancy
(ii) Atmospheric stability
(iii) Momentum of exhaust gases Identify the correct code :

A. (i) and (ii) only
B. (ii) and (iii) only
C. (i) and (iii) only
D. (i), (ii) and (iii)

46. Value education makes a student :

A. Good citizen
B. Successful businessman
C. Popular teacher
D. Efficient manager

47. Networking of libraries through electronic media is known as

A. Inflibnet B. Libinfnet
C. Internet D. HTML

48. The University which telecasts interactive educational programmes through its own channel is :

A. B. R. Ambedkar Open University, Hyderabad
B. I. G. N. O. U.
C. University of Pune
D. Annamalai University

49. The Government established the University Grants Commission by an Act of Parliament in the year :

A. 1980 B. 1948
C. 1950 D. 1956

50. Universities having central campus for imparting education are called :

A. Central Universities
B. Deemed Universities
C. Residential Universities
D. Open Universities

ANSWERS

1	**2**	**3**	**4**	**5**	**6**	**7**	**8**	**9**	**10**
D	A	A	B	A	C	D	B	B	B
11	**12**	**13**	**14**	**15**	**16**	**17**	**18**	**19**	**20**
B	A	C	A	C	D	C	C	D	A
21	**22**	**23**	**24**	**25**	**26**	**27**	**28**	**29**	**30**
C	B	C	B	D	B	A	B	A	D
31	**32**	**33**	**34**	**35**	**36**	**37**	**38**	**39**	**40**
B	C	B	C	A	A	A	A	C	D
41	**42**	**43**	**44**	**45**	**46**	**47**	**48**	**49**	**50**
B	B	A	B	D	A	A	B	D	B

SOME SELECTED EXPLANATORY ANSWERS

22. Since,

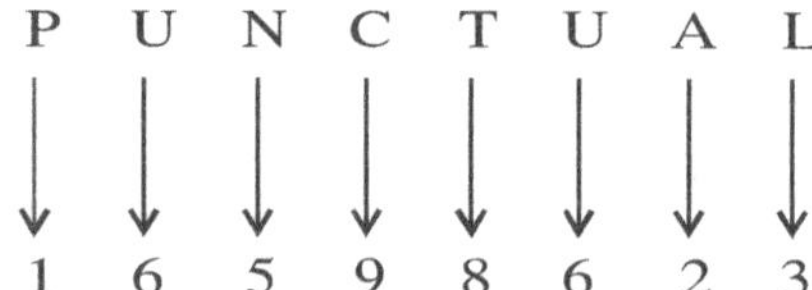

Similarly,

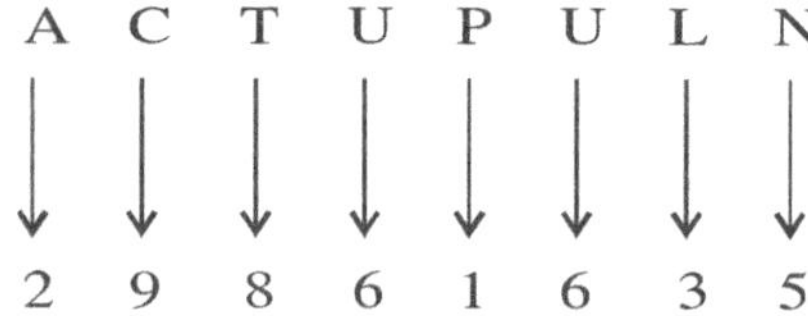

30. Hints: E $\xrightarrow{\text{Brother}}$ A $\xrightarrow{\text{Father}}$ C

C $\xrightarrow{\text{Sister}}$ D

D $\xrightarrow[\text{Son}]{}$ B

It is clear from the above figure 'E', is the Brother-in-law of 'B'.

34. Let 4th number be $3x$

$\therefore$ Average of first three numbers = $3x$

and Average of all four numbers = 5

From question

$$5 \times 4 = 3 \times 3x + x$$

$$\Rightarrow \quad 20 = 9x + x$$

$$\Rightarrow \quad x = 2$$

Previous Paper (Solved)

UGC-NET (JRF) EXAM DECEMBER, 2007

PAPER–I

Note : This paper contains **fifty** (50) multiple-choice questions, each question carrying **two** (2) marks. Attempt **all** of them.

1. Verbal guidance is least effective i the learning of:
A. Aptitudes B. Skills
C. Attitudes D. Relationship

2. Which is the most important aspect of the teacher's rle in learning?
A. The development of insight inrto what consititutes an adequate performance
B. The development of insigh into what consititutes the pitfalls and dangers to be avoided
C. The provision of encouragement and moral support
D. Te provision of continuous diagnostic and remedial help

3. The most oppropriate purpose of learning is:
A. personal adjustment
B. modification of behaviour
C. social and political awarness
D. preparing oneself for employment

4. The students who keep on asking questions in the class should be :
A. encouraged to find answer independently
B. advised to meet the teacher after the class
C. encouraged to continue questioning
D. advised not to disturb during the lecture

5. Maximum participation of students is possible in teaching through :
A. discussion method
B. lecture method
C. audio-visual aids
D. text book method

6. Generalised conclusion on the basis of a sample is technically known as :
A. Data analysis and interpretation
B. Parameter inference
C. Statistical inference
D. All of the above

7. The experimental study is based on :
A. The manipulation of variables
B. Conceptual parameters
C. Replication of research
D. Survey of literature

8. The main characteristic of scientific research is :
A. empirical B. theoretical
C. experimental D. all of the above

9. Authenticity of a research finding is its :
A. Originality B. Validity
C. Objectivity D. All of the above

10. Which technique is generally followed when the population is finite?
A. Area Sampling Technique
B. Purposive Sampling Technique
C. Systematic Sampling Technique
D. None of the above

Read the following passage and answer the questions 11 to 15 :

Gandhi's overall social and environmental philosophy is based on what human beings need rather than what they want. His early introduction to the teachings of Jains, Theosophists, Christian sermons, Ruskin and Tolstoy, and most significantly the *Bhagavad Gita,* were to have profound impact on the development of Gandhi's holistic thinking on humanity, nature and their ecological interrelation. His deep concern for the disadvantaged, the poor and rural population created an ambience for an alternative social thinking that was at once far-sighted, local and immediate. For Gandhi was acutely aware that the demands generated by the need to feed and sustain human life, compounded by the growing industrialization of India, far outstripped the finite resources of nature. This might nowadays appear naive or commonplace, but such pronouncements were as rare as they were heretical a century ago. Gandhi was also concerned about the destruction, under colonial and modernist designs, of the existing infrastructures which had more potential for keeping a community flourishing within ecologically-sensitive traditional patterns of subsistence, especially in the rural areas, than did the incoming Western alternatives based on nature-blind technology and the enslavement of human spirit and energies.

Perhaps the moral principle for which Gandhi is best known is that of active non-violence, derived from the traditional moral restraint of not injuring another being. The most refined expression of this value is in the great epic of the *Mahabharata, (c.* 100 BCE to 200 CE), where moral development proceeds through placing constraints on the liberties, desires and acquisitiveness endemic to human life. One's action is judged in terms of consequences and the impact it is likely to have on another. Jainas had generalized this principle to include all sentient creatures and biocommunities alike. Advanced Jaina monks and nuns will sweep their path to avoid harming insects and even bacteria. Non-injury is a non-negotiable universal prescription.

11. Which one of the following have a profound impact on the development of Gandhi's holistic thinking on humanity, nature and their ecological interrelations?

A. Jain teachings B. Christian sermons
C. Bhagavad Gita D. Ruskin and Tolstoy

12. Gandhi's overall social and environmental philosophy is based on human beings' :

A. need B. desire
C. wealth D. welfare

13. Gandhiji's deep concern for the disadvantaged, the poor and rural population created an ambience for an alternative :

A. rural policy B. social thinking
C. urban policy D. economic thinking

14. Colonial policy and modernisation led to the destruction of :

A. major industrial infrastructure
B. irrigation infrastructure
C. urban infrastructure
D. rural infrastructure

15. Gandhi's active non-violence is derived from :

A. Moral restraint of not injuring another being
B. Having liberties, desires and acquisitiveness
C. Freedom of action
D. Nature-blind technology and enslavement of human spirit and energies

16. DTH service was started in the year :

A. 2000 B. 2002
C. 2004 D. 2006

17. National Press day is celebrated on :

A. 16th November B. 19th November
C. 21st November D. 30th November

18. The total number of members in the Press Council of India are

A. 28 B. 14
C. 17 D. 20

19. The right to impart and receive information is guaranteed in the Constitution of India by Article :

A. 19 (2) (a) B. 19 (16)
C. 19 (2) D. 19 (1) (a)

20. Use of radio for higher education is based on the presumption of :

A. Enriching curriculum based instruction

B. Replacing teacher in the long run
C. Everybody having access to a radio set
D. Other means of instruction getting outdated

21. Find out the number which should come at the place of question mark which will complete the following series :
5, 4, 9, 17, 35, ? = 139
A. 149 B. 79
C. 49 D. 69

Questions 22 to 24 are based on the following diagram in which there are three interlocking circles I, S and P, where circle I stands for Indians, circle S for Scientists and circle P for Politicians. Different regions in the figure are lettered from a to f.

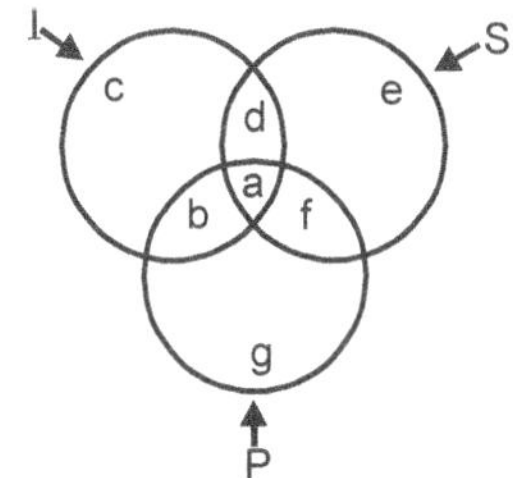

22. The region which represents Non-Indian Scientists who are Politicians :
A. f B. d
C. a D. c

23. The region which represents Indians who are neither Scientists nor Politicians
A. g B. c
C. f D. a

24. The region which represents Politicians who are Indians as well as Scientists :
A. b B. c
C. a D. d

25. Which number is missing in the following series ? 2, 5, 10, 17, 26, 37, 50,?
A. 63 B. 65
C. 67 D. 69

26. The function of measurement includes :
A. Prognosis B. Diagnosis
C. Prediction D. All of the above

27. Logical arguments are based on :
A. Scientific reasoning
B. Customary reasoning
C. Mathematical reasoning
D. Syllogistic reasoning

28. Insert the missing number 4 : 17 : : 7 : ?
A. 48 C. 50
B. 49 D. 51

29. Choose the odd worde
A. Nun C. Monk
B. Knight D. Priest

30. Choose the number which is different from others in the group
A. 49 B. 63
C. 77 D. 81

31. Probability sampling implies :
A. Stratified Random Sampling
B. Systematic Random Sampling
C. Simple Random Sampling
D. All of the above

32. Insert the missing number

$\frac{36}{62}, \frac{39}{63}, \frac{43}{61}, \frac{48}{64}, ?$

A. $\frac{51}{65}$ B. $\frac{56}{60}$

C. $\frac{54}{65}$ D. $\frac{33}{60}$

33. At what time between 3 and 4 O'clock will the hands of a watch point in opposite directions ?
A. 40 minutes past three
B. 45 minutes past three
C. 50 minutes past three
D. 55 minutes past three

34. Mary has three children. What is the probability that none of the three children is a boy?

A. $\frac{1}{2}$ B. $\frac{1}{3}$

C. $\frac{3}{4}$ D. 1

35. If the radius of a circle is increased by 50 per cent. Its area is increased by

A. 125 per cent B. 100 per cent
C. 75 per cent D. 50 per cent

36. CD ROM stands for :

A. Computer Disk Read Only Memory
B. Compact Disk Read Over Memory
C. Compact Disk Read Only Memory
D. Computer Disk Read Over Memory

37. The 'brain' of a computer which keeps peripherals under its control is called

A. Common Power Unit
B. Common Processing Unit
C. Central Power Unit
D. Central Processing Unit

38. Data can be saved on backing storage medium known as :

A. Compact Disk Recordable
B. Computer Disk Rewritable
C. Compact Disk Rewritable
D. Computer Data Rewritable

39. RAM means :

A. Random Access Memory
B. Rigid Access Memory
C. Rapid Access Memory
D. Revolving Access Memory

40. www represents :

A. who what and where
B. weird wide web
C. word wide web
D. world wide web

41. Deforestation during the recent decades has led to :

A. Soil erosion
B. Landslides
C. Loss of bio-diversity
D. All the above

42. Which one of the following natural hazards is responsible for causing highest human disaster ?

A. Earthquakes B. Volcanic eruptions
C. Snow-storms D. Tsunami

43. Which one of the following is appropriate for natural hazard mitigation?

A. International AID
B. Timely Warning System
C. Rehabilitation
D. Community Participation

44. Slums in metro-city are the result of :

A. Rural to urban migration
B. Poverty of the city-scape
C. Lack of urban infrastructure
D. Urban-governance

45. The great Indian Bustard bird is found in :

A. Thar Desert of India
B. Coastal regions of India
C. Temperate Forests in the Himalaya
D. Tarai zones of the Himalayan Foot

46. The first Indian Satellite for serving the educational sector is known as :

A. SATEDU B. INSAT - B
C. EDUSAT D. INSAT-C

47. Exclusive educational channel of IGNOU is known as :

A. Cyan Darshan B. Cyan Vani
C. Door Darshan D. Prasar Bharati

48. The head quarter of Mahatma Gandhi Antarrashtriya Hindi Vishwavidyalaya is situated in :

A. Sevagram B. New Delhi
C. Wardha D. Ahmedabad

49. Match List-I with List-II and select the correct answer using the codes given below

List-I *(Institutes)*	**List-II** *(Locations)*
(a) Central Institute of English and Foreign Languages	(i) Chitrakoot
(b) Gramodaya Vishwavidyalaya	(ii) Hyderabad
(c) Central Institute of Higher Tibetan Studies	(iii) New Delhi
(d) IGNOU	(iv) Dharmasala

Codes :

	(a)	(b)	(c)	(d)
A.	(ii)	(i)	(iv)	(iii)
B.	(iv)	(iii)	(ii)	(i)

C. (iii) (iv) (i) (ii)
D. (i) (ii) (iv) (iii)

50. The aim of vocationalization of education is :

A. preparing students for a vocation along with knowledge
B. converting liberal education into vocational education
C. giving more importance to vocational than general education
D. making liberal education job-oriented

ANSWERS

1	2	3	4	5	6	7	8	9	10
B	A	B	A	A	C	C	C	D	C
11	**12**	**13**	**14**	**15**	**16**	**17**	**18**	**19**	**20**
C	A	B	C	A	D	A	A	D	B
21	**22**	**23**	**24**	**25**	**26**	**27**	**28**	**29**	**30**
D	A	B	D	B	D	D	C	B	C
31	**32**	**33**	**34**	**35**	**36**	**37**	**38**	**39**	**40**
D	C	C	D	A	C	D	C	A	D
41	**42**	**43**	**44**	**45**	**46**	**47**	**48**	**49**	**50**
D	A	B	A	A	C	A	C	A	D

SOME SELECTED EXPLANATORY ANSWERS

21. $4 \times 2 = 8 + 1 = 9$

$9 \times 2 = 18 - 1 = 17$

$17 \times 2 = 34 + 1 = 35$

$35 \times 2 = 70 - 1 = 69$

$69 \times 2 = 138 + 1 = 139$

25.

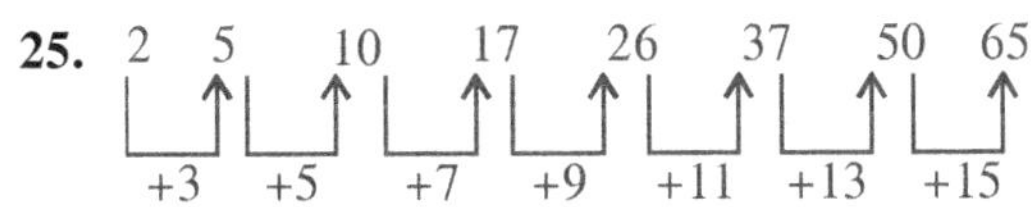

28. Since, 4 → 17 ($4^2 + 1$)

Similarly,

7 → 50 ($7^2 + 1$)

30. $49 = 4 + 9 = 13 = 1 + 3 = 4 = 2^2$
$63 = 6 + 3 = 9 = 3^2$
$77 = 7 + 7 = 14 = 4 + 1 = 5$
$81 = 8 + 1 = 9 = 3^2$

Previous Paper (Solved)

UGC-NET (JRF) EXAM
JUNE, 2006

PAPER–I

Note : This paper contains **fifty** (50) multiple-choice questions, each question carrying **two** (2) marks. Attempt **all** of them.

1. Which of the following comprise teaching skill :
A. Black Board writing
B. Questioning
C. Explaining
D. All the above

2. Which of the following statements is most appropriate?
A. Teachers can teach.
B. Teachers help can create in a student a desire to learn.
C. Lecture Method can be used for developing thinking.
D. Teachers are born.

3. The first Indian chronicler of Indian history was :
A. Megasthanese B. Fahiyan
C. Huan Tsang D. Kalhan

4. Which of the following statements is correct?
A. Syllabus is a part of curriculum.
B. Syllabus is an annexure to curriculum.
C. Curriculum is the same in all educational institutions affiliated to a particular university.
D. Syllabus is not the same in all educational institutions affiliated to a particular university.

5. Which of the two given options is of the level of understanding?
(I) Define noun.
(II) Define noun in your own words.
A. Only I B. Only II
C. Both I and II D. Neither I nor II

6. Which of the following options are the main tasks of research in modern society ?
(I) to keep pace with the advancement in knowledge.
(II) to discover new things.
(III) to write a critique on the earlier writings.
(IV) to systematically examine and critically analyse the investigations/sources with objectivity.
A. IV, II and I B. I, II and III
C. I and III D. II, III and IV

7. Match List-I (Interviews) with List-II (Meaning) and select the correct answer from the code given below :

List - I (Interviews)
(a) structured interviews
(b) Unstructured interviews
(c) Focussed interviews
(d) Clinical interviews

List - II (Meaning)
(i) greater flexibility approach
(ii) attention on the questions to be answered
(iii) individual life experience
(iv) Pre determined question
(v) non-directive

Code:

	(a)	*(b)*	*(c)*	*(d)*
A.	(iv)	(i)	(ii)	(iii)
B.	(ii)	(iv)	(i)	(iii)
C.	(v)	(ii)	(iv)	(i)
D.	(i)	(iii)	(v)	(iv)

8. What do you consider as the main aim of inter disciplinary research ?
A. To bring out holistic approach to research.
B. To reduce the emphasis of single subject in research domain.
C. To over simplify the problem of research.
D. To create a new trend in research methodology.

9. One of the aims of the scientific method in research is to :
A. improve data interpretation
B. eliminate spurious relations
C. confirm triangulation
D. introduce new variables

10. The depth of any research can be judged by:
A. title of the research.
B. objectives of the research.
C. total expenditure on the research.
D. duration of the research.

Read the following passage and answer the questions 11 *to 15 :*

The superintendence, direction and control of preparation of electoral rolls for, and the conduct of, elections to Parliament and State Legislatures and elections to the offices of the President and the Vice - President of India are vested in the Election Commission of India. It is an independent constitutional authority.

Independence of the Election Commission and its insulation from executive interference is ensured by a specific provision under Article 324 (5) of the constitution that the chief Election Commissioner shall not be removed from his office except in like manner and on like grounds as a Judge of the Supreme Court and conditions of his service shall not be varied to his disadvantage after his appointment.

In C.W.P. No. 4912 of 1998 (Kushra Bharat Vs. Union of India and others), the Delhi High Court directed that information relating to Government dues owed by the candidates to the departments dealing with Government accommodation, electricity, water, telephone and transport etc. and any other dues should be furnished by the candidates and this information should be published by the election authorities under the commission.

11. The text of the passage reflects or raises certain questions :
A. The authority of the commission can not be challenged.
B. This would help in stopping the criminalization of Indian politics.
C. This would reduce substantially the number of contesting candidates.
D. This would ensure fair and free elections.

12. According to the passage, the Election Commission is an independent constitutional authority. This is under Article No. :
A. 324 B. 356
C. 246 D. 161

13. Independence of the Commission means :
A. have a constitutional status.
B. have legislative powers.
C. have judicial powers.
D. have political powers.

14. Fair and free election means :
A. transparency
B. to maintain law and order
C. regional considerations
D. role for pressure groups

15. The Chief Election Commissioner can be removed from his office under Article :
A. 125 B. 352
C. 226 D. 324

16. The function of mass communication of supplying information regarding the processes, issues, events and societal developments is known as :
A. content supply B. surveillance
C. gratification D. correlation

17. The science of the study of feedback systems in humans, animals and machines is known as :

A. cybernetics
B. reverse communication
C. selectivity study
D. response analysis

18. Networked media exist in inter-connected :
A. social environments
B. economic environments
C. political environments
D. technological environments

19. The combination of computing, tele-communications and media in a digital atmosphere is referred to as :
A. online communication
B. integrated media
C. digital combine
D. convergence

20. A dialogue between a human-being and a computer programme that occurs simultaneously in various forms is described as :
A. man-machine speak B. binary chat
C. digital talk D. interactivity

21. Insert the missing number :
$\frac{16}{32}, \frac{15}{33}, \frac{17}{31}, \frac{14}{34}, ?$
A. $\frac{19}{35}$ B. $\frac{19}{30}$
C. $\frac{18}{35}$ D. $\frac{18}{30}$

22. Monday falls on 20th March 1995. What was the day on 3rd November 1994 ?
A. Thursday B. Sunday
C. Tuesday D. Saturday

23. The average of four consecutive even numbers is 27. The largest of these numbers is
A. 36 B. 32
C. 30 D. 28

24. In a certain code, FHQK means GIRL. How will WOMEN be written in the same code?
A. VNLDM B. FHQKN
C. XPNFO D. VLNDM

25. At what time between 4 and 5 O'Clock will the hands of a watch point in opposite directions?
A. 45 min. past 4 C. 50— min. past 4
B. $40\frac{4}{11}$ min. past 4 D. $54\frac{6}{11}$ min. past 4

26. Which of the following conclusions is logically valid based on statement given below ?
Statement : Most teachers are hard working.
Conclusions :
(I) Some teachers are hard working.
(II) Some teachers are not hard working.
A. Only (I) is implied
B. Only (II) is implied
C. Both (I) and (II) are implied
D. Neither (I) nor (II) is implied

27. Who among the following can be asked to make a statement in Indian Parliament ?
A. Any MLA
B. Chief of Army Staff
C. Solicitor General of India
D. Mayor of Delhi

28. Which of the following conclusions is logically valid based on statement given below?
Statement : Most of the Indian states existed before independence.
Conclusions :
(I) Some Indian States existed before independence.
(II) All Indian States did not exist before independence.
A. only (I) is implied
B. only (II) is implied
C. Both (I) and (II) are implied
D. Neither (I) nor (II) is implied

29. Water is always involved with landslides. This is because it :
A. reduces the shear strength of rocks
B. increases the weight of the overburden
C. enhances chemical weathering
D. is a universal solvent

30. Direction for this question :
Given below are two statements (A) and (B) followed by two conclusions (i) and (ii).

Considering the statements to be true, indicate which of the following conclusions logically follow from the given statements by selecting one of the four response alternatives given below the conclusion :

Statements :

1. all businessmen are wealthy.
2. all wealthy people are hard working.

Conclusions :

(i) All businessmen are hard working.
(ii) All hardly working people are not wealthy

A. Only (i) follows
B. Only (ii) follows
C. Only (i) and (ii) follows
D. Neither (i) nor (ii) follows

31. Using websites to pour out one's grievances is called :

A. cyberventing
B. cyber ranting
C. web hate
D. web plea

32. In web search, finding a large number of documents with very little relevant information is termed :

A. poor recall
B. web crawl
C. poor precision rate
D. poor web response

33. The concept of connect intelligence is derived from :

A. virtual reality
B. fuzzy logic
C. bluetooth technology
D. value added networks

34. Use of an ordinary telephone as an Internet applicance is called :

A. voicenet
B. voice telephone
C. voice line
D. voice portal

35. Video transmission over the Internet that looks like delayed livecasting is called :

A. virtual video
B. direct broadcast
C. video shift
D. real-time video

36. Which is the smallest North-east State in India?

A. Tripura
B. Meghalaya
C. Mizoram
D. Manipur

37. Tamilnadu coastal belt has drinking water shortage due to :

A. high evaporation
B. sea water flooding due to tsunami
C. over exploitation of ground water by tubewells
D. seepage of sea water

38. While all rivers of Peninsular India flow into the Bay of Bengal, Narmada and Tapti flow into the Arabian Sea because these two rivers:

A. Follow the slope of these rift valleys
B. The general slope of the Indian peninsula is from east to west
C. The Indian peninsula north of the Satpura ranges, is tilted towards the west
D. The Indian peninsula south of the satpura ranges is tilted towards east

39. Soils in the Mahanadi delta are less fertile than those in the Godavari delta because of:

A. erosion of top soils by annual floods
B. inundation of land by sea water
C. traditional agriculture practices
D. the derivation of alluvial soil from red-soil hinterland

40. Which of the following institutions in the field of education is set up by the MHRD Government of India ?

A. Indian council of world Affair, New Delhi
B. Mythic Society, Bangalore
C. National Bal Bhawn, New Delhi
D. India International Centre, New Delhi

41. **Assertion (A)** : Aerosols have potential for modifying climate

Reason (R) : Aerosols interact with both short waves and radiation

A. Both A. and **(R)** are true, and **(R)** is the correct explanation of A.
B. Both A. and **(R)** are true, but **(R)** is not the correct explanation of A.
C. A. is true, but **(R)** is false
D. A. is false, but **(R)** is true

42. 'SITE' stands for :

A. System for International technology and Engineering
B. Satellite Instructional Television Experiment
C. South Indian Trade Estate
D. State Institute of Technology and Engineering

43. What is the name of the Research station established by the Indian Government for 'Conducting Research at Antarctic?

A. Dakshin Gangotri
B. Yamunotri
C. Uttari Gangotri
D. None of the above

44. Ministry of Human Resource Development (HRD) includes :

A. Department of Elementary Education and Literacy
B. Department of Secondary Education and Higher Education
C. Department of Women and Child Development
D. All the above

45. Parliament can legislate on matters listed in the State list :

A. With the prior permission of the President.
B. Only after the constitution is amended suitably.
C. In case of inconsistency among State legislatures.
D. At the request of two or more States.

The following pie chart indicates the expenditure of a country on various sports during a particular year. Study the pie chart and answer it Question Number 46 to 50.

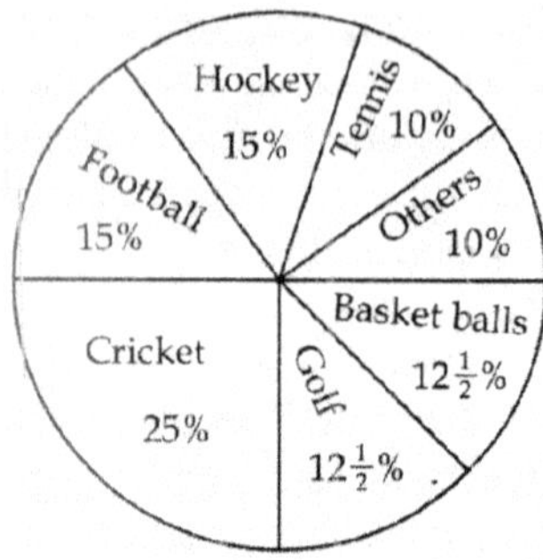

46. The ratio of the total expenditure on football to that of expenditure on hockey is:

A. 1 : 15　　B. 1 : 1
C. 15 : 1　　D. 3 : 20

47. If the total expenditure on sports during the year was Rs. 1,20,000,00 how much was spent on basket ball?

A. Rs. 9,50,000　　C. Rs. 12,00,000
B. Rs. 10,00,000　　D. Rs. 15,00,000

48. The chart shows that the most popular game of the country is :

A. Hockey　　B. Football
C. Cricket　　D. Tennis

49. Out of the following country's expenditure is the same on :

A. Hockey and Tennis
B. Golf and Basket ball
C. Cricket and Football
D. Hockey and Golf

50. If the total expenditure on sport during the year was Rs. 1,50,00,000 the expenditure on cricket and hockey together was :

A. Rs. 60,00,000　　C. Rs. 37,50,000
B. Rs. 50,00,000　　D. Rs. 25,00,000

ANSWERS

1	2	3	4	5	6	7	8	9	10
D	B	D	A	B	A	A	A	B	B
11	**12**	**13**	**14**	**15**	**16**	**17**	**18**	**19**	**20**
D	A	A	B	D	A	A	D	D	D
21	**22**	**23**	**24**	**25**	**26**	**27**	**28**	**29**	**30**
D	A	C	C	D	C	C	B	B	A

31	32	33	34	35	36	37	38	39	40
A	A	D	C	D	C	D	A	A	C
41	**42**	**43**	**44**	**45**	**46**	**47**	**48**	**49**	**50**
A	B	A	D	D	B	A	C	B	A

SOME SELECTED EXPLANATORY ANSWERS

23. Four consecutive even number—
$= x, x + 2, x + 4, x + 6$
According to question,

$$\frac{x+x+2+x+4+x+6}{4} = 27$$

$$= \frac{4x+12}{4} = 27 = 4x = 108 - 12 \Rightarrow 96$$

$$x = \frac{96}{4} = 24$$

Hence, The largest number $= x + 4$
$= 24 + 6 = 30$

24.

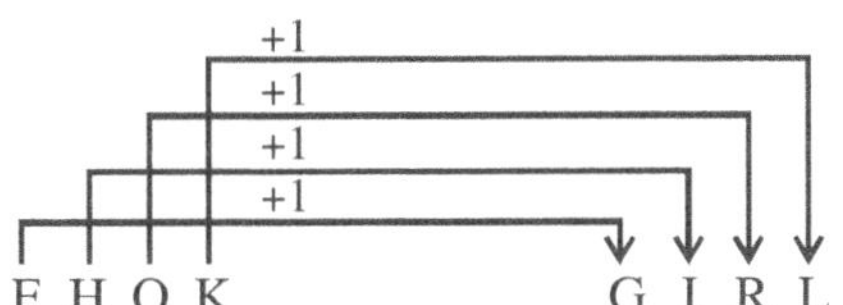

Therefore,

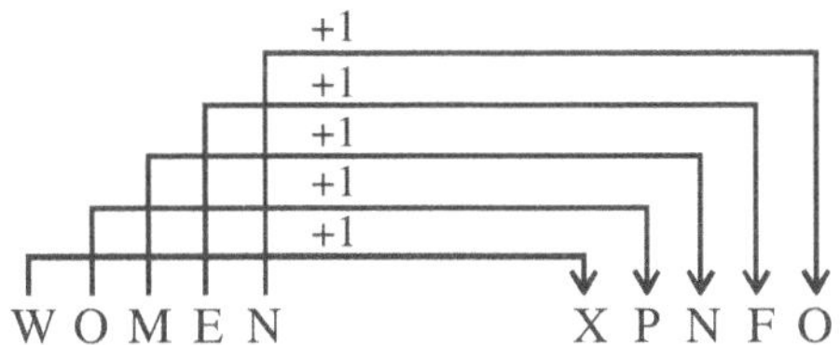

36. Area of the following states are:

Tripura	–	10,491,69
Meghalaya	–	22,429
Manipur	–	22,327
Mizoram	–	21,087

Previous Paper (Solved)

UGC-NET (JRF) EXAM DECEMBER, 2006

PAPER–I

Note : This paper contains **fifty** (50) multiple-choice questions, each question carrying **two** (2) marks. Attempt **all** of them.

1. Which of the following is **not** instructional material?
A. Over Head Projector
B. Audio Casset
C. Printed Material
D. Transparency

2. Which of the following statements is **not** correct?
A. Lecture Method can develop reasoning
B. Lecture Method can develop knowledge
C. Lecture Method is one way process
D. During Lecture Method students are passive

3. The main objective of teaching at Higher Education Level is:
A. To prepare students to pass examination
B. To develop the capacity to take decisions
C. To give new information
D. To motivate students to ask quetions during lecture

4. Which of the following statement is correct?
A. Reliability ensures validity
B. Validity ensures reliability
C. Reliability and validity are independent of each other
D. Reliability does not depend on objectivity

5. Which of the following indicates evaluation?
A. Ram got 45 marks out of 200
B. Mohan got 38 percent marks in English
C. Shyam got First Division in final examination
D. All the above

6. Research can be conducted by a person who :
A. has studied research methodology
B. holds a postgraduate degree
C. possesses thinking and reasoning ability
D. is a hard worker

7. Which of the following statements is correct?
A. Objectives of research are stated in first chapter of the thesis
B. Researcher must possess analytical ability
C. Variability is the source of problem
D. All the above

8. Which of the following is ***not*** the Method of Research?
A. Observation B. Historical
C. Survey D. Philosophical

9. Research can be classified as :
A. Basic, Applied and Action Research
B. Quantitative and Qualitative Research
C. Philosophical, Historical, Survey and Experimental Research
D. All the above

10. The first step of research is :
A. Selecting a problem
B. Searching a problem
C. Finding a problem
D. Identifying a problem

Read the following passage and answer the question nos. 11 to 15 :

After almost three decades of contemplating Swarovski-encrusted navels on increasing flat abs, the Mumbai film industry is on a discovery of India and itself. With budgets of over 30 crore each, four soon to be released movies by premier directors are exploring the idea of who we are and redefining who the other is. It is a fundamental question which the bling-bling, glam-sham and disham-disham tends to avoid. It is also a question which binds an audience when the lights go dim and the projector rolls : as a nation, who are we ? As a people, where are we going?

The Germans coined a word for it, Zeitgeist, which perhaps Yash Chopra would not care to pronounce. But at 72, he remains the person who can best capture it. After being the first to project the diasporic Indian on screen in Lamhe in 1991, he has returned to his roots in a new movie. Veer Zaara, set in 1986, where Pakistan, the traditional other, the part that got away, is the lover and the saviour. In Subhas Ghai's Kisna, set in 1947, the other is the English woman. She is not a memsahib, but a mehbooba. In Ketan Mehta's The Rising, the East India Englishman is not the evil oppressor of countless cardboard characterisations, which span the spectrum from Jewel in the Crown to Kranti, but an honourable friend.

This is Manoj Kumar's Desh Ki dharti with a difference : there is culture, not contentious politics; balle balle, not bombs : no dooriyan (distance), only nazdeekiyan (closeness).

All four films are heralding a new hero and heroine. The new hero is fallible and vulnerable, committed to his dharma, but also not afraid of failure - less of a boy and more of a man. He even has a grown up name : Veer Pratap Singh in Veer-Zaara and Mohan Bhargav in Swades. The new heroine is not a babe, but often a bebe, dressed in traditional Punjabi clothes, often with the stereotypical body type as well, as in Bride and Prejudice of Gurinder Chadha.

11. Which word Yash Chopra would not be able to pronounce?

A. Bling + bling B. Zeitgeist
C. Montaz D. Dooriyan

12. Who made Lamhe in 1991?

A. Subhash Ghai B. Yash Chopra
C. Aditya Chopra D. Sakti Samanta

13. Which movie is associated with Manoj Kumar?

A. Jewel in the Crown
B. Kisna
C. Zaara
D. Desh Ki dharti

14. Which is the latest film by Yash Chopra?

A. Deewar
B. Kabhi Kabhi
C. Dilwale Dulhaniya Le Jayenge
D. Veer *Zaara*

15. Which is the dress of the heroine in Veer-Zaara?

A. Traditional Gujarati Clothes
B. Traditional Bengali Clothes
C. Traditional Punjabi Clothes
D. Traditional Madrasi Clothes

16. Which one of the following can be termed as verbal communication?

A. Prof. Sharma delivered the lecture in the class room.
B. Signal at the cross-road changed from green to orange.
C. The child was crying to attract the attention of the mother.
D. Dipak wrote a letter for leave application.

17. Which is the 24 hours English Business news channel in India?

A. Zee News B. NDTV 24 × 7
C. CNBC D. India News

18. Consider the following statements in communication :

(i) Hema Malini is the Chairperson of the Children's Film Society, India.
(ii) Yash Chopra is the Chairman of the Central Board of Film Certification of India.
(iii) Sharmila Tagore is the Chairperson of National Film Development Corporation.

(iv) Dilip Kumar, Raj Kapoor and Preeti Zinta have all been recipients of Dada Saheb Phalke Award.

Which of the statements given above is/are correct?

A. (i) and (iii) B. (ii) and (iii)
C. (iv) only D. (iii) only

19. Which of the following pair is *not* correctly matched?

A. N. Ram : The Hindu
B. Barkha Dutt : Zee News
C. Pranay Roy : NDTV 24 × 7
D. Prabhu Chawla : Aaj taak

20. "Because you deserve to know" is the punchline used by :

A. The Times of India
B. The Hindu
C. Indian Express
D. Hindustan Times

21. In the sequence of numbers 8, 24, 12, X, 18, 54 the missing number X is :

A. 26 B. 24
C. 36 D. 32

22. If A stands for 5, B for 6, C for 7, D for 8 and so on, then the following numbers stand for 17, 19, 20, 9 and 8 :

A. PLANE B. MOPED
C. MOTOR D. TONGA

23. The letters in the first set have certain relationship. On the basis of this relationship what is the right choice for the second set ?
AST : BRU : : NQV : ?

A. ORW B. MPU
C. MRW D. OPW

24. In a certain code, PAN is written as 31 and PAR as 35. In this code PAT is written as:

A. 30 B. 37
C. 38 D. 39

25. The sides of a triangle are in the ratio of $\frac{1}{2}:\frac{1}{3}:\frac{1}{4}$. If its perimeter is 52 cm, the length of the smallest side is :

A. 9 cm B. 10 cm
C. 11 cm D. 12 cm

26. Which one of the following statements is **completely non-sensical**?

A. He was a bachelor, but he married recently.
B. He is a bachelor, but he married recently.
C. When he married, he was not a bachelor.
D. When he was a bachelor, he was not married.

27. Which of the following statements are **mutually contradictory**?

(i) All flowers are not fragrant,
(ii) Most flowers are not fragrant,
(iii) None of the flowers is fragrant,
(iv) Most flowers are fragrant.

Choose the correct answer from the code given below :

Code:

A. (i) and (ii) B. (i) and (iii)
C. (ii) and (iii) D. (iii) and (iv)

28. Which of the following statements **say the same thing**?

(i) "I am a teacher" (said by Arvind)
(ii) "I am a teacher" (said by Binod)
(iii) "My son is a teacher" (said by Binod's father)
(iv) "My brother is a teacher" (said by Binod's sister)
(v) "My brother is a teacher" (said by Binod's only sister)
(vi) "My sole enemy is a teacher" (said by Binod's only enemy) Choose the correct answer from the code given below :

Code :

A. (i) and (ii) B. (ii), (iii), (iv) and (v)
C. (ii) and (vi) D. (v) and (vi)

29. Which of the following are **correct ways of arguing**?

(i) There can be no second husband without a second wife.
(ii) Anil is a friend of Bob, Bob is a friend of Raj, hence Anil is a friend of Raj.
(iii) A is equal to B, B is equal to C, hence A is equal to C.
(iv) If everyone is a liar, then we cannot prove it.

Choose the correct answer from the code given below :

Code :

A. (iii) and (iv) B. (i), (iii) and (iv)
C. (ii), (iii) and (iv) D. (i), (ii), (iii) and (iv)

30. Which of the following statement/s are ALWAYS FALSE?

(i) The sun will not rise in the East some day.
(ii) A wooden table is not a table,
(iii) Delhi city will be drowned under water,
(iv) Cars run on water as fuel.

Choose the correct answer from the code given below :

Code :

A. (i), (iii) and (iv) B. Only (iii)
C. (i), (ii) and (iii) D. (ii) alone

Study the following graph and answer question numbers 31 to 33 :

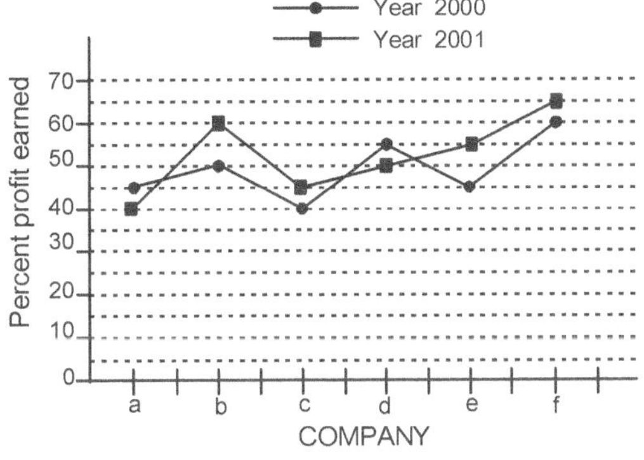

31. In the year 2000, which of the following Companies earned maximum percent profit?

A. a B. b
C. d D. f

32. In the year 2001, which of the following Companies earned minimum percent profit ?

A. a B. c
C. d D. e

33. In the years 2000 and 2001, which of the following Companies earned maximum average percent profit?

A. f B. e
C. d D. b

34. Human Development Report for 'each' of the year at global level has been published by :

A. UNDP B. WTO
C. IMF D. World Bank

35. The number of students in four classes A, B, C, D and their respective mean marks obtained by each of the class are given below :

	Class A	Class B	Class C	Class D
Number of students	10	40	30	20
Arithmetic mean	20	30	50	15

The combined mean of the marks of four classes together will be :

A. 32 B. 50
C. 20 D. 15

36. LAN stands for :

A. Local And National
B. Local Area Network
C. Large Area Network
D. Live Area Network

37. Which of the following statement is correct?

A. Modem is a software
B. Modem helps in stabilizing the voltage
C. Modem is the operating system
D. Modem converts the analog signal into digital signal and vice-versa

38. Which of the following is the appropriate definition of a computer?

A. Computer is a machine that can process information.
B. Computer is an electronic device that can store, retrieve and process both qualitative and quantitative data quickly and accurately.
C. Computer is an electronic device that can store, retrieve and quickly process only quantitative data.
D. Computer is a machine that can store, retrieve and process quickly and accurately only qualitative information

39. Information and Communication Technology includes :

A. On line learning
B. Learning through the use of EDUSAT
C. Web Based Learning
D. All the above

40. Which of the following is the appropriate format of URL of e-mail?
A. www_mail.com
B. www@mail.com
C. WWW@mail.com
D. www.mail.com

41. The most significant impact of volcanic erruption has been felt in the form of :
A. change in weather
B. sinking of islands
C. loss of vegetation
D. extinction of animals

42. With absorption and decomposition of CO_2 in ocean water beyond desired level, there will be :
A. decrease in temperature
B. increase in salinity
C. growth of phyto plankton
D. rise in sea level

43. Arrange column II in proper sequence so as to match it with column I and choose the correct answer from the code given below :

Column I	***Column II***
Water Quality	***pH Value***
(a) Neutral	(i) 5
(b) Moderately acidic	(ii) 7
(c) Alkaline	(iii) 4
(d) Injurious	(iv) 8

Code :

	(a)	(b)	(c)	(d)
A.	(ii)	(iii)	(i)	(iv)
B.	(i)	(iii)	(ii)	(iv)
C.	(ii)	(i)	(iv)	(iii)
D.	(iv)	(ii)	(iii)	(i)

44. The maximum emission of pollutants from fuel sources in India is caused by :
A. Coal
B. Firewood
C. Refuse burning
D. Vegetable waste product

45. The urbanisation process accounts for the wind in the urban centres during nights to remain :
A. faster than that in rural areas
B. slower than that in rural areas
C. the same as that in rural areas
D. cooler than that in rural areas

46. The University Grants Commission was constituted on the recommendation of :
A. Dr. Sarvapalli Radhakrishnan Commission
B. Mudaliar Commission
C. Sargent Commission
D. Kothari Commission

47. Which one of the following Articles of the Constitution of India safeguards the rights of Minorities to establish and run educational institutions of their own liking?
A. Article 19 B. Article 29
C. Article 30 D. Article 31

48. Match List-I (Institutions) with List-II (Functions) and select the correct answer by using the code given below :

List - I ***(Institutions)***	**List - II** ***(Functions)***
(a) Parliament	(i) Formulation of Budget
(b) C & A.G.	(ii) Enactment of Budget
(c) Ministry of Finance	(iii) Implementation of Budget
(d) Executing Departments	(iv) Legality of expenditure
	(v) Justification of Income

Code :

	(a)	(b)	(c)	(d)
A.	(iii)	(iv)	(ii)	(i)
B.	(ii)	(iv)	(i)	(iii)
C.	(v)	(iii)	(iv)	(ii)
D.	(iv)	(ii)	(iii)	(v)

49. Foundation training to the newly recruited IAS (Probationers) is imparted by :
A. Indian Institute of Public Administration
B. Administrative Staff College of India
C. L.B.S. National Academy of Administration
D. Centre for Advanced Studies

50. Electoral disputes arising out of Presidential and Vice-Presidential Elections are settled by:
A. Election Commission of India
B. Joint Committee of Parliament
C. Supreme Court of India
D. Central Election Tribunal

ANSWERS

1	2	3	4	5	6	7	8	9	10
D	A	B	B	D	C	D	B	D	D
11	**12**	**13**	**14**	**15**	**16**	**17**	**18**	**19**	**20**
B	B	D	D	C	C	C	D	B	D
21	**22**	**23**	**24**	**25**	**26**	**27**	**28**	**29**	**30**
C	B	D	B	D	B	B	B	A	D
31	**32**	**33**	**34**	**35**	**36**	**37**	**38**	**39**	**40**
D	A	A	A	A	B	D	B	D	B
41	**42**	**43**	**44**	**45**	**46**	**47**	**48**	**49**	**50**
A	C	C	C	B	A	C	B	C	C

SOME SELECTED EXPLANATORY ANSWERS

21. 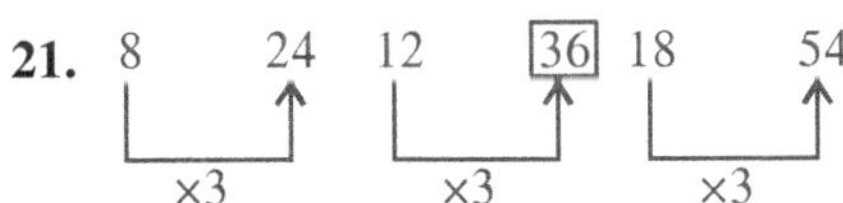

22. Since,

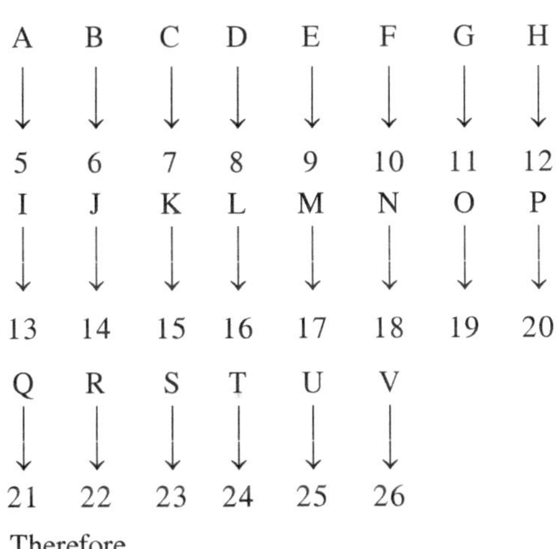

Therefore,

17 19 20 9 8
↓ ↓ ↓ ↓ ↓
M O P E D

23. Since,

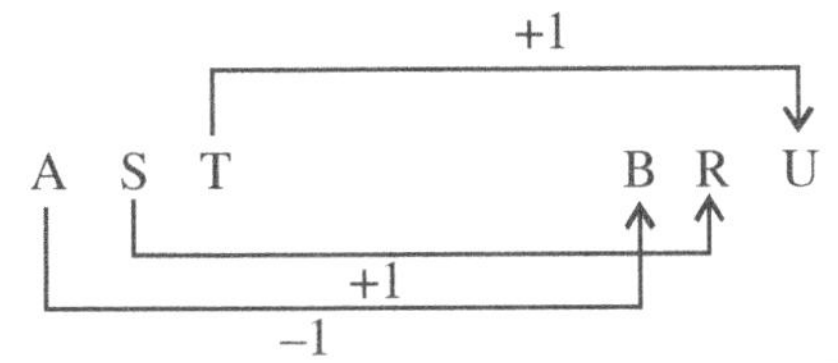

Therefore,

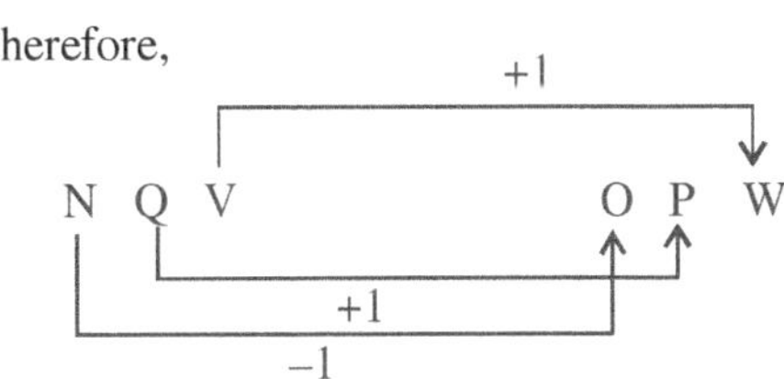

24. Since,

P A N ⇒ 16 + 1 + 14 (Sum of the position
⇒ 31 in English Alphabet)

and P A R ⇒ 16 + 1 + 18
⇒ 35

Therefore

P A T ⇒ 16 + 1 + 20
⇒ 37

25. Let the sides of the triangle are $\frac{1}{2}x, \frac{1}{3}x$ and $\frac{1}{4}x$

$$\therefore\ 52 = \frac{1}{2}x + \frac{1}{3}x + \frac{1}{4}x$$

$$= x\left[\frac{1}{2} + \frac{1}{3} = \frac{1}{4}\right] = \frac{13x}{12}$$

$$\Rightarrow 52 = \frac{13x}{12} \Rightarrow x = 48$$

$\therefore$ First side of the triangel $= 48 \times \frac{1}{2} = 24$

Second side of the triangle $= 48 \times \frac{1}{3} = 16$

Third side of the triangle $= 48 \times \frac{1}{4} = 12$

(Smalles + side)

IIIIIIIII

UGC-NET (JRF) EXAM DECEMBER, 2005

PAPER–I

Note : This paper contains **fifty** (50) multiple-choice questions, each question carrying **two** (2) marks. Attempt **all** of them.

1. Team teaching has the potential to develop:
A. Competitive spirit
B. Cooperation
C. The habit of supplementing the teaching of each other
D. Highlighting the gaps in each other's teaching

2. Which of the following is the most important characteristic of Open Book Examination system?
A. Students become serious.
B. It improves attendance in the classroom.
C. It reduces examination anxiety amongst students.
D. In compels students to think.

3. Which of the following methods of teaching encourages the use of maximum senses?
A. Problem-solving method
B. Laboratory method
C. Self-study method
D. Team teaching method

4. Which of the following statement is correct ?
A. Communicator should have fine senses
B. Communicator should have tolerance power
C. Communicator should be soft spoken
D. Communicator should have good personality

5. An effective teacher is one who can :
A. control the class
B. give more information in less time
C. motivate students to learn
D. correct the assignments carefully

6. One of the following is **not** a quality of researcher :
A. Unison with that of which he is in search
B. He must be of alert mind
C. Keenness in enquiry
D. His assertion to outstrip the evidence

7. A satisfactory statistical quantitative method should **not** possess one of the following qualities :
A. Appropriateness B. Measurability
C. Comparability D. Flexibility

8. Books and records are the primary sources of data in :
A. historical research
B. participatory research
C. clinical research
D. laboratory research

9. Which of the following statement is correct?
A. objectives should be pin-pointed
B. objectives can be written in statement or question form
C. another word for problem is variable
D. all the above

10. The important pre-requisites of a researcher in sciences, social sciences and humanities are :

A. laboratory skills, records, supervisor, topic
B. Supervisor, topic, critical analysis, patience
C. archives, supervisor, topic, flexibility in thinking
D. topic, supervisor, good temperament, pre-conceived notions

Read the following passage and answer the questions 11 to 15 :

Knowledge creation in many cases requires creativity and idea generation. This is especially important in generating alternative decision support solutions. Some people believe that an individual's creative ability stems primarily from personality traits such as inventiveness, independence, individuality, enthusiasm, and flexibility. However, several studies have found that creativity is not so much a function of individual traits as was once believed, and that individual creativity can be learned and improved. This understanding has led innovative companies to recognise that the key to fostering creativity may be the development of an idea-nurturing work environment. Idea-generation methods and techniques, to be used by individuals or in groups, are consequently being developed. Manual methods for supporting idea generation, such as brainstorming in a group, can be very successful in certain situations. However, in other situations, such an approach is either not economically feasible or not possible. For example, manual methods in group creativity sessions will not work or will not be effective when : (1) there is no time to conduct a proper idea-generation session; (2) there is a poor facilitator (or no facilitator at all); (3) it is too expensive to conduct an idea-generation session; (4) the subject matter is too sensitive for a face-to-face session; or (5) there are not enough participants, the mix of participants is not optimal, or there is no climate for idea generation. In such cases, computerised idea-generation methods have been tried, with frequent success.

Idea-generation software is designed to help stimulate a single user or a group to produce new ideas, options and choices. The user does all the work, but the software encourages and pushes, something like a personal trainer. Although idea-generation software is still relatively new, there are several packages on the market. Various approaches are used by idea-generating software to increase the flow of ideas to the user. Idea Fisher, for example, has an associate lexicon of the English language that cross-references words and phrases. These associative links, based on analogies and metaphors, make it easy for the user to be fed words related to a given theme. Some software packages use questions to prompt the user towards new, unexplored patterns of thought. This helps users to break out of cyclical thinking patterns, conquer mental blocks, or deal with bouts of procrastination.

11. The author, in this passage has focussed on
A. knowledge creation
B. idea-generation
C. creativity
D. individual traits

12. Fostering creativity needs an environment of
A. decision support systems
B. idea-nurturing
C. decision support solutions
D. alternative individual factors

13. Manual methods for the support of idea-generation, in certain occasions,
A. are alternatively effective
B. can be less expensive
C. do not need a facilitator
D. require a mix of optimal participants

14. Idea-generation software works as if it is a :
A. stimulant
B. knowledge package
C. user-friendly trainer
D. climate creator

15. Mental blocks, bouts of procrastination and cyclical thinking patterns can be won when :
A. innovative companies employ electronic thinking methods
B. idea-generation software prompts questions
C. manual methods are removed
D. individuals acquire a neutral attitude towards the software

16. Level C of the effectiveness of communication is defined as :

A. channel noise
B. semantic noise
C. psychological noise
D. source noise

17. Recording a television programme on a VCR is an example of :
A. time-shifting
B. content reference
C. mechanical clarity
D. media synchronisation

18. A good communicator is the one who offers to his audience :
A. plentiful of information
B. a good amount of statistics
C. concise proof
D. repetition of facts

19. The largest number of newspapers in India is published from the state of :
A. Kerala B. Maharashtra
C. West Bengal D. Uttar Pradesh

20. Insert the missing number :
8 24 12 ? 18 54
A. 26 B. 24
C. 36 D. 32

21. January 1, 1995 was Sunday. What day of the week lies on January 1, 1996?
A. Sunday B. Monday
C. Saturday D. None of these

22. The sum of a positive number and its reciprocal is twice the difference of the number and its reciprocal. The number is :
A. $\sqrt{2}$ B. $\frac{1}{\sqrt{2}}$
C. $\sqrt{3}$ D. $\frac{1}{\sqrt{3}}$

23. In a certain code, ROUNDS is written as RONUDS. How will PLEASE will be written in the same code :
A. L P A E S E B. P L A E S E
C. L P A E E S D. P L A S E E

24. At what time between 5.30 and 6.00 will the hands of an clock be at right angles ?
A. $43\frac{5}{11}$ min. past 5
B. $43\frac{7}{11}$ min. past 5
C. 40 min. past 5
D. 45 min past 5

25. **Statements** : I. All students are ambitious
II. All ambitious persons are hard working
Conclusions :(i) All students are hard-working
(ii) All hardly working people are not ambitious Which of the following is correct ?
A. Only (i) is correct
B. Only (ii) is correct
C. Both (i) and (ii) are correct
D. Neither (i) nor (ii) is correct

26. **Statement** : Most students are intelligent
Conclusions : (i) Some students are intelligent
(ii) All students are not intelligent
Which of the following is implied?
A. Only (i) is implied
B. Only (ii) is implied
C. Both (i) and (ii) are implied
D. Neither (i) nor (ii) is implied

27. **Statement** : Most labourers are poor
Conclusions : (i) Some labourers are poor
(ii) All labourers are not poor Which of the following is implied ?
A. Only (i) is implied
B. Only (ii) is implied
C. Both (i) and (ii) are implied
D. Neither (i) nor (ii) is implied

28. Line access and avoidance of collision are the main functions of :
A. the CPU
B. the monitor
C. network protocols
D. wide area networks

29. In the hypermedia database, information bits are stored in the form of :
A. signals B. cubes
C. nodes D. symbols

30. Communications bandwidth that has the highest capacity and is used by microwave, cable and fibre optics lines is known as :

A. hyper-link B. broadband
C. bus width D. carrier wave

31. An electronic bill board that has a short text or graphical advertising message is referred to as :

A. bulletin B. strap
C. bridge line D. banner

32. Which of the following is not the characteristic of a computer ?

A. computer is an electrical machine
B. computer cannot think at its own
C. computer processes information error free
D. computer can hold data for any length of time

33. Bitumen is obtained from :

A. Forests and Plants
B. Kerosene oil
C. Crude oil
D. underground mines

34. Malaria is caused by :

A. bacterial infection
B. viral infection
C. parasitic infection
D. fungal infection

35. The cloudy nights are warmer compared to clear nights (without clouds) during winter days. This is because :

A. clouds radiate heat towards the earth
B. clouds prevent cold wave from the sky, descend on earth
C. clouds prevent escaping of the heat radiation from the earth
D. clouds being at great heights from earth absorb heat from the sun and send towards the earth

36. Largest soil group of India is :

A. Red soil C. Sandy soil
B. Black soil D. Mountain soil

37. Main pollutant of the Indian coastal water is :

A. oil spill
B. municipal sewage
C. industrial effluents
D. aerosols

38. Human ear is most sensitive to noise in the following frequency ranges

A. 1-2 KHz B. 100-500 Hz
C. 10-12 KHz D. None of these

39. Which species of chromium is toxic in water :

A. Cr + 2
B. Cr + 3
C. Cr + 6
D. Cr is non-toxic element

40. Match List - I (Dams) with List - II (River) in the following

List -1 (Dams)	**List - II (River)**
(a) Bhakra	(i) Krishna
(b) Nagarjunasagar	(ii) Damodar
(c) Panchet	(iii) Sutlej
(d) Hirakud	(iv) Bhagirathi
(e) Tehri	(v) Mahanadi

Code:

	(a)	(b)	(c)	(d)	(e)
A.	(v)	(iii)	(iv)	(ii)	(i)
B.	(iii)	(i)	(ii)	(v)	(iv)
C.	(i)	(ii)	(iv)	(iii)	(v)
D.	(ii)	(iii)	(iv)	(i)	(v)

41. A negative reaction to a mediated communication is described as :

A. flak
B. fragmented feedback
C. passive response
D. non-conformity

42. The launch of satellite channel by IGNOU on 26th January 2003 for technological education for the growth and development of distance education is :

A. Eklavya channel
B. Gyandarshan channel
C. Rajrishi channel
D. None of these

43. Match List - I with List-II and select the correct answer from the code given below :

List -1 (Institutions)

(a) The Indian Council of Historical Reasearch (ICHR)

(b) The Indian Institute of Advanced Studies (HAS)

(c) The Indian Council of Philosophical Research

(d) The Central Institute of Coastal Engineering for fisheries

List - II (Locations)

(i) Shimla

(ii) New Delhi

(iii) Banglore Research (ICPR)

(iv) Lucknow

	a	b	c	d
A.	(ii)	(i)	(iv)	(iii)
B.	(i)	(ii)	(iii)	(iv)
C.	(ii)	(iv)	(i)	(iii)
D.	(iv)	(iii)	(ii)	(i)

44. Which of the following is not a Fundamental Right ?

A. Right to equality

B. Right against exploitation

C. Right to freedom of speech and expression

D. Right of free compulsory education of all children upto the age of 14

45. The Lok - Sabha can be dissolved before the expiry of its normal five year term by

A. The Prime Minister

B. The Speaker of Lok Sabha

C. The President on the recommendation of the Prime Minister

D. None of the above

Study the following graph carefully and answer Q.No. 46 to 50 given below it :

EXPORT OF TINS

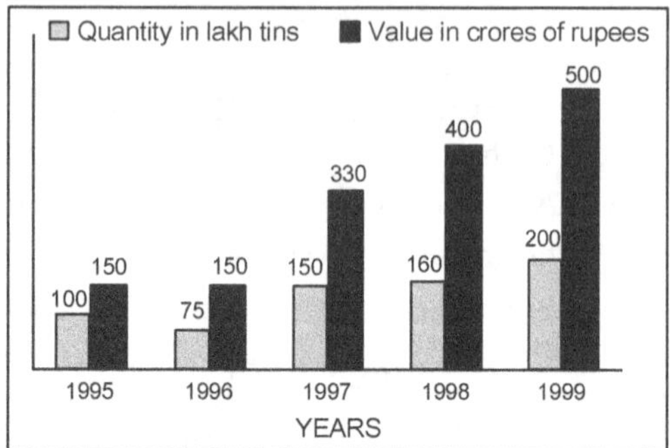

46. In which year the value per tin was minimum?

A. 1995 B. 1996

C. 1998 D. 1999

47. What was the difference between the tins exported in 1997 and 1998?

A. 10 B. 1000

C. 100000 D. 1000000

48. What was the approximate percentage increase in export value from 1995 to 1999?

A. 350 B. 330.3

C. 433.3 D. None of these

49. What was the percentage drop in export quantity from 1995 to 1996 ?

A. 75 B. 50

C. 25 D. None of these

50. If in 1998, the tins were exported at the same rate per tin as that in 1997, what would be the value (in crores of rupees) of export in 1998?

A. 400 B. 375

C. 352 D. 330

ANSWERS

1	2	3	4	5	6	7	8	9	10
C	D	B	A	C	D	D	A	A	B
11	**12**	**13**	**14**	**15**	**16**	**17**	**18**	**19**	**20**
A	B	A	A	B	A	D	A	D	C
21	**22**	**23**	**24**	**25**	**26**	**27**	**28**	**29**	**30**
B	D	B	B	C	B	B	C	A	B
31	**32**	**33**	**34**	**35**	**36**	**37**	**38**	**39**	**40**
B	A	D	C	C	A	C	D	C	B
41	**42**	**43**	**44**	**45**	**46**	**47**	**48**	**49**	**50**
C	A	A	D	C	A	A	D	C	C

SOME SELECTED EXPLANATORY ANSWERS

20.

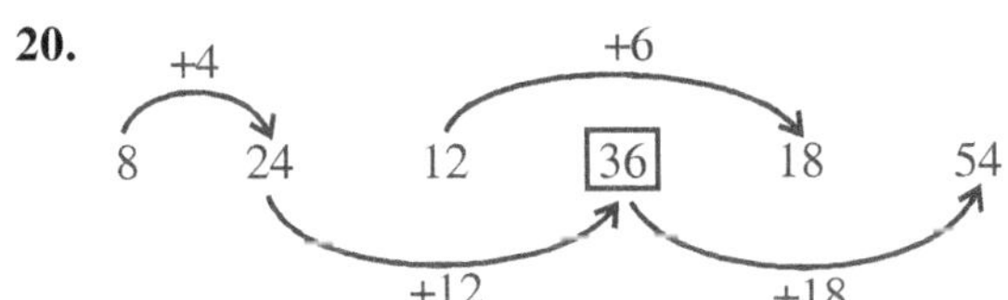

$\therefore$ Required number = 24 + 12 = 36

21. $\because$ 1st January 1995 $\rightarrow$ Sunday

$\therefore$ 31st December 1995 $\rightarrow$ Sunday

($\because$ 1995 was not a leap year)

$\therefore$ 1st January 1996 = Monday

22. $x + \frac{1}{x} = 2\left(x - \frac{1}{x}\right)$

$\Rightarrow \frac{x^2+1}{x} = 2\left(\frac{x^2-1}{x}\right)$

$\Rightarrow x^2 + 1 = 2x^2 - 2$

$\Rightarrow x^2 = 3$

$\therefore \quad x = \sqrt{3}$

23. Since,

1	2	3	4	5	6		1	2	4	3	5	6
R	O	U	N	D	S	→	R	O	N	U	D	S

Therefore,

1	2	3	4	5	6		1	2	4	3	5	6
P	L	E	A	S	E	→	P	L	A	E	S	E

Previous Paper (Solved)

UGC-NET (JRF) EXAM DECEMBER, 2004

PAPER–I

Note : This paper contains **fifty** (50) multiple-choice questions, each question carrying **two** (2) marks. Attempt **all** of them.

1. Discussion Method can be used when:
A. The topic is very difficult
B. The topic is easy
C. The topic is difficult
D. All the above

2. Which of the following is a teaching aid?
A. Working Model of Wind Mill
B. Tape Recorder
C. 16 mm Film Projector
D. All the above

3. The main aim of teaching is:
A. To develop only reasoning
B. To develop only thinking
C. Both (A) and (B)
D. To give information

4. The quality of teaching is reflected :
A. By the attendance of students in the class
B. By the pass percentage of students
C. By the quality of questions asked by students
D. By the duration of silence maintained in the class

5. The present annual examination system :
A. promotes rote learning
B. does not promote good study habits
C. does not encourage students to be regular in class
D. All the above

6. A college wants to give training in use of Statistical Package for Social Sciences (SPSS) to researchers. For this the college should organise :
A. Conference
B. Seminar
C. Workshop
D. Lecture

7. Which of the following is NOT the characteristic of a research ?
A. Research is systematic
B. Research is not a process
C. Research is problem oriented
D. Research is not passive

8. Which of the following statement is correct?
A. Discoveries are researches
B. Researches lead to discovery
C. Invention and Research are related
D. None of the above

9. Which of the following statement is correct ?
A. In research, objectives can be worded in question form
B. In research, objectives can be worded in statement form
C. Objectives are to be stated in Chapter I of the Thesis
D. All the above

10. Match List A with List B and choose the correct answer from the code given below :

List A
(a) Historical Method
(b) Survey Method
(c) Philosophical Method
(d) Experimental Method

List B

(i) Past events
(ii) Vision
(iii) Present events
(iv) Exceptional cases
(v) Future action

Code :

	(a)	(b)	(c)	(d)
A.	(i)	(iii)	(ii)	(v)
B.	(i)	(ii)	(iv)	(v)
C.	(i)	(iv)	(ii)	(v)
D.	(i)	(ii)	(iii)	(iv)

Read the following passage and answer the question numbers 11 to 15.

Each day at the Shantiniketan School starts with the Saraswati Vandana. When painting competitions are held in the school, images of Hindu gods and goddesses are most common. Sanskrit is a favourite subject of many a student. Nothing new about it except that the 1,200 - odd students studying in the Hindu - run school are Muslims.

In 1983, when Ranchodbhai Kiri started Shantiniketan in the all - Muslim Juhapura area of Ahmedabad in Gujarat, only 20 percent of the students were Muslims. But when riots involving the Muslims of Juhapura and the Hindus of nearby Jivrajpark -Vejalpur affected the locality, Hindus started migrating. Today, all the students are Muslims and the school is an unparalled example of harmony. In the 2002, when a section of inflamed Muslims wanted the school closed, the parents of the students stood like a wall behind it.

Shantiniketan's principal says, "We never thought of moving the school out of the area because of the love and affection of the local Muslims. Indeed they value the high standard of education which we have set." Such is the reputation of the school that some of the local Muslim strongmen accused of involvement in communal riots are willing to protect the school during the riots.

The parents of Shantiniketan's students believe that it's the best school when it comes to the quality of the teaching. A large number of students have gone for both graduation and post graduation studies. Significantly, the only Muslim teacher in the 40 - member teaching staff, Husena Mansuri, teaches Sanskrit. Infact, she is so happy at the school that she recently declined the principalship of another Muslim - run school.

Some of the students' entries in a recent school painting competition mere truly moving. One drew a pciture of Bharat Mata with a mosque and temple, while another portrayed a boy tying rakhi to his sister. Trully, Shantiniketan is a beacon of hope that, despite the provocations from both communities, Hindus and Muslims can live side-by-side with mutual respect.

11. How the Shantiniketan school starts the day?
A. National anthem
B. Prayer
C. Saraswati Vandana
D. Puja

12. Write the subject which is preferred by most of the students
A. Hindi B. English
C. Sanskrit D. Gujarati

13. Who protects the school during the riot times?
A. Local Muslims B. Hindus
C. Politicians D. Christians

14. Who is the teacher of Sanskrit?
A. Ranchodbhai Kiri
C. Husena Mansuri
B. Manisha Vakil
D. Husena Khatoon

15. What is the hope despite the communal riots?
A. Hindus and Muslims cannot live side by side
B. Hindus and Muslims can live side by side
C. Only Hindus can live
D. Only Muslims can live

16. Match List I with List II and choose the correct answer using the codes given below

List I *(Distinguished Ladies)*	**List II** *(Area of work)*
(a) Jhumpa Lahiri	(i) Journalist
(b) Barkha Dutt	(ii) Novel Writing
(c) Aparna Sen	(iii) Film Actress
(d) Smita Patil	(iv) Film Director

Code :

	(a)	(b)	(c)	(d)
A.	(iv)	(iii)	(ii)	(i)
B.	(ii)	(i)	(iv)	(iii)
C.	(iv)	(i)	(iii)	(ii)
D.	(ii)	(iii)	(iv)	(i)

17. Which of the following pair is not correctly matched ?
A. Aajtaak - 24 hours news channel
B. P.M. Stations - Radio
C. National Geography channel - Television
D. Vir Sanghvi - India Today

18. Which is the oldest soap opera telecasted in India?
A. Kahani Ghar Ghar Ke
B. Buniad
C. Humlog
D. Saas bhi Kabhi Bahu Thee

19. Which satellite channel uses the adline, "Knowing is everything"?
A. BBC World B. Star
C. Sony D. Zee

20. Which is the "First made in India" Kids channel of television ?
A. Cartoon Network
B. Walt Disney
C. United Home Entertainment's Hungama TV
D. Nick Jr.

21. The letters in the first set have certain relationships. On the basis of the relationship which is the right choice for the second set?
BF : GK : : LP : ?
A. JK B. QU
C. VW D. RQ

22. If the BLOOD is coded as 24113 and BRUST as 20678, then code for ROBUST is :
A. 620781 B. 012678
C. 678102 D. 610732

23. A bag contains an equal number of one rupee, 50 paise and 25 paise coins. If the total amount in the bag is Rs. 35, how many coins of each type are there?
A. 15 B. 18
C. 20 D. 25

24. In the sequence of numbers
$\frac{2}{3}, \frac{4}{7}, X, \frac{11}{21}, \frac{16}{31}$
the missing number X is :
A. $\frac{8}{10}$ B. $\frac{6}{10}$
C. $\frac{5}{10}$ D. $\frac{7}{10}$

25. If A stands for 5 , B for 6, C for 7, D for 8, and so on, what do the following numbers stand for :
22, 25, 8, 22 and 5 ?
A. PRIYA B. NEEMA
C. MEENA D. RUDRA

26. Which of the following statements are always true ?
(a) A wooden table is a table
(b) Now, it is raining or not raining
(c) The sun rises in the East every day
(d) A chicken comes out of a hen's egg
Choose the correct answer from the code given below :
Code :
A. (a) and (c)
B. (a), (c) and (d)
C. (a) and (b)
D. (b) and (c)

27. Which of the following statements are mutually inconsistent?
(a) Mostly poets are not egoistic
(b) Mostly poets are humble
(c) Some poets are egoistic
(d) Some poets are not non - egoistic
Choose the correct answer from the code given below :
Code :
A. (a) and (d) B. (b) and (c)
C. (a) and (c) D. (c) and (d)

28. Which of the following statements is/are absolutely impossible?

(a) A woman giving birth to her own grandchild
(b) A man attending his own funeral
(c) The Sun not rising in the East some day
(d) Cars running without petrol

Choose the correct answer from the code given below :

Code :

A. (a) and (b) B. (c) and (d)
C. (b) D. (a)

29. Which of the following are incorrect ways of arguing?

(a) If horses are cows, and if cows are sheep, then all horses must be sheep.
(b) If top actors are famous, and Shah Rukh Khan is famous, then Shah Rukh Khan is a top actor
(c) Lata is the second sister of Raju, hence Raju is the second brother of Lata
(d) A is not equal to B, but B is equal to C, hence A is equal to C. Choose the correct answer from the code given below :

Code :

A. (a), (b) and (c)
B. (a), (c) and (d)
C. (b), (c) and (d)
D. (a), (b) and (d)

30. Which of the following statements say the same thing?

(a) "I am clever" (said by Rama)
(b) "I am clever" (said by Raju)
(c) "My son is clever" (said by Rama's father)
(d) "My brother is clever" (said by Rama's sister)
(e) "My brother is clever" (said by Rama's only sister)
(f) "My sole enemy is clever" (said by Rama's only enemy) Choose the correct answer from the code given below :

Code :

A. (a), (c), (d), (e) and (f)
B. (a) and (b)
C. (d) and (e)
D. (a) and (f)

Study the following graph and answer Question Numbers 31 to 33:

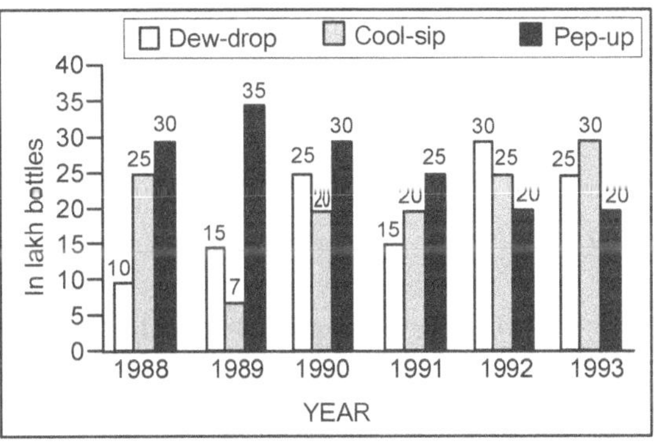

31. In which year was the sale of 'Pep - up' the maximum?

A. 1990 B. 1992
C. 1993 D. None of the above

32. In the case of which soft drink was the average annual sale maximum during the period 1988 -1993.

A. Pep - up only
B. Cool - sip only
C. Cool - sip and Dew - drop
D. Pep - up and Dew - drop

33. What was the approximate percent drop in the sale of Pep - up in 1990 over its sale in 1989?

A. 5 B. 12
C. 14 D. 20

34. The "Report on Currency and Finance" for each of the financial year in India is published by:

A. Reserve Bank of India
B. Ministry of Finance
C. Planning Commission
D. Central Statistical Organisation

35. The number of students in two classes A and B and the respective "mean" of the marks obtained by each of the class are given in the following table :

	Class A	**Class B**
Number of Students	20	80
Arithmatic Mean	10	20

The combined "mean" of the marks of the two classes will be :

A. 18 C. 10
B. 15 D. 20

36. ICT stands for :

A. International Communication Technology
B. Intera Common Terminology
C. Information and Communication Technology
D. Inter connected Terminals

37. Which of the following statement is **NOT** correct?

A. Computer is capable of processing only digital signal
B. Computer is capable of analysing both quantitative and qualitative data
C. Appropriate software is required for processing the data
D. Computer is capable of processing digital as well as analog signals

38. Which of the following is the appropriate definition of Information Technology?

A. Information Technology refers to the use of hardware and software for processing information
B. Information Technology refers to the use of hardware and software for distribution of useful information
C. Information Technology refers to the use of hardware and software for storage, retrieval, processing and distributing information of many kinds.
D. Information Technology refers to the use of principles of Physical sciences and Social sciences for processing of information of many kinds.

39. Which of the following statement is correct ?

A. Virus improves the speed of processing information through computer
B. Internet does not allow the virus to spread
C. Virus is a part of software
D. Virus is an operating system

40. Which of the following is correct statement?

A. Computers can be used for diagnosing the difficulty of a student in learning a subject
B. Psychological testing can be done with the help of computer provided a software is available
C. A set of instructions is called a programme
D. All the above

41. Global warning during winter becomes more pronounced at the :

A. Equator
B. Poles
C. Tropic of Cancer
D. Tropic of Capricorn

42. In the study of man - environment interaction, the statement of Miss Semple that "the humans are solely the product of their environment", is :

A. An opinion
B. A prejudice
C. A fact
D. A widely accepted phenomenon

43. In analysis of man - environment relationship Pragmatic Possibilism implies that :

A. There is no limit for man to exploit resources of earth
B. There are limited possibilities to explore earth's resources
C. The man has to watch and assess the situation and then go ahead with resource utilization
D. The man has to keep in mind only his basic needs while planning to harness the potential of resourceful earth

44. Arrange Column II in proper sequence so as to match it with Column I and choose the correct answer from the code given below :

Column I *(Activity)*	**Column II** *(Noise level)*
(a) Hearing	(i) 30 dB
(b) Whispering	(ii) 1 dB
(c) Interference with sleep	(iii) 60 dB
(d) Normal talk	(iv) 30 - 50 dB

Code :

	(a)	(b)	(c)	(d)
A.	(i)	(ii)	(iii)	(iv)
B.	(ii)	(i)	(iv)	(iii)
C.	(iv)	(ii)	(iii)	(i)
D.	(iii)	(i)	(ii)	(iv)

45. The maximum loss of forest lands in India is caused by :
A. River valley projects
B. Industries
C. Means of transportation
D. Agriculture

46. In which year the University Grants Commission was established?
A. 1948 B. 1944
C. 1953 D. 1960

47. Another name of Basic Education or Nai Talim is :
A. Compulsory Education
B. New Education Policy
C. Wardha Education Plan
D. Sarva Shikshya Abhiyan

48. The Idea of 'Democratic Decentralisation' in India was popularised by :
A. A.D. Gorwala Committee, 1951
B. Paul H. Appleby Committee, 1953
C. B.R. Mehta Committee, 1957
D. Ashok Mehta Committee, 1978

49. In India, a political party is recognised as a National or Regional Party by the :
A. President of India
B. Election Commission of India
C. Law ministry in consultation with the Law Commission of India
D. Union Parliament in consultation with the State Legislatures

50. Which of the following factors is/are responsible for the increase of the role of Government in Developing Countries ?
(a) Economic Planning
(b) Rising expectation of People
(c) Privatisation
(d) Emergence of the concept of Welfare State

Select the most appropriate answer from the code given below :

Code :
A. (a) and (d) B. (a), (b) and (d)
C. Only (c) D. Only (d)

ANSWERS

1	**2**	**3**	**4**	**5**	**6**	**7**	**8**	**9**	**10**
A	D	C	C	D	C	B	B	D	A
11	**12**	**13**	**14**	**15**	**16**	**17**	**18**	**19**	**20**
C	C	A	C	B	B	D	C	A	C
21	**22**	**23**	**24**	**25**	**26**	**27**	**28**	**29**	**30**
B	B	C	D	D	B	A	C	C	A
31	**32**	**33**	**34**	**35**	**36**	**37**	**38**	**39**	**40**
D	A	C	A	A	C	D	C	C	D
41	**42**	**43**	**44**	**45**	**46**	**47**	**48**	**49**	**50**
B	A	C	A	D	C	C	C	B	B

SOME SELECTED EXPLANATORY ANSWERS

22. Since,

D	B	L	O	R	U	S	T
↓	↓	↓	↓	↓	↓	↓	↓
3	2	4	1	0	6	7	8

Therefore,

R	O	B	U	S	T
↓	↓	↓	↓	↓	↓
0	1	2	6	7	8

23. Let the total number of each type of coins is x.

$\therefore$ From question

$$100x + 50x + 25x = 3500$$

$$\Rightarrow 175x = 3500$$

$$\Rightarrow x = \frac{3500}{175} = 20$$

IIIIIIIII

www.ingramcontent.com/pod-product-compliance
Lightning Source LLC
LaVergne TN
LVHW080453160826
845677LV00006B/1343

* 9 7 8 9 3 8 7 6 0 4 6 4 3 *